The
Craft
of
Argument

Joseph M. Williams
University of Chicago

Gregory G. Colomb
University of Virginia

New York • San Francisco • Boston
London • Toronto • Sydney • Tokyo • Singapore • Madrid
Mexico City • Munich • Paris • Cape Town • Hong Kong • Montreal

Editor-in-Chief: Joseph P. Terry
Acquisitions Editor: Susan Kunchandy
Associate Development Editor: Bennett Morrison
Marketing Manager: Carlise Paulson
Supplements Editor: Donna Campion
Production Manager: Joseph Vella
Project Coordination, Text Design,
  and Electronic Page Makeup: Thompson Steele, Inc.
Cover Designer/Manager: John Callahan
Manufacturing Buyer: Roy Pickering
Printer and Binder: Courier-Westford
Cover Printer: The Lehigh Press, Inc.

For permission to use copyrighted material, grateful acknowledgment is made to the
copyright holders on pp. 467–468, which are hereby made part of this copyright page.

Library of Congress Cataloging-in-Publication Data

Williams, Joseph M.
    The craft of argument / Joseph M. Williams, Gregory C. Colomb.–1st ed.
      p. cm.
    Includes bibliographical references (p. 467) and index.
    ISBN 0-321-01264-X (alk. paper)
      1. English language–Rhetoric. 2. Persuasion (Rhetoric) 3. Report
writing. I. Colomb, Gregory G. II. Title.

PE1431 .C65 2001
808'.042–dc21
                                             00-039087
                                                CIP

Please visit our website at http://www.ablongman.com

ISBN 0-321-01264-X

1 2 3 4 5 6 7 8 9 10–CRW–03 02 01 00

Brief Contents

Contents

APPENDICES

READINGS

Topical Contents
of the
Writing Process Sections

Preface for Teachers

In this book, we explain written arguments in a way that is not wholly new, but new enough to need some explanation. Readers looking for certain standard topics will not find them here:

- We offer no account of syllogistic reasoning because we can find no good evidence that teaching it improves the quality of anyone's thinking or writing.

- We do not treat "arguments about values" as a category distinct from fact or policy because we believe the traditional tri-part division obscures a more basic distinction. We do, however, show students how values influence both their arguments and their readers' responses to them.

- We give little attention to fallacies, though readers who want a list of them will find one in Appendix 1. We have instead tried to integrate critical thinking with our discussion of argument and writing in every chapter.

Readers will also find topics new to books on argument. We have brought together recent work in areas rarely visited by composition specialists: decision theory, cognitive biases, attribution theory, linguistic stylistics, text linguistics, problem formulation, and ordinary logic.

- In the last twenty-five years, research has flourished on the issue of "cognitive bias," which differs from fallacies as usually described. Cognitive biases are widely shared habits of mind that lead us astray, but that can be guarded against through the discipline imposed by careful argument.

- Cognitive scientists have also helped us understand how we actually interpret cause-and-effect relationships, assign responsibility to human agency, and categorize what we experience.

- We understand better how the structure of the problem occasioning an argument shapes it.

Though few if any of these insights have found their way into standard texts on written arguments, they are all relevant to rhetoric and critical thinking. We have integrated this work with more familiar work in composition so that it requires no expert knowledge to teach. Indeed, it supports a good deal of familiar common sense about thinking and arguing soundly.

We have also tried to synthesize two aspects of argument usually kept distinct: dialectic and rhetoric. Since Aristotle, dialectic has been defined as seeking truth through questioning and answering, a topic now pursued by those characterizing their work as "pragma-dialectical." In contrast, rhetoric has been defined as the means to find persuasive ways to support a claim already known, expressed by a monologic voice that acknowledges other views only to rebut them.

We present a view of argument in which questions and answers not only seek truth, but also generate the means of persuasion that rhetoric seeks, a thread that may remind some readers of Bakhtin. We show students how to develop written arguments by drawing on speech genres they already know and use, encouraging them to create for their arguments the dialogues that mature writers have with readers, either real before they write or imagined as they draft and revise. To help students internalize that dialectic, we suggest ways that they can engage readers, classmates, and writing groups in conversations that develop and test their claims. We cover that ground in a section in early chapters called "Writing Collaboratively."

What we do share with many recent books on argument are some of Stephen Toulmin's central insights :

- All arguments are sustained by a logic of question and answer.

- Arguments differ in different fields but have a common family structure.

- That structure cannot be a syllogism, because an argument consists of a network of elements that include more than a claim and its premises.

- We best express those elements not as formal symbols but in ordinary language, as answers to a few questions such as "What are you claiming?" and "What do you have to go on?"

But as important as Toulmin's insights are, we believe that those who uncritically embrace his formal layout of arguments make a pedagogical and theoretical mistake. Recall that he represents the elements of an argument like this:

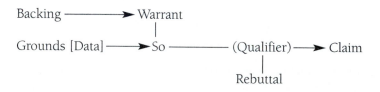

He intended that layout to explain how arguments in different fields differ. We aim to teach students how to make sound arguments, so we modified his layout in six ways, some minor, others major:

1.   **We removed the arrows from the diagram.** Toulmin designed his layout to represent how a mind reasons from grounds to a claim, guided by a warrant supported by backing and constrained by qualifiers and rebuttals. But that grounds-to-claim flow is psychologically unrealistic, particularly when we think abductively (as we do most of the time) from a hypothesis (a provisional claim), to a search for supporting grounds, and then back through the elements of the layout to confirm the hypothesis. And in any case, we want our layout to help students not only to understand the structure of arguments, but to create them and anticipate how readers experience them, particularly when those elements appear in different orders. Our layout does not represent "real time" reasoning, but only those relationships among the elements of argument that help us think about argument from the three perspectives of maker, reader, and critic.

2.   **We dropped the element called "backing."** Toulmin needed "backing" to explain how arguments differ among different fields of study, because it is in their different ways of backing warrants that fields differ most significantly. In the law, a warrant is backed by statutes or tradition, in the sciences by detailed observation, in religion by revealed principles of faith, and so on. But we are not centrally concerned with distinguishing arguments in one field from those in another. Moreover, since a warrant is often a general claim derived from another argument, backing is just another term for the grounds supporting that claim used *as* a warrant. Backing is therefore redundant. (We discuss these matters more fully in the Teacher's Guide.)

3.   **We dropped "qualifier" as a separate element.** We thought about this change a lot, because qualifications such as *probably* and *certainly, all, most,* and *some, can* and *may* are crucial not just to the substance of an argument, but to the experience of reading it and judging its writer's character, or *ethos*. But a qualifier is not, as Toulmin suggests, a discrete filter that assigns a level of probability to a claim. Rather, qualifiers appear everywhere in an argument: in claims, but also in evidence, reasons, warrants, and rebuttals. None of those considerations are relevant to his project, but they are to ours. So we treat qualification as a matter of precision and as a stylistic issue affecting ethos. We do not ignore qualification; we emphasize it by distributing it through every element of an argument.

4.   **We replaced the single element called "grounds" (or "data") with two, reasons and evidence.** In arguments about significant issues, careful readers want more than mere reasons. They expect to see the "foundation" on which those reasons rest, what we call in ordinary language, "hard evidence." This distinction reflects a psychological and social imperative: Readers want to see how a claim rests on something outside of—and more "solid" than—mere assertion. And in many fields readers are conditioned not just to demand evidentiary support for reasons, but to test its solidity.

We also distinguish between evidence "itself" and reports of it used in an argument. To some students (and teachers), this will seem to split hairs, but students must recognize how their prototypical image of evidence—a smoking gun, fingerprints—differs from what in fact they can offer in its stead—a *description* of the smoking gun, an *image* of fingerprints. We want students to understand that writers offer not evidence itself but only reports of it so that they will realize that every representation of evidence, even numbers, "spins" it in some way, simplifying it, making it tidier than it is. They will then be more critical of what they read and, when they write, more careful to earn their readers' trust by reporting evidence accurately and citing its sources.

5.   **We replaced "rebuttal" with "acknowledgment and response."** Many have noted that Toulmin's treatment of rebuttals is problematical. In ordinary language, a rebuttal is what we offer to oppose an objection. But Toulmin used the term to refer to constraints on the range of a claim:

> Since Harry was born in Bermuda, he is a British subject, *unless he has renounced his citizenship, or one of his parents was a diplomatic representative, or* . . .

Writers rarely state these constraints, because they are default conditions that readers usually assume. But writers often raise objections and offer rebuttals as we ordinarily understand them. They even raise alternative positions that they do not treat as objections to be rebutted.

So for *rebuttal* we substitute *acknowledgment & response,* a term more inclusive and less confrontational. No mature argument would be complete if it failed to acknowledge and respond to other points of view—objections, but also qualifications, alternative claims, alternative interpretations of evidence, and so on. And while the response might be a rebuttal as we usually understand it (a counterargument), it need not be: Mature arguers concede the force of valid alternatives. (Our term also covers the less common cases included in Toulmin's term: when a writer raises a default constraint as a possible objection that he rebuts.)

6.   **We offer a new, quasi-formal account of how warrants work, and a common-sense means to test them not for truth, but for soundness.** It is common to assert that for an argument to work, its warrant must be true. But so far as we know, no one has explained how a warrant, reason, and claim can all be true but fail as an argument. For example,

> You should eat fish*claim* because it does not raise your cholesterol *reason* since, as we all know, we should eat foods that provide roughage.*warrant*

Each of those three elements is true, but the warrant does not link the reason and claim soundly.

We offer what we think is an intuitively satisfying explanation for how warrants bridge a reason and claim, and when they do not, why they fail—something that Toulmin did not address, even in his textbook with Riecke and

Janik.[1] In this discussion, we introduce a pattern of reasoning that some readers may think is merely a synthesis of categorical and conditional reasoning. We agree, except for the words "merely" and we would add, "which reflects naturalistic explanations of reasoning better than syllogisms."

7. A final difference between this book and others is one of degree. Just as we have emphasized the role of sound thinking in writing good arguments, we have also tried to demonstrate in every chapter how the writing process supports sound thinking. So rather than segregate advice about writing into separate chapters, we distributed it through every chapter, connecting specific advice about planning, drafting, and revising to related issues of sound reasoning and arguing.

Having emphasized our differences from standard argument texts, we should note what we share with them: We aim at helping students develop a public voice appropriate to a variety of civic, professional, academic, and other forums. We think that readers are likely to assent to a claim only when they see good reasons and evidence, when they understand the logical connections between reasons and claims, and when they see their concerns and questions acknowledged and answered. We view argument not as a coercive device, nor even as a product of human rationality (though it is), but as a competence by which rationality is shared.

We have been struck by how closely we tracked issues in Aristotle's *Rhetoric*. As did he, we base our discussion of argument on the occasions that motivate it. He focused on public events: trials, funerals, and political deliberations—occasions that called for oral argument. That led him to categorize arguments by the typical problems that such occasions addressed: what people should believe, what they should value, and what they should do—the familiar categories of forensic, epideictic, and deliberative, which have come down to us roughly as fact, value, and policy.

But the more we thought about the problems that motivate argument, the more we were drawn to an account that we think is deeper and more general than the traditional tri-part distinction. We argue that the problems that motivate arguments are of two general kinds that we call *conceptual* and *pragmatic*. They may seem to match the traditional categories of fact and policy, but those categories are less distinct than they appear: arguments that seem to be about what to believe (fact) are often covert arguments about what to do (policy), and arguments about what to do always turn on embedded arguments about what to believe. And any argument categorized as one of values devolves into one of fact (belief) or policy (action).

But whatever kind of argument we make, we make it not just to gain adherence to a claim, but to solve the problem that occasioned the argument in

[1] Stephen Toulmin, Richard Rieke, and Allan Janik, *An Introduction to Reasoning* (New York: Macmillan, 1979).

the first place. How we build an argument to support a solution depends how we frame the problem it solves. So to understand how to make a sound argument, students first have to understand the problem that occasioned it.

We have been surprised by other links to Aristotle. We also focus on style and on the psychology of readers, neither of which claims much space in most current textbooks on argument. Not surprisingly, we discuss those issues differently, but we share his sense of their relevance. Our discussion of warrants turned out to track his discussion of special and general topics. And as he did, we exclude syllogistic logic from rhetoric, relying instead on warranted reasoning. To reach that end, he imported enthymemes, which are like syllogisms but, as he says, address matters that are only probable. Warrants are the typically silent member of an enthymeme.

As was his goal, ours is also relentlessly "how to." We present an analytical apparatus intended to answer the practical questions of readers and writers as they try to understand and discuss two questions:

- What elements of argument do readers need to reach a sound conclusion?

- How do we combine and arrange those elements so that readers experience our argument as we want them to?

We hope this book encourages students and teachers to think about argument more deeply than they otherwise might. But we have tried never to forget that this is a book about writing, written to students for whom writing may not come naturally. So we have included in each chapter a "Writing Process" section, sometimes as long as the chapter itself, that gives writers advice stated directly and explicitly.

Some Thoughts on Teaching This Book

This book comprises five parts and two appendices.

- In Part 1, we survey argument and its relationship to problem solving.

- In Part 2, we look at the five elements of an argument in more detail.

- In Part 3, we discuss reasoning, particularly about meaning and causation.

- In Part 4, we discuss the role of language and its devices in arguments.

In the Readings, we include sample arguments that students can analyze and respond to with arguments of their own.

This is important: After you finish Part 1, you can go directly to any of the other parts. After Part 1, no part depends on any other, so you can teach them in any order. You can also teach the chapters within Parts 2 through 4 in whatever order best suits you and your students, or even assign chapters individually, so that particular students can work on particular issues.

In addition to the Writing Process sections, every chapter also includes a number of "Inquiries." You can tell your students to ignore these entirely, ask them to pick one or two to think about, or assign them as topics for papers. Some are even worth a research paper. Under no circumstances can students do all of them. Some are so difficult that we expect them merely to pique interest and stimulate thinking. None of them, so far as we know, has just one right answer.

You'll find more specific advice about teaching with this book in the Teacher's Guide, but we can summarize our approach here: Use this book not to create your syllabus but to support your students' experience of making arguments. If you have assignments that engage their interests and abilities, start by discussing them in class. (We'll suggest others in this book and the Teacher's Guide.) *Then* use the book to build on that experience. If students read chapters *after* a class of making and critiquing arguments, it will help them organize and consolidate knowledge and skills activated in classroom experience. Of the teachers who used earlier versions of this book, the most successful subordinated it to free-for-all exchanges in class. The least successful assigned chapters without the context of a dynamic experience of making arguments, thus turning the reading into empty memorization of lists and principles. So use this book to support rather than constrain your teaching.

A Message to Students

What Is Argument?

Our aim in this book is to help you do in writing what you do a dozen times a day speaking: settle a contested issue by reaching an agreement based on good reasons.

> You: Let's catch the Bruce Willis movie. I hear it's pretty wild.
>
> Friend: There's a party over at Jan's. Let's go there.
>
> You: Her parties always end up with the cops banging on the door.
>
> Friend: We'll go just for a while. Besides that only happened twice.
>
> You: But you said you wanted to see the Willis movie, and so do I.
>
> Friend: We can see it tomorrow.
>
> You: I have to work tomorrow.
>
> Friend: OK. Maybe I'll go to Jan's later.

Conversations like that are often about trivial matters, but not always:

> Friend: It's stupid for the government to sue cigarette companies over lung cancer and heart disease. People know what they're doing when they start smoking.
>
> You: Yeah, but they try to hook kids. Are you saying an 11-year-old can make that choice intelligently?
>
> Friend: Well, why don't their parents pay more attention to them?
>
> You: Because no one can watch kids every minute. Some parents work.
>
> Friend: You've got a point. But anyone can quit if they want to.
>
> You: That's not so. My uncle has emphysema and he still has to smoke.
>
> Friend: He could quit if he really wanted to. He just needs a little willpower. My mom quit.
>
> You: That's easy for you to say.

On issues from what movie to see to the guilt of cigarette manufacturers to international terrorism, we make claims, offer reasons, and respond to questions, objections, and alternatives. These conversations let us find civil, rational ways to settle disputes, decide what to believe, conduct business, set public policy, and much more. It's how people in every society spend a good part of their day. In fact, it's part of what distinguishes us from the other creatures of the earth.

We call that universal social activity *argument*. That word sets off alarm bells for many people because it evokes images of quarreling or worse. But we hope to rehabilitate that image of argument by focusing not on its tone but on its form and intention. We'll show you how we use argument not to upset social relationships, but to establish and strengthen them.

We make an argument when we

- offer a claim and reasons to support that claim,

- to someone not inclined to accept what we say at face value,

- in order to solve the problem that motivated us to make the claim in the first place.

We can do that amiably or belligerently, but in either case we profit from an argument only when we know what problem we can solve by making one. Arguments are ways of solving problems.

An argument is different from two other kinds of writing that you may have done before, summary and expressions of personal opinion.

- *Summary:* When you summarize, you report others' ideas without coloring them with your own. You don't just mindlessly compress the original, of course. You have to decide what is relevant to your readers, then express it in your own words. When you write arguments, you may have to summarize background, evidence, or other arguments, but you use that summary as *part of* your argument, to support a claim based on what *you* understand and think. Summaries are useful, but not as important in sound decision making as good arguments.

- *Personal opinion:* An expression of opinion and an argument differ in how you treat your readers. In an opinion paper, you tell readers only what you think, not why they should think so too. You can ignore their views and make claims you don't support. That's why opinion papers have little place in academic, professional, or civil life (unless you are so important that your opinion counts for a lot, just because of who you are). If you want readers to take your opinions seriously, you have to support them; that is, you have to offer an argument that gives readers good reason to think they are sound.

In this book, we want to show you how experienced writers think about and make written arguments.

- They know that the point of an argument is not always to win, but to address a problem that can be solved only with the agreement of others.

- They know that they cannot verbally coerce others into that agreement, but must listen to their questions and objections and, when they write, acknowledge and respond to some of them, even if they have to imagine a voice asking those questions on their readers' behalf.

- They know that good arguments and good thinking go hand-in-hand, that the harder they think about the quality of their argument, the more they improve the quality of their thinking, and vice versa.

- They know that they cannot invent new forms every time they write a new argument, that readers expect to see familiar forms, and that writers can use those conventional forms not just to organize their arguments but to discover them.

- Most importantly, they know something so obvious that it escapes most of us: Even when they don't "win" their argument, they gain something just as important when they earn their readers' respect with an argument that seems amiable, reasonable, and thoughtful.

We want you to understand some other things as well:

- why the ethical dimensions of argument are important in making sound ones;

- how and why arguments differ in different fields;

- why making academic arguments is so difficult for students just entering the academic world;

- how you can use what you learn about making an argument to understand those of others.

People have been making arguments since humankind began to talk, and have been making arguments about making arguments for at least two or three thousand years. So you won't be surprised to learn that some aspects of making arguments are still today topics of intense study, discussion, and even more argument.

Some of those recurring questions are difficult to understand and explain. Many students have wondered why they need to distinguish between their evidence and the mere reports of it they include in their arguments. Every student who has ever tried to understand something we call *warrants* has found them tough going, whether they read about them in this book or in others. Our chapters on reasoning, meaning, and causation address issues that philosophers have argued over for 2,500 years. They demand close reading. The two of us wrangled over them at length, often getting into arguments, sometimes so heatedly that we later had to apologize to each other. When you are committed to an idea, it's not always easy to argue in the amiable way we recommend. But when you argue to solve a problem, not just to win, you can preserve the spirit of collaboration that good argument requires.

Why Study Argument?

If you are reading this book in a first-year writing course, you might be surprised by what your teachers ask you to write. And if you don't understand how they judge what you write, you may be more surprised by their comments—and disappointed with your grades. We realize that some of you already know what to expect, especially if you've been in college for a while. But having worked with so many students who don't, the two of us decided we should talk about these issues anyway. If what we say is familiar, you can still learn by hearing it from a teacher's perspective.

In this class, your job is not just to build on writing skills you already have, but to use them in a new way. We've known many students, whether they just graduated high school or were out working for a while, who were surprised not just by how much they had to write, but by how it was judged. Most students begin college assuming that they can go on doing a kind of writing called "knowledge-telling": In high school, they told their teachers what they already knew, in correct English sentences, assembled into coherent paragraphs. In the best cases, students repeated what they had learned; in the worst, what they thought their teachers wanted to hear. So they think that in college they will do the same thing, only about more complicated topics.

In fact, your college teachers will expect you to do something different. We ask you to write papers for many reasons, but rarely just to report what you've read or heard in class. Most teachers, most of the time, will expect you to explain and support not *their* position, but *yours*. We want you to lay out a claim that *you* have come to believe and to explain why you believe it, in more detail than you may think necessary. That doesn't mean we expect your claim to be unique, only that you reached it because you thought through the reasons, evidence, and alternative views.

But you will be expected to write a paper that shows not just what you believe but what you can bring readers to accept. You do that in two ways:

- when you think about what you've read and heard long enough to draw your own conclusion, and

- when you show readers why they should accept your position, or at least respect it as thoughtfully plausible.

In making such arguments in writing, you do what you have done many times in conversation: you put your own ideas into dialogue with those of others. You enter into an imagined conversation with someone not inclined to accept your claim just because you make it. One of our aims is to show you how to create that kind of dialogue in your thinking and then represent it in writing.

We teachers expect something else. We won't be satisfied that you just support a claim. We expect you to make that claim in order to accomplish something: either to call for an action that solves a problem or to answer a puzzling question.

We'll explain why arguments that call for action are more common in the business and professional world and arguments that answer questions more common in the academic world. Your teachers will often ask you to make arguments about ideas that have no obvious connection to a problem in the "real world," except your understanding of it: Can chimps count? Where did weaving originate in the ancient world? How did the social structure of the South contribute to the Civil War? For many students, arguments like that seem airy exercises, theoretical speculation useful to no one. That's why we will discuss in detail what we call "conceptual problems," the kind you will increasingly be expected to pose and solve as you progress through your academic career. You won't understand how the academic world works until you understand why such questions are so important to your teachers and why they expect you to support your answers with a sound argument. We offer this discussion as a kind of primer in academic studies that you may not get elsewhere.

The two of us have known many students who find it difficult to accept the idea of making and supporting claims of their own. So, based on questions we have heard many times before, we want to anticipate those you might have and respond to them now, before they become an obstacle to your reading (we're trying to do what we will repeatedly advise you to do—think ahead about the questions and objections your readers might have, then acknowledge and respond to them).

Some students resist the notion that we actually care about their ideas:

> *You don't really expect me to build an argument around my own ideas, do you? If my ideas are right, you already know them. So why try to convince you of what you already know? I'm here to learn from you: just tell me what to say and I'll say it.*

There is a grain of truth in that concern if we're talking about take-home exams intended to measure what you have learned. For most other papers, though, while we care intensely whether you get the facts right, we care more about how you use them to make a plausible case for your views.

Other students, especially in literature classes, think they should write only about their personal responses:

> *Why do I have to support my ideas with reasons and evidence that satisfy you? My feelings and ideas are good enough for me.*

To be sure, it is better to have some ideas than none. And you do learn what you think by writing it out for no one but yourself. But as important as that may be, your teachers want to help you prepare for a time when people will read what you write not because they are paid to, as your teachers are, but because they think you have something to say that they should know. They will have little interest in knowing just your feelings and opinions. Even when you write about your most private thoughts, you have an opportunity to practice writing for readers who, you hope, will take your ideas seriously, whether they share your feelings or not.

Other students worry that they have nothing to say:

> *I can't solve important problems like abortion or gun control. And what do I know about what documents Thomas Jefferson used as models for the Declaration of Independence?*

Those who think that shortchange their intelligence. You may not now be able to change the mind of an experienced historian, but you can write an argument that she will respect and that encourages her to respect the quality of your mind.

Finally, some students shy away from argument altogether:

> *Arguments make me uncomfortable. I feel pushy trying to get people to change their minds. I don't like shouting or the idea of winners and losers. Besides, I don't think it's right to take sides all the time.*

That view of argument is widespread, but it defines argument too narrowly. You don't have to get into an argument every time you offer one. We two have been making an argument for the last several pages, giving you what we hope are good reasons to consider something that you might not be inclined to accept: that many, perhaps most of your papers in high school did not make arguments, and that most of the papers you write in college must. But we haven't shouted, and we hope you don't feel we've tried to push you around.

We do acknowledge the force of one concern that some students express:

> *Arguments rarely settle anything.*

On some recurring issues, that's true—most people have views on issues such as abortion and gay rights that are so deeply entrenched in their system of values that no argument can (or should) change them. But such intractable issues are rare. And even in those cases, argument has a place: When we all make the best, most reasonable arguments we can, we understand one another better and at least make it possible to respect one anothers' reasons for holding the beliefs we do. A good argument does not have to earn others' agreement to earn their respect.

There is a term for the image that you project in making an argument others respect: your *ethos*. Image has such a bad reputation these days that we hesitate to offer it as a reason for learning how to make sound arguments. But when the evidence is uncertain, when opposing points of view both seem to have force, when we aren't clear about what to think or do, we tend to give weight to those who project the ethos of someone reasonable, thoughtful, and mature. Over time, the ethos you project in individual arguments becomes your enduring reputation. And when you earn the reputation of someone who makes reasonable, thoughtful, mature arguments, you earn a fair hearing even from those inclined to disagree.

Now here's a final warning: Much of our advice about planning, drafting, and revising arguments may seem formulaic and mechanical. Some of you will think that an advantage: *Great! Just tell me what to do and I'll do it.* Others will bristle that it stifles your creativity: *I want my writing to be mine, not the product of your formulas.*

We hope that you will all learn both how to lean on our models when you need to and how to set them aside them when you can. You know how to do that if you've ever learned a sport such as golf or tennis or a performance art such as dance or music. You don't practice the whole skill all at one, but one part at a time: plant your feet this way, hold your hand that way. When you put the parts together in a game or performance, you at first seem to move by the numbers, more clunky than creative. But once you learn the parts well enough not to think about every conscious move, there comes a moment when you go with the flow, putting the moves and pieces together into a seamless, flowing performance.

That's how you'll learn to make arguments. You may at first feel you are writing by the numbers, that your arguments are mechanical and formulaic. But as you master the parts, they will disappear into the flow of drafting, and your arguments will seem more natural and organic. It's then that you can be as creative as you wish. With rare exceptions, creative people work within boundaries and forms that they *knowingly* adapt or even break. Shakespeare was perhaps the most creative person who ever wrote in English, but he worked within conventions that all his contemporaries recognized. When he broke those boundaries, he knew what they were and what he was doing.

We hope that you learn the forms of argument well enough to use them creatively. But when you struggle because time is short or the issue too complex, you'll have something to fall back on that will help you assemble the pieces into a seamless, flowing argument that puts your ideas—and you—in the best light.

How to Use This Book

We designed this book so that you can use it to suit your particular needs and circumstances. We hope you will find our ideas so interesting, our advice so useful, and our words so engaging that you'll read through from cover to cover. But we also know that everyone is busy and life is short. So on the chance that you don't find the topic of argument as fascinating as we do, we've tried to make this book easy to use when you're just searching for some particular information or advice. Before you can decide how to use this book to meet your needs, however, you have to know how we put it together.

We've organized this book into five parts:

- In Part 1, (Chapters 1–3), we present an **overview of the nature of argument**. Try to get through these chapters quickly, because they will help you write complete arguments from the start.

- In Part 2, (Chapters 4–8), we lay out the **five elements of an argument** in detail, explaining how to use each one to develop your argument and test your thinking. Your teacher may ask you to work through these chapters in sequence, or to look at individual chapters as specific issues arise in your writing.

- In Part 3, (Chapters 9–11), we focus on the **reasoning, meaning, and causes** that go into an argument. These are the most advanced chapters in the book.

- In Part 4, (Chapters 12–13), we discuss the role of **language** in argument. We show you how to write clearly and vividly and how to use language in deliberately persuasive ways. You may not want to wait until the end to read these chapters, especially Chapter 12, because they will help you revise your papers.

- At the end of the book you'll find three sections of **readings**. Your teacher may ask you to study them as examples of argument or to write about issues they raise.

We have divided each chapter into three sections that approach the material from different points of view. We designed them to work together:

- The main body of each chapter explores one aspect of arguments. It will help you understand the rationale behind our advice about writing them. Use this section to put our specific advice into a larger context and to guide your thinking about the Inquiries.

- The Writing Process section offers nuts-and-bolts advice about how to use what you learn in the main body. Our advice is divided into five units: (1) thinking–reading–talking, (2) preparing and planning, (3) drafting, (4) revising, and (5) working collaboratively.

- In the Inquiries, we present questions and activities to help you explore issues in that chapter, to spark your thinking about your experience writing and reading arguments. You might use them to prime your thinking before you start reading a chapter; afterwards, use them to pursue ideas that interest you.

Each section also has its own individual use:

- If you are most interested in the theory of argument and sound reasoning, read the main body of the chapters.

- If you want to know only how to write, concentrate on the instructions and checklists in the Writing Process section. We've collected many of them on pages 214. You'll find a list of the topics of our advice in the Topical Contents of the Writing Process Sections on page xv.

- When you want to brainstorm ideas for class discussion or paper topics, read the Inquiries to find ones that catch your interest.

Most chapters also include shaded boxes that present background information, interesting examples, and other matters that we think will give you perspective on the chapters. Other boxes with borders present examples that illustrate matters discussed in the chapter. We intend these boxes only as supplements to your reading, so don't let them interrupt your flow.

In Chapters 1 through 8, we include a Writing Projects section with assignments for written arguments. Chapters 2, 3, 5, and 6 contain Sample Essays for you to analyze and in some cases revise. Your teacher may ask you to do some of these assignments. If not, you can learn something by reading them and then imagining how you would follow their instructions.

Finally, we conclude every chapter with a brief summary of its main points. We hope you won't substitute reading the summary for reading the chapter because we do not explain the principles we list there. But some of you may find it useful to read the summary before you read the chapter to organize your thinking. Also, you may benefit from reading through all the summaries just before you begin writing a new paper, especially if it is for another class.

Acknowlegments

As we say in a few places in this book, writers need the help of readers because there is one thing we can never know: what it's like to be our readers. We two have been immeasurably helped by those readers who reviewed this book during its development. They told us things that we could never have known (and sometimes didn't want to hear). But they read our work better than we ever could, and we are deeply grateful for their careful, always helpful comments, even when they stung. Students who profit from this book can thank the following reviewers, as do we: Jonathan Ayres, The University of Texas; R. Michael Barrett, University of Wisconsin, River Falls; David Blakesley, Southern Illinois University, Carbondale; Stuart C. Brown, New Mexico State University; Jami L. Carlacio, University of Wisconsin, Milwaukee; William J. Carpenter, University of Kansas; Peter Dorman, Central Virginia Community College; Ellen Burton Harrington, Tulane University; Eleanor Latham, Central Oregon Community College; Carol A. Lowe, McLennan Community College; Margaret P. Morgan, University of North Carolina, Charlotte; B. Keith Murphy, Fort Valley State University; Twila Yates Papay, Rollins College; CarolAnn H. Posey, Virginia Wesleyan College; Deborah F. Rossen-Knoll, Philadelphia College of Textiles and Science; Mary Sauer, Indiana University Purdue University Indianapolis; Laura Wendorff, University of Wisconsin, Platteville

We are especially grateful to those who taught versions of this book in its formative stages and to their students, both of whom provided invaluable feedback: Thomas Fischer, Paula McQuade, Dev Parikh, Peter Sattler, Brian Wagner, and Carol Williams.

We would also like to thank Ben Morrison and Elinor Stapleton for seeing this manuscript through to production, and Anna Hirsch, for her reliable work tracking down sources and helping assemble the index. We would especially like to thank Anne Smith, who had the faith in us to back this project, even when we told her that it wouldn't be your ordinary book on argument.

And finally, those closest to us.

There is no way to say how much the growing family has meant to me. The best days have been when we've all been together—Christopher, Oliver, Megan and Phil, Dave and Patty, Joe and Christine. And of course Joan, she who for many years has put up with my "Just one more minute." Her deep well of patience and good humor still flows more generously than I deserve.

—JMW

I was born to a clan of arguers, and my daughters have inherited the tradition. But what they learned along with their love of argument was that good argument never threatens love. Robin, Karen, and Lauren have kept me on my toes, my arguments well-tested, and my heart full. This last they got from their mother, my companion for more than thirty years. Sandra has always been the heart of it all.

—GGC

PART 1

The Nature of Argument

In this first part, we present the essentials of argument.

- In Chapter 1, we discuss the place of argument in our social, professional, civic, and even mental lives. We explain it not as antagonistic confrontation aimed at imposing agreement on others, but as a civil conversation aimed at solving a problem in a way that meets everyone's best interests.

- In Chapter 2, we discuss five questions whose answers help you organize the arguments you make in cooperation with others. They are questions that you must answer every time you converse with those whose opinion you value. We show how by asking those five questions of yourself, you can create the substance and plan of a written argument.

- In Chapter 3, we discuss why we make arguments at all—to solve problems. We explain the two kinds of problems that occasion most written arguments: (1) pragmatic problems, which you can solve only by getting readers to act or at least to support an action, and (2) conceptual problems, which you can solve only by helping readers understand something better. We then discuss how to frame an argument by articulating the problem and its solution in a way that motivates readers to read.

CHAPTER 1

Argument and Rationality

In this chapter, we introduce our view of argument: Argument is not combat or coercion, but a way to find and test good solutions to tough problems with the cooperation of others. Bad arguments can divide us, but good ones strengthen the fabric of our communities—academic, professional, and civic—by helping us justify not just what we do and think, but why others might do the same. Even when our arguments don't succeed, they help us understand why we differ.

What Is Argument?

How many arguments have you heard or read today? Probably more than you can count. Television and talk radio are so full of them that arguing seems to be a national sport—and the nastier the better. Some talk shows are framed less as a conversation between thoughtful adults than as a battle between adversaries eager to shout each other into silence. Politicians attack each other so fiercely that many of the best flee public service. And when the politicians aren't attacking each other, plenty of columnists on both the right and left do so with venomous pleasure.

This image of argument as war is entrenched even in our language: Opposing sides *attack* each other, *advancing* claims, *marshaling* reasons and evidence, and *defending* them from *counterattack*. They try to *shoot down* each other's claims and *undermine* each other's position, until one side claims *victory* and the other admits *defeat*. So it's not just the likes of Jerry Springer who encourage verbal violence; the English language itself inclines us to imagine argument as a form of close combat.

But ignore hostile confrontations. How often can you recall people trading claims over issues as trivial as the future of the Rolling Stones or as important as the morality of suicide, then quietly and amiably supporting their claims with reasons and evidence? As calm as they are, those exchanges are also arguments, because an argument is not defined by its hostile tone, but simply by people exchanging and testing claims and reasons in search of a solution to a problem:

- Your friend says she doesn't want to eat Japanese because she had Korean last night, but you want vegetarian so you compromise on Indian.
- Your teacher is skeptical of a claim that apes can count because it is based on flawed data. You mention an article claiming that they communicate by sign language, which seems harder than counting, but your teacher criticizes those studies too.
- You tell your boss that the new software can't generate up-to-date sales reports. He says it would cost too much to replace it, but wants you to find out more and report back.

In countless conversations like these, we offer each other claims and reasons to solve problems ranging from where to have lunch to the origin of the universe.

Even if you spent the day alone reading a book, you probably had a silent argument with its author. You read, *Cloning has no moral implications,* and think, *Wait a minute. Every action has moral implications. I wonder how he would explain. . . .* As you might guess, we are making an argument with you right now, offering what we hope you will see as good reasons to accept our claim—that an argument need not be colored by antagonism, that it is not something we have but something we collaboratively *make* to solve a problem in a way that serves everyone's best interests. And we hope you are thinking to yourself, *Wait a minute. I don't agree because . . .*

You may even have argued with yourself, if in your own mind you had to wrestle with a vexing personal question: *So what do I do about my chem class? I have no shot at med school if I don't get at least a B. But can I? It would mean no social life for the rest of the term. And do I really want med school? . . .* We make arguments with others, face-to-face or in writing, or even between two sides of our own divided mind.

The Source of the Word *Argument*

Occasionally, we'll discuss the original meaning of an important term, because earlier meanings can illuminate current ones. The original meaning of *argument,* for example, was to "make clear." The Latin word for silver, *argentum,* comes from the same root. The two words are related in that what shines is often clear.

What Good Is Argument?

When we make an argument not to defeat others but to enlist them in solving a problem, we put our views into dialogue with theirs so that we can test them and, if we hear good reasons, improve them. We all benefit from such arguments, because no one person has all the evidence or understands every aspect of a problem. We can all afford to lose an argument; what we cannot afford to lose is the opportunity to work together to find sound reasons for believing and acting as we do.

Argument Makes Us Rational

It is easier to say what rationality is not than what it is: It is not a body of facts or rules of logic. Nor does it have anything to do with education or intelligence. It doesn't even mean being right, because we can rationally believe what is false. For thousands of years it was "rational" for educated and intelligent people to think that the world was flat and that the sun went around it, because that's what their best evidence told them.

We start to become rational as children when we want reasons for thinking or doing what we are told. But as we mature, we have to develop other aspects of rationality. We have to acquire the self-control to size up a problem before jumping to a solution, a pause that gives us time to exercise other rational competencies:

- the patience to gather information from remembered experience, direct observation, or active research, and the judgment to know when to stop;
- the ability to use that information as evidence in reasoning our way to a sound conclusion.

But even that is a limited kind of rationality, something, it is claimed, chimps can do. We become most humanly rational when we can reflect on our own reasoning, when we exercise:

- the resolve to look for evidence that might contradict our solution (but also to know when to stop looking);
- the courage to change our mind when the weight of evidence contradicts our beliefs (but also the confidence not to change important beliefs lightly);
- the imagination to evaluate the long-term consequences of believing in or acting on our conclusions (but not at the expense of not believing or acting when belief or action is necessary);
- most important, the ability to reason about our reasoning, to recognize and question assumptions, inconsistencies, and contradictions (but not to try to resolve every conceivable contradiction).

At least that's how we're supposed to think rationally. The fact is, hardly any of us does so consistently, no matter how intelligent, well educated, or experienced we are. Just about all of us reason in ways that are quick and simple, bounded by short-term self-interest. What's remarkable is that even when we rely on quick and simple thinking, we still make so many good decisions. But when we make spectacularly bad ones, we can almost always point to the same cause: We didn't step back to assess whether we drew a sound conclusion based on good evidence, or whether we reached the conclusion we did just because we wanted it to be true. If so, we didn't exercise our deepest rationality.

So rationality is not just thinking soundly. It's sound thinking about the soundness of your thinking, a competence that depends on your ability to listen to another voice questioning your reasoning. It's best when you find others to ask those questions for you. But when you can't, you have to imagine that voice murmuring insistently, *But wait. What about . . . ? Do you think your conclusion is sound simply because you want it to be? What would you say to someone who said . . . ?* In short, rationality is the ability to conduct arguments—with others when you can, but with yourself when you must.

How Common Are Critical Thinkers?

One researcher wanted to find out how well we can question our own beliefs. She interviewed 160 people about problems such as the causes of unemployment and school dropouts. Those interviewed ranged from ninth graders to high school dropouts to college graduates to experts in the social problems that were the topic of the questions. When someone offered a cause, the questioner followed up with questions like these:

- How do you know that is the cause? What evidence would you offer?
- How would someone disagree with you? What evidence might he offer?
- What would you say to that person to show he was wrong?
- Is there any evidence that would show your view to be wrong?
- Do experts know for sure what the cause is?
- Is there more than one point of view about the cause? Could more than one point of view be right?

Fewer than half of those asked could think of any evidence to support their views. Though two out of three could think of an alternative view, fewer than half could think of an argument that might support it, and even when offered a counter-argument, fewer than half could think of an answer to it. In other words, most of those she questioned could not imagine another point of view based on sound reasoning, or think of any good evidence to support their own!

Source: From Deanna Kuhn, *The Skills of Argument* (New York: Cambridge University Press, 1991).

Arguments Sustain a Civil Community

Rationality defines our humanity, but we are also social creatures who live and work with others whose views often differ from our own. So if you hope to be part of a rational community, you must be able not only to *form* rational beliefs, but to *explain* them, to give others good reason to believe that your thinking deserves if not their agreement, then at least their respect. Even when no one agrees with your claim, you still succeed if others think you made your argument thoughtfully and supported it with reasons that would seem reasonable, were they in your shoes.

When your arguments are consistently sound, you gain another social benefit: the durable reputation of someone who thinks well. In every argument you make, you project an image, a character or personality that some call your *ethos*. Some of us project an ethos that others don't much like: aggressive, quick to judge, impatient, closed minded, even abusive. Others project an ethos that seems thoughtful, open minded, confident but not smugly sure that they have all the right answers, the kind of ethos that thoughtful people tend to trust. Once you earn a reputation for judicious thinking, you enjoy the confidence of those whose judgment matters most. This is particularly important when issues are complex and uncertain, because it's on those occasions when we depend as much on the character of the person making an argument as on its actual substance.

Arguments Define Academic and Professional Communities

Arguments, especially written ones, are also the lifeblood of academic and professional communities. Scientists, engineers, lawyers, agricultural agents, college professors and countless others—they all make arguments to support solutions to the problems in their fields. They make those arguments first in their own minds, then talking with colleagues, then in writing.

Most professional communities make arguments to address problems that can be solved only if someone *does* something.

Problem: The Malaysian economy has collapsed.

Solution: What we should do is lend it money.

Argument: If we do not, our own economy will suffer . . .

We call these *pragmatic* problems, problems that left unsolved will have consequences that we—and we hope others—can't tolerate. So we propose *doing something* to eliminate their consequences.

In academic communities, on the other hand, researchers often dig into problems with no idea of proposing any action. Instead, they make an argument only so that we will *understand* something better:

Problem: We do not understand how European trade influenced the Malaysian economy in the seventeenth century.

Solution: It created a commercial class of merchants and traders who . . .

Argument: . . .

Academic communities also call questions like these *problems,* but they are a different kind of problem. They are *conceptual* problems that we typically phrase as questions: *How big is the universe? Do birds really descend from dinosaurs? How did European trade influence the Malaysian economy in the seventeenth century?* Such problems may be "about" the world, but arguments supporting their solutions don't explain what we should do to improve it, but rather only how we can better understand it. Researchers may believe that in the long run the more we know about the world, the better we can deal with it, but their immediate aim is not action, but understanding. Those who work on questions like these sometimes call what they do "pure" research. We'll discuss both kinds of problems in more detail in Chapter 3.

Whatever kind of problem a writer poses, she commonly has to make an argument to support her solution, so that others in her community can reflect on it, test it, maybe improve it, or if necessary, reject it. As we enter the third millennium, we depend on sound knowledge created by arguments at least as much as we depended a century ago on steel, coal, and electricity. And just as our forebears had to learn to judge the quality of cars, houses, and other products of the Age of Industry, so must we learn to judge the quality of our understanding in the Age of Information.

IN THE READINGS

The Variety of Arguments

On pages 359-466 you'll find brief readings that we will use as examples and you can use for some of your writing projects. From time to time, we'll include a box about the readings or experiences that the two of us have had, pointing out how aspects of argument work in practice.

For example, some students who read this book in manuscript wondered whether people really have to make arguments as often as we claim. One said, *Since I'm going to be an architectural engineer, I'll just be doing what my clients ask, so what does this have to do with me? I don't want to argue with my client.* He got an answer from a practicing architect (Colomb's brother), who started by recalling all the arguments he had to make as part of a bridge restoration project for the city of Chicago. When he got to about twenty, we asked, *And how many had to be in writing?* He answered by pulling out a two-inch thick file of proposals, reports, letters, memos, and so on—all written arguments.

Arguments Enable Democracy

Arguments are also central in our civic lives, because raising problems and debating solutions is at the heart of this messy way of governing ourselves that we call democracy. A dictator doesn't have to make arguments, because no one dares question his claims, much less his reasons. But in a democracy, those who govern are, at least in principle, obliged to answer our questions. We elect people to think about our problems, to ask questions, and to make arguments on our behalf, and we pay journalists, commentators, and political analysts to write books, articles, and editorials that contribute to those debates. Our designated questioners might not ask the questions we want them to; often we don't even know what questions they should ask. But whenever a government official is asked a question, he is reminded that he is in principle answerable to us. If our leaders ever thought they could have their way without giving us good reasons, our democracy would end.

Of course, even your best argument won't always succeed, especially when it threatens your reader's self interest and she has more power or prestige than you. Some claim that power, not reason is what finally counts, so rational arguments are exercises in futility. But that view both ignores occasions when good arguments have prevailed and excuses those who exercise their power from having to justify their arbitrary use of it. In the short run, they may still get their way, but a weak argument reveals their shoddy thinking.

Developing Democracy Means More Arguments

Sumalee Limpaovart thought she was simply a mother protecting her child. But she found herself a warrior in the front lines of a struggle for democratic openness that is being fought today in Thailand and across East Asia. When her six-year-old daughter was rejected by an exclusive government school earlier this year, Mrs. Sumalee did something that would have been unthinkable here only a few years ago: She challenged the decision, using a new freedom of information law to demand the test scores of the other children. In the end, Mrs. Sumalee found what she had suspected: One-third of the students admitted had failed the entrance exam but had been accepted because of their families' status or gifts to the school.

It was just one of the many small, sharp battles that have multiplied in recent years as a bolder, better-educated middle class begins to rise up against the paternalistic order of the past. As they do so, a society built on harmony and civility is becoming increasingly argumentative, confrontational, and noisy.

Source: From *New York Times*, August 10, 1999.

What's Not Argument, or at Least Not a Good One?

Explanations

Some claims and reasons look like arguments, but are not. Consider this pair of statements:

> I have to go home. ₁ₗₐᵢₘ I'm so tired I'm making mistakes. ᵣₑₐₛₒₙ

I have to go home. _{claim} I'm so tired I'm making mistakes. _{reason}

That first sentence is a claim and the second a reason, but we cannot know whether they constitute an argument until we know the speaker's intention:

Ron: Leaving? About time. You've been working for hours.

Tanya: I have to go home. _{claim} I'm so tired I'm making mistakes. _{reason}

Tanya offers Ron a reason not to *convince* him of her claim that she should go home (he seems to think she should), but to *explain* why she must. Contrast this:

Ron: You're not leaving, are you? Don't leave! We need you!

Tanya: I have to go home. _{claim} I'm so tired I'm making mistakes. _{reason}

Tanya offers the same claim and reason, but now to *convince* Ron to accept a claim that she thinks he will not accept just because she makes it. That's not an explanation; now it's an argument about the solution to a problem.

For an exchange to be an argument, it has to meet two criteria:

- The first is its form. To make an argument, you have to offer someone a claim (a statement that makes clear what you want that person to believe or do) and support it with at least one reason (a statement that gives that person a basis for agreeing).

- The second criterion concerns the intention of the participant. You make an argument when the other person will agree with your claim only if you earn her assent by giving her a reason that she thinks is a good one.

For an exchange to be a *thoughtful* argument, however, it has to be more than a one-sided list of reasons:

- You make an argument that is both sound and fair when you not only offer your own claim and reasons, but also acknowledge and respond to views that might qualify or even contradict them. Tanya is obliged to answer if Ron says to her: *But you promised you would stay longer.*

We use explanations and arguments for different ends, but we often have to weave them together when we argue about complex issues. You might, for example, argue that we should be allowed to invest some of our social security taxes in the stock market, but in doing so, you would have to explain how the market works, because we have to understand it before we believe what you say about it.

Persuasion

Here are three other forms of persuasion that may seem like arguments but lack a key quality of sound and fair ones: (1) negotiation, (2) propaganda, and (3) coercion.

Negotiation seems like argument when you and another person trade claims and reasons about, say, the price of a car. But when you negotiate, you both can offer any reason to reach an outcome that you both can live with. You might not lie, but you are not obliged to be candid. So you are not unethical when you keep the highest price you will pay secret. But when you collaborate on an argument to address a serious problem, secrets encourage a distrust deadly to the spirit of inquiry. For example, you would betray business colleagues if you claimed that you negotiated a good price for company cars but kept extra costs secret.

Propaganda resembles argument when it offers claims and reasons. But propagandists don't care whether the reasons are any good, only whether they work, usually by playing on the emotions of their audience. Nor do they care what anyone else thinks, except to know what beliefs they have to defeat. Least of all do they care whether another point of view might change their own. When you make a serious argument, you must be open to opposing claims and reasons.

Coercion solves problems by open threat, by making the cost of rejecting a claim intolerable. It usually takes the form of *Agree or I will hurt you.* Though we think of coercion as a paddle, a carrot can also coerce when it is a bribe: *Agree and I will reward you.* Those who present themselves as authoritative also seek to coerce, expecting us to assent just because they ask us to: *Agree because I know better.* So do those who try to shame us into agreement: When Princess Leia of *Star Wars* pleads, *Help me Obiwan Kenobe, you're my only hope,* he must either help her or seem to betray his deepest values.

Negotiation, propaganda, and coercion are not always irrational, or even unethical. We coerce, propagandize, and negotiate with children, but we call it parenting. Nor would we be irrational not to negotiate with terrorists holding hostage a school bus full of students. Our challenge is always to know what form of discourse best serves the cause of a civil and just community. (Some writers distinguish between *convincing*—getting someone to believe something—and *persuading*—getting someone to do something. It's a useful distinction, but the fact is that few people make it in their casual speaking and writing.)

Fair Argument Persuades with Reasons

When Colomb was a boy, his school had a vice principal called the "Prefect of Discipline" who kept in his office a paddle known as "The Persuader." That paddle influenced Colomb's thinking and occasionally his actions, but getting paddled was not a form of argument, any more than are the insults of those talk radio and TV participants who shout others into silence.

Stories

Stories are as old as arguments, maybe older, but they appeal to a different form of thinking and usually to our feelings. In many ways, stories are more persuasive than arguments because they have three powerful advantages:

- When you tell a good story, you seem to describe what "really" happened "out there" so vividly that its truth is apparent to the mind's eye of your listener. When you make an argument, however, you have to offer sequences of abstract reasons and claims that must not only reflect your own internal reasoning, but accommodate that of your readers.

- When you tell a good story, you usually hope listeners will at least for a time suspend their critical judgment, not to object *Wait a minute, that can't be so!* but instead to wonder only *What happened next?* When you write a thoughtful argument, you expect, even hope that readers will question your reasons. You tell stories hoping your readers will suspend their disbelief; you make arguments that acknowledge their doubts. In fact, some put so much faith in the power of stories to reveal the truth of experience that they claim it is morally wrong even to question them, so long as they seem to be sincerely told and offer insight into some larger truth.

- When you tell a story especially well, it can create in listeners awe, fear, pleasure, disgust, and so on. When you make an argument, you hope to create a more ineffable sense of intellectual pleasure, a good feeling, but one usually less viscerally compelling than anger or delight.

Inexperienced writers typically go wrong when they think that merely by telling a good story, they make a good argument. But as we shall see, a story can never itself be a claim, or even a reason. That's why so many moral tales end with an explicit message like, *So be careful what you wish for.* Lacking such a moral flourish, a story forces us to infer the claim it is supposed to illustrate; which is to say, we can read into a story almost any claim we want. Stories can, however, count as illustrations or evidence in support of a reason. And since they have such power, experienced writers use them often, but only as part of a larger argument.

How Arguments Go Bad

Though argument is central in our social, professional, and mental lives, it can create discord when we manage it badly. Combative argument stops rational thinking, but so do claims and reasons that might seem reasonable to us but wholly irrational to others. This is particularly true in multicultural settings. For example, recent conflicts in southeastern Europe have created an immense human tragedy. The facts are clear: More than 600 years ago, Turkish forces inflicted on Serbs in the province of Kosovo a defeat so great that it has become part of Serbian cultural memory. Much later, Kosovo was inhabited by ethnic Albanians, who by early 1999 constituted about 90 percent of its population. Many Serbs believed that to recover their national honor they had to drive out the Albanians and reclaim Kosovo as their own, which their government tried to do. Many in the rest of the world believe it is irrational to think that a defeat six centuries ago demands retaliation today. *They're mad!,* people claim.

The problem is that some aspects of every culture can seem mad to others. The United States, for example, seemed irrational to many in the rest of the world in the way we dealt with President Clinton's efforts to cover up his sexual misconduct, because they don't share values and assumptions so deeply entrenched in our thinking that we can scarcely express them clearly. When that kind of deep disagreement on fundamental values occurs, different communities often can't get beyond simply trading claims: One side thinks it irrational to question such values, while the other side thinks it irrational not to.

Does that mean that different cultures can never agree? On some issues, perhaps not, especially when our assumptions are so deeply buried in our minds that we have to excavate them (see p. 183). But if arguments can't settle certain issues, they can help us understand why not. Just discovering our deep assumptions is a challenge, one that face-to-face conversation can sometimes help solve, but that more often requires the patience to explore in the cooler, more thoughtful form of writing.

In a society of diverse values, we need more than good will and tolerance. To respect the views of others, we also need to understand why they hold them.

This book is about making written arguments based on a model of civil conversation. That, however, is just another way of saying it's about using our powers of human rationality to address problems and questions whose solutions and answers are not obvious to everyone.

Logic, Character, Emotion / Logos, Ethos, Pathos

We hope you've noticed that we have not identified rationality as cold logic. You would seem irrational if you never felt emotion as you made or read some arguments. No rational person could read or write a study on the Holocaust or slavery and feel nothing. In fact, we gauge the importance of a problem largely by how strongly we *feel* about its consequences. And since no one can check all the evidence and consider all the alternatives in arguments about complex issues, we often evaluate an argument partly by how we feel about its writer.

Nor is it irrational to listen to your feelings carefully. We have all reached a logical conclusion, only to discover that it doesn't feel right. But when we have to support a *claim* based on feelings alone, how do we show that our feelings are more reliable than those of someone else? Or, since our feelings can also mislead us, how do we know they are reliable at all? We can't *justify* a decision simply by saying how strongly we feel about it, either to ourselves or to someone else. We have to explain our decision—and our feelings—in ways that seem rational. And that means with good reasons.

Those who write about arguments distinguish three kinds of force in them:

- When we appeal to logic, we base our position on what is called *logos*—the topic of most of this book.

- When we project a trustful character, we hope readers will respond to our *ethos*. (We discuss this force throughout this book, as well.)

- When we appeal directly to the feelings of readers, we appeal to their *pathos*. (We raise this issue mainly in Part 4.)

It is sometimes useful to separate these appeals for analysis, but in practice they are so intertwined that to distinguish them may be mere hairsplitting.

WRITING PROCESS 1
Argument and Rationality

We aim to help you make sound written arguments. Unfortunately, many writers have habits that keep them from doing that. They read with no sense of purpose, taking copious notes on everything. Then they plunge into drafting and go where chance takes them, or they plan in painful detail, then write up their argument exactly according to the plan. Experienced writers know that they have to think, prepare, and plan before they draft, but they also expect to make discoveries as they draft and revise, particularly as they imagine how their readers will respond to their reasons and evidence.

That's a lesson many inexperienced writers take a long time learning. When they read an argument in a newspaper or magazine, they see only the neatly printed product, not the hours of drafting, revising, editing, and re-editing that went into it. And so they think that professionals just dash off a draft, maybe spell-check it, and print it out. And to be sure, some talented writers do just that. The other 99 percent of us wish we could. We have to plan, draft, re-plan, re-draft, revise, re-draft, revise again, . . . until we run out of energy, interest, or time.

To start you on that learning curve, in each chapter we discuss strategies that experienced writers use to produce effective arguments in a reasonable time. We organize this advice into four categories (1) Thinking-Reading-Talking, (2) Preparing and Planning, (3) Drafting, and (4) Revising. Those steps look like a linear sequence, but don't try to follow them step-by-step. Be ready to loop back and forth.

Because your readers are as important in this process as you are, we include in the first few chapters sections on working with those who can stand in for your real reader. Experienced writers know that they can better anticipate how readers will respond when they share their work with others *as they go*.

Thinking-Reading-Talking

You begin working on your paper long before you take your first notes or sketch your first outline. In these sections, we show you how to use your time after you get an assignment but before you begin to draft. Since you will read mostly arguments, you can use what you know about writing them to help you read them more effectively. And the best way to understand what you read is to write. Mark up what you read: underline, highlight, comment in the margins. Talk back to the writer by writing out your questions or reservations. (Of course, you know not to mark up anything from a library. So work on a photo-copy or use post-it tags.)

Get an Overview

Start by skimming to create a framework for more careful reading. Ask these questions of your authors:

- What problem do you solve here? What question do you answer?
- What is your solution to the problem, your answer to the question?
- If I agree, do you want me just to think something or to do something?
- What main reasons support your claim? What evidence do you offer?

Why not just start at the first word and read straight through? Because once you have a framework, you can read faster, understand better, and remember longer. Here is a procedure for skimming to create that informed framework:

Articles

1. Locate where the introduction stops and the body begins. That may be marked with a heading, extra space, or other printed signal.
2. Skim the introduction, focusing on its end. You are most likely to find there a statement of the problem or question that the author addresses. Highlight it. You may also find the main point, the answer to the question, the solution to the problem. If so, highlight it too.
3. Turn to the conclusion and skim it. If the Main Point was not at the end of the introduction, you should find it here. Highlight it.
4. Look through the body for headings that indicate how the article is organized and its sequence of topics.
5. Skim just the first paragraph or two of each main section.

Books

1. Read the table of contents and the opening section that contains an overview. It might be called "Introduction," "Preface," or "Chapter 1."
2. Focus on the beginning and conclusion of the overview, looking for a statement of the issue, problem, or question the book addresses.
3. Read the conclusion, noticing how it relates to the overview. Look for the main point. Highlight or summarize it.
4. Skim the first and last few paragraphs of each chapter.

Web Sites

Many of the texts posted on Web sites have the same structure as published articles, and you can use the approach above. Otherwise, do this:

1. Look for an overview or introduction. You might find it on the home page or on a page all its own.
2. Look for a site map to see how it is organized into topics and sections. If you find no map, read through the major links on the home page.

Once you have a general sense of a text, question it as you read it. Record disagreements, questions, alternative points of view. This is a useful habit, because it helps you imagine your readers doing the same with you. The more you talk back to what you read, the better you can anticipate how your readers will talk back to you.

When you've finished a section, write—or at least mentally rehearse—a brief summary of what you've read. By mentally summarizing, you help fix in your memory a clearer and more permanent image of it. Think of it as your "elevator story"—what you would tell someone about that article or book between the first and the tenth floor.

Preparing and Planning

One thing that distinguishes expert writers is the quality of their preparation. They invest time up front to inform themselves and to prepare and plan their arguments, because experience has taught them that the more they prepare the better they write. Nothing replaces experience, but what you can learn to do consciously now, you will later do automatically. Along the way, you'll discover the rituals of planning and preparation that work best for you, what you can do in your head, and what you have to write out.

Focus on Your Problem

Start planning your argument by being clear about what you want it to achieve. What do you gain if readers assent to your solution? What do you lose if they don't? What counts as success and failure? Do you propose ways to improve the world or just ways to understand it better? Decide what kind of problem you are addressing:

- Your problem is *conceptual* if you want readers simply to *understand* something better. What do you want readers to *understand* about Super-K and Wal-Mart?

  Megastores force small family stores out of business, replacing the intimate spaces of small stores where neighbors could meet with huge impersonal barns where everyone is a stranger, thereby eroding community values.

- Your problem is *pragmatic* if you want readers to *do* something or to support an action:

> Because large megastores erode the quality of community life, this county should pass zoning laws to keep K-Marts out of rural areas.

The language that explicitly signals a pragmatic problem includes words like *should, must, have to,* and *ought to.* But you can signal readers that you want them to act, or at least support an action with other words:

> By creating new zoning laws, we could . . .
>
> The creation of new zoning laws would . . .
>
> Without new zoning laws, we are . . .

Inexperienced writers commonly—and mistakenly—assume that when they don't explicitly say what they want their readers to *do,* their readers will still "get it." Since readers often don't get it, however, it is usually better to be explicit.

Think about Your Readers

Of course, what counts as a problem for you might not for your readers. You might think that rising college tuition is a problem, but someone who just graduated might not. So once you understand what you want your argument to accomplish, you have to anticipate how your readers will think about it. Don't imagine yourself behind a podium reading your argument to a faceless crowd in a dark auditorium. Imagine sitting across a table from some amiable but feisty friends who interrupt you with hard questions, objections, and their own views. To imagine your argument in that situation, you have to figure out what their questions and objections might be. It's what experienced writers do as a matter of course.

But they don't just imagine readers; they try to check them out.

- Before an architect draws up a proposal, she finds out everything she can about her clients, from their finances to their family habits.

- Before a lawyer drafts a pleading, he checks out the judge who will hear the case by reading her decisions and asking other lawyers about her.

- Before a technical writer produces a software manual, he conducts surveys and focus groups to find out what users know and need to know.

Of course, in a first-year writing class you can't do all that research, but you can do some, and more as you advance in your studies.

Real Versus Stipulated Readers

You may, however, have problems if your teacher tells you that your real reader—teacher, grader, or classmate—is not the one you must address: *You are a researcher at Ace Advertising, working on the new V-Sport Vehicle account, and your manager asks for an analysis of how Ford and Chrysler ads appeal to people under age twenty-five.* No ad manager will read your paper, but your teacher will try to judge it as if she were one. So you have an actual reader (your teacher) and a stipulated reader (the imagined manager). In that situation, all you can do is try to imagine yourself in the shoes of your stipulated reader, then decide whether your real reader will imagine the same thing. It's an uncomfortable situation.

If your assignment stipulates your reader is "the general public," you also have a problem because there is no such reader. But if that's your assignment, assume (though it is not true) that this "general public" reads editorial pages in newspapers such as the *New York Times* and articles in the *New Yorker,* the *National Review, Scientific American,* and so on. Alternatively, assume that the "general public" is like yourself. They have read what you have, but have not discussed it and want to hear more on the subject.

Use Sources to Learn about Readers Indirectly

If your sources address readers like yours, study how they imagine them.

- Note what they assume you know; it will be in what they *don't* say. Is there background information that you wish the writer had explained? If writers don't explain it, they probably assume you know it.

- Note what they assume you do not know. You will find that in background information, terms or concepts that they define, principles of reasoning they explain or defend.

- Note what evidence they explain and what they just mention and assume you will accept. When writers explain evidence, they may believe it is new or controversial. When they mention it without comment, they are likely to believe that it is familiar to their readers.

Talk to Readers

The best way to find out about readers is to talk to them.

- Find out what they already know and believe.

  Suppose Elena is preparing a proposal for a Center for English Language Studies to help students whose first language is not English. She could visit administrators to find out what they know about ESL students, whether they have dealt with the issue before, who will have a say in approving her proposal, and so on.

- Find out how they react to your argument.

  Once Elena has a proposal, she could visit readers to gauge their reactions to it. Do they think there is a problem? Do they think resources should be invested in other services? Do they have a cheaper alternative? Readers often judge an argument more generously when they are familiar with it before they read it.

Of course, for most students, talking to readers means talking to a teacher. But that's not a bad thing. Not only will it help you anticipate your teacher's concerns, but it will prepare her to read your argument more generously by giving her a stake in seeing your paper succeed.

Here's the best advice we can give when you can't talk to readers directly: Imagine someone who is smart and amiable but inclined to disagree with you, and write to that person.

Drafting

At this moment, you may not yet be working on a complete argument, but even for a short one, think of the "writing" part as two stages: drafting and revising. Try not to be too critical of your own writing *as you write*. Don't go only where your plan takes you; be open to surprises. When you revise, you can be critical, but you'll write better and faster if you draft first and revise later.

To Outline or Not to Outline

Experienced writers have mixed feelings about outlines. When the two of us left high school, we were glad to be shut of roman numerals and letters, always a "ii" for every "i." We don't make elaborate outlines any more, but we do depend on scratch outlines for the general shape of our arguments. If you like formal outlines, use them. But don't reject a scratch outline just because you reject a formal one. Find the kind of outline that works best for you, even if it is only a list of topics. Whatever it is, start a serious first draft only when you have one.

When to Begin Drafting

It might seem logical to begin drafting only after you've figured out the solution to your problem. But that can be a mistake, because one way of discovering your solution is to do exploratory writing to help you understand your problem better. Start by formulating a few tentative solutions—call them *hypotheses*. You don't have to be dead certain you are on the right track; think of this early writing as an opportunity to "audition" claims that you might be able to support later (one student compared this process to dating: no commitment, just interest). Once you can articulate even a tentative claim, list reasons that would encourage a critical reader to take it seriously. That list can become your scratch outline *after* you arrange those reasons into an order that makes sense to your reader.

Styles of Drafting

Some writers draft slowly and carefully, others as quickly as they can. Draft in whatever way works for you. But while there is no best way, most experienced writers are closer to quick than to careful.

- *Quick drafters* don't stop to find exactly the right phrase, because they expect to revise. When they get on a roll, they leave out quotations, data, even whole paragraphs that they know they can fill in later. When they bog down, they jump ahead or go back to parts they skipped, edit for grammar and spelling, or look for that right word. Quick drafters know they risk rambling, however, so they leave time to reorganize and rethink their argument. So if you draft fast, start early.

• *Careful drafters* have to finish one sentence before they can begin the next, get each paragraph right before they move on to another. Slow and careful drafters need meticulous plans. But even small changes can cascade, each requiring another, finally requiring bigger changes than the original plan allowed. So if you draft slowly, plan carefully.

Revising

Experienced writers know their real work begins after they have a draft in hand. They know that once they figure out what they can say, they still have to say it in ways that meet their readers' needs and expectations. In fact, some experienced writers spend more time revising than drafting.

Your biggest obstacle in revising will not be too little time, but too much memory. None of us can read our own work as our readers will, because we remember too well what we wanted to mean when we wrote it. So we read into our writing what we want readers to get out of it. Given that problem, you have to get distance on your drafts. One strategy is to set it aside until it is no longer fresh in your memory. Another is to ask someone to read it back to you, out loud. A third is to revise in a way that sidesteps your too-good understanding of your own thinking. In later chapters, we'll explain how to do that.

Working Collaboratively

Why Collaborate?

Making an argument ends not when you finish it but when your readers respond to it (and not even then if you respond to their responses). So create imaginary readers or enlist real ones to help you anticipate their responses. Your teacher knows how this works: she has worked with reviewers, editors, and colleagues on almost everything she has published. Some students fear that working together is dishonest, but it doesn't have to be if you don't depend on others to draft your paper. Instead use them to get feedback on your outlines and drafts. Revise for yourself on the basis of their responses. You might also let your teacher know what you are doing.

That risk aside, you benefit from working with others in many ways.

1. Since you can't read your own work as your readers will, you see your work more objectively.

2. Since you must make arguments in dialogue with others, you learn how to anticipate their questions and objections. You learn to listen and respond to other points of view.

3. By practicing the skills of civil disagreement, you learn to ask hard questions in an amiable way and then to listen to answers.

4. You learn to interact with others in ways that project a credible character, what we've called your ethos. You project an ethos in many ways, but none more directly than in how you respond to questions and objections.

5. You learn to critique the arguments of others. As you advance in your studies, you will have to think critically about what you read. And in the workplace, where collaboration is the norm, you are likely to be responsible for responding critically *and helpfully* to the work of colleagues and eventually to the writing of those who work for you. That may seem distant, but you can prepare yourself for that task by practicing thoughtful, generous, and helpful criticism now.

Our Many Collaborators

We got lots of help writing this book. Early drafts were critiqued by more than a dozen readers. We also got help from teachers who listened to our ideas at conferences and workshops or used the manuscript in classes. Some of their students wrote us responses, even e-mailed us.

At times the process was painful. Early reviewers said things like "I'm afraid to say that unless [this book is] revised extensively, it will prove to be a great disappointment to many who [use] it." But even after we revised for years, some reviewers were still not satisfied: "The text seems in a very early stage of completion. . . . It feels as if the authors were more concerned with being done than with complete coverage. . . . I hope that these [problems] are indeed [be]cause of the youth of the script." We didn't like reading comments like that, but they helped.

Setting up a Writing Group

The best way to help one another is to create a writing group. You have to invest time organizing it, but it is an efficient way to improve your writing. Find three or four people you can disagree with amiably and who can meet at an agreeable time—not at eleven the night before a paper is due. You will need to exchange work to review ahead of meetings. Unless everyone is at the earliest stages of preparing, group members should circulate something for each meeting—a draft, an outline, even just a list of ideas. The group should also respond to one another's work in writing: lists of comments, marked up drafts, and so on.

Groups work best with a *Facilitator* and a *Recorder* (pass the jobs around).

- The Facilitator keeps the group on task, makes sure everyone participates and deflects debate when it gets prickly. At the end of the meeting, she has the group set an agenda for the next one.
- The Recorder records what each person agrees to do for the next meeting and if possible, reminds everyone by e-mail.

The most delicate task is keeping everyone working productively. There are some predictable problems of group behavior:

- One or two people dominate the conversation or remain silent.
- One or two become the "experts" on whom the others rely.
- One or two are regularly discounted.

In each case, the problem is as much with the group as with the person. Someone can dominate or be silent only if the group allows it. You guard against that by giving everyone a specific task. If everyone has a task, the group will not suffer from some members' not pulling their weight.

INQUIRIES

These inquiries offer a wide range of questions, puzzles, things to do, suggestions for class discussions, short papers, and even research papers, all intended to help you understand the nature and uses of argument. There are three kinds of inquiries: A **Reflection** *asks you to think. A* **Task** *asks you to do something and discuss it. A* **Project** *asks you to engage in active research. Most chapters have too many inquiries for anyone to complete, so don't try to do them all. Pick those that interest you, especially if your teacher asks you to prepare some for class discussion.*

Reflections

1. Imagine that someone discovers a group of people isolated in some part of the world and claims that they are "completely irrational." Can you imagine what would count as evidence that a whole society is completely irrational? Could an irrational society survive?
2. How is it possible for two rational people who agree on the facts to come to diametrically opposite conclusions? Or is it impossible?
3. Have you ever been in a conversation where you thought you were simply explaining something while the other thought you were making an argument? What caused this confusion?
4. Must we know the truth about something before we can think about it rationally?
5. How often do you argue because you want someone to do something rather than believe something? Why does anyone bother to argue over

mere beliefs? What difference does it make whether we agree on ideas? When was the last time you changed what you did on the basis of changing what you believed? What was the most important time?

6. We can only speculate how rationality evolved, much less why. Here is a fable about its origins:

> At first, our forebears solved problems like the disputed ownership of a rock by hooting at or beating on each other until one retreated. The first advance in the technology of dispute resolution occurred when one of them found he could effectively claim ownership of the rock by clubbing the other with it. It was a pivotal moment: No longer was size or strength the only means of persuasion; humankind had developed the intelligence to make tools, especially those we call weapons. But the greatest change in our means of persuasion occurred when our ancestors replaced stones with words. Imagine that it might have happened like this: Once, when one of our forbears wanted to settle the question of who owned a useful rock, he uttered the equivalent of "Mine!" The other one in the confrontation might have just lunged at the one claiming the rock, but instead did something that must have amazed the other. She (or he) asked something like "Why?", an act that transformed a physical confrontation into a verbal one. Then the first one did something more amazing yet. Instead of ignoring the question and just whacking the other with the rock, he (or she) offered the other a reason: "I found it." But the most amazing moment of all came when the other agreed: "OK, your rock." When they settled the issue not with blows but with good reasons, they together created the kind of talk we call argument and marked the beginnings of shared rationality, the ability to share our beliefs and the reasons that make us hold them, in the hope that others will agree.

In that story, humans began to offer claims and reasons to avoid violence. Can you imagine other ways that argument could have originated? (One of us [JMW] thinks this story must have a nub of truth; the other [GGC] thinks it unlikely.) Since we can never know for sure, you can be as fanciful as you like. Is the idea of "origin" even possible to speculate about? Does the fact that our metaphors for argument are so predictably drawn from images of combat offer any assistance here?

7. What metaphors do we use when we talk about reasoning? Are they as misleading as those we use for argument? Here is an example:

> I tried to resist the force of her logic, but it was so overwhelming that I could not stand up to it. I was simply compelled to accept her reasoning.

8. What metaphors do we use when we talk about expressing an opinion? (You might look up the original meaning of *express*.) Are they misleading? Here is a pair of passages that depend on different metaphors:

> It is important for me to *express* my ideas *honestly,* so I *lay out* my thoughts on the page as directly as I can. When I just *let it flow,* when I can *pour* my ideas out without any interference, I write most sincerely.

> It is important for me to *share* my ideas in a way that makes them *attractive* to readers. I try to *dress them up* with good reasons, to *show* them to *best advantage* and *hide* any weaknesses or rough spots.

If those two speakers argued in the way they describe, how would their arguments differ?

9. What metaphors other than combat might describe arguments? Try out these: game, exploration, love affair. Imagine how arguments would work if we talked about them in those terms. Now invent a new metaphor. Could these new ways of describing an argument change how you understand arguments and how they might work? Are there any advantages to keeping the metaphor of argument as war?

Tasks

10. Sketch supporting reasons for a position on one of these issues: (a) Computers seem to behave in ways that we would never call irrational, but would we want to call them rational? (b) How about animals? What would count as rational or irrational behavior in a dog? A chimp? A spider?

11. List the sorts of occasions in which public figures at least seem to listen to questions and answer them. How do they most commonly duck their responsibility to the questioner?

12. We've suggested that people make arguments to solve problems. Are there arguments that we have just for the sake of having them, regardless of whether the outcome resolves an issue? List some occasions when you have participated or witnessed such an argument. Was it appropriate in the circumstances?

13. In your experience, are children more likely to argue just for fun than adults? Boys more than girls? Men more than women? People at home more than people at work? Why?

14. Recall an occasion when someone spoke or acted in ways that you judged irrational. What factors led you to think so?

15. Is it rational always to be completely rational? If not, list some occasions when you think that it is better not to be rational. Why would it be wrong to be rational on those occasions? Compare your list with those of your classmates. If you have items on your list that they do not, what reasons can you offer for adding those items to their lists? Or for deleting them?

16. Are arguments good for anything other than getting someone to accept your opinion or grant your request? Find an example of an argument: (a) that succeeds but does not achieve agreement; (b) that achieves agreement but does not solve the problem that occasioned it; (c) that gets another to say *I don't agree, but I see your point.* What good is this last response? Has the argument failed?

Projects

17. Keep a diary for a day (or at least a few hours) in which you record how often you felt you had to give reasons to someone before that person

would do or believe something you wanted that person to. Which occurred more often, arguments over what to think or what to do?

18. At what age do children begin to offer reasons for their claims? At what age do they understand the question, *Why do you think that?* How would we know whether they understood the question but couldn't answer it, or just didn't understand the question? At what point are we ready to say that a child becomes rational? If you can observe children interacting, watch how they make arguments. Do they negotiate? Coerce? Propagandize?

19. Watch some talk shows that feature pundits debating each other, like *Cross-Fire* or the *Capital Gang.* Rarely do the participants end up agreeing on anything. Why do they argue then? Why does anyone watch?

20. Some inexperienced writers are surprised that they are expected to convince a teacher of something. They wonder, *Isn't my job just to show my teacher what I know?* Survey five or six students to find out what they thought their goals were when they wrote in high school. Was it to show the teacher what they had learned? To give back what the teacher said in class? To express an opinion? To support a claim that the teacher might not be inclined to agree with? To practice making good arguments? Now survey some teachers in your current classes. Ask them what they want students to achieve in their papers. How much agreement is there?

WRITING PROJECTS 1
Project 1.1

Context.   What follows are scenarios in which you have been asked to participate in a discussion group, by someone who wants you to think about a problem that you can help solve.

Task.   You haven't been asked to prepare a formal report, only to think. To help you do that, you've been given an outline of points to make notes on. In each scenario, you can be assured that everything you say will be kept confidential. Pick one scenario. Read the request and write out a page or two of notes that will help you discuss the issues in question but that are also clear enough for you to share. Bring your notes to class, one copy for yourself and one to turn in.

Scenario 1.   From your high school: *We hope you are off to a good start in college and feel prepared for your work. Your Old High School has received a grant of money to improve teaching. To decide how to use these funds, we want to find out how you judge the teaching you experienced. What qualities did you admire most in your best teachers? What qualities did you like least in those who helped you the least? In other words, what can your best teachers teach your other teachers? To make the best use of your time, here is a list of topics you might think about. Thanks for your help.*

1. What qualities in your best teachers did you admire most?
2. What qualities distinguished the teachers who helped you least?
3. What larger problem can you see arising if we don't help our weakest teachers improve?
4. Can you suggest two or three specific ways to solve this problem?
5. What do you think will be the biggest obstacles to solving it?
6. Can you give us a story about the best and worst teaching you had?
7. If someone questioned your analysis, what is the strongest "hard evidence" that you could offer to back up what you say?

Scenario 2.   From your college: *We are conducting a self-study to determine how to improve the quality of student life. We hope your experience has been good, but we know that in every complex process, there are glitches. We invite you to a discussion with a few classmates to help us find out how to fix those glitches. To make the best use of your time, here is a list topics you might think about. Thanks for your help.*

With respect to your daily life as a student,

1. What do we do best right now?
2. What problem do you think we should focus on?
3. If we do not solve this problem, what larger problem do you think might arise?
4. Can you suggest two or three specific ways to solve this problem?
5. What do you think will be the biggest obstacles to fixing it?
6. Can you describe in detail an example of this problem?
7. If someone questioned your analysis, what is the strongest "hard evidence" that you could offer to back up what you say?
8. Can you cite others who feel the same way, not by name but by recounting their experiences?

Scenario 3.   From a former employer: *We here at [your former employer] have embarked on a self-study to find out how we can become a better company. We are asking former employees how we could improve our operations, from our treatment of customers to employee relations. To make the best use of your time, here is a list of topics you might think about. Thanks for your help.*

With respect to our day-to-day operations,

1. What do we do best right now?
2. What problem do you think we should focus on?
3. If we do not solve this problem, what larger problem do you think might arise?
4. Can you suggest two or three specific ways to solve this problem?
5. What do you think will be the biggest obstacles to fixing it?

6. Can you describe in detail an example of this problem?

7. If someone questioned your analysis, what is the strongest "hard evidence" that you could offer to back up what you say?

8. Can you cite others who feel the same way, not by name but by recounting their experiences?

Scenario 4.   From any other organization you have been a member of, fill in the blanks to suit an organization you know, such as a church or civic group, a sports or hobby club, and so on: *We here at [organization] have embarked on a self-study to find out how we can achieve our mission more effectively. We are asking members how we could do our work better. To make the best use of your time, here is a list of topics you might consider. Thanks for your help.*
With respect to our day-to-day operations,

1. What do we do best right now?

2. What problem do you think we should focus on?

3. If we do not solve this problem, what larger problem do you think might arise?

4. Can you suggest two or three specific ways to solve this problem?

5. What do you think will be the biggest obstacles to fixing it?

6. Can you describe in detail an example of this problem?

7. If someone questioned your analysis, what is the strongest "hard evidence" that you could offer to back up what you say?

8. Can you cite others who feel the same way, not by name but by recounting their experiences?

Project 1.2

Context.   A common charge against advertising is that it appeals to our basest emotions—insecurity, pride, greed, lust, and so on. If that were true, advertising would be a dangerous influence on us, like pornography. But is that a fair charge? Is it true of all ads?

Scenario.   One of your classmates has attacked advertising as morally degrading, and when you tried to respond in class, you realized you hadn't thought through the issues. Alternatively, someone has defended advertising as decent and useful, and you think it is a dangerous. The topic will come up again in the next class, and this time you want to be prepared.

Task.   Find three print ads that you think appeal more to your rational powers than to your emotions. Photocopy the ads and prepare notes that would let you respond to someone charging that advertising is intellectually corrupt. Try to find a second ad for a similar product that does appeal to base emotions, so that you can make your point by contrasting the two. Or prepare the opposite case. (*Note:* Do not defend or attack advertising as commercially necessary, as a way to communicate news about a product to the public. Focus on advertising strictly in terms of its moral, ethical, and intellectual qualities.)

Project 1.3

Task.   Select one of the Tasks or Projects (or even a Reflection) from pp. 22-25 on which you can take a strong position. Work up notes for an argument that might support that position.

Project 1.4

Task.   If you have a recent paper, work up notes on an argument someone could make to support a position different from yours. Do this only if you can make a case for that position.

Project 1.5

Scenario.   Your class is reading a variety of articles about student life, with each student reading different articles. You have been assigned the article by Carol Trosset, "Obstacles to Open Discussion and Critical Thinking: The Grinnell College Study." (pp. 361-368) Your teacher has asked you to focus on this question: *Does this article reflect your own experience?* You will have to summarize and respond to the article in class, confirming, contradicting, or qualifying the author's claim.

Task.   Write detailed notes outlining the argument of the article along with a possible response, agreeing or disagreeing.

CHAPTER 1 IN A NUTSHELL
About Your Argument . . .

We do not define arguments by their abrasive tone, the belligerent attitudes of the parties to it, or by the desire to coerce our audience into accepting our claims. Instead, we define an argument by two criteria:

- Two (or more) people want to solve a problem, but they don't already agree on a solution.
- They exchange reasons and evidence that they think support a solution, responding to one another's questions, objections, and alternatives.

We make arguments not just to settle disagreements. Good arguments help us explore questions and share reasons for our beliefs, so that even when we and our readers can't agree, we can at least understand why.

. . . and About Writing It

Your first task in writing an argument is to understand the problem that occasions it. Why (other than the fact that your teacher assigned it) are you writing it? What do you want it to achieve?

- Do you want your readers just to understand something better, with no expectation that they act? If so, why is that better understanding important?

- Do you want your readers to do something? If so, what action do you want them to take? How do you know it will work, that it is feasible, that solving it will not cost more than the problem, and that it won't create a new problem?

Once you understand your problem, speculate about a few solutions. Pick one that seems promising, then list reasons that would encourage readers to agree. You can use that list as a scratch outline or, if you wish, expand it into a formal one.

Draft in whatever way feels comfortable: quick and messy, or slow and careful. If you are quick, start early and leave time to revise. If you are slow, plan carefully and get it right the fist time, because you may not have time to fix it later.

CHAPTER 2

Argument as Civil Conversation

In this chapter, we show you how to build an argument out of the answers to just five kinds of questions that we ask one another every day. Then we show you how to use these questions to have a conversation with yourself to help you develop a written argument that your readers will judge to be thoughtful and persuasive.

You make arguments so often that you probably never reflect on how you do it. You know you have to make a claim and support it, but what do you support it *with?* And what do you say to those who question your logic? How do you keep the conversation amiable while wrestling with challenging questions (two more combat metaphors)? Some people do that while projecting in either speech or writing, an ethos that strikes us as thoughtful and judicious. They do that in two ways:

- They build arguments out of elements that they know we look for when we consider their claim.

- In written arguments especially, they respond to questions that they know we would ask, were we there to ask them.

When we read such arguments, we feel we are dealing with people who deserve at least our respect, because they have respected us by acknowledging our views and expectations.

It's easier to build that confidence in conversation than in writing, because others are there to ask questions. When someone doesn't understand part of your argument, she can ask you about it. If you answer respectfully, you not only create the building blocks of your argument but project the amiable ethos of someone who makes reasonable arguments.

It is harder to imagine answering those questions when you are "conversing" with a pad or computer screen. But it is a skill you must learn, because even a written argument has to be the product of a collaborative dialogue with other voices, sometimes real, but more often voices you must imagine on behalf of your readers. Fortunately, you have asked and answered such questions countless times. Moreover, there are only five kinds.

When you answer the first two, you create the core of your argument, your claim and your reason(s) for believing it:

1. What's your point? What are you saying, in a nutshell? In short, what are you **claiming** that I should do or believe?

2. What makes you believe that? Why do you think your claim is sound? What's behind it? What **reasons** can you offer to support it?

The next two questions help you establish the soundness of your reasons. They are more challenging than the first two:

3. On what grounds do you base those reasons? Can you back them up with facts? On what **evidence** do they rest?

4. Can you explain how your reasons are *relevant* to your claim? What logic connects your reason to your claim? What general principle (we'll call it a **warrant**) makes your so-called reason *count as* one?

The final question asks you to imagine your argument from your readers' point of view and to respond to their doubts and reservations:

5. But have you considered . . . But what about . . . But what would you say to someone who said/objected/argued/claimed . . . ? In short, what is your **response** to alternatives, objections, and other points of view?

When you ask and answer those five kinds of questions, you create the basis for a sound written argument. In this chapter, we look at those questions as they occur in conversation, then discuss how to assemble their answers into a written argument that will at best win over your readers (another combat metaphor), but at least encourage them to believe that you have been thoughtful, judicious, and fair.

Argument's Roots in Civil Conversation

Here is a conversation among Sue and Raj, two friends home on spring break from different colleges, and one of their high school teachers, Ann. After chatting about Raj's school for a while, Ann asks Sue about hers:

Ann: So what's new at your school?

Sue: I've been tied up with a student government committee working on something we're calling a "Student Bill of Rights."

Ann: What's that?

Sue: Well, it's an idea about how to improve life on campus and in class.

Ann: What's the problem?

Sue: We think the school is just taking us for granted, not giving us the services we need to get a good education.

Raj: What's your idea?

Sue: We think the university should stop thinking of us only as students and start treating us like customers.

Ann: Customers? What's behind that?

Sue: Well, we pay a lot of money for our education, but we don't get near the attention customers do.

Raj: Like how?

Sue: For one thing, we can hardly see teachers outside of class. Last week I counted office hours posted on office doors on the first floor of the Arts and Sciences building. [She pulls a piece of paper out of her backpack.] They average less than an hour a week, most of them in the afternoon when a lot of us work. I have the numbers right here.

Ann: Can I see?

Sue: Sure. [She hands the paper over.]

Ann: [reading] Well, you're right about that one floor in that one building, but I wonder what a bigger sample would show.

Raj: I agree about office hours. We've got the same problem at my college. But I want to go back to something you said before. I don't see how paying tuition makes us customers. What's the connection?

Sue: Well, when you pay for a service, you buy it, right? And when you buy something you're a customer. We pay tuition for our education, so that means we're customers and should be treated like one.

Ann: But an education isn't a service. At least it's not like hiring a plumber. Doctors get paid for services, but patients aren't customers.

Raj: What if someone said that your idea means we just buy a degree? And what about the saying, *The customer is always right?* My test answers aren't always right. I don't want teachers pandering to me like advertisers do.

Sue: Nobody wants anyone to pander to us. We just want to be treated reasonably, like better bus service from off-campus dorms or the library to be open if we need to study late. And most of all, we want teachers to be more available. A lot of us work when we're not in class. Why should we have to take off work?

Raj: You're right about teachers. I've had trouble seeing my psych prof.

Ann: How about the idea of students as clients? When you go to a lawyer, he doesn't tell you what makes you happy just because you pay him. And good lawyers worry how you feel, so maybe it should be the same with a university. Maybe a school should treat students like clients.

Sue: "Students as clients." Doesn't sound as catchy as students as customers, but it's worth talking about. Thanks for the idea. I'll bring it up.

Sue offered a claim about students as customers that Raj and Ann helped her test and develop by asking her just five kinds of questions. Let's look at this conversation from that perspective.

Two Friendly Questions About What Sue Thinks

When Ann asks Sue what is happening at her school, Sue raises the problem that motivates the rest of the discussion:

Ann: So what's new at your school?

Sue: I've been tied up with a student government committee working on something we're calling a "Student Bill of Rights."

Ann: What's that?

Sue: Well, it's an idea about how to improve life on campus and in class.

Ann: What's the problem?

Sue: We think the school is just taking us for granted, not giving us the services we need to get a good education.

Ann and Raj then ask the two questions about the gist of Sue's argument.

What are you claiming?

Raj: What's your idea?

Sue: We think the university should stop thinking of us only as students and start treating us like customers. _{claim/solution}

What are your reasons?

Ann: Customers? What's behind that?

Sue: Well, we pay a lot of money for our education but don't get near the attention customers do. _{reason}

Sue welcomes those two questions, because they invite her to share what she thinks and why she thinks it.

The Difference Between Claims and Reasons

Some students puzzle over the difference between claims and reasons, saying that a reason is itself a kind of claim. In fact, we could call reasons subclaims, because they need to be supported, usually with evidence. But we use these two different terms to emphasize that you use claims and reasons differently. For example, the same statement can be a reason or a claim, depending on how you use it:

> **Children who watch lots of violent entertainment tend to become violent adults,** _{claim} because they slowly lose their ability to distinguish between reality and fiction. _{reason}

> Violence on television and in video games should be reduced _{claim} because **children who watch lots of violent entertainment tend to become violent adults.** _{reason}

Your **claim** states the solution to your problem; your **reasons** are statements that encourage your readers to accept your claim as sound.

Two Challenging Questions about the Basis of Sue's Argument

At this point, Ann and Raj understand the core of Sue's position. If they agreed, they could let the matter drop. Or if Ann felt defensive about criticism of other teachers, she could counterattack: *That's a silly idea!* Or she might not be convinced but still think that Sue's problem is worth considering. If so, she could explore it further by asking two more questions about the basis of Sue's argument.

In conversation, however, this is a step that many of us are reluctant to take because we shrink from seeming to challenge what others say. *After all, everyone's entitled to their opinion. What right do I have to question it?* We are indeed all entitled to our opinion, but not to everyone's assent to it simply because we assert it. In fact, a civil society depends on our asking one another tough questions about important issues and getting responsive answers. We have an obligation to help make the claims we accept as sound as possible by questioning one another, in the spirit not of belligerent confrontation, but of amiable inquiry.

So in that spirit Ann and Raj ask Sue two questions that may seem to challenge her, because they imply that they do not accept her claim and its support at face value. But Ann and Raj ask these questions not to prove Sue wrong, but to understand better why she thinks she's right:

On what evidence do you base that reason?

Sue: Well, we pay a lot of money for our education, but we don't get near the attention customers do. _{reason}

Raj: Like how? *[What evidence do you base that reason on?]*

Sue: For one thing, we can hardly see teachers outside of class. Last week I counted office hours posted on office doors on the first floor of the

Arts and Sciences building. [She pulls a piece of paper out of her backpack.] They average less than an hour a week, most of them in the afternoon when a lot of us work. I have the numbers right here. <small>summary of evidence</small>

Ann: Can I see? [*What hard evidence do you base your summary on?*]

At this point Ann verges on seeming really uncivil, because she implies that she does not trust Sue's report. But she is not overtly *disagreeing* with Sue, only trying to understand the basis of her claim. Sue agreeably offers Ann her data:

Sue: Sure. [She hands the paper over.]

With a little help from her friends, Sue has assembled the core of her argument and tethered it to the first of two anchors that every argument needs: the evidence on which she bases her reason.

| **CLAIM** | *because of* | **REASON** | *based on* | **EVIDENCE** |

How does your reason support your claim?

Every argument needs an anchor in sound evidence and another in sound reasoning. But if Ann and Raj ask for that second anchor, they may seem to challenge Sue even more sharply. They will ask not for additional evidence, but for something more fundamental: the logic behind her reasoning.

Raj: I agree about faculty hours. We've got the same problem at my college. But I want to go back to something you said before. I don't see how paying tuition makes us customers. What's the connection?

Sue's reason is factually correct: Students do pay good money for their education, but Raj doesn't see how that is   to Sue's claim that they are *therefore* customers. Raj does not see how Sue's claim follows from her reason.

To answer Raj's question, Sue has to think about her own thinking, to offer a general principle that shows why she thinks her reason is relevant to her claim. This is an element of argument that challenges every one of us: How do we justify the logic of our argument? Sue answers,

Sue: Well, when you pay for a service, you buy it, right? And when you buy something you're a customer. <small>general principle</small> We pay tuition for our education, <small>reason</small> so that means we're customers and should be treated like customers. <small>claim</small>

There are technical terms for a general principle that connects a reason to a claim. Some call it a *premise,* others an *assumption.* When that premise is explicitly stated, most people who write about arguments these days call it a *warrant:* Like all warrants, Sue's has two parts:

(1) a general circumstance, which lets us draw

(2) a general inference.

Graphically, it looks like this:

| (1) General circumstance | — lets us draw → | (2) General Inference |

| (1) person pays for service _{reason} | so | (2) person is a customer. _{claim} |

If Raj and Ann believe Sue's warrant, Sue can apply it to her specific circumstance and then from it draw a specific claim:

| When a person pays for a service, | | that person is a customer. _{warrant} |

| Sue pays for her education, _{reason} | so | she is a customer. _{claim} |

Warrants are more than statements of static facts. They are dynamic principles that justify (warrant) the specific inference we draw from a specific circumstance. (We should alert you that everyone struggles with warrants—including the two of us. They are the most abstract and difficult element of an argument. If you are uncertain about them now, rest easy. We devote all of Chapter 7 to them.)

The answers to those two questions about evidence and warrants provide the two anchors for Ann's argument, but they don't guarantee its ultimate success, because every participant in an argument brings to it her own views and experiences. And that's what motivates the fifth—and toughest—question.

The Most Challenging Question: But What About . . . ?

Once Raj and Ann think they understand the general contour of Sue's argument, they can ask the most overtly challenging question: *But what about . . . ?* In face-to-face arguments, you have the advantage of hearing others' objections and questions directly, so you can answer them right then and there. In fact, you must. But when you write, you can only *imagine* your readers' questions, objections, and alternative views. You must create a voice in the back of your mind, insistently asking, *But what about . . . ? But what would you say to someone who argued . . . ?* How well you imagine and respond to those questions affects how your readers judge the quality of your mind, especially your willingness to examine your own views critically—in short, your ethos as a thoughtful and fair partner in cooperatively making an argument.

You must expect lots of questions and objections. Here are some that Sue and Raj offered:

- Ann objected that Sue's warrants do not apply to her facts:

  But an education isn't a service. At least it's not like hiring a plumber. Doctors get paid for services, but patients aren't customers.

- She also questioned the quality of Sue's evidence about office hours:

  Well, you're right about that one floor in that one building, but I wonder what a bigger sample would show.

- Raj points out a cost of accepting Sue's claim, one perhaps greater than the cost of the existing problem:

  What if someone said that your idea means we just buy a degree? And what about the saying, *The customer is always right?* My test answers aren't always right. I don't want teachers pandering to me like advertisers do.

- Ann offers an alternative solution and a bit of an argument of her own:

  How about the idea of students as clients? When you go to a lawyer, he doesn't tell you what makes you happy just because you pay him.

Raj and Ann could have asked Sue many more questions:

Exactly what do you mean by "enough" office hours?

Do you have any other reasons to think you aren't being treated well?

What do you think teachers would say about that idea? Or parents? Or state legislators?

Do you think you could actually get the school to adopt that policy?

But each of those questions is just a variation on one of the other five: *What do you mean by* asks that the claim be stated more clearly; *Do you have any other reasons* asks for more reasons; *What do you think teachers would say* and *Do you think you could actually* are two implicit objections/reservations.

When you make a claim, you must *as a matter of course* expect readers to think of objections and alternatives, and you must acknowledge and respond to them. Some students doubt that. *Why are we obliged to imagine other views and maybe even let them change our own? Isn't our job to stand up for our own beliefs?* True enough, but when you address a problem with a lot at stake, it is in your own best interests to find its best solution, regardless of the solution you want. Furthermore, in a conversation, you would seem not just arrogant but foolish to ignore questions and objections. You carry no less an ethical burden when you write. What makes that burden so heavy in writing is that you must write not only in your own voice, but on behalf of others.

Questions Versus Answers in the College Curriculum

Researchers have found that students starting college differ from their teachers in how they value questions and answers. Many first-year students think that their goal is to learn the facts and when asked, report them back accurately. But most teachers say that what they most want from students is not just answers but questions—critical thinking about what they hear and read, testing claims against alternatives and available evidence. That difference often causes difficulty for students and teachers alike. Here is a test to help you know whether your attitudes about teaching and learning might conflict with those of your teachers. Do you agree with the following?

1. If professors stuck to facts and theorized less, I'd get more out of college.

2. The best thing about science courses is that problems have only one right answer.
3. It's annoying to listen to a lecturer who can't decide what he really believes.
4. It wastes time to work on problems with no clear-cut, unambiguous answer.
5. Educators should know by now which is the better teaching method, lectures or small discussion groups.
6. Once a person has all the facts, most questions have only one right answer.
7. A good teacher keeps students from wandering off the right track.

If you mostly agree, you can expect your values to conflict with those of your teachers, who mostly disagree.

Source: From M. P. Ryan, "Monitoring Text Comprehension: Individual Differences in Epistemological Standards," *Journal of Educational Psychology* 76, (1984): 250.

Review: Modeling an Argument

So far, we have simply listed the five key questions. You might get a better grasp on how they work together if we show you how they combine into an argument, the way that atoms combine into molecules. We'll also give you some diagrams to help you visualize an argument as a system of five elements, because some of us understand an abstraction better when we can picture it. But if you find our words easier to understand than the diagrams, ignore the diagrams.

The Core of an Argument: Claim + Support

In its simplest form an argument is just a claim and its support. The claim states something that you want readers to believe or do:

> Because major college sports have degenerated into a corrupt, money-making sideshow that is eroding the real mission of higher education, reason they must be thoroughly reformed. claim

We can represent the relationship between a claim and its support in this diagram of the core of an argument:

> **REASON**   *therefore*   **CLAIM**

That diagram does not represent the only order of the elements. We could reverse them:

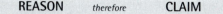

> **CLAIM**   *because of*   **REASON**

Major college sports must be thoroughly reformed, _{claim} because they have degenerated into a corrupt, money-making side-show that is eroding the real mission of higher education. _{reason}

To be consistent in what follows, we'll keep the claim on the left.

Anchoring the Core: Evidence and Warrants

In casual conversations, we might support a claim with just a reason:

Larry: We'd better stop for gas here. _{claim}

Curly: What reason do you have for saying that?

Moe: Because we're almost empty. _{reason}

Curly is unlikely to respond, *What evidence do you base that reason on?* or *Why should the fact that we're almost empty mean that we should stop for gas?* But when an issue is contested, readers usually want to know both that you've based your reason on reliable evidence and that your reason is relevant to your claim.

Evidence

That argument about college athletics could use some evidence:

Major college sports must be thoroughly reformed, _{claim} because they have degenerated into a corrupt, money-making side-show that is eroding the real mission of higher education. _{reason} **In the last three years, we have had dozens of reports of students receiving money for their athletic achievements and even more of athletes being exempted from academic requirements that all other students must meet.** _{evidence}

Reasons and evidence might seem to be just different words for the same thing, but they are not:

- You think up reasons and express them only in words.
- You don't "think up" evidence (or at least you shouldn't). Evidence must seem to come from "out there" in the world, something you can point out to your reader.

For example, we can't point at athletics degenerating into a sideshow, but we can point at someone handing athletes money or exempting them from academic requirements. (We discuss evidence in more detail in Chapters 5 and 6.)

To emphasize the difference between reasons and evidence, we represent the core of an argument like this:

| **CLAIM** | *because of* | **REASON** | *based on* | **EVIDENCE** |

Think of evidence as anchoring your argument in facts.

IN THE READINGS . . .

Reasons and Evidence

In "Lies, Damn Lies, and Statistics," Jonathan Rauch defines the "strange but common animal, the policy lie" with a story about how Barry McCaffrey, President Clinton's drug czar, used evidence (p. 456). When the Dutch challenged McCaffrey's claim that their liberal drug policy was an "unmitigated disaster," he offered as a reason another claim, that the Dutch murder rate was double that of the United States. When this too was challenged, McCaffrey reported as evidence Interpol statistics that he acknowledged might not be accurate: "We have said if we are wrong, speak to Interpol—it's not our statistics, it's [their] reporting." (If this seems to make no sense, remember that he is a politician.) In exposing McCaffrey's "policy lie," Rauch reports several kinds of evidence to show that the Netherlands is in fact safer than the United States. Read the passage, picking out those places where Rauch reports evidence. How does he make his evidence seem more credible than McCaffrey's? Does he persuade you that it's better?

Warrants

Readers may agree that what you offer as a reason is based on good evidence, but still deny that it supports your claim because your reason doesn't "count" as one. In that case, they are asking what anchoring principle justifies connecting your reason to your claim, what we've called a *warrant*. If readers accept your warrant, then whenever you can point to a *particular* circumstance of the first kind, you can infer a *particular* circumstance of the second kind. Here's an example:

> **When an institution has its most eminent faculty teach first-year classes, it can justly be said to put its educational mission first.** _{warrant} We have tried to make our undergraduate education second to none _{claim} by asking our best researchers to teach first-year students. _{reason} For example, Professor Kinahan, a recent Nobel Prize winner in physics, is now teaching physics 101. _{evidence}

Along with evidence, warrants anchor the central core of an argument. We can add warrants to our diagram in a way that shows it holding a claim and its supporting reason together, "bridging" the reason and claim:

WARRANT

CLAIM   *because of*   **REASON**   *based on*   **EVIDENCE**

The History of *Warrant*

Our term *warrant* is the same word as in *search warrant* or *arrest warrant*, documents that permit you to do something and protect you once you have. *Warrant* is closely related to *guarantee,* and in a sense, a warrant guarantees that a reason relates to a claim. Both *warrant* and *guarantee* can ultimately be traced back to a word meaning to "guard." And that, finally, is what a warrant does: It guards your reasoning from error as you link a claim and its reasons.

IN THE READINGS . . .

Warrants

When Jonathan Rauch defines a "policy lie" in "Lies, Damn Lies, and Statistics" (p. 468), he articulates just one warrant: "A mistake uncorrected is no longer a mistake." When we unpack this proverb-like warrant, it looks something like this:

> When someone does not correct a public statement that he knows is false, that person is guilty of a kind of lie.

Why is this the only principle of reasoning that he states explicitly? Presumably, he thought he did not need to remind readers of the others. For example, he relies on but does not state this warrant:

> When an immoral act damages the lives of many people, it is more immoral than one that damages only a few.

Since this is a familiar moral principle, Rauch probably expected his readers to recognize and apply it. But since he explicitly stated his "mistake" warrant, we can infer that he probably believed his readers would not take it for granted.

The Fifth Question: Acknowledgments and Responses

Readers are likely to have alternative views that a thoughtful writer must acknowledge and respond to. We might argue, for example, that famous researchers don't make good teachers, a view that a skilled writer anticipates:

> When an institution has its most eminent faculty teach first-year classes, it can justly be said that it puts its educational mission first. ₍warrant₎ We have tried to make our undergraduate education second to none ₍claim₎ by asking our best researchers to teach first-year students. ₍reason₎ For example, Professor Kinahan, a recent Nobel Prize winner in physics, is now teaching physics 101. ₍evidence₎ **To be sure, not every researcher teaches well, but recent teaching evaluations show that teachers such as Kinahan are highly respected by our students.** ₍acknowledgment and response₎

We can add acknowledgments and responses to our previous diagram to show that they address all the other parts of an argument (we add the questions to this last diagram):

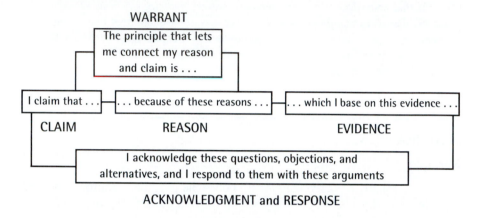

IN THE READINGS . . .

The Questions of Argument

In "On the Uses of a Liberal Education" (p. 369), Mark Edmundson raises many questions. Some anticipate objections: "But wait . . . Can I extend my view from Charlottesville to encompass the whole country . . . ?" (p. 372). Others introduce not objections but Edmunson's own points. Pick out all the places where Edmundson either anticipates readers' objections or states a question of his own.

- Are the objections he anticipates ones you might actually raise?
- Does raising them make him seem more thoughful? More concerned about you?
- Are his other questions ones you might actually raise yourself?
- How do they affect your sense of his ethos?

Crafting Written Arguments

When you ask and answer the five questions of argument in conversation, you don't organize them in advance; you and your partner just go where the conversation takes you, rarely in a straight line to a conclusion. We manage well enough, though, because the back-and-forth helps us clarify our points, elaborate on difficult concepts, even figure out what claim we can plausibly make. But when we write, we have to decide by ourselves what to say and in what order, with no second chances.

Although you can vary the order of elements in a written argument in many ways, there are some standard orders you can rely on. For example, the default order for the first three elements is CLAIM + REASON + EVIDENCE. You can sandwich them between an introduction that states the problem and its solution and a conclusion that restates your Claim:

1. **Problem:**   What problem does this argument solve?

2. **Claim/Solution:**   What do you claim is its solution?

3. **Reasons:**   What reasons do you offer in support?

4. **Evidence:**   What evidence do you base those reasons on?

5. **Restatement:**   What is your solution again?

We can't tell you exactly where to put the other elements—warrants and responses—except to put them near what they apply to:

- Locate warrants just before or after the claim they apply to, so that readers understand how they connect your reason to your claim. (We know this matter of warrants is still murky. We promise it will become clearer.)

- Locate acknowledgments and responses to questions or objections where you suspect readers will think of them. Alternatively, put them all after the core of your argument.

Here is a simple plan for an argument with one reason:

Introduction: Problem to be solved + Claimed solution
Body:
    Warrant
    Reason + Evidence
    Responses/Acknowledgments
Conclusion: Restatement of problem + Claimed solution

Sue could organize a written argument following that standard plan. In a one-paragraph introduction, she states her problem and solution:

> Recently, student government has been studying complaints about life Midwest U. Some are minor, such as the bursar's office closing at 2 P.M. But others are major, such as teachers not keeping enough office hours. This problem suggests that the university cares little about our needs, apparently thinking of us only as transients, paying to be here but deserving little consideration. If this issue is ignored, we risk gaining the reputation of a "student unfriendly" place that will gradually erode our reputation and ultimately threaten the quality of our education. _{problem} We believe the university should think of us not just as students, but also as customers vital to its success. _{claimed solution}

Then she lays out the body of her argument:

> When someone pays for a service, she deserves to be treated as a business treats its customers. _{warrant} Even though we pay for the services of teachers, _{reason 1} we don't get the consideration that good customers do. _{reason 2} For one thing, many faculty do not keep enough office hours._{reason 3 supporting reason 2} In a survey of Arts & Sciences Hall, office hours averaged less than an hour a week. _{reason 4 supporting reason 3} (The data are attached. _{report of evidence}) No business would survive if it treated customers like that. Of course, this is only a small sample, _{acknowledgment of anticipated objection} but it indicates a wider problem. _{response}
>
> Admittedly, we cannot push the analogy too far—the university can't educate us if it treats us like customers in all respects, especially in class. _{acknowledgment of alternative} Still, if thinking of us as customers leads it to make our experience more productive, then we think the principle of "student as customer" is worth considering. _{response/Main Claim}

In our examples, we've made sure that every sentence answers one of our five questions, but not every sentence in every argument has to, because as you make an argument about a complex issue, you may also have to explain certain aspects of it. If, for example, you argue that the cost of gasoline additives is more than their benefits, you might first have to help readers understand the chemistry of carbon-based combustion.

Thickening Your Argument

Unfortunately, a written argument as undeveloped as that is unlikely to win assent to the solution of a problem as complex as whether a college takes its undergraduates seriously. Experienced writers know that we reject arguments that seem so "thin," "undeveloped," or worst of all, "simplistic." When we make such judgments, we implicitly think something like this:

- You offer only one reason for treating you like a customer, that you pay for your education. I need more than that before I accept your claim.

- You offer some evidence, but I need more and some assurance that it is sound. You say teachers keep too few office hours, but you surveyed the offices on only one floor in one building.

- You offer a warrant but not a case that it is in fact true. Why do you think that just because someone pays for something, that person is a customer?

- You acknowledge that you have too little evidence about office hours, but you claim in response that even that little evidence shows there's a problem. I need supporting reasons and evidence before I accept that.

You build a nuclear argument out of the answers to the five core questions, but you almost always have to treat each reason, warrant, and response *as a claim at the center of its own argument,* supporting each answer with its own reasons, evidence, warrants, and responses. In so doing, you "thicken," "broaden," and "deepen" your main argument by developing supporting arguments inside it. Readers judge an argument to be thoughtfully complex when they see nuclear arguments assembled into larger and more complex ones, just as simple cells assemble into more complex organisms.

In Chapters 4 through 8, we look in closer detail at each of these elements. In the next chapter, we look at why we make arguments at all.

WRITING PROCESS 2
Argument as Civil Conversation

Preparing and Planning

Three Strategies for Designing an Argument

There are three strategies for finding a plan or blueprint for your argument:

1. Do not plan at all: Just let the argument fall onto the page as it happens to. Some great writers do that, but the rest of us try it at some risk.

2. Create a new plan for every new argument. To do that you have to know exactly who your readers are, what they know, what reasons they find compelling, what they don't understand, what the complexities of the subject are. The problem with this strategy is that you ignore the benefits of experience. The number of possible plans is a fairly small set that experienced writers improvise on, the way a musician vamps on a tune or a basketball player varies the practiced moves of a set play.

3. Follow exactly whatever stock plan you get from teachers, editors, or textbook writers like us. The problem with this strategy is that while some stock plans are reliable, many are not.

Our advice is to combine the second and third strategies. We offer some stock plans that we think are reliable, but we also suggest ways to adapt them to your situation. Think of these stock plans as external support for a structure as you construct it but that does not look like the finished work. Use our stock plans in the same way. After you frame your argument, build it roughly according to the plan, but don't let it tyrannize your thinking or writing.

Four Stock Plans to Avoid

Here are some stock plans to avoid:

- **Five paragraph essay.** You may have mastered this form in high school:

  Introduction: There are three reasons why tooth flossing is important.

  Body: Reason 1, Reason 2, but most important, Reason 3.

  Conclusion: So now we see there are three reasons to floss.

That plan rarely accommodates complex problems, and under any circumstances it reminds teachers of high school essays.

- **Narrative of your thinking:** A blow-by-blow account of how you thought your way through a problem will engage those interested in the workings of your mind, but most of us will care more about what it creates. When you write a single unrevised draft, you probably recorded only a history of your struggle to write it.

- **Summary of your sources:** When you make an argument based on something you have read, avoid a summary that tracks the order of its ideas. You will seem only to rehash them, with nothing new from you.

- **Thing One and Thing Two:** If you write about two or more clear-cut objects, such as two people, books, or places, avoid organizing your paper in two parts, the first based on Thing One, the second on Thing Two. In comparing *Romeo and Juliet* to *West Side Story,* for example, don't devote part one to *Romeo and Juliet* and part two to *West Side Story.* Instead, organize your argument around aspects of the two works, such as their contrasting themes, actions, emotional impact, and so on. If you cannot avoid the obvious organization, at least insert into the second part phrases that recall and connect it to the first: *In comparison to Romeo and Juliet . . . , In contrast to Romeo and Juliet . . . , West Side Story shares with Romeo and Juliet. . . .* Otherwise, your argument will read like two unconnected summaries.

Sketch a Plan for Your Argument

Before you draft, make an outline, no matter how sketchy. As you gain experience, you may get by with just a scratch outline—even one you don't have to write down. But in your early papers, you're likely to need all the help you can get. Here's a low-cost way to plan a paper systematically:

1. **Sketch the problem or question and a plausible solution or answer.**

   Binge drinking is a problem, but the university has not been able to control it with rules banning drinking. $_{problem}$ We have to do a better job of identifying the few students who binge dangerously. $_{solution}$

2. **At the tops of separate pages, state the reasons that would encourage readers to agree.** Assume that you need more than one and probably more than two or three. If you think of more than five, pick only the most persuasive ones.

   R1: Some students will drink no matter what anyone says.

   R2: When rules are ignored, students disrespect the administration.

   R3: Only a few students are the real problem drinkers.

   R4: Blanket prohibition deprives responsible students of a right.

3. **After each reason, sketch the evidence (data, facts) that support it.** This is the hardest step. You can think up reasons, but you have to hunt

down evidence. If you can't think of any, you at least know what you have to look for.

4. **On the same pages, sketch alternative solutions, additional evidence, or objections that your readers might raise; then respond to them.**

A. It has been claimed that student drinkers cannot be controlled through education. But researchers at the University of Washington have found otherwise. _{response} In their study, . . .

B. It is true the administration has a legal responsibility to set rules that protect students. However, a rule that cannot be enforced protects no one. _{response} We have seen this happen before when . . .

Order the Elements of Your Argument

Once you have the elements, you have to put them into a coherent order.

Where Does Your Main Claim Go?

You have two choices, and each implies a different "social contract" between you and your reader:

•	State your main claim at the end of the introduction and again in the conclusion.

When you do that, you in effect say to readers: *Now that you know my problem and its solution, you are in control of your reading. You know the most important things I have to say, so you can stop reading, read on to the end, skim, or skip around to find what interests you most.*

•	Save your main claim for the conclusion.

When you make readers wait for your conclusion, you in effect say to them: *I am in control here. You will have to follow me as I reveal my reasoning to you. Stay with me every step of the way, and in the end I will reveal my main claim.*

Sometimes we accept that second contract with pleasurable anticipation, but only if we want to follow the twists and turns of an intellectual journey. In fact, some teachers, especially in the humanities, tend to like that kind of "discovery" organization. They enjoy watching an argument unfold like a mystery story. Most of us, though, want to control our own time, so we prefer to see the clearest statement of your main claim early, at the end of your introduction. That sounds cut-and-dried, but in a world where we all have more to read than time to read it, few of us have the leisure to see how it all turns out.

Some students hold back their main claim, fearing that if they "give it away" too soon, readers will lose interest and stop reading. That's a mistake. What motivates us to read is a problem in which we have something at stake. If you pose an important problem, we will read on, even if we see your solution in the introduction. Conversely, no one is motivated to read about a trivial question just because you hide its answer.

Other students think that if readers might resist their main claim, they should sneak up on it. Holding off a contentious claim works occasionally. But you have to be a skilled writer to lure us toward an unwelcome conclusion that we don't see coming a long way off. And even if you do pull that off, we may feel you have tricked us into agreement. Your best chance to win over hostile readers is not to manipulate them, but to acknowledge differences from the start. If their minds are so set against your claim that they refuse even to consider your argument, you won't persuade them in any event. But if you approach them as readers who give fair hearings even to positions they do not like, they may not accept your claim but may at least acknowledge that you have good reasons for believing it.

If you do decide to hold off your main claim until the conclusion, you have to give readers plenty of guidance about what is coming. You do that by ending your introduction with sentences that don't reveal your main claim but do set in motion the central concepts that you will develop in the body of your argument. Compare the following two ways of ending an introduction to an argument about binge drinking:

> In fact, **times** have **changed,** and universities have to **understand** how they have if they are to address **drinking** effectively.

> In fact, the **traditional role** of a university, **in loco parentis,** is more **complex** now than a generation ago, because it involves issues of **civil rights, privacy,** and **student autonomy.** Not until it **understands** where it **stands, legally, pragmatically,** and **morally,** can this university formulate workable **policies** on the problem of **binge drinking.**

The boldfaced words in both tell us what to expect, but the second version does it a lot better than the first, because it states more specifically what themes the argument will develop. Of course, once you announce those specific themes, you have to develop them in what follows.

Neither social contract, point-first or point-last, is intrinsically better. They're just different, each implying a different relationship among the author, reader, text, and circumstances. It's safe to assume, though, that most of us most of the time prefer to see a point early because that lets us control our own time better.

Where Do Reasons Go?

Your reasons should go in the body of the argument, of course, with a different section devoted to each one. The question is how to order the sections. You can use standard orders: simple to complex, more important to less important (or vice versa), more familiar to less familiar, and so on. Or you can find your own order. But in either case, readers are likely to judge your argument incoherent if they cannot see any principle behind your order. So either say what principle you are following (as we did at the start of this chapter, p. 31) or introduce each section with transitional words such as *More important, therefore,* and *on the other hand.* (For more detailed advice on ordering reasons, see pp. 133–35 in Chapter 5.)

Just as you had to decide where to announce your main claim in your whole paper, you also have to decide where to put each reason within its own section. Since a reason is the point of its section, you can put it at the end of the introduction to that section or in its conclusion. Here too, the default choice is to state the reason/point of a section early, at the end of its introduction.

Where Does Evidence Go?

Your evidence will make up a large part of the body of each section. If you put the reason in the introduction, subreasons and the evidence will follow the main reason. You can, however, reverse that order by saving the reason (that is, the point of the section) for its conclusion. When you move from evidence to a reason, you suggest that you are thinking your way toward that reason. But that can be a problem when readers have no idea what the evidence is relevant to until they get to the reason at the end. So if you present evidence before its reason, introduce it with a sentence or two that explain the general issue that the evidence relates to. You can even state the reason first, then jump to the evidence and work your way back to your reason, restated in the conclusion of that section. This is an issue we address in more detail in Chapter 6.

Where Do Warrants Go?

This is the hardest choice, because you first have to decide whether to include warrants at all. You can usually omit them if your readers share your values, assumptions, definitions, and so on. If not, you have to state your assumptions as warrants, typically before the reasons they apply to. For example, after reading the following little argument, a reader could reject the claim at the end simply by objecting that what children watch is irrelevant to their psychological development:

> Every day, children are bombarded by TV violence. reason The average child sees almost twelve acts of violence a day, most more graphic than necessary, few causing permanent damage, and even fewer condemned or punished (Smith 1992). report of evidence When that kind of violence becomes a pervasive part of their experience, restatement of reason it is likely to damage their psychological development. claim

On the other hand, if the writer can first get readers to agree on a general principle about the influence of example on child development, she is more likely to get agreement later that her reason supports her claim:

> Most of us believe that when children enjoy stories about admirable actions, they are more likely to become healthy adults. warrant Isn't it likely, then, that when they see degrading behavior, they will be hurt by it? warrant Every day, children are bombarded by TV violence. reason The average child sees . . . evidence . . . [watching TV violence] is likely to damage their psychological development. claim

The argument now begins with two warrants, followed by reasons, evidence, and a claim. A reader may be more inclined to think that the reason supports the claim if she first accepts the general principle (*when children see degrading behavior, they are hurt by it*). Of course, if the reader might reject those warrants, the writer has to back them with their own supporting arguments.

Where Do Acknowledgments and Responses Go?

Ideally, you acknowledge and respond to questions or objections the moment they occur to your readers. Unfortunately, few of us are smart enough to predict when that will be. But just by acknowledging *some* objections and responding to them *anywhere,* you show readers you are aware of at least some alternative views, if not theirs in particular.

All of this suggests the stock plan we sketched earlier:

1. Introduction: Problem + Solution
2. Body:

   Warrants
   Reason 1 + Evidence + Acknowledgment/response
   Reason 2 + Evidence + Acknowledgment/response
   Reason 3, 4, etc.
   General Acknowledgments and responses

3. Conclusion: Solution restated.

How Closely Should You Follow This Plan?

We know that plans like these seem formulaic, and it is true that if you rely on them mindlessly, you may seem to display a "write-by-the-numbers" mind-set. Think of a plan not as a blueprint but as a freehand sketch that you flesh out and modify, as you draft. Don't fret if at first following a plan feels awkwardly mechanical. Remember when you learned to drive, dance, play a musical instrument, or play a new sport. Every move seemed clunky. But as you improved, the stiffness disappeared into a flowing, seamless activity. As you gain experience making arguments, you'll know when to forget these plans altogether and let your intuition (backed by experience) be your guide. Even then, however, it's still a good idea to have *some* plan in mind before you start.

Finally, consider whether some issues might puzzle your readers. Have you used terms that they might not know? Is there context or history that they could be unaware of? Have you referred to processes or events unfamiliar to them? If so, you will have to weave an explanation of those matters through your argument, shaping it so that it serves your aims.

Drafting

When to Stop Planning and Start Drafting

You are ready to draft only when you have a general idea of a claim you can make, some reasons to support it, evidence to back up those reasons (facts, quotes, data, and so on), and at least a sketch of the order for those elements. But since it is so much easier to keep reading than to start writing, too many of us just go on researching in order to put off the tougher job of drafting. Set a deadline to start drafting by back-planning from your due date: Decide how much time you need to draft, then add 20 percent. Then add more time to revise (if you are a quick drafter, figure on as much time revising as drafting; if you are slow and careful, about half as much); finally, add time to proofread the final draft.

Draft a Working Introduction

You may have been told to write introductions last, after you have drafted something to introduce. That's a good idea, but it's also smart to sketch a working introduction to focus your thinking as you draft. Try this plan:

1. **Start with a sentence or two of shared context for your problem:**

    For centuries, drinking has been a part of college life. For some students, it is almost a rite of passage. But it has become deadly.

2. **Add a sentence or two that articulates the problem:**

    To control the risk, the university wants to pass regulations banning alcohol at all student events, even fraternity and sorority parties.

3. **In a sentence or two, state what is bad about the problem, what it does or will cost readers:**

    Students will ignore these rules, which will encourage contempt for the university's authority. And if the rules are enforced, responsible students will be deprived of a legal right.

4. **End your introduction with the gist of your solution to the problem:**

    Student Government must join the Greek Council in opposing these rules and support instead educational programs.

Build Each Section Around a Reason

If your paper is short, with each section consisting of only a paragraph or two, draft straight through from beginning to end. But in a longer paper, you may find it helpful to draft each section separately. Do the following for each section longer than one paragraph (at this drafting stage, start each new section on a new page):

1. **Begin with a mini-introduction** (at least a sentence, perhaps a paragraph for a longer section). The mini-introduction should state
   - the part of the problem or question you will address in the section, and
   - the major reason that will be its point/claim.

2. **Draft the body of the section around the reasons and evidence supporting the claim of the section.** Include relevant acknowledgments and responses.

3. **If a section is longer than a few paragraphs, end it with a sentence or two that sums up or otherwise concludes it.** Readers should know when they end one section and what they should remember from it as they move to the next.

After the sections are drafted, do this:

1. **Reconsider their order.** Put the sections in an order that best helps readers to follow your logic. Try out different orders.

2. **Begin the first sentence of each section with a transition that relates what you discussed in the previous section to what you will discuss in the next one.** The simplest transitions are *first, second, as a result,* and so on, but you can also build transitions by beginning a section with words that are familiar from the previous one.

Revision

Match Your Introduction to Your Conclusion

Leave time to revise, but when time runs out, here is a quick fix that ensures that your introduction and conclusion at least do not contradict each other.

1. **Draw a line or add an extra space after the introduction and before the conclusion.** Readers become confused when they can't see those boundaries. If you can't find them easily, your readers may not find them at all.

2. **Highlight the Main Claim of your paper.**
   - If you stated the main claim at the end of the introduction, highlight it, there and again in the conclusion.
   - If you stated the main claim for the first time in the conclusion, also highlight the last sentence or two of the introduction.
   - If the main claim is anywhere else, revise.

3. **Compare the highlighted sentences in your introduction to those in your conclusion.** If they do not harmonize, revise the introduction to

match the conclusion because what you wrote last probably reflects your best thinking. The two main claims should not be identical, but they should at least seem related. For example, this student's conclusion contradicted his introduction:

- Claim in introduction: Treatment of racial issues in Japanese newspapers strongly affects Japanese views of racial differences.

- Claim in conclusion: Thus we see that Japanese attitudes toward race have many sources, from old cultural patterns to international television such as CNN.

If you have time, repeat this process for each section longer than a page: In its introduction and conclusion, highlight the reason/claim that is its point; put it at the end of the introduction if you can, or at least in the conclusion; if it's in the introduction, be sure that it harmonizes with the point in the conclusion, but avoid restating it in exactly the same words.

Working Collaboratively

Pre-analyze Drafts Before You Circulate Them

You can help colleagues give you better advice if before you circulate your papers you pre-analyze them so that they can see their parts. You might use subscripts, as we have, to indicate what element you think a sentence represents. You can show how your paper is organized by adding headings to signal its introduction, major parts, and conclusion. In that way, readers can see its overall structure. At least put an extra space between your introduction and body, between major sections in the body, and between your body and conclusion. Set your word processor to put line numbers down the margin, if it can, to help readers refer to specific passages.

Keep Your Eyes on the Page

You don't help a writer with generalizations like *This is disorganized* or *Your argument is thin.* Such comments tell the writer you have a problem, but not what causes it. More useful are comments that focus on specific sentences on the page: *On lines 9–17 of page 3, I can't tell which reason connects to the evidence about TV viewing,* or *I think you need more reasons to support the claim about history on page 2.* Or *on p. 3, what would you say to someone who said . . . ?* The Facilitator should encourage everyone to refer to specific places on the page. If someone says the language is too colloquial, the Facilitator should ask, *Can you read examples?* If the writer says, *What I wanted to do was show that . . . ,* the Facilitator should ask, *Would you read the part where you do show it?*

Ask Specific Questions

If you ask specific questions, you avoid vague praise or complaints, so the Facilitator should not start with *Well, what do we think?* You can find specific questions in the "Writing Process" sections; they are collected on pages 214-23.

For example, you can help each other develop arguments by asking the five questions: (1) What are you claiming? (2) What are your reasons? (3) What evidence do you base them on? (4) What warrant connects your claims and reasons? (5) What about this alternative? When you share outlines, you can use the scheme laid out in "Sketch a Plan for Your Argument" (p. 46). Or you can practice writing introductions by having each person fill in the four steps in "Draft a Working Introduction" (p. 51). Our checklists are not just for you to work on your papers in private; they can help you read and comment on the work of your colleagues.

Phrase Criticism in Terms of Responses, Suggestions in Terms of Principles

Helpful comments do not make colleagues respond defensively. You make yours helpful when you explain them from the point of view of your experience reading the argument rather than the writer's failure to make it.

Criticism

You can express your criticism from three points of view:

- You can locate a problem in the writer: *You are disorganized.*
- You can locate a problem in the paper: *This paper is disorganized.*
- You can locate a problem in your response: *When I read this paper, I couldn't see how X relates to Y.*

If you criticize the writer or the paper, you can sound too personal. But if you describe your response, you not only lessen the chance that the writer will become defensive but help him focus attention where it should be: on the reader.

- Rather than say, *You are unclear* or *This is unclear,* say, *I don't understand.*
- Rather than say *You are confusing* or *This is confused,* say, *I am confused.*
- Rather than say *You don't offer any evidence,* say, *I didn't see anything here that I could accept as evidence.*
- Rather than say *You don't acknowledge this alternative,* say, *What would you say to someone who said . . . ?*

Suggestions

You can also express suggestions from three points of view:

- You can talk in terms of what's wrong and exactly how to fix it: *This reason lacks support, so why don't you back it up with evidence.*

- You can talk about a general principle: *Each reason needs evidence your readers do not question.*
- You can talk about a specific fix from your point of view: *I would feel more confident about this claim if I saw some evidence right here.*

The most helpful approach combines these suggestions. If you offer only a revision, you just do the writer's work. If you offer only a general principle, you don't help her apply it to her particular text. If you offer only a personal response, your suggestion may seem idiosyncratic. When you offer a generalization and show how it applies to *what is on the page,* the writer knows why you made the suggestion and can more easily see the benefit of your revision.

Be Flexible When You Question One Another's Drafts

As you evaluate how well your colleagues' papers match the features you look for, don't turn our suggestions—or yours—into rigid rules. We describe default patterns that are common, predictable, and generally reliable, but they are *not* your only choice. Don't try to force your argument into our mold if your colleagues can give good reasons to choose otherwise.

INQUIRIES

Remember that these Inquiries offer a wide range of questions, puzzles, and other things to do. Most chapters have too many for you to complete, so pick and choose the ones that catch your interest.

Reflections

1. Some reject rationality as a means to enlightenment: Mystics and spiritualists seek understanding from spheres of experience other than the merely intellectual or physical; subjectivists depend on feeling, impressions, intuition, and so on. How would a mystic or a subjectivist defend, justify, or explain mysticism or subjectivism without offering good reasons? How would a mystic or subjectivist show another mystic or subjectivist that he had reached a mistaken conclusion? Does that question even make sense?

2. Here is an example of the most common way that one partner in a dialogue deliberately derails a conversation. What is it?

   Myles: You've claimed that if you are elected, you will balance the budget by cutting waste. Can you tell us what you will cut?

   Kwan: Unless we resolve to take some tough actions, this state will be bankrupt in five years. We can't just go on spending, spending, spending. We've got to stop it somewhere.

3. Some say that ethos and reputation work best in the dark: they have the most effect on those who know least about the issue being debated.

They believe that the more you know about the person (as opposed to just an image) and the more you know about the facts of the case, the less you should be influenced by ethos or reputation. Do you agree that if an argument is strong enough, the character of the person making it should not matter? What if two people make equally strong arguments, but one seems trustworthy and the other doesn't? Why do ethos and reputation matter to you, if they do?

4. When is a written argument more appropriate than a conversation? When is a conversation more appropriate than a written argument?

Tasks

5. The first question asked in the Bible is in Genesis 3.9: "Adam, where are you?" Read the whole passage. Why is the first question in human history (according to the Bible) asked not by Adam or Eve but by God? Why would God ask a question at all? Don't we ask questions to find out something we don't know? Where is the next question in the Bible? What do you make of it? Who asks it? Why?

6. How much are you influenced by reputation? Identify people whose judgment you trust, including public figures and people you know personally. List the features in their *manner* of arguing. Are they passionate or reserved? Do they qualify their statements or speak with unqualified certainty? Do they acknowledge the contributions of others? Do they use statistics? Anecdotes? What is their tone? Is there a pattern in the attributes of arguers you trust? If so, what does that say about you?

7. Are there questions other than the five listed in this chapter that you *must* imagine yourself answering before your listener or reader would understand your argument? How about these?

> How do you feel about that?
>
> How sure are you?
>
> What is the source of your evidence?
>
> Can you define . . . ?

8. The five questions underlying argument can be asked in relatively explicit ways or with just "Umm" or "Oh?" Observe two or three conversations in which people make arguments. Notice how many different ways they ask others to expand and explain their arguments. Are their questions explicit or implicit? How often do people push enough to get the hard evidence on which someone bases a claim?

9. The next time you disagree with someone, spend a few minutes asking the other person questions to help you understand what that person's argument *is*. Ask about general principles. Offer alternatives in the form of questions: *How would you answer someone who said. . . .* Do some ques-

tions elicit more heated responses than others? How do you feel about asking them?

10. If you subscribe to an e-mail discussion list, choose a series of postings that make arguments.

11. Are arguments at work different from arguments in school? If you have a job, notice how people make arguments with those above them, below them, and on the same level. Do they offer as much evidence as academic writers do? Do they acknowledge alternatives? What would explain the differences?

12. Ask your writing group or roommate to ask you the five questions. Which questions are hardest to answer? When do you find yourself feeling a bit annoyed? When are you *very* annoyed? Can you explain why some questions are more vexing than others?

Projects

13. Many teachers and departments keep model essays of the kind of writing you are expected to do. (Your writing center may also keep models.) Work with classmates to analyze model papers. If you are in a first-year writing class, concentrate on introductory courses in a variety of disciplines. Once you have some models, group them in terms of how they seem to you now. Then try again after you have studied the parts of an argument.

14. Collect some papers you have written. (Hold on to them because you will be asked to analyze them over the next few chapters.) Select the shortest, least developed one. How would you thicken its argument?

15. Are advertisements arguments? Few say explicitly, *Buy this car!* or *See this movie!*, but they still try to get you to do something specific. Most of them give reasons, and the photograph or drawing of the product seems to count as something like evidence, something you can see with your own eyes. Try analyzing them as arguments. What difference does it make whether we call them arguments or not? Look for advertisements that seek to persuade by means other than reasons and evidence. Can you find an ad that acknowledges another point of view?

WRITING PROJECTS 2
Project 2.1

Task.   Organize the notes you assembled for the Writing Projects in Chapter 1 under headings that you can turn into a scratch outline of an argument addressed to those who asked you to help solve their problem, or if your teacher asks you, into a full written argument itself. Before you assemble an argument, work your way through the questions listed below for Project 2.2.

Project 2.2

Scenario.   You have been asked to contribute to a "Forum" on the issue of "Students as Customers," published by the student newspaper in response to a statement approved by (choose one: Student Government, the Faculty Senate, a dean of your school, the state legislature). Your argument is one of several, and not the first in the series. Assume that the statement takes a position opposite to yours.

Task.   Read the material on "Students as Customers," and decide where you stand: Should students be treated as customers? Outline an argument to support your stand. Before you do, work your way through the questions listed below.

Questions

1. What position do you take, exactly?
2. What do you think is at stake here? What difference does it make whether your group's problem is solved, whether we think of advertising as irrational, or whether the university thinks of you as a customer, student, or client?
3. Why do you take that position? What reasons do you have for wanting to think or do_____ ?
4. That's only_____reasons. Can you think of at least one or two more?
5. What hard evidence do you have to go on? What facts and data can you offer to back up your reasons?
6. If you had to imagine how your readers will state their position, what would they say? What reasons do they have for believing their claims?
7. How do you respond to those reasons? Why do you not accept them?
8. What experiences might they have had that are relevant to their reasons?
9. What objections do you think they will make to your position?
10. What are your basic assumptions? Is your position a specific example of a more general principle?
11. What principles do your readers have that differ from yours?

Project 2.3

Context.   The issue of lying became a topic of national concern when President Clinton admitted he lied about his private affairs. The responses ranged from, *Oh, everyone lies about sex* to *Any lie is grounds for impeachment!* In fact, lying has been a matter of moral concern for thousands of years, with philosophers of all schools examining different kinds of lies in different situations. The materials on lying (pp.441-466) lay out some of the issues.

Scenario 1.   You are a candidate for office in student government. At a public meeting, someone asks you about your position:

> We all tell little lies very day. We tell a friend not to fear the worst about a test, when we know he has probably failed it. We know government officials sometimes lie. The Secretary of State says she is on vacation when she is really in secret negotiations. No one expects us to be 100 percent truthful 100 percent of the time. But we have a right to expect that as a student government official, you won't lie to us all the time. Can you give us a sense of how you decide when a public figure can legitimately tell a lie? I'd like to hear some specific examples of when you'd lie and when you wouldn't, and the general principles by which you'd decide those cases.

Task 1.   Write a two- or three-page answer to that question. To help yourself think through the issues, answer—or better, discuss with someone else—the questions on p. 60. Use the answers to build your argument.

Scenario 2.   You are being interviewed for a job with considerable responsibility and the salary to go with it. The interviewer makes this statement:

> Our company has a reputation for integrity, so we try to hire people with high personal standards. Now we know that we all tell each other little white lies. But we can't afford to lose our reputation as people of integrity, because our business depends on trust. I'd like a sense of where you draw the line between white lies and serious lies. For example, suppose you're doing business with one of our best customers who happens to be anti-gay or pro-gay, pro-life or pro-choice, and she asks you where you stand. If you knew your position opposed hers and you suspected she might take her business elsewhere if she knew what you thought, would you lie? I'm interested in how you make decisions in tough cases. Do you have any general principles about when to tell the truth and when not?

Task 2.   Write up two or three pages laying out your position. Write it as if you were proposing a company-wide policy. And don't use that example about the customer. Find new ones. To help yourself think through the issues, answer—or better, discuss with someone else—the questions on p. 60. Use the answers to build your argument.

Scenario 3.   Your best friend is in a class whose instructor suspects students have been buying term papers off the Internet. Your friend did not but knows who did, and her teacher asks her for the names. If she doesn't give him the names, he will try to get her disciplined in some way. She asks you whether she should refuse to answer or to lie and say she doesn't know who plagiarized. You tell her she should follow her conscience. She decides to lie and say she doesn't know. But the plagiarists are caught and reveal that in fact, your friend did know. She tells the administration that you told her to follow her conscience. Now you are in trouble, because you knew that someone knew about plagiarism and you did not turn that person in.

Task 3(a).   Write a defense of your own action in a letter to the Disciplinary Committee. To help yourself think through the issues, answer—or better, discuss with someone else—the questions below. Use the answers to build your argument.

Task 3(b).   Write a defense of your friend's action in a letter to the Disciplinary Committee. Even if you don't ultimately approve of her action, make the best case for it that you can. To help yourself think through the issues, answer—or better, discuss with someone else—the questions below. Use the answers to build your argument.

Scenario 4.   Your school is considering an honor code that obligates everyone to turn in not only known cheaters and plagiarists, but anyone who knows about cheaters and plagiarists but does not turn them in.

Task 4.   Write a paper supporting or opposing that proposal. To help yourself think through the issues, answer—or better, discuss with someone else—the questions below. Use the answers to build your argument.

Scenario 5.   Your workplace is suffering from internal theft. Your employer proposes that not just the thieves but anyone who knows of theft and does not report it will be fired. You are on a union committee negotiating with the company about that policy.

Task 5.   Write a position paper for your committee on that issue. To help yourself think through the issues, answer—or better, discuss with someone else—the questions below. Use the answers to build your argument.

Questions

1. What is the problem? What is at stake in whether readers agree or not?
2. What position do you take? That is, what are you claiming?
3. What reasons do you have for taking the position you do?
4. What hard evidence do you have to back up your reasons?
5. How will your readers state a position different from yours?
6. What reasons do they have for believing their position?
7. How do you respond to those reasons? Do they have a point? Why do you reject them?
8. Those who disagree may have had experiences relevant to their reasons. Can you imagine what they might be?
9. What objections might they make to your reasons and evidence?
10. Can you say what your basic assumptions are?

Project 2.4

Context.   The most common objection to all lying is the "slippery slope" argument: If you tell a little lie, you inevitably go on to tell a bigger one, and then a bigger one yet, and pretty soon, you're lying whenever it's convenient.

Scenario.   For a workshop on morality in public life, you have been asked to read the materials on lying and respond to the question of whether one lie always leads to ever bigger ones. Take whatever position you want on this issue; the audience consists of people exactly like those in your class.

Task.   Write your statement.

Project 2.5

Context.   Science has always raised ethical questions, and no science has raised more puzzles than biology, from gene splicing to biomedical technology. To help people understand these issues, the Center for Biomedical Ethics at the University of Virginia publishes a monthly web column, *Judgment Call*. It addresses ethical questions, including links to background information. You can find it at www.med.virginia.edu/bioethics/judgmentcall.htm.

Scenario.   You serve as an intern for Senator X from your state. She has to keep up on biomedical issues because many biotech companies have located in your state.

Task   Your job is to keep the senator up to date on biotechnology issues, including the matters raised in *Judgment Call*. Select a column from the archive, decide the position you would take on the issue raised in the column; assume the senator probably supports your position. Lay out an argument the senator can make for the position you have chosen. Be sure to address the major points supporting other positions.

SAMPLE ESSAYS

Here are two essays on binge drinking. They respond to a proposal that a university should notify parents when students under twenty-one are caught drinking by university officials, even if no charges are filed. Most students and some faculty oppose it. To help you focus on the substantive elements of these arguments, we have selected essays that won't distract you with complex language or grammatical errors. So don't get caught up in *how* these essays make their points (we'll come back to that later); focus on their substance. Read both, then look at the two tasks that follow.

Student Privacy and Drinking

1   University President, Albert Tanaki, recently proposed that the university should notify parents whenever a student is caught drinking before the age of twenty-one. Tanaki says this will help prevent students from binge drinking. This is wrong because students have rights to privacy and the university should
5   respect them. Tanaki also fails to realize that present-day student life is surrounded by alcohol.

The first aspect in which I feel that Tanaki's proposal is wrong is when he suggests that the university owes it to parents to tell them that their son or daughter is drinking in school. This suggestion clearly violates students' rights to
10 privacy. Young people who do not go to college do not have anyone calling their parents when they get caught drinking before twenty-one. When students are home for the summer, they do not have parents following them around and looking over their shoulder constantly to see whether they are drinking. Parents realize that their children have privacy rights and do not interfere with their social
15 lives. Besides most parents don't care whether their college-age children drink. But even if they don't care themselves about our drinking, parents will get upset with us if they get a notice from the university that we were caught drinking.

Another way in which Tanaki's proposal is wrong is that students will think of the university as the enemy if it does not respect their rights to privacy. The
20 university should not act like a high school and "rat" on students every time they have a problem. It doesn't have parent-teacher conferences, so why should it notify parents about drinking?

University students do not even like it when the university mails grades home to parents. (Other schools mail grades only to the students because they know
25 that grades are a student's private property that she can decide for herself to share with her parents or not.) If the university becomes a tattle-tale, students will have a bad attitude toward it, which would cause them to participate less in university social activities and look for social life away from campustown, where there will be even more drinking. Besides their bad attitude will spill over and
30 harm their studies.

This brings me to my next point that no matter what the university does about student drinking, students are still susceptible to drinking in any environment they live in. It is obvious that Tanaki is looking to eliminate student drinking and protect students from harm by violating their rights to privacy, but Tanaki is
35 totally ignorant of the era in which we live. In the 90's, life is not as it used to be in the past and drinking is an obvious part of everyday college life; therefore, I feel that getting students in trouble with their parents may not influence whether they drink as much as Tanaki thinks. We live in a time in which young people feel it is necessary to drink in order to fit in with the crowd. Their parents
40 drink, their friends drink, and even their teachers drink. President Tanaki may say that it is wrong for students to drink, but he has lots of alcohol at the faculty parties at his house on Marrs Hill, right in the middle of the campus.

Furthermore, you can't go to any kind of student party that does not have drinking around you. It is not just the Greek parties that have liquor everywhere.
45 Most dorm parties, even in the first year dorms, have alcohol that anyone can drink. Students bring alcohol and other drugs as well to concerts at University Hall. When there is not a concert, students have to go to campustown bars to hear live music since first-year students cannot keep a car at their dorms. The city

50 says it is legal for students under twenty-one but over eighteen to go into bars for the music, and it is obvious that they would then be around people drinking. It is a mistake if anyone thinks that students can live in an environment in which they are surrounded by alcohol and never have it pass their lips. As Billy Joel says, "We didn't start the fire." It was our parents and people like President Tanaki who put us in an alcohol environment.

55   In conclusion, I would like to state that Tanaki's proposal is a complete infringement of the privacy rights of students and won't work anyway. I also feel that instead of trying to tattle on students to their parents, he should do something to make the social life of first-year students better so that they do not have to drink because there is nothing better to do at night. It is obvious that the

60 university needs a better solution to the problem of binge drinking than invading the privacy of every student who takes one drink.

Binge Drinking and Parental Notification: Students' Rights to Privacy or Parents' Right to Know?

1   When University President Albert Tanaki announced that he wanted to notify parents when students under twenty-one were caught drinking by university police, there was an uproar among students and faculty. The Student Council passed a resolution the next day stating that "any invasion of student privacy is

5 wrong." Council Chair Susan Ford wrote in the *Student Daily*, "This is morally wrong, legally wrong, and besides it won't work." It is understandable why students have gotten so upset over Tanaki's proposal. But by thinking only about how the proposal impacts on their rights, students and the faculty who have come out in support of them have forgotten about the rights of their parents.

10   The first thing most people have said against the proposal is that it treats students like children instead of adults who have a right to privacy. Well, students do not live in the world of adults. Adults work to pay for their food, housing, phones, computers, and transportation. Students get them free. They even get free condoms. It is true that some students work part time, but that barely covers

15 their spending money in most cases. That is not the world of adults. It is obvious that if you do not have the responsibilities of adults then you cannot expect to get the rights of adults.

On the other hand, students who say they have a right to privacy are not entirely wrong. Most students had privacy rights when they still lived at home.

20 Five of the six people living in my dorm suite had the right to keep our parents out of our bedrooms. Most high schools cannot go into a student's locker unless the police are looking for drugs or guns. Students should not have less right to privacy at college than they did when they were younger. That does not necessarily mean,

however, that students get all the privacy of adults just because they are in
25   college.

In addition to the question of whether students deserve all the rights of
adults, we have to consider how much privacy adults get. Privacy invasions exist
on a continuum. There is a huge difference between sneaking pictures of someone through their bathroom window and telling parents when you break the law
30   by doing something that could harm you forever. What if you overheard your best
friend talking about suicide when he was having a private phone conversation?
Would you protect his privacy? Or would you tell someone who can help him?
Which is the greater evil, to violate someone's privacy or to let them harm themselves? Telling parents about a student's drinking may be an invasion of their
35   privacy and treating them like a child, but it is also doing something to keep them
from harming themselves. There is not a huge difference between telling someone to stop a student from killing themselves and telling parents about a student
doing something as stupid and dangerous as getting drunk enough to get caught
by university police.

40   The one point that no one has considered, however, is the rights of parents.
They are the ones who finance our academic joy ride. They pay for our tuition,
board, books, and just about everything else we take for granted. They don't pay
for these things just so that we don't have to work like adults. They pay because
we are their dependents and they are investing in our future by paying for our
45   education. But when people make investments, don't they watch where their
money goes? Silicon Valley investors keep track of what the companies they
invest in do with the money they give them. As investors in a start-up company
(us), our parents have a right to know what we are doing with the money they
give the university for us. As their dependents, we should not forget that beggars
50   cannot be choosers.

Just because the student opposition to the proposal looks at things from a
self-interested perspective and does not consider the rights of parents, that does
not mean that the proposal is a good one in every way. I think the proposal is on
the right track and is generally a good idea if the university only notifies parents
55   when a student is seriously drunk and not just sneaking one beer. But both
President Tanaki and the opposition act as though all university students live in
dorms and do their drinking on campus or in campustown so that university
police might catch them. What about students who have moved out of the dorms
and live in apartments? There are hardly any juniors or seniors in my dorm. What
60   about students who live at home? About one-third of university students never
live on campus. According to the figures on the registrar's Web page, 36 percent
of this year's first-year students do not live in dorms. Besides, students who are
over twenty-one can have drinking problems as much as those under twenty-one
can. The student who died from binge drinking last year was a senior and so prob-

65 ably over 21. The registrar does not give figures for this, but my first-year classes have lots of students who are older and probably have a family of their own. What about them?

When you consider all of the factors, President Tanaki's proposal may not be perfect but it does not look like an evil invasion of privacy as the opposition says 70 it is. It is an invasion of students' privacy, but for a good cause. It also protects the rights of parents, who as long as they are paying have the right to know what we are up to. Most of all, it lets parents do something to help their troubled children who risk their lives when they engage in binge drinking. I believe that rather than selfishly oppose the proposal, students should work with President Tanaki to 75 create one that can help deal with the problem without invading students privacy rights any more than is necessary.

Task 1.   Identify the elements of argument in each essay. Make a copy and mark it up with different colored highlighters, or use line numbers to identify specific sentences. Indicate in which sentence or sentences the writer does the following:

1. States the **main claim** or point of the essay. Is that claim repeated elsewhere in the essay?

2. States the **main point** of each body paragraph (ignore the introduction and conclusion). These points should be major **reasons** supporting the main claim, and will themselves be claims that the rest of the paragraph supports.

3. Presents information that you regard as hard **evidence,** or as close to hard evidence as you can reasonably expect the writer to get.

4. **Acknowledges** an objection or alternative point of view. Indicate next to each one whether the writer seems to respect the alternative (R), is neutral toward it (N), or is disrespectful (D).

5. **Responds** to an objection or alternative point of view. Indicate next to each one whether the writer seems to respect the alternative (R), is neutral toward it (N), or is disrespectful (D).

6. States a general principle or **warrant** that explains why a reason supports a claim.

Task 2.   Write a brief answer to the question below. Don't get caught up in whether you agree or not; focus on *how* the writers make their case. Use the results of your analysis in Task 1 as evidence to support the claims you make in your answers.

Which essay seems more like an amiable conversation in which the writer answers the five questions and considers the views of others? Why?

CHAPTER 2 IN A NUTSHELL
About Your Argument . . .

We build arguments out of the answers to just five kinds of questions we ask one another every day:

1. What are you claiming?
2. What reasons do you have for believing that claim?
3. What evidence do you base those reasons on?
4. What warrant makes your reasons relevant to your claims?
5. But what about . . . ?

In conversation, someone asks you those questions, but when you write, you have to ask those questions on your readers' behalf. Your biggest challenge will be to answer the fifth: *But what would you say to someone who said . . . ?*

You anchor your argument on two of those answers: on evidence and on warrants. If your readers do not accept those elements, you can't make an argument at all. You must report evidence explicitly; you leave most warrants implicit, if you and your readers share assumptions. But you usually have to state them when you address contested issues. All of us assume that we and our readers share more than we actually do, so it is wise to be more explicit than you think you have to be.

The answers to those five questions constitute the core of a simple argument, but each reason, warrant, and response to a different point of view can also serve as the claim of another, subordinate argument. That's "thickening" your argument.

. . . and About Writing It

As we said at the end of Chapter 1, you have four initial tasks:

- Understand the problem that occasions your argument.
- Formulate some hypotheses that might be good candidates for a solution.
- Pick the best candidate.
- List the reasons that encourage your reader to agree with your solution.

Avoid these stock plans:

- The five-paragraph essay
- A narrative of your research and thinking
- A summary of your sources
- Organizing parts around things rather than ideas and concepts

Once you have reasons to support your claim, think about evidence to back up those reasons. Then imagine someone asking *But what about . . . ?* Here is a plan for drafting your argument:

- Sketch the problem and its solution.
- List reasons that you think your readers would accept as sound.
- Articulate the evidence on which you think those reasons rest.
- Order those reasons in a way that will make sense to your reader.
- Imagine objections and respond to them.

Draft a working introduction:

- Start with a sentence or two of shared context for your problem.
- Add a sentence or two that articulates the problem.
- State what is bad about the problem, what it costs readers.
- Finish with a sentence that sketches the gist of a solution.

Set off your introduction and conclusion from the body of your paper, then compare the last sentence or two in your introduction with the most important claim in your conclusion. If they do not complement each other, change them so they do. (You will most likely have to change the one in the introduction.)

If you can, do the same in each major section: Set off its introduction and (if it has one) conclusion and compare them. The main point in each section should probably appear at the end of the introduction to its section.

CHAPTER 3

Motivating Your Argument

In this chapter we discuss how you can motivate readers to read your argument carefully by posing a problem they care about. We distinguish two kinds of problems— pragmatic and conceptual—and show why it is important to keep them distinct. We then discuss how to write introductions and conclusions that "frame" your argument in ways that help readers understand and remember it.

You can occasionally choose whether to make an argument face-to-face or in writing, but usually you have no choice. You have to make your case in person if you need a personal touch or have no time to write; you have to write if you can't meet readers in person or they want to read your argument before discussing it. Writing has other advantages: When you write, you can better control the flow of your ideas, explain complex issues patiently, and test your argument before sending it off it to critical readers. And those readers can study your argument, reviewing what they cannot remember.

Writing also has disadvantages: You may lack a sense of what your readers are like—amiable or prickly, generous or difficult—and you can't respond immediately to their doubts, questions, or misunderstandings. You can only try to anticipate them and hope for the best. When you write, you also lose one way to get your readers to take your argument seriously: Face-to-face, you can draw others into it with your body language, the passion in your voice, even the look in your eye. If, for example, you ran into a dean after a bad experience at the student health service, you could visibly communicate your frustration right there, and the dean would probably respond more intently than if he were in his office reading an angry letter. Human presence engages us as writing rarely can.

When you make an argument in writing, then, you have to overcome its impersonal distance by offering readers not only good reason to accept your claim, but before that, good reason to engage with you at all. The most devastating response to an argument is not disagreement but indifference. In this chapter, we discuss how you motivate readers to think not *So what?* but *Oh! I see!* And what motivates *I see* is their seeing a problem in need of a solution.

Two Kinds of Problems

Most arguments are occasioned by one of two kinds of problems. One kind leads us to ask, *What must be done to improve this situation?* The other, *What must I learn to understand this issue better?* We'll call them *pragmatic* problems and *conceptual* problems. Readers expect you to write about them differently, so you need to understand what distinguishes them.

Pragmatic Problems

A pragmatic problem is the kind you try to avoid or eliminate, like AIDS, genocide, sagging profits, rising tuition—whatever makes you angry, sad, pained, guilty, embarrassed, ashamed, discouraged, or even just annoyed, for yourself or empathetically for others. You solve a pragmatic problem only when someone *does* something that breaks the chain of causes and effects that leads to the feelings you and, more importantly, your readers want to eliminate or avoid.

Pragmatic problems motivate written arguments everywhere in the professional world and in academic areas such as business, engineering, and architecture, where writers propose what to do about problems ranging from ineffective advertising to maintaining old bridges. A pragmatic problem can be as minor as a loud radio or as immense as global warming. But they all have this in common: Those who pose pragmatic problems must get readers to see that if the problem is not solved, someone they care about (maybe themselves) pays a cost.

Conceptual Problems

A conceptual problem, on the other hand, is more like an intellectual puzzle, something we can state as a question: *Why don't apes cry? What did Thomas Jefferson really think about slavery?* Left unsolved, purely conceptual problems like those might not cause anyone sadness or pain, but not knowing frustrates a fundamental human need to know more about the world and to understand everything about it better, even its most trivial aspects, such as why the biggest nuts in a can always end up on top. Such questions don't motivate everyone, but they do motivate researchers to seek their answers.

The value of spending money on answering such questions seems dubious to some practical minded people, especially politicians. *Who cares,* they ask, *why the biggest nuts end up on top? How will that make the world a better place?* But scholars defend "pure" research of this kind because it simply helps us understand the world better. That was the defense of a University of Chicago professor who, puzzled by the mixed nuts phenomenon, spent a lot of time figuring it out. For him, satisfying his intellectual curiosity was its own reward. And as it turned out, his answer now helps shipping companies pack granular materials more efficiently, construction companies build tougher roads, and drug companies make better pills. In fact, this same scientist recently answered another apparently pointless question: Why does a coffee stain dry up not as a uniformly colored blob, but as a ring? Seems like trivial pursuit, but his answer may help make paint more uniform and computer circuits more exact. (The answer has to do with surface tension, capillary action, and evaporation.)

The Ties Between Conceptual and Pragmatic Problems

Although you have to make different kinds of arguments to solve pragmatic and conceptual problems, the two are often connected. Many researchers work on a conceptual problem expecting its answer to help solve a pragmatic one; they call such research *applied.* When researchers work on a conceptual problem with no immediate practical goal, they call their research *pure.* But even then, their answers often point to solutions to pragmatic problems they had not thought of, as in the mixed nuts problem. You can never tell how valuable an answer might be until you find it.

On the other hand, pragmatic problems always come with conceptual problems built in, because before we can know what to do about something, we first have to understand it. For example, we will be able to take some *action* to solve the pragmatic problem of a failing Social Security system only when we solve the conceptual problem of *knowing* how much money we will save by delaying retirement and *understanding* how society will change if people have to work longer. Solving that pragmatic problem depends on first solving a bundle of conceptual ones because successful action depends on sound knowledge and understanding.

A common mistake among inexperienced writers is to pose one kind of problem and then solve the other. It's important to know what kind of problem you pose, because not only do you have to write about the two kinds differently, but you have to be sure that the problem you pose is the one you solve.

The Structure of Pragmatic Problems

We'll start with a pragmatic problem too simple to write about. Imagine you are driving to a final exam that you must pass to graduate. Your teacher said that anyone missing the exam fails the course. You partied last night, then slept through the alarm. You'll probably be late, but even if you make it, you'll probably fail, because you didn't study. You hit a huge traffic jam; now you *know* you won't make it. Do you have a problem?

Your situation seems to have the makings of one, because it is going to end up making you feel very bad indeed.

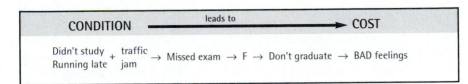

Then you glance at the car next to you and see your instructor! As you slump down out of sight, you realize you no longer have a problem; in fact, you are in the middle of its solution!

How did what seemed like the last straw of a big problem actually solve it? That traffic jam suddenly became a solution when it no longer cost you anything—failing the exam and not graduating. On the contrary: it created a benefit—the test is put off, and you can study for it. Now the situation looks like this:

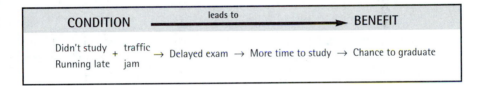

No cost, all benefit, no problem. By this definition, having a painless disease that will kill you tomorrow is not a problem if an asteroid is going to kill everyone on earth today.

In short, every pragmatic problem has two parts:

Part 1: Any event, condition, situation, or circumstance that unsettles your world. We'll call this part of a problem its **destabilizing condition.**

We usually name a problem by naming just its condition: alcoholism, racism, cancer, AIDS. But there's another half to a problem:

Part 2: That destabilizing condition must have an effect that you believe will make you—or someone you care about—feel bad. We call this part of a problem its **cost.**

If cancer, like freckles, had no bad effect, it would be no problem.

When you write an argument addressing a pragmatic problem, you must make your readers see this two-part structure, especially the costs of leaving the problem unsolved, because it is the costs *they* want to avoid that will motivate them to read your argument. Sometimes, you don't have to state the cost, because it's so obvious, but more often you do. Researchers repeatedly warn that doctors routinely give too many antibiotics to patients with minor viral infections. What's the problem?—which is to say, what's the cost?

Identifying Costs

Since readers are motivated to read by the significance of costs to *them,* you must think about your problem from their point of view. To do that, imagine someone repeatedly asking *So what?* until your answer makes her say, *Oh no! What do we do?* For example,

> There's a hole in the ozone layer
>
> *So what?*
>
> Less ozone means more ultraviolet light.
>
> *So what?*
>
> More ultraviolet light means more skin cancer.

If she again asks *So what?,* you might question her moral rationality. But if you still needed to motivate her to care, you'd have to try one more time:

> More skin cancer will lead to higher health care costs and many deaths.

If, however improbably, she again asks *So what?,* you have failed to state your problem in a way that makes her accept it as hers. At that point, you can only shrug, baffled that she lacks human feeling and cannot recognize her own best interests. But if she says, *What do we do?,* you have identified costs that motivate her to see her problem.

"Why Do I Have to Learn this Jargon?"

Some students wonder why they should learn new terms like *conceptual problem, pragmatic problem,* and *destabilizing condition.* They ask, *If making arguments is, as you say, something I do every day, why do I need new words to talk about it?* Well, you are used to making arguments, but probably not to analyzing them. Studying argument is no different from studying chemistry or sociology: you have to discuss concepts for which you have no everyday terms. When you are new to a field, its new terms always sound like jargon. But after a while, they become part of your thinking, no more difficult than *molecule* or *demographics.*

The Nature of Conceptual Problems

A conceptual problem also consists of a destabilizing condition and its resulting cost, but it feels very different from a pragmatic one.

The Destabilizing Condition in Conceptual Problems

In contrast to the endless variety of destabilizing conditions of pragmatic problems, the destabilizing conditions of conceptual problems are always the same kind.

Part 1: In a conceptual problem, the destabilizing condition is always a gap in knowledge or understanding, a discrepancy, puzzle, anomaly, contradiction, uncertainty—a mental itch that you have to scratch.

You can always state the destabilizing condition of a conceptual problem as a question:

How many stars are in the sky?

How does watching TV affect the development of young children?

The Consequences of Conceptual Problems

Conceptual and pragmatic problems also differ in the effect of that destabilizing condition. Remember that in a pragmatic problem the cost of a destabilizing condition is an effect that makes us unhappy: Miss an exam → fail the course. The effect of a conceptual problem is so different that instead of a palpable cost we'll call it a *consequence:*

Part 2: In a conceptual problem, the consequence of a destabilizing condition is something else that you don't know, but that is more significant than the condition.

We understand that what you just read may seem baffling: A conceptual problem consists not of *one* thing you don't know, but of *two.*

Here's how it works: Suppose you don't know something (a destabilizing condition)—*How many stars are in the sky?* or *How does watching TV affect children?* Imagine someone asks, *So what if you don't know that?* You explain the consequence by stating something else you don't know because you don't know the first thing:

If we can't answer the question of how many stars are in the sky, condition / first question then we can't answer a more important question: Does the universe have enough mass for gravity to hold it together? consequence / larger question

If we can't answer the question of how TV affects children, condition / first question then we can't answer a more important one: Does passive entertainment stunt intellectual growth? consequence / larger question

If the second question is one your readers want answered, then you have identified a consequence to them that makes the first question worth asking: By answering the first, you may be able to answer the second, more important question.

We could, of course, imagine someone asking again,

So what if you don't know whether there is enough mass in the universe to hold it together?

At that point, we could offer an even larger question:

If we can't answer the question whether the universe has enough mass for gravity to hold it together, second question then we can't answer an even more important one: Will the universe one day cease to exist? consequence / larger question

But more likely, we'd just shrug and think, *Wrong audience*. We all choose to pursue some questions and ignore others, because some problems interest us and others don't. Researchers depend on the interest of their particular audience, usually people much like themselves, to take their particular conceptual problems seriously. But that means finding the right audience and then articulating the problem in a way that catches their interest. And that's why those just getting started in their academic studies sometimes have a problem "finding something to write about." They have not yet developed particular intellectual interests in special areas; as a consequence, they have no problem to solve, which is to say, no reason to write an argument supporting a solution.

Pure Research and Larger Questions

One "pure" research question long debated by historians has recently been brought closer to an answer. Its answer does not change much in the world, but it does help us understand part of our history:

Did Thomas Jefferson have children with his slave Sally Hemings?

DNA evidence suggests that he might have, but so what if we never find out? *Well, the historians answer, until we know, we can't answer bigger questions:*

Until we know whether Jefferson had children with Hemings, we can't know whether his actions contradicted his claims about equality and morality.

But so what if you don't know?

Until we know, we can't evaluate his ideas about equality.

But so what if you can't?

Until we can evaluate those ideas, we won't understand a figure we treat as a national hero and a source of our key political principles.

Some would still ask, *So what? Who cares?* Well, many do care. And for a few people this conceptual problem applies to a pragmatic one: Who can lie in the Jefferson family cemetery at Monticello? On May 16, 1999, the recognized descendants of Jefferson met to decide whether to let Hemings' descendants be buried there. They voted to study the matter further.

The Wider Coherence of Conceptual Problems

Pragmatic and conceptual problems differ in another way, one that also makes conceptual problems especially difficult for those new to a field. As we've said, you solve a pragmatic problem when you do something to eliminate or ameliorate its costs. It's a bottom line measure: Does your solution improve things or not?

But when we evaluate the answer to the kind of conceptual problem common in college, we want it to be consistent with everything else we know and believe about the subject, including our political and ideological values. So a solution has to fit our mental landscape. That's why some historians refuse to consider DNA evidence showing that Jefferson could have fathered Heming's children, because the very idea that he had sex with a slave contradicts everything they believe about him. They cannot make it fit their system of values and beliefs.

Here's another example: *Why did the mammoth, camel, and other large mammals disappear from North America about 12,000 years ago?* Not much seems to ride on the answer, beyond understanding ancient ecological history. But one proposed answer generates ideological heat. Some researchers claim those creatures died out from climate change or disease; others claim they were hunted to extinction by the earliest Native Americans. The heat comes from those who believe that Native Americans lived in harmony with nature and so *in principle* could not have wiped out a dozen species of large mammals, as modern Europeans almost wiped out the buffalo. So no matter the evidence, it *must* have been the changing climate that killed them.

This need to make new ideas cohere with old is what makes academic conceptual arguments so challenging, especially for those new to a field. When students make a claim about a conceptual issue, they typically know fewer of the facts, principles, theories, data, and arguments than their teachers do. So they don't know what system of settled beliefs their argument must fit.

That's also why those who make a living solving conceptual problems rarely accept wholeheartedly anyone's solution to any problem. We can be certain about a conceptual claim only when we are certain that nothing we can ever know will contradict it. But new evidence can appear at any time, so we can never be drop-dead certain about anything we think we know.

"What Questions Are You Asking Yourself?"

That question was put to several prominent researchers by the *New York Times*. Here are some of their responses. Note that all but one are problems of pure understanding.

- What is the crucial distinction between inanimate matter and an entity which can act as an "agent," manipulating the world on its own behalf, and how does that change happen?—Philip Anderson, physicist and Nobel laureate.
- Why is music such a pleasure?—Nicholas Humphrey, psychologist.
- How can we build a new ethics of respect for life that goes beyond individual survival to include the necessity of death, the preservation of the environment and our current and developing scientific knowledge?—Mary Catherine Bateson, anthropologist.

- Which cognitive skills develop in any reasonably normal human environment and which only in specific sociocultural contexts?—John T. Bruer, President, James S. McDonnell Foundation.

- What might a second specimen of the phenomenon that we call life look like?—Richard Dawkins, evolutionary biologist.

- What goes on inside the head of a baby?—Freeman Dyson, physicist.

- With the ever-growing dominance of corporate forms of control in everyday social life, how do we reconcile our notions of personal liberty and autonomy rooted in Enlightenment political thought?—Edward O. Alumna, sociologist.

Source: New York Times, December 30, 1997.

Framing Pragmatic Problems

When you motivate readers to read your argument closely, they understand it better and remember it longer. You motivate them to read closely by stating a problem they want to see solved. So at the center of every introduction, you must state your problem in a way that helps them see their stake in its solution, its costs or consequences to *them.* We now show you how to write an introduction that does that. We discuss pragmatic problems first, then conceptual ones.

The Heart of Your Introduction: Conditions and Costs

At the heart of every introduction should be your problem. If you state that problem explicitly, you will state a destabilizing condition and its pragmatic cost or conceptual consequence. Some costs may seem too obvious to state, but it's risky to assume that your readers understand them as you do. For example, binge drinking has obvious costs, but different readers may well see different ones:

It threatens the lives of the drinkers and those around them.

It is a moral weakness.

It tarnishes the image of the university.

It exposes the school to legal action for the damage it causes.

Moreover, each cost implies that we could solve the problem in a different way:

Since it threatens lives, ban it entirely.

Since it erodes moral values, teach stronger moral virtue.

Since it makes us look bad, create a public relations campaign to make us look good.

Since it exposes the school to legal action, hire good lawyers.

Each cost also implies the values not only of the writer, but of the implied reader as well: One implies that readers feel anguish over injury and death, another that they fear loss of prestige, another loss of money, another moral guilt. Each of those fears implies a different system of values.

Contrast how these three introductions articulate the problem:

1. When students drink, many "binge," consuming large amounts of alcohol at one sitting until they pass out, a behavior that has spread even to women. _{destabilizing condition} (*So what?*) We may not be able to eradicate drinking, but we can do something to control it. _{promise of solution}

2. When students drink, many "binge," consuming large amounts of alcohol at one sitting until they pass out, behavior that has spread even to women. _{destabilizing condition} (*So what?*) Bingeing is, tragically, far from harmless. In the last six months, binge drinking has been cited in three deaths from alcohol poisoning, two from falls, and one in a car crash. It injures not only drinkers but those around them. It crosses the line from fun to reckless behavior that, if uncontrolled, will kill and injure still more students. _{costs} We may not be able to eradicate drinking, but we can control its costs by educating first-year students how to manage its risks. _{promise of solution}

3. When students drink, many "binge," consuming large amounts of alcohol at one sitting until they pass out, behavior that has spread even to women. _{destabilizing condition} (*So what?*) This behavior not only tarnishes our image, but exposes us to liability if a student injures himself or others. Until this problem is solved, we risk criticism from the state legislature, with possible cuts in our budget, and increased insurance costs, either of which will force us to delay salary increases. _{costs} We may not be able to eradicate drinking, but we can control its costs by educating the public and the legislature that the problem is caused by lax parenting. _{promise of solution}

The first introduction implies that binge drinking is bad, but doesn't say why— it offers no costs. The second and third motivate readers to read, because they specify the costs of binge drinking. But they appeal to different values: in (2), concern for the injury and death of others; in (3), the reader's self-interest in the college.

Negative Costs versus Positive Benefits

The best way to motivate readers is to describe costs they want to avoid. But you can state disagreeable costs in a positive way by phrasing them as potential benefits they might want to attain. Here the writer first states a cost directly, then restates it as a benefit:

> Bingeing is, tragically, far from harmless. In the last six months, it has been cited in three deaths from alcohol poisoning, two from falls, and one in a car crash. It injures not only drinkers but those around them. **Bingeing crosses**

the line from good times to reckless behavior that, if uncontrolled, will kill and injure still more students. _{costs} We cannot eradicate drinking, but we must do something to control it. _{solution} If we can reduce it even slightly, **we will not just save those who binge from injury or even death, but mitigate the damage they do to those around them.** _{costs restated as benefits}

You might think that stating a cost as a loss or potential gain is just a stylistic nicety, but some good research suggests that we are motivated more by the fear of loss than by the attraction of possible gain. For example, the consequence of the hole the ozone is objectively the same, whether we describe it as costing 10,000 deaths, or, if we can fix it, as an opportunity to save 10,000 lives. But we tend to react more keenly to the fear of lives certainly lost than to lives possibly saved.

The Core of Your Introduction: Common Ground and Solution

So far, we've seen that at the heart of your introduction is your problem:

> **INTRODUCTION**
>
> . . . . + [Destabilizing Condition + Costs] _{problem} + ...

Most introductions have two more parts. Right after readers learn of the problem, they look for its solution (or at least a gesture toward it). But before the problem, readers usually need to see some familiar context for it, what we'll call *common ground*. Schematically, a full introduction looks like this:

> **INTRODUCTION**
>
> Common Ground + [Destabilizing Condition + Costs] _{problem} + Solution

We'll discuss the solution first, then the common ground.

Solutions

Once you pose a problem, readers usually look for the gist of its solution, a sentence (or two) that sketch its general contours. For example, we might end that introductory paragraph about bingeing with this specific solution:

> . . . Bingeing crosses the line from good times to reckless behavior that, if uncontrolled, will kill and injure still more students. _{costs} **We may not be able to end drinking, but colleges must start educating students how to manage its risks, just as we now educate them about sexual harassment and other social problems on campus.** _{solution/main claim}

Though it is a bit of a cliché, a rhetorical question can achieve the same end:

> We may not be able to end drinking, but is it possible to educate students in how to manage its risks, just as we now educate them about sexual harassment and other social problems on campus? _{solution/main claim}

But some writers only sketch a solution, implying that they will eventually offer it, but not until their conclusion:

> . . . Bingeing crosses the line from good times to reckless behavior that, if uncontrolled, will kill and injure still more students. _{costs} **We may not be able to stop drinking entirely, but it is a problem we can no longer ignore. The right solution is not obvious, but finding one must be an integral part of our educational mission.** _{promise of solution to come}

That last sentence only promises a solution, but it introduces concepts—*integral part of our educational mission*—that suggest where the writer goes from there.

If you do not state your solution but only promise one, you risk seeming to hide something. At best, you help readers less than you might to understand the rest of your argument. But there is a way to avoid those risks: State your problem so precisely that readers can infer your solution. For example, readers cannot predict what specific solution will follow this introduction:

> When students drink, many "binge," consuming large amounts of alcohol at one sitting until they pass out, behavior that has spread even to women. _{destabilizing condition} Bingeing is, tragically, far from harmless . . . It crosses the line from fun to reckless behavior that, if uncontrolled, will kill and injure still more students. _{costs} **We may not be able to stop drinking entirely, but it is a problem we can no longer avoid. The right solution is not obvious, but finding one must be an integral part of our educational mission.** _{promise of solution to come}

But if the writer states the problem in detail, readers have a much better idea of what is to come, even if the writer does not specifically state the solution at the end of the introduction:

> Increasingly, except for driving under the influence, students are unaware of the specific risks of excessive alcohol consumption. When students first arrive on campus they gravely underestimate the risks they face. Fewer than 40 percent even know about the toxic effects of alcohol, and most of that 40 percent think those effects occur only with long-term drinkers. Yet the university does nothing during orientation or later to inform students what those risks are and how students can manage them. So, many students "binge," consuming large amounts of alcohol at one sitting until they pass out or worse. _{destabilizing condition} Bingeing is, tragically, far from harmless . . . It crosses the line from fun to reckless behavior that, if uncontrolled, will kill and injure still more students. _{costs} We may not be able to stop drinking entirely, but it is a problem we can no longer avoid. Finding a solution must be an integral part of our educational mission. _{promise of solution to come}

Is it fair to say that most readers can predict that the solution to this problem will involve informing students about the risks of drinking during orientation? When we see a problem stated that explicitly, we can predict the gist of its solution. So if you think you must hold back your solution until the end of your argument, consider stating your problem in enough detail that readers will have an idea of what its general contours will be.

EXAMPLE

A Problem That Forecasts Its Solution

> *In some cases, it's not necessary to state a solution because the problem is framed so specifically that its solution is obvious. Here is the skeleton of an argument about doing historical research on the Internet. Notice that at the end of the introduction, the writer does not specify a solution because it is so obvious.*

Does the Internet help college students learn? Enthusiasts proclaim it has made a world of information available to any freshman with a computer. Skeptics warn that cyberspace is so full of junk that research in it will never amount to anything more than garbage collecting . . . I concede that the skeptics have a case. _{common ground} But the problem with doing research on the Internet is not about garbage. It's that, by doing all their homework on the Internet, _{destabilizing condition} students may develop a misunderstanding of research itself and even of the subjects they are studying. _{cost—end of introduction}

Historical research takes place in libraries and archives, but it is not a straightforward process of retrieving information. _{reason 1} You may open a box of manuscripts . . . but . . . every document . . . must be read between the lines and related to all the surrounding documents. . . .

Moreover, most documents never make it into archives . . . _{reason 2}

[Moreover] . . . no digitized text can duplicate the original—its handwriting or typography, its layout, its paper . . . _{reason 3}

[Finally d]igitizers often dump texts onto the Internet without considering their quality as sources, and students often fail to read those texts critically. . . . _{reason 4 end of body of argument}

Such thoughts touch off Luddite fantasies: smash all the computers and leave the Internet to drown in the ocean of its own junk. But that way madness lies, and my students have taught me that, if handled with care, the Internet can be an effective tool . . . Instead of turning our backs on cyberspace, we need to take control of it—to set standards, develop quality controls and direct traffic. Our students will learn to navigate the Internet successfully if we set up warning signals and teach them to obey: Proceed with caution. Danger lies ahead. _{solution /main claim}

Source: From Robert Darnton, "No Computer Can Hold the Past,"
New York Times, June 12, 1999.

Common Ground

Experienced writers motivate readers by describing the costs of a problem so that they understand what they risk if it is left unsolved. But even before that, writers often use another device to encourage readers to take their problem seriously. They open with a statement of what we call *common ground;* then they contradict it, something we did in opening this paragraph. In the first sentence, we stated something we thought you knew and would accept as unproblematic:

> Experienced writers motivate readers by describing the costs of a problem so that readers understand what they risk if it is left unsolved.

That was our common ground. In the next sentence we then tried to surprise you with something we thought you did not know:

> But even before that, writers often use another device to encourage readers to take their problem seriously.

In that sentence, we wanted to destabilize what we hoped you would take as unproblematic. To be sure you didn't miss that, we opened it with a *but.*

Here, for example, is a widely known fact about drinking:

> Drinking has been a part of American college life since the first college opened its doors more than three centuries ago, and ever since it has been an accepted, even celebrated part of growing up. _{common ground}

Once we establish that as our common ground, we can destabilize it with a *but, however,* or some other term signaling that what you thought you knew is at least incomplete, maybe even wrong:

> Drinking has been a part of American college life since the first college opened its doors more than three centuries ago, and ever since it has been an accepted, even celebrated part of growing up. _{common ground} **But** in recent years a new, dangerous kind of drinking known as binge drinking has become common. _{destabilizing condition}

Writers sometimes omit common ground when they address a well-known problem. In that case, they begin by stating the problem directly:

> The rise in fatalities and injuries _{cost} as a result of binge drinking on college campuses _{destabilizing condition} has convinced many college administrators that it is time to address the problem directly. Many have instituted new rules regulating drinking on college property, one of which is claimed to work: banning all alcohol in dormitories. _{solution}

But a skilled writer can use all of that as common ground by contradicting it with a *but* or *however* and then telling you something you did not know:

> . . . one of which is claimed to work: banning all alcohol in dormitories. _{common ground} Such a blanket prohibition, **however,** is likely to do more harm than good. _{destabilizing condition} First, it will cause students to . . . _{cost 1}

In other words, we can use *anything* as common ground, if readers accept it and we can upset it with a destabilizing condition.

Let's go back to the boxed argument about research on the Internet. The writer opens with common ground in the form of one understanding of the problem:

> Does the Internet help college students learn? Enthusiasts proclaim it has made a world of information available to any freshman with a computer.

> Skeptics warn that cyberspace is so full of junk that research in it will never amount to anything more than garbage collecting. . . . I concede that the skeptics have a case. _{common ground}

He then destabilizes that shared understanding by redefining the problem:

> But the problem with doing research on the Internet is not about garbage. It's that, by doing all their homework on the Internet, _{destabilizing condition} students may develop a misunderstanding of research itself and even of the subjects they are studying. _{cost}

With this frame for the problem, we have a model introduction with four elements:

INTRODUCTION

Common Ground + [Destabilizing Condition + Costs] _{problem} + Solution

---

Some writers, however, use one more element to set up these four.

Prelude

You may recall being told to "catch your readers' attention" by opening your essays with an interesting anecdote, a striking fact, or a quotation. What catches our attention better is a problem that we think needs a solution. But opening with something catchy can work, if it encapsulates and vividly introduces key concepts related to the problem. To name this device, we'll borrow a term from music: *prelude*.

Here are three preludes you could use to open an argument about bingeing.

1. You can open with a fact that you hope will startle your reader:

   > A recent study on student drinking reports that at most colleges three out of four students "binged" at least once in the previous 30 days, drinking more than five drinks at a sitting. Almost half binge once a week, and those who binge most are not just members of fraternities, but their officers. _{fact}

2. You can start with a quotation, familiar or not:

   > "If you're old enough to die for your country, you're old enough to drink to it." How many times have you heard that justification for allowing 18-year-olds to drink? _{quotation}

3. You can present a concrete example of your problem, the most common prelude:

   > When Jim Shay, president of Omega Alpha, accepted a dare from his fraternity brothers to down a pint of whiskey in one long swallow, he didn't plan to become this year's eighth college fatality from alcohol poisoning, but he did. _{anecdote}

And of course, you can combine all three:

"If you're old enough to die for your country, you're old enough to drink to it." Tragically, Jim Shay, president of Omega Alpha, won't have a chance to do either. When he accepted a dare from his fraternity brothers to down a pint of whiskey in one long swallow, he didn't plan to become this year's eighth college fatality from alcohol poisoning, but he did. According to a recent study, at most colleges, three out of four students at most colleges have, like Jim Shay, drunk five drinks at a sitting in the previous 30 days. And those who drink the most are not just members of fraternities, but, like Shay, officers. _{prelude}

Drinking, of course, has been a part of American college life since the first college opened. . . . _{common ground} But in recent years a new, dangerous kind of drinking known as "binge drinking" has become increasingly common. _{destabi-lizing condition}

Preludes are rare in writing in the natural and social sciences, but they are often used in the humanities and in writing for the public. You use a prelude best to introduce key themes that your argument will pursue, particularly by representing your problem in a vivid and concrete example.

Here is the complete structure of an introduction:

INTRODUCTION

Prelude + Common Ground + [Destabilizing Condition + Costs] + Gist/Promise of Solution

---

You don't need all five elements in every introduction. You can mix and match them to create introductions of more or less complexity. The only element you always need is a destabilizing condition (if its cost is obvious). For a long argument, you can expand each of the first three elements into a paragraph or more, creating an introduction two or three pages long.

Framing Conceptual Problems

An introduction to a conceptual problem has the same parts as a pragmatic one. It differs in the substance of its destabilizing condition, something we don't know or understand, and its consequences, a second thing we won't know until we know the first. Here are two introductions of different quality:

1. Ernest Hemingway's *A Farewell to Arms* blends the themes of love and war and other themes based on love and death. The main themes of love and war and bliss and tragedy develop and intermix. The result is a fusion of the idyllic or comic, and the tragic or disturbing which is affected by war. With meticulous care, it follows the development of the psychological characteristics of the two lovers, Catherine Barkley and Frederic Henry. Hemingway represents average human beings in their emotions, thoughts, and actions in a natural world of love and war. (*So what?*)

2. Though Flannery O'Connor's stories give us insight into Southern culture, critics have criticized her attitude toward race, calling it the product of "an imperfectly developed sensibility" and claiming that "large social issues as such were never the subject of her writing." _{common ground} But that criticism ignores her religious beliefs, which caused her to view racism not just as a social issue but as the symptom of a larger spiritual and religious crisis._{destabilizing condition} (*So what?*) If we fail to recognize her views on these spiritual issues, we risk overlooking her insights into sources of racism that are deeper and more harmful than mere social or cultural causes. _{consequence} Her stories show that her treatment of racism as a spiritual crisis is more sympathetic to equality than is apparent and suggests an understanding of racism that set her apart from liberals of her time. _{answer/main claim} Once we recognize the spiritual basis of her thinking, we see her works in a new and surprising light. _{cost restated as benefit}

The first introduction goes nowhere. Not only do we not know the question, but we don't know what part is supposed to be familiar common ground and what part is a claim that needs to be supported. The second has all four elements.

IN THE READINGS

Introductions

You can see in the readings that writers follow the pattern for introductions in so many ways that we notice the pattern only when we look for it. Here is an outline of the very long introduction to Pamela White's "'Drinking Age Has Simply Got to Go,' Say Campus Riots" (p. 423) (the numbers refer to paragraphs):

[1]The young are always the first to recognize hypocrisy. . . . So it's no wonder that Boulder's young adults are incensed over the state's drinking laws. _{prelude}

[2]Last weekend marked the first anniversary of the University Hill "beer" riots. . . .

[3]Old people, like me, have responded . . . with scorn. . . .

[4]Our disgust with the violence and its emotional and financial costs is well-justified. Violence can only be justified in cases of self-defense, and, even then, it is a tragedy. Rioting should never be condoned. _{common ground}

[5]But when we casually dismiss the root of these young people's anger, we are missing the point. _{destabilizing condition} Their frustration has less to do with a desire to drink booze and more to do [with] social justice. _{consequence}

Paragraphs 6 through 12 elaborate the consequences.

[13]I suppose the nation could choose to . . . . _{rejected solution}

[14]It might also be a good idea to . . . . _{rejected solution}

^{15}Still, the best solution might be the most difficult . . . . we should abolish the drinking age completely. ~solution~

Problem Solving Versus Problem Posing

There is a kind of argument, particularly common in newspapers and magazines, that aims not at solving a problem, but only at posing one. We have to call its problem a conceptual one because the writer wants us only to believe that a problem exists. Instead of building the introduction around a full statement of a problem and ending it with a solution, he devotes most of the introduction to describing the destabilizing condition, making that his main claim. Then in the body of the argument, he shows that the problem exists by describing its costs in some detail, turning each one into a reason supported with evidence. The writer doesn't claim to know how to solve the problem, but he does claim that a solution must be found. In effect, the whole argument has roughly the same structure as an introduction.

The outlines shown here present the differences between problem-solving and problem-posing arguments.

Problem-Solving Argument
Introduction
 (Prelude)
 (Common Ground)
 Destabilizing Condition
 Costs
 Gist of Solution/Claim

Body
 (Warrants)
 Reasons supporting Solution
 Acknowledgment/Response

Conclusion
 Solution/Claim restated

Problem-Posing Argument
Introduction
 (Prelude)
 (Common Ground)
 Destabilizing Condition/Claim

Body
 (Warrants)
 Costs as Reasons supporting Claim
 Acknowledgment/Response

Conclusion
 (Gesture toward a Solution)

EXAMPLE

A Problem-Posing Argument

In this essay, the writer works harder at posing a problem than at solving it. He opens with common ground that he destabilizes by claiming that research papers he recently received were worse than those in past years because they were researched on the Internet.

Sometimes I look forward to the end-of-semester rush, when students' final papers come streaming into my office and mailbox. I could have hundreds of pages of original thought to read and evaluate. Once in a while, it is truly exciting, and brilliant words are typed across a page in response to a question I've asked the class to discuss. _{common ground}

But this past semester was different. I noticed a disturbing decline in both the quality of the writing and the originality of the thoughts expressed. What had happened since last fall? Did I ask worse questions? Were my students unusually lazy? No. My class had fallen victim to the latest easy way of writing a paper: doing their research on the World Wide Web. _{destabilizing condition}

He then goes on to specify the costs of that destabilizing condition, how they were worse:

It's easy to spot a research paper that is based primarily on information collected from the Web. First, the bibliography cites no books, just articles or pointers to places in that virtual land somewhere off any map: http://www. _{reason 1} Then a strange preponderance of material in the bibliography is curiously out of date . . . _{reason 2} Another clue is the beautiful pictures and graphs that are inserted neatly into the body of the student's text. They look impressive . . . but actually they often bear little relation to the precise subject of the paper. _{reason 3}

The author gestures toward a solution at the end, but nothing in his argument supports it, so it is just a way to bring his argument to a close.

I'd like [my students] to . . . ponder what it means to live in a world where some things get easier and easier so rapidly that we can hardly keep track of how easy they're getting, while other tasks remain as hard as ever—such as doing research and writing a good paper that teaches the writer something in the process. Knowledge does not emerge in a vacuum, but we do need silence and space for sustained thought. Next semester, I'm going to urge my students to turn off their glowing boxes and think, if only once in a while.

Source: From David Rothenberg, "How the Web Destroys the Quality of Students' Research Papers," *Chronicle of Higher Education*, August 15, 1997.

Writing Conclusions

Conclusions are more variable than introductions, but in a pinch, you can map yours onto the elements of your introduction. Just reverse their order in your conclusion:

1. Start by stating (or restating) the gist of your claim.
2. Explain its significance by answering the question *So what?* Answer in a new way, if you can. But if not, restate what you offered in the introduction.

3. Suggest a further question or problem that needs to be resolved. This is like the destabilizing condition, something not known. In effect, you answer the question *Now what?*

4. End with an anecdote, quotation, or fact. If possible, it should balance your prelude. We'll call this the *coda.*

For example, here is a paraphrase of the introduction to that Flannery O'Connor paper on page 84.

1. [no prelude]
2. Critics have said O'Connor did not have a social conscience. _{common ground}
3. But she viewed racism not as a social issue but as the symptom of a spiritual crisis. _{destabilizing condition} (*So what?*)
4. If we ignore this, we miss her insights into sources of racism that are deeper than cultural conflict. _{consequence}
5. Her treatment of racism as a spiritual crisis is more sympathetic to equality than is apparent. _{answer/main claim}

To create a workable conclusion, the writer could have started it by restating her main claim, adding a new consequence, and then raising new questions to pursue.

> So those who claim that O'Connor was indifferent to racism fail to see how she saw past the surface of the black-white conflict to find a deeper crisis of faith—the modern failure to recognize the healing knowledge that comes from profound suffering. _{main claim restated} (*So what?*) Indeed, these insights into the human condition put her among a select few Southern writers who first saw the deep failure of the modern world to deal with human differences not just as economic or social problems, but as spiritual ones. For example, . . . _{new consequence / significance} (*Now what?*) Seen in this light, a rereading of her private correspondence would almost certainly show that . . . . _{new questions to pursue}

We could, if we had a striking quote, add it to the end as a coda.

There are other patterns for conclusions, but this one will work when you can't come up with anything better.

Introductions and Conclusions as a Way of Thinking

Some think schematic plans cramp creative thinking. In fact, they focus your thinking, each step increasing your opportunity to be creative.

- When you select a common ground, you have to think about what your readers believe that your problem will unsettle.
- When you state the destabilizing condition, you have to think about what part of the troubling situation your solution will change.
- When you ask *So what?*, you have to think about which possible costs your readers will be least willing to pay, or which larger questions they will most want answered.

- When you think about preludes and codas, you think about the key concepts that you must forecast or the best ways to encapsulate your problem in a pithy, vivid way.

Though some students fear that this pattern is boring, you can use it in so many different ways that your readers will notice it only when they look for it. But even if your introductions at first seem mechanical, you will eventually learn to make them feel natural.

WRITING PROCESS 3
Motivating Your Argument

Thinking-Reading-Talking

Use Problem Statements to Focus Your Reading

In your reading, look at introductions carefully, because they tell you what the writer thinks is important.

- The common ground gives what the writer thinks is important context. What other writers does she respond to? What views does she claim hers will replace? Most important, what will her solution change?
- The destabilizing condition is what has to be changed in a pragmatic problem; in a conceptual one, it is the gap in knowledge or understanding to be resolved.
- The costs or consequences indicate why the writer thinks the problem is worth solving.
- The solution tells you how to read what follows.

If you don't find the problem in the introduction, look for it in the conclusion.

Preparing and Planning

From a Topic to a Problem

Most arguments assigned in a class are likely to be short—three to five pages, probably in response to something you read. But if you are writing a research paper, you may have to find your own problem. Here are four steps to find a problem, starting from scratch: (1) find a topic, (2) narrow it, (3) question it, and (4) turn the questions into a problem.

Step 1: Find a Topic That Interests You
If your assignment doesn't specify a topic, find one that interests you. Worry later whether it will interest others.

For General Topics
1. What would you like to know more about if you were free to explore any of your interests? Once you can name a topic, think about its history, economics, politics, and possible controversies related to it.
2. What are politicians *not* talking about that they should? If you invited your governor to speak on campus, what topic should she address?
3. What makes you angry about public issues? Finish this sentence: *What gripes me about politics / teaching / education / movies / radio / TV / advertising is . . .*
4. Browse a big magazine rack until you find a title that grabs your interest. Skim the article to see if you'd like to know more.
5. Join an e-mail group or visit a Web site on a subject that interests you. Look for debates, misunderstandings, questions. Search archived messages and related sites.
6. What courses will you take next term? If you can find a topic related to one of them, you get a head start on your work.

For Topics in a Particular Field of Study
1. Ask your teacher which issues that you have discussed in class are hotly contested.
2. Browse through an encyclopedia in the field you are studying.
3. Ask a teacher or librarian for journals that review the year's work in your field of interest.

We cannot exaggerate how important it is to find a topic that will hold your interest over several weeks. If your topic bores you, you will bore your reader.

Step 2: Turn Your General Topic into a Specific One
A topic looks like an entry in a library catalog or encyclopedia:

AIDS	Balance of trade	Jefferson-Hemings debate
Homelessness	Evolution of birds	Campaign finance reform.

Too often, inexperienced writers think that once they have a topic, they have their problem. They do not. You have to turn a general topic into a more specific one by adding relationships, connections, characteristics, implications, and qualities:

SIMPLE TOPIC		SPECIFIC TOPIC
Territorial behavior in ground squirrels	→	The **acquisition** of territorial **protection** behavior in young ground squirrels and its **similarity** to behavior of **human children**

SIMPLE TOPIC	SPECIFIC TOPIC
Calvinism in Lincoln's "Gettysburg Address" and other speeches →	The **influence** of Lincoln's Calvinist **beliefs** about **destiny** on his **justification** for the **need for political and personal sacrifice** in the "Gettysburg Address" and other speeches

We realize you might be puzzled after reading these suggestions: *How can I "add relationships, connections . . . " until I know something about the topic?* In truth, you can't. That's what makes it hard to write a research paper in a course with no specialized content. You have to come up with a topic and develop it in a vacuum. Before you can narrow it, you'll have to read around a bit. But you might find what follows useful.

Step 3: Question Your Topic

Try rephasing your topic as a question, especially as a *how* or *why* question. Note that you can ask these questions in two ways. Try both: *How* can mean either *in what manner* or *by what means:*

> In what manner/By what means did Lincoln's Calvinist beliefs about destiny influence the way he justified the need for political and personal sacrifice in the "Gettysburg Address" and other speeches?

And *why* can mean either *for what reason* or *what caused:*

> For what reason did Lincoln think/What caused Lincoln to think his Calvinist beliefs about destiny were relevant to the need for political and personal sacrifice?

Now ask four more questions. The first two decompose your topic into its parts:

1. What are the parts of each thing you are writing about and how do they relate to one another?

   What are the elements of Lincoln's Calvinist beliefs about destiny? Did one of them in particular cause Lincoln to believe sacrifice was necessary? How did the element of destiny relate to the elements of punishment?

2. What is the history of your topic? How did it begin and how does it end? What are its stages?

   How did Calvin's ideas reach Lincoln? How does Lincoln relate his ideas to those of the founding fathers? How were his speeches influenced by traditional patterns of oratory?

Two more questions ask how your topic is part of a larger whole:

3. How is each thing you write about part of a larger unit or category? How is each one like something else?

   Were Lincoln's beliefs part of a larger philosophy? Were they shared by others? Were Lincoln's calls for sacrifice similar to those of others?

4. How is your topic part of a larger history?

   What did those before Lincoln think about destiny? How have those after him thought about it?

A fifth question inquires into the qualities of your topic.

5. Is Lincoln's use of these ideas effective? Traditional? Innovative? Mistaken? Simple?

After you ask several questions, pick two or three that most catch your interest.

Step 4: Turn Questions into a Problem

The more you read and think about your topic, the better you develop your questions into a problem. If you feel confused, here is a formulaic way to do that.

For a pragmatic problem, decide what condition must be changed, and why. Fill in the blanks in these three steps. At the end of the second, imagine your reader asking *So what?*

1. I am working on the problem of_____

   2. in order to find out how to change_____*(So what if you don't?)*

      3. so that you/we/someone can avoid the cost/gain the benefit of_____.

Here are some ways to complete these statements:

1. I am working on the problem of traffic congestion after football games,

   2. in order to get traffic through city streets efficiently, *(So what if you don't?)*

      3. so that town businesses will not suffer from traffic gridlock.

For a conceptual problem, you depend even more on questions, because your best ones define its heart, what you don't know. *Why* and *how* questions are particularly useful. Again, imagine someone asking *So what?* at the end of the second step:

1. I am working on the issue of_____

   2. in order to find out why/how/when/what_____*(So what if you don't find out?)*

      3. so that I can understand better why/how/when/what_____.

Again, some ways to complete these:

1. I am working on the issue of the appeal that the Taj Mahal has in the West,

2. because I want to find out what causes Europeans to think of it as the only masterpiece of Indian architecture, (*So what? What if you never find out?*)

3. so that I can understand better why people tend to misunderstand the art of other cultures by focusing on a few notable but not representative works.

This is a formulaic way of framing a project, but a formula may be what you need when your head is spinning with a buzz of facts and ideas.

Some writers can't think of a way to spell out that last step (. . . *so that I can understand better how* . . .). If you are in the early stages of your research, don't spend time trying to figure out what larger question you want to answer. Work on the second step (. . . *in order to find out why* . . .). Have faith that you will discover how to complete the third step once you are close to finishing. It is almost always late in the game that any of us sees clearly the full significance of our work. Only then can we really answer that toughest question of all, *So what?*

Revising

Test Your Problem Statement

Once you finish a first draft, revisit your introduction to make sure it matches the argument you have made. Ask these questions:

1. If you have a prelude, does it introduce themes that you develop through the rest of the argument?

2. Does your common ground state something readers believe and that you will at least supplement, if not correct?

3. Does the destabilizing condition contradict or at least qualify that common ground?

4. Do your costs or consequences answer the question *So what?*

5. (a) Does your introduction conclude with the solution to the problem and Main Claim of your argument?

   (b) If you have reason to withhold your solution/Main Claim until the conclusion, does your introduction end with a sentence that introduces the key concepts that the rest of your argument develops?

Also check your conclusion:

1. Does the main point in your conclusion restate, complement, or at least not contradict the Main Claim in your introduction?

2. Have you suggested the significance of your Main Claim? In a pinch, you can restate the costs from the introduction as benefits.

Check for Common Themes in the Title, Claim, and Body

Even a brief introduction should create a conceptual frame to guide readers through your argument. Here is a way to be sure they stay on track. No test better predicts whether readers will think your argument is coherent.

1. Find the sentence that states your main claim and circle three or four key concepts in it, especially concepts that *you* contributed and were not given by the language of your assignment.
2. If you held off stating your main claim until your conclusion, also circle three or four key concepts in the sentence or two at the end of your introduction.
3. In the body of your paper, circle the words that you circled in (1) and (2).
4. Underline words in the body that closely relate to those you circled.

Now scan the body of your paper:

1. If the words you circled in your introduction and conclusion don't match, revise your introduction to fit your conclusion.
2. If you have neither circled nor underlined many words in the body, you have gotten off track.
3. If you circled few words but underlined many different ones, change some of the underlined words to words you circled.
4. If you notice words in the body that do not appear in the introduction or conclusion, revise your introduction and conclusion so that they do.

Build a Title Out of Your Circled Words

Your title should preview the key themes and concepts in your argument, so it should include the words that you circled in your introduction and conclusion. We suggest a title consisting of two lines, separated by a colon. Such titles may feel stiff, but they give you two chances to help your reader know what to expect. For example, if you were assigned to write about the motives for the Crusades, the least useful title would be one every reader could predict:

Motives for the Crusades

You help readers more with a title that names concepts that appear often in the discussion and that forecast your main claim:

The Political and Social Motives for the Crusades: Papal Efforts to Unify a Divided Church and Empire

If you are working in a field that encourages section headings, use this technique to create a one-line heading based on words in the point of each section.

Working Collaboratively

Ask So What?

Besides providing a fresh eye for one another's papers, your group should routinely work through the checklists in the Writing Process sections. The most important question to keep asking is *So what? What is the significance of your problem? Why should readers care about your answer? What are the consequences to them of answering it? What cost do they pay if you don't? How do they benefit if you do?* At first you may feel rude asking and you may be annoyed when asked. But if you ask early, often, and amiably, you'll get used to it.

INQUIRIES

Reflections

1. Pure researchers defend their work by arguing that without it we would still be in the Dark Ages. Does that seem a reasonable defense? Without tangible consequences to judge by, how do you know when pure research is pointless and wasteful or worth the effort? For example, one researcher dug up the body of Jesse James to see whether he was actually shot in the back, as legends say. Is it worth disturbing the dead to find that out? Can you think of any good reason to dig up someone who died a century ago?

2. The question of whose children are whose is but one of many historical questions that can now be answered with scientific tests. In the Hemings-Jefferson case, the test was performed on tissue from Sally Heming's youngest son, Eston, and five acknowledged descendants of Jefferson. But what if it would have been necessary to exhume Jefferson's body to conduct the test? If the decision was yours, would you give permission to exhume Jefferson to obtain a sample for scientific testing? Should his heirs have a say? What if Jefferson were not a national hero, but an ordinary person?

3. A skeleton was found in Washington State that may predate even the Native Americans who settled in the area and to have features of Caucasians. Native Americans in the area want to rebury the skeleton as one of their ancestors just as it is; the National Park Service wants to test the skeleton, claiming it might not be a Native American ancestor and, under any circumstances, is so unusual that it deserves further study. How should we settle this kind of question? On the one side are the religious beliefs of Native Americans, on the other scientific interest in a skeleton that could rewrite the prehistory of America. Native Americans frame this matter as a pragmatic problem, the National Park Service as a conceptual one. How would you decide what kind of problem it should be?

4. Some scholars argue that all knowledge is worth having, no matter how esoteric. Here are two things you not know: (a) How many hairs were on Abraham Lincoln's head when he was assassinated? (b) What was John Wilkes Booth thinking about the moment he shot him? If you could know only one or the other, which would you choose? How would you justify your choice? What would you say to someone who said they are equally unimportant, so it really doesn't matter?

5. Some cultures avoid questioning established knowledge and beliefs. What do you make of a society that does not value new knowledge? Is it appropriate to make a value judgment about such societies? Is it possible to want to know too much? Are there some things we should not know?

6. We talked about ways to motivate readers to care about your problem by getting them to care about its costs. But every cost can be restated as an opportunity to gain a benefit:

   Bingeing crosses the line from good times to reckless behavior. If it cannot be controlled, it will kill and injure still more students. _{cost}

   Bingeing crosses the line from good times to reckless behavior. If it can be controlled, we can save the lives of many students. _{benefit}

   What difference does it make whether you state consequences as a cost or as a possible benefit? Which do you think motivates readers more? (Try a thought experiment: When would you be more likely to risk going into a busy street to retrieve a twenty dollar bill, when the bill happens to blow past you or when it falls out of your pocket?)

Tasks

7. Pick a pragmatic problem that affects you right now—crowding in the dorms, difficulties registering for classes, over-large classes, lack of Internet access, etc. List everyone who could conceivably help you solve it—friends, roommates, parents, teachers, school officials, etc. Then list the costs that might motivate each of them to act to solve the problem. Don't focus on the costs your problem exacts on you, but on those it exacts on them.

8. The film *Contact* is, among other things, a parable about the value of pure research. Watch the film with friends, if possible. How do you respond to its defense of pure research? What do your friends think? Is it reasonable for the movie to portray the National Science Advisor who is skeptical of pure research as a villain? What do you think of the way the movie uses the romance between the two main characters to contrast the scientist's faith in research with the religious leader's faith in God? What about the industrialist's claim that he funds pure research to "give something back" to humanity?

9. Here are two introductions that address the same issue. Explain why one poses a problem and the other doesn't.

A.   In the last few years, children have been taught to read by two methods. Some have been taught to read by the phonics method, in which children sound out words they don't know, letter by letter, until they can pronounce the word. Then if they don't know the meaning, they look it up in a dictionary. Others have been taught to read by the "whole word" method, in which they guess at the meaning of word from its context. These two methods are common today, and each has its adherents.

B.   School boards have been debating whether to teach reading by the phonics method, in which children sound out letters, or by the "whole word" method, in which they try to understand the meaning of a word from its context. Each side has accused the other not only of failing to teach children to read effectively, but of inculcating children with their ideological beliefs. The phonics side claims that "whole word" teachers undermine mental discipline in favor of sloppy guessing, while the "whole word" side accuses the phonics teachers of suppressing children's intellectual and imaginative powers. If our schools make the wrong choice, we can expect that our children will suffer in ways that go beyond reading ability. The best method, though, is as we might expect: some of both.

10.   Look over papers you have written in other classes. Did they address pragmatic or conceptual problems? Look especially at papers written in your humanities classes. Did you have a problem at all?

Projects

11.   You probably think of poetry, drama, and fiction as being far from argument. Nevertheless, pick a favorite poem, story, novel, or play, and imagine that the author wrote it as the solution to a conceptual problem. Write an argument claiming that your poem, story, or play solves that problem. (This is easier with satire and other forms that seek to teach readers lessons.) Be sure not to confuse the problem that the characters in the story have with the problem that the author wanted the story to solve in the real world.

12.   Look at the introductions to three editorials or editorial columns in your local newspaper and analyze how they formulate problems and motivate readers.

WRITING PROJECTS 3

Project 3.1

Context.   Today, politicians increasingly depend on consultants and pollsters to decide what positions to take on controversial issues. Rather than rely on their own sense of right and wrong, they want to know how the voters will react to one decision or another.

Scenario. You have an internship in the campaign office of a local candidate for Congress. Your candidate intends to position himself as a new kind of politician who listens to the people rather than to the pollsters and political consultants. Your boss has just read an editorial in the student newspaper complaining that politicians always talk about the same problems but never address the ones that matter most to people. Since his district includes the university, he wants you to talk to some of your classmates and identify problems that students think politicians should talk about but don't.

Task 1. Survey students to find out what problems they think politicians, especially local ones, should talk about but don't. When you have a list of ten or so items, group them into three or four categories. Write a report to your boss, briefly outlining the four or five kinds of problems students think are important. Be sure to explain why they count as problems and what costs students think they are paying.

Task 2. Form two-partner teams in which one person lives on campus and one lives at home. The on-campus partner should survey students on campus (as in Task 1). The off-campus partner should survey people in his or her neighborhood. When each of you has a list of ten or so items, group them into four or five categories. Write a brief report to your boss outlining the difference between students' perceptions of important problems and those of the local community. Be sure to focus on costs.

Task 3. Decide what you think is the most important problem your candidate should address. Write a report in which you identify the problem and explain why it is important, why the voting public will care about it, and why your boss will benefit by talking about it. Be sure to focus on costs.

Project 3.2

Context. Some students object to required courses that have no obvious relevance to their careers. Colleges praise the value of a "liberal education," preparing students to think critically, to expand intellectual horizons, and so on, but many students look upon this as propaganda. What would count as evidence that such courses do what supporters claim they do? One kind of evidence might be self-reports of those now working in a profession. How do they feel about the liberal arts courses they took? If they did not take any such courses, do they regret it?

Scenario. You have been asked to write a feature article for your school newspaper that argues for or against requiring students to take liberal arts courses.

Task. Interview a few people who graduated from college at least three years ago. Choose those whose judgment you trust. Report their views about taking courses that had no direct relevance to their work today. Do they wish they had taken more? Do they wish they had not bothered with any? This is a project where collaborative work will be particularly useful, because if each member of the group can talk to one or two people, the whole group can share the evidence.

Project 3.3

Context.   Some critics think we are becoming a "nanny state" where the federal government wants to guard us from every risk of modern life. And so we have laws banning smoking, requiring motorcycle helmets and seat belts, and so on. Some also claim that people are becoming interested in extreme sports such as skate boarding, rock climbing, and mountain biking because they reject the risk-free world that the nanny state seems to create. Those who court risk argue that it gives life an edge that humdrum existence lacks, and it's no one's business but their own whether they risk their own lives. Others say people can do what they want, only as long as they alone pay the price if the worst happens. This means that you can bike without a helmet as long as no one else pays when you are injured—no rescue teams or paramedics supported by tax dollars, no disability, no insurance. If we all have to share in the costs associated with your risky behavior, then you don't have a right to take those risks. Why should we (they say) pay for the consequences of your recklessness?

Scenario.   You have an internship in the Washington office of your local member of the House. Congress is considering a law regulating rock climbing, hang gliding, mountain biking, skate boarding, roller blading, sky diving, and all other "sports involving inordinate risk" on federal property or sponsored by organizations receiving federal funds. According to the proposed law, you must get a license to do any of those things, and to get a license you must demonstrate that you have taken a certified safety course, that you own and use appropriate safety equipment, and that you are insured against injury and death.

Task.   Your boss wants a "position paper" that summarizes the issues raised by this law. She doesn't want you to tell her how to vote. In fact, she is the kind of person who gets bent out of shape when anyone tells her what to think. So you have to lay out the problem in a way that she sees as entirely objective and neutral. All she wants is three or four pages to help her understand the problem.

Project 3R

For the next five chapters, we will include writing assignments for an ongoing research project. Each step in the project will show you how to use the material in that chapter to produce a substantial research paper. If you have one due at the end of the semester, start now; you'll do a better job if you don't rush. If you have only a few weeks to devote to your project, follow these steps but more quickly. We assume that during these weeks you are researching your topic.

Scenario. You have just begun a class on a subject you have always wanted to study: the anthropology of the South Seas, the sociology of sport, the history of the blues, the economics of the fashion industry, the automobile in American popular culture—whatever strikes your fancy. Your teacher conducts the class as a seminar: each student selects an aspect of the topic, researches it, and presents a research paper to the class. Everyone is as interested in the topic as you are, so assume that your imagined classmates can't read enough about it.

Task 1. Your first task is to interest your teacher and classmates in your problem. Using the four steps presented in "From a Topic to a Problem," (p. 88) select a general topic, then narrow it to a specific problem. Focus on *how* and *why* questions; avoid those that ask for simple yes/no answers. Write a one-page proposal that states your research question/problem and explains how it relates to the general topic of your imagined class and why your classmates should care about it. If the subject matter is new to you, you will have to do some reading to discover why others are (or should be) interested in it and what information is available.

Task 2. Exchange preliminary proposals with two or three classmates. Make brief written notes on your reactions, comments, and suggestions; give the notes to the writer, but also explain them in person. After reading your classmates' notes, sketch a preliminary introduction and conclusion for your proposed paper. At this point, you can only guess how you will answer your question, but you should be able to sketch a working version of the common ground, destabilizing condition, and consequences.

SAMPLE ESSAYS

Here are the introductions to the two essays presented in Chapter 2. (You can review these essays on pp. 61-65):

Student Privacy and Drinking

1   University President, Albert Tanaki, recently proposed that the university should notify parents whenever a student is caught drinking before the age of twenty-one. Tanaki says this will help prevent students from binge drinking. This is wrong because students have rights to privacy and the university should respect them. Tanaki also fails to realize that present-day student life is surrounded by alcohol.

> ### Binge Drinking and Parental Notification:
> ### Students' Rights to Privacy or Parents' Right to Know?
>
> When University President Albert Tanaki announced that he wanted to notify parents when students under twenty-one were caught drinking by university police, there was an uproar among students and faculty. The Student Council passed a resolution the next day stating that "any invasion of student privacy is wrong." Council Chair Susan Ford wrote in the *Student Daily,* "This is morally wrong, legally wrong, and besides it won't work." It is understandable why students have gotten so upset over Tanaki's proposal. But by thinking only about how the proposal impacts on their rights, students and the faculty who have come out in support of them have forgotten about the rights of their parents.

Task 1.   Pick out the elements of each introduction. In which sentences does the writer state:

- Common ground
- Destabilizing condition
- Costs or consequences
- Solution or promise of solution

If you can't find a sentence that explicitly states one of the elements, indicate which sentence comes closest to stating it. Then try to formulate an explicit statement of it for yourself.

Task 2.   Review both essays (pp. 61-65). Identify the Main Claim in each. Is it a solution to the problem? Is it a viable solution?

Task 3.   Using your own words, reformulate the problem for each essay. Restate the problem or find a new one so that you state a problem that is solved by the main claim of the paper. State each part of the problem separately:

Destabilizing condition:

Cost or consequences:

Solution/main claim:

Task 4.   Write a new introduction for one or both essays. Not only should your introduction include all four elements, but it should also give readers a rich cognitive framework for the essay. Make sure that your statement of the problem and solution introduce the main themes repeated through the rest of the essay.

CHAPTER 3 IN A NUTSHELL
About Your Argument . . .

We make arguments to solve two kinds of problems, pragmatic and conceptual. Both kinds of problems have the same structure:

> **Problem = Destabilizing Condition + Cost/Consequence**

But what goes into that structure is different. This is what happens with a pragmatic problem:

- The destabilizing condition can be, literally, any situation, condition, event at all, so long as it has a cost.
- The cost answers the question *So what?* The answer always points to some form of unhappiness, pain, loss, distress—something that you and your readers want to avoid.

And this is what happens with a purely conceptual problem:

- The destabilizing condition is always some gap in knowledge or lack of understanding.
- The consequence of that gap answers the question *So what?* The answer always points to another gap in knowledge or lack of understanding, but one that is more significant, more consequential than the first.

What is tricky about solutions to conceptual problems is that they must not only solve the problem, but do so in a way that is coherent and consistent with everything else that is known about the subject.

A kind of mixed problem is the object of what we call *applied* research: we try to solve a conceptual problem hoping eventually to solve a pragmatic one.

Introductions to conceptual and pragmatic problems have up to four elements:

- An opening prelude that offers an anecdote, fact, or quotation that forecasts or encapsulates the problem.
- Common ground, some belief or idea that the audience holds that is not quite right, or is at least incomplete.
- Your problem, which consists of two parts:

  A destabilizing condition

  A cost or consequence of that condition

- The gist of your solution, or at least a sentence that introduces some of the key concepts that the rest of the argument will use in getting to the solution.

Many introductions do not have all of these elements. Preludes are more common in journalistic or popular writing, less so in academic or professional writing. If the problem is well-known and on readers' minds, you don't need common ground. In some cases, the cost of the problem is so obvious that it's not necessary to state it.

You can map your conclusion onto your introduction:

- Recapitulate your Main Claim (or express it for the first time).
- Describe why your claim is significant.
- Add what is yet to be done, how your argument is incomplete.
- Close with a coda that echoes the prelude.

. . . and About Writing It.

Your first job is to transform your topic into a problem.

1. Narrow your topic by adding to it as many qualifiers and modifiers as you can.
2. Ask questions about its relations to other things, about its own history, about its role in a larger history, and about its qualities.
3. Focus on your problem by running through this formula every so often. For a pragmatic problem, you can follow this scheme:

    1. I am working on the issue of _____
        2. in order to find out how to change_____ (*So what?*)
            3. so that you/they/someone can avoid the cost/gain the benefit of _____.

For a conceptual problem, you can follow this one:

1. I am working on the issue of_____
    2. in order to find out why/how/when/what_____ (*So what?*)
        3. so that I can understand better why/how/when/what _____.

Be sure that throughout your introduction, but particularly in the last couple of sentences, you use concepts central to the rest of your argument. Do this:

- Circle the key words in your introduction and conclusion.
- In the body of your argument, underline those words or words related to them. Look for both synonyms and homonyms.

If you underline few words in the body of your argument, you may have gotten off track. Even if you haven't, your readers will think so. Insert those circled words and words related to them. If you can't do that easily, you have to start over. Now do the same thing for each major section.

Finally, create a title out of the most important words you have circled.

PART 2

Developing Your Argument

In this section, we explore in more detail the five elements that constitute the substance of an argument.

- In Chapter 4, we discuss what counts as a reasonable and thoughtful claim. We show you how to formulate a claim in more detail than you might finally need in order to help you plan an argument that your readers will judge to be clear and coherent.

- In Chapters 5 and 6, we show you how to support a claim with reasons and evidence. We distinguish between reasons and evidence, and then we make a finer distinction: between the evidence "itself" and what you actually offer in most arguments, which is not evidence, but reports of it.

- In Chapter 7 we discuss an issue that has vexed students of argumentation for the last 2,500 years: Some call this element a *premise, assumption,* or a *general* or *specific topic.* We call it a *warrant.* Warrants express principles of reasoning so deeply entrenched in our thinking that we are rarely conscious of them. But to understand how an argument works, you cannot afford to ignore them.

- In Chapter 8, we discuss acknowledgments and responses, and we show you why it is important to imagine your readers asking questions, raising objections, and offering alternative points of view, and then to respond to them. No habit of mind is more important than being aware that your point of view is but one of many and that an effective argument cannot ignore the views of others.

CHAPTER 4

Articulating Claims

In this chapter, we look in more detail at your main claim, the solution to your problem, the statement that the rest of the argument supports. Here we show you how to develop claims that readers judge to be thoughtful and that can guide you through the process of drafting the rest of the argument.

At the center of every argument is your main claim, the point you want to make, the solution to the problem that caused you to make an argument in the first place. *Claim,* though, has two meanings: When you claim *that* something is so, you also make a claim *on* your reader to think about it. You justify that claim on their time only if your argument offers them something in return. That's why we stress that a claim is not just a statement that you want readers to agree with, but the solution to a problem that you think they should care about.

The tough part, of course, can be finding such a claim. Sometimes you don't have to search. If you believe human cloning is wrong, you know where you stand when you're asked to make an argument about it. But on other issues, you may have no ready answer: Should insurers be allowed to do genetic screening for a tendency to alcoholism? Should parents be held responsible for their children's crimes? In this chapter, we focus not on finding that solution but on expressing it as your main claim.

Exploring Claims Without Rushing to Judgment

Whatever strategies you follow to solve your problem, you can't wait until you've looked at all the evidence before you start formulating and testing likely solutions. So formulate two or three plausible ones as soon as you can.

That's what expert problem solvers do. They attack a problem by sizing it up quickly, then spinning off a tentative solution or two, which they treat as hypotheses that they test against their data. Although they try to delay settling on one solution until they think they understand enough of the facts, they start with one or more initial hypotheses to guide their thinking. Otherwise, they would not know what evidence to look for or how to evaluate what they found.

Less successful problem solvers also jump to a quick solution, but instead of testing it, they concentrate on confirming it. They don't make that mistake intentionally; it's just that our minds are built to make quick judgments. It's a habit of mind that, in the short run, helps us manage crises. But it's risky when your problem has long term consequences. The business world has a maxim about people who always come up with the same quick solution: *To a person with a hammer, every problem is a nail.* If profits are falling, the ad manager thinks the company needs more advertising; the operations manager thinks it should modernize the plant; while the personnel manager wants to invest in recruiting and training. Each might be partly right, but when they insist on their pet solution to the exclusion of others, they risk missing the best solution, because all they see is a nail that matches their particular hammer.

Admittedly, our advice is hard to follow, but here it is: Formulate a few tentative solutions to a problem sooner rather than later, but hold them lightly as you test them against the evidence. Resist doing what most of us do too easily: Jump into a simple conclusion that we can't climb out of. You can't change human nature, but you can deflect your tendency toward hasty, superficial judgments with patient reasoning, especially by talking things over with others. Focus on finding claims from the outset, but keep testing, revising, and reshaping them.

Rushing to Judgment

After two boys killed four schoolmates and a teacher in Jonesboro, Arkansas, in 1998, the media were filled with instant answers to the problem of why the boys did it: It was media violence, or our violent culture, or too many guns, or hate Websites, or the breakdown of the family, or just the kids' evil character. Most of those claims were based not on evidence but on what people were predisposed to believe. Then when a year later, two boys killed even more people at Columbine High School in Littleton, Colorado, they offered the same all-purpose answers that said more about their assumptions than about the real sources of the problem.

What Counts as a Successful Claim?

When you make a claim, you have to aim at two kinds of success. You achieve the obvious one when your argument earns your readers' assent. But well before that, it has to earn their interest and respect. In the last chapter, we discussed how a well-framed problem motivates your readers to read. You add to that motivation when you locate its solution at the end of your introduction as your main claim. We have no sure way to help you find the best of all claims, but we can offer some advice about how to evaluate and develop the best one you can find so that your readers will at least give it a fair hearing.

Is Your Claim Pragmatic or Conceptual?

Above all, readers want to know what you want them to do: to think or to act? The solution to a conceptual problem asks readers to *understand* or *believe* something:

> Not only do students whose first language is other than English do better in class when they receive tutorial help, but in the long run they require less faculty time.

The solution to a pragmatic problem asks them to *do* something (or endorse an action). Such claims are typically built around a *should* or *must*:

> State U. should increase the budget for tutorial help for students whose first language is not English.

If you trust readers to read between the lines, you can imply the need for an action, hoping they will infer it:

> Since students whose first language is other than English require less faculty time when they receive tutorial help, State U. could save money by increasing the budget for tutors.

Most of us, though, think readers can infer more than they do. So when in doubt, *explicitly* state what you expect of them. Be clear about the kind of claim you are making: Do you want readers to understand something, with no intent that they act? Or do you want them to perform (or at least support) an action?

Especially when you make a pragmatic claim, state it affirmatively and specifically. A negative goal does not provide a plan of action; a positive goal does. Compare:

> The university should stop using its teaching evaluation form because it does not reveal feelings about learning.

> The university should develop a new teaching evaluation form that tells faculty whether their students think they are learning useful skills.

Values Claims

Claims that assert something is right or wrong, good or bad, are often called "values" claims. Some values claims are covert pragmatic claims because they imply that you should do something, without stating exactly what that action is. In "Turkey Police, Beware" (p. 438) Richard Berman explains values that he expects us to act on:

> In an effort to change American eating habits to conform to their puritanical vision, groups such as the Center for Science in the Public Interest, the Vegetarian Society,

and People for the Ethical Treatment of Animals are perverting the way Americans look at food.

In saying that, he implies that we should do something, but doesn't say what: maybe ignore extreme claims in the news, or cook a traditional Thanksgiving turkey, or eat in a restaurant (Berman is founder of a restaurant association). By not specifying a solution, he relieves himself of the obligation to defend it.

On the other hand, a values claim is conceptual when it implies only that we should approve or disapprove, and nothing more:

As President, John Kennedy was inspirational, but as a person, he was sexually corrupt.

That claim does not ask us to do anything, only to think and feel as the writer wants us to: to disapprove of Kennedy's character. While there might be some distant *so don't you be like that* behind the claim, our negative judgment alone solves the conceptual problem posed by the writer.

Whether you assert a values claim that is pragmatic or conceptual, you still have to make the same kind of argument with reasons, based on evidence, governed by warrants. You still have to acknowledge and respond to other views. What's tricky about a values claim is that it always reflects beliefs, definitions, and values that transcend the particular issue you address. So we will agree that Kennedy was corrupt only if we already hold moral principles that a writer can appeal to. If not, then the writer has to lay down warrants about what we believe is good or bad, then argue that the warrants are true.

Is Your Claim Worth Contesting?

Even if readers have no settled beliefs about a topic, they will—or should—adopt an amiably skeptical attitude: *Well, your claim sounds interesting, but let's see your support.* You are in trouble if instead your readers think, *That's obvious!* A claim is worth supporting only if readers might *contest* it. You have no good reason to ask for their time if they already believe your claim or are indifferent to it. For example, how would readers respond to claims like these?

1a. Education is important in our society.

2a. We should not ridicule the way people look.

3a. I will summarize current views on the disappearance of frogs.

Can you imagine a reader thinking, *Wow! If that's so, I'll have to change my mind about education/ridicule/frogs?* Not likely. Those claims don't need an argument, because it's hard to imagine anyone bothering to contest them.

Here's a quick way to assess whether a claim is contestable: Revise it into its negative form (or a negative claim into its affirmative form) and assess whether it still seems plausible or significant.

1b. Education is **not** important in our society.

2b. We **should** ridicule people's appearance.

3b. I will **not** summarize current views on the disappearance of frogs.

Claims (1b) and (2b) seem self-evidently implausible, so they fail the test. If no one is likely to believe the opposite of a claim, then everyone is likely to agree with the original claim. The negative claim (3b), on the other hand, seems trivial. If the negative is trivial, then the affirmative will be too. In none of these cases is the claim worth supporting, because no one would contest it.

We must note, however, that the history of human thought has been revolutionized by those who contradicted claims that at the time seemed self-evidently true:

The sun does not go around the earth.

Human beings have not always looked as they do today.

We do not consist of solid matter.

We cannot rule out as forever false the claim that education is unimportant (some groups in fact believe it). You would make your reputation if you could convince us of that, but it would take a powerful argument to do so.

Can Your Claim Be Proved Wrong?

At least in principle, you should phrase your claim so that it can be proved wrong (the technical term is *disconfirmed*). Now that may seem odd. Don't we make claims we can prove, not ones our readers can *disprove*? In fact, a careful writer makes a claim only when he believes that his readers can *at least in principle* find evidence that would make him give it up.

For example, suppose you wanted to argue that ghosts do not exist. If you were unsure what kind of evidence readers would find convincing, you might ask (or imagine asking) them,

Can you think of any way you and I can test whether ghosts exist? Is there any evidence that would prove to our mutual satisfaction that they do or do not? In short, what will it take to change our minds?

Suppose your readers responded,

I cannot imagine even in principle any evidence that would prove that ghosts do not exist, because for me, *nothing* can disprove (or prove) that our souls survive death.

If you agree that no evidence can prove or disprove the survival of our souls after death, then there is no possibility of an argument, because an argument depends on reasons and evidence.

All parties to an argument must agree to a first principle of the social contract governing cooperative arguments: *Both reader and writer must be able to imagine that there could be evidence that would change their beliefs.* If you cannot think of evidence that might change your reader's mind, you have no good-faith basis for making an argument based on evidence; but neither do you have a good-faith basis if you cannot think of evidence that might change *your* mind.

Now this principle does not disparage beliefs in ghosts or anything else we can't prove. We are entitled to believe whatever we please, for any reason, or even for no reason at all. Nor does it prevent us from *explaining* our beliefs. But when we make public claims about our private beliefs and then make an argument that we want readers to spend time on, we must first open our own minds as much as we ask them to open theirs.

Is Your Claim Reasonable on Its Face?

Once you have a claim that readers can both contest and at least in principle disprove, you must start listening to that voice in the back of your mind asking questions they are likely to ask, questions like these:

- Is your solution **feasible?**

Tanya is unlikely to get a hearing from the dean if she suggests that the problem of weak teaching could be solved by shifting half the athletic budget to create a Teaching Resource Center. But the dean might listen if she suggested a small tax on research grants to subsidize one.

- Is your solution **ethical** (or **legal, proper, fair,** etc.)?

She would overreach if she proposed that the administration secretly monitor classes, but she might get a hearing if she suggested that faculty be encouraged to observe one another's teaching.

- Is your solution **prudent?** Might it create a problem worse than the one it solves?

She would have no chance of getting the dean to cut the salary of faculty with poor teaching evaluations because it would incite a rebellion. But he might consider merit raises to reward good teaching.

What Degree of Acceptance Do You Seek for Your Claim?

Some writers think that agreement is all-or-nothing, win-or-lose, agree-or-die. But that's shortsighted. Readers might not accept a big claim about a big problem, but they might accept a modest one about part of it. For example, Elena might think her college devotes too few resources to helping international students with their English, but she also knows that administrators are unlikely to spend lots of money on a new language center. If, however, she can get them just to *consider* increasing the budget for tutors, she will achieve an important interim outcome. Modest success is not total failure.

So when you begin formulating a claim, think how you want your readers to take it. Do you want them to

- **respect** your reasons for making your claim and, by extension, you;

- **approve** of your claim and the argument supporting it;
- **publicly endorse** your claim as worth everyone's serious consideration;
- **believe** in your claim and in your argument supporting it; or
- **act** as you propose, or actively support someone else's action?

Only the last two count as complete success for those who see argument as a win-or-lose proposition. But those who take that view must fail more often than they succeed, because few arguments completely convince anybody of anything. Your argument is a total failure only when your readers scoff not only at it, but at you, rejecting both as not worth their time, much less their respect.

Articulating Claims Thoughtfully

At some point—sooner better than later—you have to get your hypotheses out of the dark warmth of your mind into the cold light of print. But once you have drafted it, you have to ask: *Does this claim encourage readers to judge it—and me—as thoughtful?* Sad to say, we cannot teach anyone how to be thoughtful. We can only describe what encourages readers to think that a claim is at least not simplistic. Compare these:

> TV makes crime seem a bigger problem than it really is.

> Though violent crime has dropped in most parts of the country, many believe it has increased in their own neighborhoods because night after night their local TV news shows open with graphic reports of murder and mayhem, making it seem that violence happens every night just outside their front door.

The second claim is potentially more interesting, because its verbal complexity reflects the complex situation it describes.

We are *not* asserting that a claim bloated with ideas is always better than a slender one of few words. Too many words can obscure key issues, and a few well-chosen words can focus readers on what's important. But inexperienced writers commonly make claims that are too thin rather than too thick.

It is often impossible to express a complex solution to a complex problem in a single sentence, but for a few pages we will pretend that we can, because it's useful to try. You can always revise it later. You enhance the complexity of a claim in two ways: develop its conceptual richness and elaborate its core.

Developing Conceptual Richness

Compare these claims:

> The **effects** of the Civil War are still **felt** today.

> The **divisiveness** from the Civil War still **shapes** the **political discourse** of **North** and **South** at the **turn of the twenty-first century,** reflecting their **antithetical views** about the **relationship** between **state** and **federal powers** and the **authority of government** over **individuals.**

The first feels "thin." It mentions *effects* that are *felt* in some vague way. The second expresses a richer set of concepts (in fact, some might think too many). A claim rich in concepts does two things:

- When you formulate a claim that includes many specific concepts, you obligate yourself to develop them in your argument.
- When readers find those concepts at the end of your introduction and then see them again in the body of your argument, they are more likely to think your argument is coherent.

So when you think you have a good claim, spend a minute or two making its language even more specific than you think necessary. You can always pare it back when you revise.

Elaborating the Core of Your Claim

At the core of every claim is a simple proposition, like this:

American colleges could do something about tuition. claim

But that claim is thin bordering on simplistic: What does *do something* mean? We make it richer by making it more specific:

American colleges could slow tuition increases to half their rate. claim

But we can also elaborate it in two other ways:

1. Add a reason-clause beginning with *because* or *if,* or a phrase beginning with *by* or *in order to.*

Compare these two claims:

American colleges could slow tuition increases to half their rate. claim

American colleges could slow tuition increases to half their rate, claim **if they cut administrative costs** reason 1 **and had their faculties teach more.** reason 2

The first claim states a proposition that is still rather bare bones. In the second elaborated one, readers can see the gist of a solution in the *if*-clause and thereby better anticipate the rest of the argument.

2. Add a concession-clause beginning with *although, while,* or *even though* or a phrase beginning with *despite, regardless of,* or *notwithstanding.*

Compare:

Colleges could slow tuition increases to half their rate, if they cut administrative costs and had their faculties teach more.

Although the costs of maintaining the physical plants of American colleges are rising and scientific advances require them to update research facilities continually, acknowledgment of alternative point of view colleges could slow tuition increases to half their rate, if they cut administrative costs and had their faculties teach more.

That first claim states a view as if it were simple and unqualified. The second acknowledges a complicating fact.

If you stretch your claim sentence too far (like the one above), you can divide it. The most convenient place is usually after an *although*-clause. Make that clause a separate sentence and begin the next sentence with *but, however, even so, nevertheless,* etc. (incidentally, it is *not* a grammatical error to begin a sentence with *but* or *however*):

> The costs of maintaining the physical plants of American colleges are rising steadily, and scientific advances require them to update their research facilities continually. **But / Nevertheless / Even so / However,** colleges could slow tuition increases to half their rate, if they cut administrative costs and had their faculties teach more.

Again, your goal is to write complex claims not for the sake of dazzling readers with their complexity, but to force yourself to think harder than you otherwise might. You do that when you deliberately (and temporarily) create claims that are rich in specific concepts and elaborated with reasons and acknowledgments. You can always edit a hyper-complex claim into something more manageable.

WRITING PROCESS 4
Finding and Articulating Claims

Preparing and Planning

Developing a Rich Claim

State Your Claim in Specific Language
Once you have a rough statement of your claim, find the most specific and evocative words you can to state it.

1. For each key noun in your claim, ask the question *What kind of*_____? Then ask again for each of those terms.

   For example, for the claim *The effects of the Civil War are still felt today,* ask, *What kind of effects? Political divisiveness, regional prejudice, ideological differences?* Then for the term *ideological differences,* ask, *What kind of differences? States' rights, ideas about individual freedom, right to work laws, Bible belt fundamentalism?*

2. For each key verb in your claim, ask the question, *How _____?*

   For example, *How are effects are felt? By the regions mistrusting one another, by the South voting as a political bloc, by the South seeing federal efforts*

*toward desegregation as an imposition from the North, by old divisions influ-
encing new attitudes?*

3. For each new term, look for related words that may express your ideas
more explicitly. Ask the question_____*as opposed to?*

For example, *Divisiveness* as opposed to *disruption* or *disagreement; influence* as opposed to *determine* or *shape; ideology* as opposed to *views,
ideas, opinions;* and so on.

4. Once you have generated a rich set of concepts, rewrite your claim
including those that best reflect the concepts you expect to develop in
your argument:

The **divisiveness** from the Civil War still **shapes** the **political discourse**
of **North** and **South** at the **turn of the twenty-first** century, reflecting
antithetical views about the **relationship** between **state** and **federal
powers** and the **authority government** should have over **individuals.**

Elaborate the Core of Your Claim

On p. 112, we sketched a way to systematically develop your claim:

Although_____

   [I claim]_____

     because_____

Obviously, you can't build all that complexity into one sentence, so you have to
edit it when you draft. For now, though, you can use that structure to outline
not just the contours of your claim, but the major elements in your paper.

Qualify Inappropriate Certainty

When you settle on a main claim, don't present it in a way that leaves no room
to question it.

Every American college would stop tuition increases if it just slashed
administrative costs and got all of its faculty to teach more classes.

When readers read such an extreme claim, they wonder, *How can you be so sure?*
Worse, they have a visceral feeling of irritation, even anger. This is a case where
you want to seem modest, even deferential. Contrast that flat-footed certainty
with this more nuanced claim:

Many American colleges **could** slow their rates of tuition increases, if they
could cut administrative costs and get **more** of their faculty to teach more
classes.

You invite readers to question your good judgment if you imply that your
claims are 100 percent right and all-inclusive. But if you over-qualify, you give
them reason to doubt your confidence. In either case, your ethos suffers.

It's a balancing act. Compare these three claims:

1. Research proves that people with a gun at home more often kill themselves or a family member than protect themselves from intruders.

2. **Some recent** research **seems** to **suggest** there **may** be a **risk** that **some** people with a gun at home **could** be **more prone** to use it to kill themselves or a family member than to protect themselves from **potential** intruders.

3. **Recent** research **suggests** that people with a gun at home **are more likely** to use it to kill themselves or a family member than to protect themselves from intruders.

Most academic and professional readers would judge (1) as too absolute and reject (2) as wishy-washy, but find (3) confident yet temperate, because it comes closest to the Goldilocks rule: not too certain, not too uncertain, maybe not just right, but close. (How's that for hedging?) Experienced writers know that they can rarely assert a claim with 100 percent certainty, even when they in fact feel that certain.

Here is some vocabulary that expresses civil diffidence (use in moderation):

- **Quantity:** Instead of *all, every,* or *each,* write *many, most,* or *some.*

- **Frequency:** Instead of *always* write *often, usually, frequently,* or *predictably;* instead of *never,* write *seldom, rarely,* or *infrequently.*

- **Probability:** Instead of *certainly* or *impossible,* write *probably* or *unlikely;* instead of *it is,* write *it may be, might be, seems to be,* or *appears to be.*

- **Proof:** Instead of X *proves, demonstrates, establishes,* or *shows* Y, write X *suggests, points to, argues for, leads us to believe,* or *indicates* Y.

After these steps, your claim will probably be too complex, but wait to edit it until after you've drafted some of your paper. Be sure to use the terms that specifically name the concepts you develop through the body of your argument.

Certainty in Eighteenth-Century Politics and Twentieth-Century Science

Those who think that hedging is mealymouthed might note this advice from Benjamin Franklin describing how he deliberately created an ethos of judicious moderation by speaking

> . . . in terms of modest diffidence, never using when I advance anything that may possibly be disputed, the words *certainly, undoubtedly,* or any others that gave the air of positiveness to an opinion; but rather say, *I conceive,* or *I apprehend a Thing to*

be so or so It appears as to me, or I should think it so or so for such and such Reasons, or I imagine it to be so, or it is so if I am not mistaken. This habit I believe has been of great advantage to me... To this habit (after my character of integrity) I think it principally owing that I had early so much weight with my fellow citizens when I proposed new institutions or alterations in the old, and so much influence in public councils when I became a member.

That advice is relevant today. Among those who make arguments for a living, scientists may distrust certainty the most because they know that scientific truths change. You can see this not only in the way they test claims, but in the language they use to make them. Here is how a science journalist describes how some scientists commented on some recently released research:

Notice the qualifiers on belief: "pretty much," "more or less," "don't particularly disbelieve." Scientists are great suspenders of belief. They know that their measurements often have large margins of error, their experimental devices are often relatively inadequate, and their own understanding incomplete. They know that the world is complex, interconnected, subtle and extremely easy to get wrong. Geologists once believed that the Sudbury mineral complex in Ontario, the source of most of the world's nickel, precipitated out of a melt formed when the liquid in the earth's middle rose up through the crust. But after finding shattered rock, microscopic mineral grains subjected to intense pressure, and other signs of a great impact, they now believe the nickel formed when a 6-mile-wide meteorite hit the Earth so hard that the crust melted.... Geologists will mostly believe that until more evidence comes along.

Source: From Ann Finkbeiner, "In Science, Seeing Is Not Believing," *USA Today*, October 21, 1997.

INQUIRIES

Reflections

1. Are those who make conceptual arguments responsible for what others do with their claims? Is a scientist who discovers something that someone uses to create new weapons responsible for their consequences? Should a geneticist get credit when his discoveries help doctors save lives? If so, should he be blamed if those same discoveries are used in immoral ways? What about a political scientist whose ideas about limiting the power of government inspire someone to bomb a federal building? What principle might we use to make distinctions among these cases? Could you make a case that some claims should never be made? What about a discovery that makes it possible for anyone to build an atomic bomb in his kitchen? What might be the unintended consequences if researchers kept secret discoveries that they thought might be potentially dangerous?

Tasks

2. Suppose you have been asked for suggestions about recreational facilities, intramural sports, cultural activities, or some other part of your college life. Make a snap judgment about what you think is a problem and offer a quick and easy solution. Now work through whether you have identified the real problem. Assume that quick, unreflective judgments are usually wrong.
3. Try the negation test (pp. 108-09) on the claims in some of your old papers. What does it tell you about the significance of your claims?
4. What kinds of claims have you made most often in your papers, calls for action or claims that something is true? Try revising each claim that explicitly calls for an action into a claim that only implies one, and vice versa.

Projects

5. Suppose you are a leader in a national student organization dedicated to reducing the costs of a college education. Sketch a plan of action for asking college presidents to support a policy that will lower tuition. What role would negotiation or mediation have in your plan? Propaganda (advertising, public relations, etc.)? Coercion (demonstrations, civil disobedience, lobbying legislators, etc.)? How would argument fit in your plans?
6. Look in your old papers for the qualities of good claims (pp. 106-11). Look especially for signals of cause and effect (*because, so, in order to,* and so on) and reservation (*despite, although, while,* and so on). If your claims seem thin, elaborate them in ways we've suggested (p. 112).

WRITING PROJECTS 4
Project 4.1

Context.   In the fairest arguments, writers present the positions of those with whom they differ in a way that their "opponents" would accept as accurate. But nothing is more common than for writers of opinion pieces in newspapers and magazines to distort the positions of those they oppose. It is likely that the three organizations named by Richard Berman in "Turkey Police, Beware" (p. 438) would reject his characterization of their beliefs. You can find information about the organizations and their positions in the library and on the Web (www.cspinet.org; www.vegsoc.org; www.cyberveg.org; and www.peta-online.org).

Scenario 1.   You have an internship with one of three organizations: Center for Science in the Public Interest, Vegetarian Society, or PETA [choose one]. Your job is to monitor the press for mentions of the organization.

Task 1(a). Berman's essay has landed on your desk. Your job is to draft a letter to the editor of the *Washington Times* correcting Berman's characterization of your organization and its position.

Task 1(b). Berman's essay has landed on your desk. Your job is to draft an opinion piece that counters Berman's essay without responding to it directly.

Scenario 2. You have an internship with the Guest Choice Network, the restaurant association founded by Berman.

Task 2(a). Berman has been notified by the *Washington Times* that it has received a response from one of the three organizations [choose one], accusing him of misrepresenting them. The paper would like to have a letter from Berman responding to their letter (nothing sells papers like controversy). Your job is to draft a letter proving that the organization is as extreme as he said it was.

Task 2(b). Berman reads in the *Washington Times* a response from one of the three organizations [choose one], accusing him of misrepresenting them. He wants you to draft another essay, this time focusing on just the one organization, arguing that it takes extremist positions concerning food.

Project 4R

Scenario. In Project 3R in Chapter 3 you shared your problem statement with your teacher and classmates. They agree that your problem has promise, but your teacher wants to be sure that you can answer the question that you propose.

Task. Write a formal proposal for a research paper in which you do the following:

- state your research question/problem
- explain how your question/problem relates to the topic of your imagined class
- state its consequences explicitly, what is not now known that your readers should want to know
- offer some speculative answers
- explain what kind of support you might find to back up your answer(s).

You can make each of these items a separate section with its own heading. You might also decide to reorder items. As you speculate about answers, avoid rushing to judgment. Append to your proposal a revised version of your preliminary introduction and conclusion.

CHAPTER 4 IN A NUTSHELL
About Your Argument . . .

Claims are at the heart of every argument. They are your main point, the solution to your problem. Though you should try to formulate a tentative claim or hypothesis as soon as you can, you must also work hard to keep your mind open to giving it up in favor of a better one. That's why it's important to imagine a number of hypotheses and hold them all in mind as you work your way toward a best one.

Your claim should have these qualities:

- It should be clearly conceptual or pragmatic and assert what readers should know or what they should do.
- It should be something that readers are inclined not to agree with without seeing your good reasons. It should be contestable.
- It should in principle be capable of being proved wrong, because you can imagine evidence that would make you give it up. It should be disconfirmable.
- It should be feasible, ethical, and prudent. It should be reasonable.

Be clear to yourself the degree of assent you seek. Decide what you want your readers to do:

- Respect your reasons for making your claim.
- Approve of your claim and the argument supporting it.
- Publicly endorse your claim as worth serious consideration.
- Believe your claim and the argument supporting it.
- Act as you propose.

. . . and About Writing It

Work toward a claim that has these qualities:

- Its language is explicit and specific. It previews the central concepts that you will develop in the rest of the argument.
- It is elaborated with clauses beginning with *although* and *because*. If you think that makes the claim too long and complex, then break it into shorter sentences.
- It is hedged with appropriate qualifiers such as *many, most, often, usually, probably,* and *unlikely* instead of *all, always,* and *certainly.*

CHAPTER 5

Reasons and Evidence

In this chapter, we focus on the support you need to make a claim seem credible and convincing. In particular, we distinguish three kinds of support that you need to keep straight: reasons, evidence, and reports of evidence. We also show you how to arrange reasons into an order that is useful to readers.

Those who make a flat claim, expecting us to agree just because they say so, risk seeming at least uncivil:

> TV's obsession with sexuality damages the social and emotional development of our preteens. _{claim}

We expect some qualification and at least one reason in its support:

> **Though the TV industry has improved children's daytime programming,** _{acknowledgment} its prime-time obsession with sexuality **may** be damaging the social and emotional development of **many** preteens _{claim} **because so many of them model their behavior on what they see adults do.** _{reason}

But careful readers expect more than just a reason. Saying that preteens base their behavior on what they see on TV does not mean that in fact they do. Though that assertion is a reason supporting a main claim, it is also a claim that itself needs support. What is that reason based on, other than the writer's opinion? Thoughtful writers create a broader and deeper base of support by treating their reasons like claims in need of more reasons, finally basing all their reasons on sound evidence.

Reasons and Evidence as Forms of Support

As we saw in Chapter 1, the language we use about *having* an argument implies combat. But when we describe *making* one, we sound less like commandos than like construction workers. We *support* claims with reasons that in turn *rest on a*

120

firm base of sound evidence. That *grounding* on *solid footing* should be so *unshakable* that critics cannot topple our argument by *undermining* its *foundation*.
Such language visualizes an argument like this:

These metaphors are useful, but to understand how we actually plan and draft arguments, we need four more terms with more literal meanings: *fact, data, evidence,* and *reasons*. The first two we can define easily:

- A *fact* is a statement in words or symbols that readers don't contest: *The capital of Ohio is Columbus.*

- *Data* (the singular is *datum*) are sets of facts. We can summarize data in words: *In 1980, Abco's market share was 19.4%; by 1990, it had slipped to 11.7%; but recently has grown to 22%.* But more often, data are arrayed in a table, graph, or chart:

Abco Market Share (%)

1980	1990	1999
19.4	11.7	22.0

Facts and data, however, are inert information serving no purpose until we use them as *evidence* supporting *reasons* that in turn support claims. Here is a brief argument assembled out of those elements:

Although television has improved its after-school programming, its prime-time shows may be undermining the social and emotional development of many preteens _{claim} by exposing them to sexually explicit behavior that encourages them to engage in sexplay before they understand its consequences. _{reason} In his report on the relationship between TV watching and sexual experimentation, for example, Kahn (1996) evaluated children ages 10-13 who regularly (three times in four weeks) watch sexually oriented shows on television (more than five references to or images of sexual conduct). He found they are 40% more likely to engage in sexual play than those who do not watch such programs at all. _{evidence}

That is the core of an argument in a standard form: Claim + Reason + Evidence.

Distinguishing Reasons and Evidence

The difference between reasons and evidence seems intuitively obvious, but it is more complex than it appears. On the one hand, we often use those terms synonymously:

What *reasons* can you offer to support your claim?

What *evidence* can you offer to support your claim?

But we also distinguish them in sentences like these:

We need to think up *reasons* to support our request.

We need to think up *evidence* to support our request.

Before I accept your *reasons,* I have to see the *evidence* they rest on.

Before I accept your *evidence,* I have to see the *reasons* it rests on.

Most of us find the first sentence in each pair natural, the second a bit odd.

One source of the difference is the metaphorical images that we associate with reasons and evidence. With evidence, we use metaphors like *solid* or *hard* that incline us to see evidence as being in the world, "outside" our subjective experience. Reasons metaphorically come from "inside" our minds. Weak reasons are illogical; weak evidence is soft. So readers are inclined to test your evidence by whether they could see it for themselves if you told them where to look. You can't tell them where to go look for reasons.

Since we assume evidence is at least in principle *public* and *sharable,* readers ask certain questions about it:

- Where did you get your evidence? What are your sources? Are they sound?

- How did you collect it? What methods and devices did you use? Could I see it for myself?

- What are its limitations? Is it reliable? What problems did you have collecting it?

On the other hand, they are unlikely to ask where you got your reasons or how you thought them up, because they know they originated in your mind.

Recall the conversation among Sue, Ann, and Raj: When Sue claimed that her school did not treat students well, she offered as a reason that teachers kept too few office hours. She based that reason on facts that she reported—the actual hours posted: *Prof. X, Monday, 4–5 PM, Prof. Y, Friday 4–4:30 PM,* etc. Those names and numbers were not her reasons, not her judgments or opinions, but what she hoped her friends would accept as evidence, as facts independent of her reasons. Figuratively, Sue's argument looked like this:

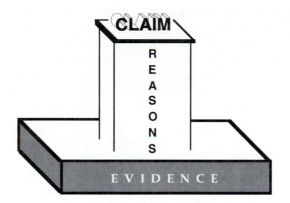

When we read reasons that we think lack a foundation of evidence, we are likely to judge them to be "mere opinion," and mere opinion is, to continue the construction metaphor, "too flimsy" to support reliable claims about weighty problems.

You can use that construction image of claims, reasons, and evidence as a useful way to think about the core of an argument. But when we examine it more closely, it turns out to be a bit misleading. In what follows, we make a distinction that some of you will think is academic hairsplitting. But we think it is important in understanding how arguments really work. (If you don't care that what you *call* evidence rarely is, skip to p. 127.)

Origins of the Words *Reason* and *Evidence*

The original meanings of *reason* and *evidence* illuminate their different uses in arguments:

- *Reason* is related to *rational.* It goes back to the Latin *ratio,* "to calculate or think." We seem to construct reasons in our minds.

- *Evidence* is related to *vision* and *evident,* as in *self-evident.* It goes back to *e-videre,* "to see." We seem to see evidence out there.

Primary and Reported Evidence

As disconcerting as it may seem, what we call evidence almost never is. It is instead only a report of it, or even a report of a report of it. Evidence "itself" cannot be "in" an argument, if we define evidence as something objective, the stuff we—or someone—can find out in the world. In a murder trial, the evidence "itself" might be an actual "smoking gun," but in the argument we can only refer to it; in an argument about unemployment, we can only refer to the evidence, actual people losing and finding jobs; in an argument about cosmology, we can only describe or depict the evidence, an actual star collapsing into a black hole. What we offer as evidence are only *reports of evidence* that describe, picture, refer to, talk about those actual guns, people, and stars.

Even when you've seen the "real" evidence out in the world with your own eyes, you can bring it into your written argument only by representing it in words, numbers, or images. And whenever you represent evidence, you change it—smooth it out, tidy it up, make it more coherent, more regular, more systematic than the "stuff out there" really is. You have to select just a few details and leave out a multitude of others, because it would be humanly impossible to represent them all. So what you ask your readers to go on is not the evidence, but only your selective report of it.

We emphasize this distinction because the word *evidence* carries so much authority, seems so weighty and objective that when someone offers what he claims is "hard" evidence, we may be already half convinced that it has an objective reality that we cannot question. But it is not objective: What we call evidence is always a report of it selected and shaped to fit an argument.

Representations as Evidence

Some students wonder about quoted words and photographs. Aren't they "the evidence itself"? But they are also representations. Even when we quote words correctly, we take them out of context, so readers may understand them in ways that their context would contradict. When a painting is reproduced, it is changed in obvious ways. And even when we reproduce a photograph as exactly as possible, it is still seen on a different paper, in a different context, with a different purpose.

You should strive to report evidence with as few alterations as possible. But remember that just as a picture of an apple is not an apple, so a report of evidence is not the evidence.

Once you grasp that distinction, you can understand why careful readers care so much that your reports of evidence be reliable and from a good source. That's why they expect you to tell them where you found the evidence you report, whether you gathered it personally or are reporting it from others, and if so, from whom. That's why readers expect footnotes to assure them that, if they wanted to, they could track your reports back as close as they can get to the evidence "itself." Evidence is only as sound as the chain of reports leading to it, and the last link in that chain is always you.

Recall again that in the discussion among Sue, Ann, and Raj, the question of evidence turned on that very issue:

Sue: We pay a lot of money for our education, but we don't get anywhere near the attention customers do. _{reason}

Raj: Like how? [*i.e., What evidence do you base that reason on?*]

Sue: For one thing, we have trouble seeing teachers outside of class. Last week I went to every office on the first floor of the Arts and Sciences building and counted the hours posted on the doors. [She pulls a piece of paper out of her backpack.] They average less than an hour a week, most of them in the afternoon when a lot of us work. _{report of evidence}

Ann: Can I see?

Sue: Sure. [Sue hands the paper over.]

When Ann looked at the numbers, she still was not looking at the evidence "itself": that is still attached to doors. Sue's friends must assume that she copied those hours accurately and reported them fairly. (But see also Reflection 1 on p. 138)

If the distinction between evidence and reports of it is accurate, then Sue's argument can *not* look like this:

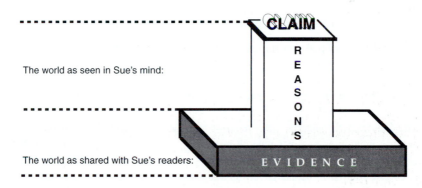

Instead, her argument must look like this:

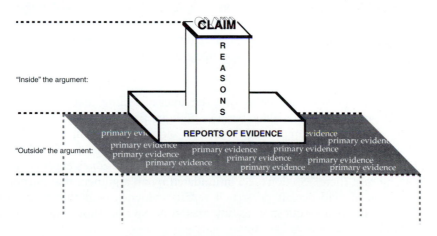

What Sue offers as evidence *inside* an argument can be only reports that we hope are reliably grounded on evidence *outside* the argument. But readers almost never get to observe that evidence directly (or even the first-hand reports of it). So from their point of view, an argument really looks like this:

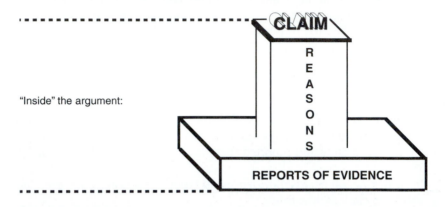

"Inside" the argument:

On the Evidence for Warm-Blooded Dinosaurs

Even when it seems we can hold evidence "itself" in our hands, we may be holding only a report of it. Not too long ago, some paleontologists announced that they had uncovered the heart of a dinosaur, the first one ever found. After some examination, they found to their amazement that it had two chambers, evidence, they said, that the dinosaur it came from may have been warm-blooded. The evidence that they had to point to, however, was not the actual heart of that dinosaur, because what they had was not the heart tissue itself but a fossil stone casting created by natural processes—nature's "report" of the evidence. Moreover, what the scientists pointed to as evidence was not the fossil casting but a series of two-dimensional CAT-scans of its internal structure which they assembled into a three dimensional model. Their evidence that dinosaurs might have been warm-blooded is a three dimensional model that reports on a series of two-dimensional images that report on a stone fossil that reports on an organ that no longer exists. The hard question is how much each of those reports distorts that once-beating heart (if it is in fact a heart, which some paleontologists doubt).

At this point you may be getting the uneasy feeling that reasons and reports of evidence are a lot alike, because both are products of a mind sifting, shaping, reflecting, and reporting. If so, you see something important about arguments. Reasons and what we call evidence (actually reports of evidence) are both products of our minds working on reports of someone's experience of something "out there." So don't feel intimidated by an argument that purports to offer lots of evidence. It doesn't; it *reports* evidence, and that report of evidence is as open to question as any reason is. So you should question it accordingly.

If it is your report of evidence, your readers will ask how you got it, whether you gathered it personally or are reporting it from others who did (or from reports of reports), and if so, from whom. That's why you must develop the reputation of someone who reports evidence accurately, because the last person in the chain of trust is you. When you betray that trust, you lose credibility, not just for the argument you happen to be making, but possibly for all the ones you will make again. When that happens, you compromise your ethos.

How Far Are You from Your Evidence?

Suppose your friend Al offers you a fact from what seems an unimpeachable source:

> Al: I heard something on Geraldo last night that you might be able to use in your paper: He said the crime rate has been falling for a decade.

> You: I can't believe that. Crime is up.

> Al: No, it's a fact. He quoted a new FBI report. It shows that crime is down. You could look it up.

Even if Geraldo quoted accurately, how does the FBI know that crime is down? The *actual* evidence is fewer individuals committing actual crimes. But that evidence has disappeared into the past. Those crimes were recorded by police officers who listened to reports of what victims and witnesses remembered and criminals sometimes confessed to. Then someone in each police department entered those reports in the FBI database; someone else compiled the statistics; someone else reported them in a summary; and finally someone else reported them in an FBI report you could find in your library. We usually know even the most reliable evidence only through reports of reports of reports.

Multiple Reasons

Even when you base a reason on lots of (reports of) evidence, readers are reluctant to accept a significant claim based on just one reason. So you usually have to support it with more. Those reasons can relate to your claim in two ways: You can offer reasons that support the claim in parallel, all of them supporting the claim directly; or you can offer reasons as a series, with each supporting the next one and resting on the one before, the last one resting on evidence (or a report of it).

Multiple Reasons in Parallel

When you offer several reasons that each support your claim separately, they are *parallel* reasons. It's the standard plan for the five-paragraph essay:

There are three reasons [or two, four, or five . . .] why we should curb binge drinking. _{claim} First, it gives the campus a bad image. _{reason 1} For example, Small College has become known as . . . _{report of evidence} Second, it exposes us to substantial legal liability. _{reason 2} At least four cases have been filed . . . _{report of evidence} Third and most important, however, it leads to injury and even death. _{reason 3} In the last six months alone, . . . _{report of evidence}

Each parallel reason stands independently of the others. Take one away and the claim might slump, but the other reasons can still support it. Reasons in parallel look like this:

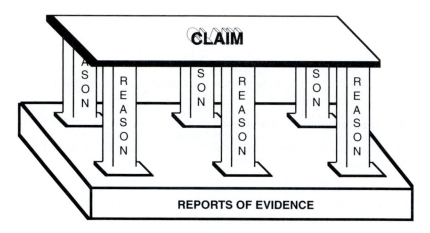

When you add parallel reasons, you thicken your argument, and you thicken it further when you find evidence to support each reason.

Multiple Reasons in Sequence

You can also add reasons that support a claim, not separately in parallel, but in a series, each reason resting on another, the last one resting on reports of evidence:

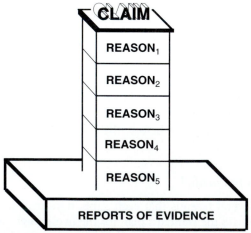

(Or imagine these reasons sideways, as links in a series of steps from here to there—choose whatever visual metaphor best helps you think about the links between reasons in a series.)

For example, in this next argument, the writer bases a main claim on three linked—or better, perhaps, "stacked"—reasons and one report of evidence. (Notice that in this case, the writer *starts* the argument with a report of evidence, then reasons his way *upward,* though downward on the page, toward his claim):

> The National Association for Educational Progress has reported that between 1990 and 1998, while academic performance in mathematics has risen 1.3%, reading and writing scores have remained level, but noted that their results are statistically unreliable, because different states give different tests that cannot be correlated, and some do little testing at all. _{report of evidence} That lack of sound data deprives local taxpayers of the ability to judge how well their schools and their children are doing in comparison not just to the rest of the United States, but more important, to the world. _{reason 1 based on evidence} As a result, we cannot be confident that schools are teaching and our children learning the intellectual skills to face the challenges of the third millennium. _{reason 2} In short, this nation needs a system of national tests that will benchmark performance in secondary education so that we can measure intellectual skills in a consistent and useful way. _{claim}

- That argument opens with a report of evidence: *statistics on educational performance are unreliable.*

- That supports a claim that serves as reason 1: *[Therefore] we cannot judge educational performance.*

- Reason 1 in turn supports another claim that serves as reason 2: *[Therefore] we cannot be confident that our children will face new challenges.*

- Reason 2 supports the main claim: *[Therefore] we need a system of national tests.*

Notice that we could just as easily have reversed the order:

> This nation needs a system of national tests that will benchmark performance in math, reading, and writing so that we can measure educational performance in a consistent and informative way. _{claim} We need such tests so that we can be confident that our children will have the intellectual skills to face the challenges of the third millennium. _{reason 2} But at the present time, local taxpayers cannot judge how well their schools and their children are doing in comparison not just to the rest of the United States, but more important to the world, because we lack sound data about educational performance. _{reason 2 based on evidence} The National Association for Educational Progress has recently reported that between 1990 and 1998, while academic performance in mathematics has risen 1.3%, reading and writing scores have remained level, but noted that their results are statistically unreliable, because different states give different tests that cannot be correlated, and some do little testing at all. _{report of evidence} Only a system of national testing will provide us with that sound data. _{claim restated}

Experienced writers create arguments like these by laying deeper and deeper foundations for their claims (another of those building metaphors), thereby thickening their arguments. The risk of such an argument is that if readers miss just one intermediate step, they lose track of the logic, and the argument collapses.

Using Reasons to Help Readers Understand Evidence

If evidence anchors an argument, you might wonder why we bother with reasons at all. Why not just base a claim directly on reports of evidence? Sometimes we do that:

> The demographic future of counties in this part of the state is predicted by their employment trends. _{claim}

County	Industry	Population by County			
		1985	1995	Change	% change
Tuttle	Farming	200,502	100,400	(10,102)	-50.7
Oswego	Farming	150,792	90,614	(6,178)	-39.1
Clark	Mnfctrng	120,651	250,266	12,615	100.2
Perko	Mnfctrng	92,047	276,890	184,843	300.1

reported evidence

After reading that claim, a careful reader could eventually figure out the connection—more manufacturing means more people; farming means fewer. But a reason that interpreted the data would make the data clearer:

> The demographic future of counties in this part of the state is predicted by their employment trends. _{claim} **Those that are primarily agricultural are losing population, whereas Clark and Perko, with a strong manufacturing base, have doubled and even tripled in population.** _{reason}

Given that one sentence, we now know how to interpret the table.

Some fear that if readers can figure out how a report of evidence supports a claim, they insult them when they spell out the obvious. And it is true: no one wants to read the obvious. But all of us, experienced and inexperienced alike, overestimate what readers can understand on their own. So you usually do them a service when you add a reason that summarizes what is important in your report of evidence, making it clear how it in fact supports your claim.

Readers also look for help when your evidence is a quotation. Here is a passage that bases a claim about Hamlet directly on the evidence of a quoted passage:

> When Hamlet comes up behind his stepfather Claudius while he is at prayer, he demonstrates a cool and logical mind. _{claim}

> Now might I do it [kill him] pat, now he is praying:
> And now I'll do't; and so he goes to heaven;
> And so am I reveng'd. . . . [Hamlet pauses to think]
> [But this] villain kills my father; and for that,
> I, his sole son, do this same villain send to heaven[?]
> Why, this is hire and salary, not revenge. _{report of evidence}

Many readers find that argument a bit hard to follow. Nothing in the quotation seems obviously to support a claim about Hamlet's cool reason. The writer forces us to figure it out on our own. Compare this version:

> When Hamlet comes up behind his stepfather Claudius while he is at prayer, he demonstrates a cool and logical mind. _{claim} **At first he impulsively wants to kill Claudius instantly, but he pauses to reflect. If he kills Claudius while praying, he sends his soul to heaven. But Hamlet wants him damned to hell forever. So he coolly decides to kill him later:** _{reason}
>
> > Now might I do it [kill him] pat, now he is praying:
> > And now I'll do't; and so . . . _{report of evidence}

That reason tells us what to see in the quotation so that we understand better how it supports the claim.

A detailed report of evidence seldom speaks for itself. Without a reason to speak for it, readers often struggle to understand what it signifies. They have to work less hard when you add a reason that both supports the claim *and* explains the evidence. Visually, it looks like this:

So when you offer evidence in the form of quotations, images, or data in tables and charts, don't just attach it to a claim. Add a reason that tells your readers what you want them to see in the evidence that is relevant to the claim.

WRITING PROCESS 5
Reasons and Evidence

Preparing and Planning

Be Aware How Your Reasons Color Your Claim (and You)

Your reasons can color how your readers respond not only to your argument but to you. Suppose Jorge claims that plagiarism from the Internet is increasing and should be curbed, offering these reasons:

R1: Plagiarism prevents good students from standing out with higher grades.

R2: It erodes the foundations of trust that a community depends on.

R3: If the public learns about it, it will make the university look bad.

R4: It makes students think they can get something for nothing.

Each reason casts a different light on the kind of person Jorge imagines his reader to be, but also reflects on his claim and even on himself.

When you offer a reason, you imply a warrant that reflects a principle of reasoning or action that in turn reflects a set of beliefs and values. Even if your claim is true, your reason could "poison" both it and your ethos. So once you have a list of possible reasons, test each one for how it reflects on both you and your reader:

1. State the general principles or warrants that connect each reason to the claim.

   W1: When something prevents good students from standing out, it should be curbed. Plagiarism makes it hard for our better students to stand out, so it should be curbed.

   W2: When something undermines the moral fabric of a community, it should be curbed. Plagiarism undermines the moral fabric of our community, so it should be curbed.

   W3: When something might bring bad publicity, it should be curbed. Plagiarism makes us look bad, so it should be curbed.

   W4: When something makes students think they can get something for nothing, it should be curbed. Plagiarism makes students think they can get something for nothing, so it should be curbed.

2. Ask whether that principle reflects the values of your readers.

Most readers are likely to respond more positively to an appeal implying that they care about the moral fabric of our community than to one based on bad publicity or students not getting due credit.

Ordering Multiple Reasons

As we said on p. 127, when you have more than one reason, they will relate in one of two ways:

1. They will be like a set of parallel columns, all supporting the main claim.
2. They will be like a series of steps or a tower of blocks, each leading to or supporting the next.

Ordering Parallel Reasons

If you have parallel reasons supporting a claim, you have to arrange them in an order that creates the right impact and that readers will think is coherent. Some writers don't arrange reasons at all, leaving them in the order they popped into mind, which is rarely best order. Experienced writers arrange parallel reasons in an order that helps readers and explicitly signal what that order is.

Ordering Reasons by Their Substance. The reasons themselves may suggest a principle of order. Historical reasons have a default chronological order, reasons referring to different countries can be organized into a geographical order, and so on. For example, to explain the causes of the Holocaust someone might offer these four parallel reasons, each independently supporting the claim:

1. The Allied nations did not try to stop the Holocaust for political reasons.
2. Anti-Semitism had a long history in Germany.
3. Hitler and those around him were uniquely evil.
4. Jews did not resist soon enough or strongly enough.

It's hard to see a principle in that order. An order based on chronology would be clearer: 2 (history) –3 (Hitler's evil) –4 (weak resistance) –1 (failure of Allies).

Ordering Reasons by Readers' Responses. A better way to order parallel reasons is by how you want readers to react to them. One principle of order is relative *strength*. For example, the reasons for the Holocaust might be ordered from what readers would take to be weakest to strongest, or vice versa, depending on whether we want to make a quick impact or to build toward a climax. Of course, readers differ in which reasons they judge strong or weak.

A second principle of order based on readers' responses is relative *acceptability*. Even when readers think a reason is strong, they may still not like hearing it. For example, it is likely that Jews, Germans, and those associated with the Allies would each resist most strongly the reason that assigns responsibility to one of them. Members of each group would probably want to see other causes acknowledged before the writer focused on their own responsibility.

Another principle of order is relative *complexity*. Readers grasp simpler reasons more easily than complex ones. (What is easier or more difficult, of course, depends on what they know.) For example, to explain why our ability to learn language is not like our ability to learn chess or geometry but is based on a genetically determined competence, someone might give these three reasons:

1. All human languages have a set of common features reflecting abstract principles of syntactic organization and phonological expression.
2. Children all over the world learn to talk at about the same age.
3. Chimpanzees, the most intelligent nonhuman, can't learn the grammatical structures that two-year olds master easily.

The first reason is extremely difficult to grasp in detail; the second easier; and the third easiest of all. If so, readers would understand the argument better if those reasons were in reverse order.

Finally, reasons can be ordered by *familiarity*. (This too depends on particular readers.) Readers understand familiar reasons more readily than unfamiliar ones. For example, of the three reasons about learning language, the first is least familiar to most readers, the second most familiar for anyone who has been around children. So for them, the best order is 2-3-1.

If these principles of order conflict, the simplest principle is to put your strongest reasons last, if you are writing for a reader who you trust will read to the end of your argument. If you fear that your reader will stop reading, put your strongest reasons first. Under any circumstances, choose *some* principle of order and make it clear to your readers.

Ordering Reasons in a Series

When you offer a series of reasons, each one not supporting the claim directly, but linked to the one before and after it, you have to look for completely different principles of order.

Process Orders. If your reasons reflect some external process, you can order them to reflect its sequence. Begin at the beginning of the process and move to its outcome, like this:

> When buyers are satisfied with the quality of the product and then the quality of service when it breaks down, _{step 1} they are likely to become loyal customers. _{step 2} Loyal customers are important, because they don't need advertising or a high-powered sales force to convince them to buy that product again. _{step 3} So the more loyal users a product has, the more profits a company can expect. _{claim}

Or you can begin with the outcome and move back to its beginning, like this:

> Manufacturers increase profits and sales _{step 3} when they create loyal customers who bought their product once and return to buy the same product a second time, _{step 2} without the need of advertising or a high-powered sales force. Customers become loyal when they are satisfied with the product, which depends on two things: the quality of service, but more importantly

the product's intrinsic quality. _{step 1} Therefore, while manufacturers should focus on both the quality of their service and the quality of their product, they should emphasize product quality. _{claim}

Both orders make sense. Which you choose depends on how you want readers to think about the process. The last step is the one they focus on most closely, so choose the order that focuses them on what you want them to emphasize.

Reasoning Orders. You can order sequential reasons to follow not an external process but the internal process of your readers' logic. In the next example, the writer reports Thomas Jefferson's order of reasoning. The second reason depends on the logical principle stated in the first, and the third reason depends on the second (and the writer bases it all on the reported evidence of Jefferson's words):

> When Jefferson wrote "all men are created equal" with "certain inalienable rights," _{evidence} he laid down the first principle of civil society—we all have intrinsic rights that cannot be taken away. _{reason 1} To protect those rights, we establish government, _{reason 2} but when government tries to take those rights away, we have the duty to replace it with one that will protect us. _{reason 3} In a democracy, we do that by the vote. But when a government is a ruthless tyranny, we have the duty to throw off its rule by force, if necessary. _{claim}

The reverse order is possible, but harder to follow.

We can't tell you how to choose among these orders: that depends on your knowing your argument, your situation, but most of all your readers. So try different orders on surrogate readers. Under any circumstances, though, always question an order that you did not *choose*. Never assume that the order in which you wrote down reasons is the order that best helps readers grasp them.

Have a Plan for Gathering Evidence

Gathering evidence is like diamond mining; you have to know where to look, but more important, what to look for; then you have to process lots of dross to find a single gem; and even the gems need polishing. When you assemble an argument, you need an idea about the kind of (reports of) evidence you are looking for and where to find them. Many inexperienced writers start mounding up notes the moment they have a topic. If you do that, you risk "boiling the ocean," because so much data is available on every aspect of every topic that it would take weeks to sample even a small part of it, then months to sort it out. You avoid aimlessly and endlessly collecting data if you plan before you look. Here are some ideas.

1. **Use your problem and possible solutions to plan your search.** To decide what data are worth collecting, state as best you can your problem, a few hypothetical solutions, and some reasons that might support

them. Then ask yourself what kind of evidence would support those reasons. When you do not have a problem to help you select evidence, you are likely to end up with an indiscriminate data dump—everything you could find about X, as some of you may remember from a high school "research" paper.

2. **Think about readers: What kind of evidence do they expect?** Not only must your evidence suit your claim and reasons, it must also suit your readers. For example, what *kind* of data would convince your *particular* reader that extrasensory perception exists: A striking anecdote about your experience? Objective data generated by controlled experiments? Testimony from someone they trust? Only their own personal experience of it? Before you start searching, imagine as specifically as you can what kind of evidence your readers would count as conclusive before you ask whether you can find it. Use that imagined evidence to establish a benchmark against which to test what you find. Of course, you cannot use invented evidence in your argument.

3. **Weigh the cost of the search against the value of the evidence.** How long will it take to find the best sources of evidence, and what risk is there that you will find none at all? Hedge your bet by gathering the easiest evidence to find first, just to be sure you have some. For example, if Elena had only a few weeks to prepare her argument supporting a Center for English Language Studies, she would not have time to identify and survey every college with such a center. So she would have to settle for a less reliable phone survey of the few centers she knew about.

4. Decide on the most likely source of data. There are several options to consider:

   • **Libraries:** A college library can provide most of the data you need as "outside" support for your arguments. The trick is knowing how to find them. We can't tell you how to use a library, but every library has a tour, and most librarians are eager to help. An hour or two invested in learning how to find resources in different fields will pay off in time saved later.

   • **The Internet:** The Internet is an increasingly important source of information, but right now, it is like an undiscriminating library without librarians. Unlike publishers and libraries, the Internet has no gatekeepers that screen for quality. It offers a lot information, much of it reliable, but much that libraries do not think worthy of inclusion. So it is a case of "Browser beware." At the very least, be sure you know who, if anyone, stands behind the information in a site. Search engines will help you find sites and even individual pages, but usually too many. Once you find a relevant site, you may or may not find the help you need in zeroing in on specific information. You can improve your search results if you learn to use what is called a "Boolean" search—an Internet screening device that utilizes keywords—for example, "X and Y and not Z"—to narrow down topics.

By all means use the Net, but until it evolves the selectivity and quality controls of libraries, use it for these purposes, cautiously:

- To survey what information is available.
- To get public materials. Most major newspapers and magazines maintain web sites with information on recent articles, sometimes the articles themselves. You can also find information on companies, civic or political groups, government departments, and so on.
- To get copies of information found in libraries. Many college libraries offer electronic access to articles, abstracts, and databases.
- To find information too recent to be found in libraries. Many government reports are released first on the web, then in print.
- To supplement information that you find in libraries. Some journals conduct net-based discussions among readers and authors. Others use the web to archive data and ancillary information not included in printed texts.
- To find information that libraries don't collect. For example, a student interested in steel pan music found that many steel bands have their own web pages.

- **People:** You may need support beyond the written word. For example, Elena's work on ESL tutoring would depend on information gathered directly from students. When you use people as sources, plan carefully so that you avoid wasting not just your time, but theirs. Prepare your questions, not to read them like a script, but to stay focused. Use a tape recorder, and get everything you need the first time.

- **Direct Observation:** Many questions are best answered through field studies or controlled experiments conducted in ways a discipline requires. In a writing class, it's not likely you'll have to collect empirical evidence, but you might construct a problem that needs it: How do instructors in different departments mark their papers? Do some bars encourage binge drinking more than others? Record the activities on the spot, then report only the data that your *records* support, not what you have to recall after you realize that you did not record information you should have. Be sure to tell readers how you collected the data. And if you have data that call your claim into question, you have an obligation to your readers to account for that, as well.

- **"I search":** In some classes, teachers expect students to gather most of their evidence from personal reflection: not *research* but *I search*. If your assignment calls for this kind of evidence, guard against the deceptions of memory: We are all prone to remember what we think ought to have happened rather than what did. And never treat this kind of evidence as an "outside" source.

5. **Sample the evidence.** You can't always do this, but it improves your chances of success. For a survey, test it in a trial run or focus group. For evidence in books or articles, skim a few introductions and abstracts to see whether they look promising. For direct observation, make a quick visit to the site to see what there is to see.

6. **Take stock as the evidence mounts.** Some students turn off their judgment when they start gathering evidence or reports of it, reading book after book, taking endless notes before they realize that most of what they have is irrelevant to any claim they might make. Some researchers just can't stop gathering ever more data, usually because they have no plan, no hypothesis, no idea where they are going. But at some point, enough is enough. So from time to time, step back to consider the value of what you have collected. Otherwise you risk wasting more time than you have. However, avoid the other common mistake of assuming that you have done your job when you have found any evidence at all. Teachers most commonly complain that students offer too little evidence.

Drafting

Balance Reasons and Evidence

Beware the data dump. Some writers worry that readers will distrust their reports of evidence, so they compensate by dumping on them buckets of undigested data and quotations. Not long ago, one of our children was writing her first paper in a college writing class. In preparing her first draft, she assembled more than ninety quotations. When her father suggested that she might have trouble squeezing nine pages of quotes into five pages of argument, she acknowledged she might have gone overboard collecting evidence. Readers want reliable reports of *relevant* evidence, not all the data available on some topic.

Beware as well the opinion piece. Some writers who can't find evidence or reports of it build their arguments out of unsupported opinion. We are all entitled to opinions, but we are not entitled to our readers' time to read them. We have to earn that time with good reasons and the evidence they rest on.

INQUIRIES

Reflections

1. Sue copied the office hours from the schedules posted on professors' doors. But are the actual, physical pieces of paper listing office hours the "hard evidence" that "proves" that on average teachers are in their offices for less than an hour a week?

2. Here is something that some people might take to be a "fact" and there-fore usable as evidence in favor of allowing people to carry concealed weapons:

> According to an NRA press release, states that have passed laws allow-ing citizens to carry concealed weapons in public have experienced on average a 4.6 percent drop in daylight assaults and robbery.

How many removes from the primary evidence itself would you esti-mate that report of evidence is?

3. How close to the primary evidence itself are these: (a) a musical score; (b) musical recordings made from that score; (c) color reproductions of oil paintings in art history books; (d) full-size exact reproductions of etchings in art books; (e) a videotape of an automobile accident; (f) a tape recording of a meeting; (g) a transcription of that tape recording; (h) a drawing of a witness in a courtroom; (i) a photograph of a witness in a courtroom.

4. What counts as evidence for being in love? For sexual fidelity? For God directly telling someone to do something? For pain that disables some-one from working?

5. Which of the following statements is closer to the truth? Does it matter?

Most of the important questions in the world are those for which we have no good evidence to decide either way.

Most of the important questions in the world are those for which we have no good reasons to decide either way.

6. When Jefferson says "We hold these truths to be self-evident," what does he base that on?

7. Consider these three statements:

   a. The comments on my history paper did not provide specific advice about improving the next paper.

   b. The comments on my history paper averaged about six words, and all of the comments expressed only approval or disapproval.

   c. The comments on my history paper were very brief and uninfor-mative.

All might be true, but which seems closest to representing what's "out there," independent of anyone's judgment? Can you order them as a claim supported by a reason supported by evidence? "X because Y because Z"?

8. Some people refuse to judge any reason good or bad, because any reason is a good one for the person offering it. If so, then all reasons are equally good. They are in effect just opinions, and everyone's opinion is as good as anyone else's. Do you agree that all opinions are equally good? If you do, then some philosophers would claim that you have contradicted yourself. Have you?

Tasks

9. Pull out those old papers you've been working with. Select one that has the most evidence. Identify each report of evidence and grade it on a four-point scale:

   4 = as close to primary evidence as anyone could get
   3 = your own report of primary evidence that you directly collected or experienced
   2 = your secondhand report of what is reported by the person who directly collected or experienced the primary evidence
   1 = your third- or fourthhand report of what someone else reported that someone else reported.

   What is your average score? Could you have raised it if you had looked further?

10. This exercise asks you to see how arguers can gain your trust by exploiting your bias to think of evidence as "out there in the world." Find a textbook that relies on complex data (experimental psychology, physics, economics). Pick out reports of evidence offered as factually true, beyond question (look for tables and graphs). Do you understand that evidence? Does it seem to you self-evident, obvious in the external world? What would you have to believe to accept this evidence as "given." Now find the same thing in a newspaper or newsmagazine, then in a television newscast.

11. The next serious disagreement you get into, try to establish what you and the other person are willing to accept as evidence. How hard is it to do that? Is there any disagreement about what to count as evidence?

Project

12. Select one of your old papers, and imagine that you intended it for a reader who does not trust you and will question your reported evidence. What would you need to bolster each of the reports of evidence in your paper? Do some research to see whether you can get it. (You may not be able to put your hands on the evidence now, but you should be able to find out whether it is at least out there.) For quotations, imagine that your reader suspects that you quoted out of context. How could you show that you did not?

WRITING PROJECTS 5

Project 5.1

Context.   One good way to develop an argument is to adapt a related argument that you or your readers find convincing. For example, in literature classes students often develop arguments about a book not discussed in class by applying to it the general structure of argument and some of the evidence used to discuss a related book that was assigned for class. This is also a common practice among professionals, such as management consultants. When they investigate the case of one client, they often make arguments similar to those they have previously made for other clients. This is not plagiarism, as long as you acknowledge your source and no one is fooled into thinking that you built the argument from scratch.

Scenario.   You work part-time as a work-study student in the dean of students office. Your boss, the dean, has been pressured by parents and the surrounding community to curb binge drinking among students. She has resisted that pressure because she believes that any antidrinking measures would infringe students' rights and hamper their growth as adults. She asked you to research the issue, and you provided her with a number of articles, including Camille Paglia's "Wisdom in a Bottle: 'Binge Drinking' and the New Campus Nannyism" and Jacob Sullum's "Smoking and the Tyranny of Public Health." The dean likes Paglia's piece and has been echoing its argument in her own statements. You have told her that you think Sullum's argument is more appropriate.

Task 1.   Your boss sends you the following e-mail: "I've been thinking about your concerns about using Paglia's argument, and you may have a point. I'm going to be visiting high schools for the next few days, but I'll check my e-mail. Send me a brief summary about the problems you see in Paglia's case and why you think I should use Sullum's instead." Write an e-mail memo to send to your boss.

Task 2.   Your boss wants a quick-and-dirty outline of an argument about drinking parallel to Sullum's argument about smoking. Outline Sullum's main reasons. Create a new outline by adapting, replacing, or deleting specific reasons so that the argument now applies to binge drinking.

Task 3.   Your boss wants a more detailed outline that she can use as "talking points" when she speaks around campus and in the community. Add evidence to support each reason. You can borrow Sullum's evidence when it applies; when it doesn't, find evidence focused on drinking rather than smoking.

Task 4.   Your boss wants you to ghostwrite an essay for the student newspaper. She will rewrite your argument to make it suit her style, but she wants a complete and polished draft from you.

Project 5R

Scenario.   Your proposal for a research paper has been accepted and you will be working on it for weeks. Your teacher wants to keep up with your progress by seeing your work along the way. You have two options: create a detailed outline by following steps 1, 2, and 3a (best for slow and careful drafters), or create a scratch outline and begin drafting by following steps 1, 2, and 3b (best for quick and dirty drafters).

Task.   Follow these steps:

• **Step 1:**   Determine the major sections of your paper. After selecting the most promising answer to your research question, list the major reasons in support of that claim in an order that will help your readers understand it. Try several stock orders (familiar to unfamiliar, simple to complex, less to more controversial, etc.) as well as others that come to mind. You now have a rough outline of the major sections in your paper to share with your classmates.

• **Step 2:**   Sketch a brief introduction to each section that states what part of the main question/problem you address in that section. End it with the reason that will be the main claim/point of that section.

• **Step 3a**   (for slow and careful drafters): Create a detailed outline for the section using the procedures in Step 1. Under each reason, indicate what evidence you offer to support it. If you already have evidence, summarize it. If not, summarize the kind of evidence you expect to collect and how you expect to get it.

• **Step 3b**   (for quick and dirty drafters): Draft each section including evidence you have collected. Otherwise indicate the kind of evidence you will look for. If you think that you can find a particular kind of evidence, summarize it. Indicate clearly that you have not yet checked your sources. (You can start these paragraphs with a note to yourself, *Although I have not yet looked, I expect that [SOURCE] will show that . . . .*)

SAMPLE ESSAY

The essay that follows uses evidence gathered from sources. You may not yet be writing papers as fully researched as this one, but even a shorter essay has to use its sources well. Read the essay and do the following:

Task 1.   Pick out the reasons and evidence in the essay. This will be easiest if you make a copy and mark it up with different colored highlighters. Otherwise, use line numbers to identify specific sentences. (Save your marked up copies; you'll need them again.)

1. How many reasons are supported with specific evidence? How many have no evidence at all?

2. On average, how many items of evidence does the writer present in support of each of the major reasons? (You can estimate this.)

3. Estimate the following: (a) What percentage of the evidence in this paper is reported primary evidence (one step away from the evidence itself; that is, the writer observed or collected it directly)? (b) What

percentage is secondary evidence (two steps away from the evidence itself; that is, the writer reports on evidence reported by someone who observed or collected it)? (c) What percentage is tertiary evidence (three or more steps away)?

Task 2:   Answer the following questions, using your analysis in Task 1 as evidence for your claims.

1. In general, does the evidence in this essay support its reasons?

2. Assuming that you accept those reasons, how well do they support the claim "that guns were not popular in America until after the Civil War, and that the reasons people began to buy guns had more to do with money than with patriotism"?

3. How well do they support the claim that "People should not be duped into thinking that supporting gun control laws is unpatriotic or un-American"?

4. Does the presentation of evidence in this essay make the writer seem more or less credible? Why?

Guns in America

1   If you listen to the NRA, owning a gun is the ultimate symbol of American freedom and democracy. So most people believe them when they say that gun ownership has been a part of America since the Revolution and that it is a violation of basic American beliefs when the government tries to take away the
5   people's guns. But this is just propaganda. The claim that for our forefathers owning guns was a patriotic duty is erroneous. History shows that guns were not popular in America until after the Civil War, and that the reasons people began to buy guns had more to do with money than with patriotism. People should not be duped into thinking that supporting gun control laws is unpatriotic or un-
10   American.
        It is true that in colonial days many Americans owned guns, but they faced many dangers, and there was no police force to protect you. The rule was, defend yourself or die. But later, when the country became more civilized, people stopped owning guns. According to historian Michael Bellesiles, "It would appear that at
15   no time prior to 1850 did more than a tenth of the people own guns" (1966). This conclusion is based on surveys done by the states to see how many people owned guns so that they could serve in state militias. The state of Massachusetts counted all the guns owned by private citizens, and in every survey until 1840 it found that less than 11 percent of the people owned guns. "At the start of the
20   War of 1812, the state had more spears than firearms in its arsenal" (Economist, 1999). Also, guns were not the sort of thing people bought for a hobby, as they do today. The first magazine devoted to guns was not published until 1843.

One example of heroic gun owners that gun supporters talk about is the Minutemen of Massachusetts. These were farmers who, on a minute's notice,
25 formed an army to defeat the British at Lexington and Concord, supposedly shooting the British soldiers from behind fences and hedges because they were great marksmen. But they were really a minority. Bellesiles did a study in which he checked wills and "probate inventories" (records of personal possesses when people died) between 1765 and 1790, and he found that less than 15 percent
30 of all households had guns, and that more than half of the guns were broken (Bellesiles, 1966). So by the time of the Revolution most Americans had already stopped owning guns. In 1793, less than twenty years after the Revolution, Congress passed a law to buy 7,000 muskets because it was worried that so few people owned guns that the country would not be able to defend itself
35 (there was still no army). But the people didn't want the guns. From 1808 to 1839, the government had a program to give a gun to every white male who belonged to a state militia, but only half the militias bothered to ask for them (*Economist,* 1999). This was not because the militia members already owned guns, but because they didn't care about owning guns. In the 1830s, the
40 general sent down by the federal government to lead the Florida militia in a war against the Seminoles, Winfield Scott, complained that the militia had almost no guns.

The militias are another example of heroic gun owners held up by gun supporters. But they were mostly a joke. Militia members were mostly "town
45 paupers, idlers, vagrants, foreigners, itinerants, drunkards and the outcasts of society," according to the adjutant general of Massachusetts (*Economist,* 1999). It was even more of a joke to think of them as marksmen like the Minutemen. In Pennsylvania, one militia held a shooting contest, but no one hit the target and the winner was the one who came closest. According to the newspaper, "The size
50 of the target is known accurately, having been carefully measured. It was precisely the size and shape of a barn door" (Bellesiles, 1998). Most militias stopped having shooting practice because it was embarrassing how badly they shot. In 1839, the Secretary of War complained that militias were "armed with walking canes, fowling pieces or unserviceable muskets" (*Economist,* 1999).
55 If you go by the movies, everyone had a gun in the Wild West. But Robert Dykstra says that it was more peaceful in cattle towns like Tombstone, Arizona, or Dodge City, Kansas, than in the cities in the east. It is true that most cowboys carried rifles on the trail (mostly for hunting) and some of them carried pistols. But when they came to a town, they did not have to defend themselves against
60 the dangers of the trail, so they left their guns behind because most cattle towns had strict anti-gun laws and the Sheriff would take them away. "During its most celebrated decade as a tough cattle town, only 15 persons died violently in Dodge City, 1876–1885, for an average of just 1.5 killings per cowboy season" (Dykstra, 1968). Living in these towns was more like *The Little House on the Prairie* than the

65 *Wild Bunch.* Maybe the movies have so many guns in Westerns because gunfights are exciting and add to the action, or maybe they are just trying to support the myth that America is the land of the free and home of the brave because it is the home of the gun.

Why did most Americans not own a gun before the Civil War? There were
70 two reasons. First, they didn't need them. It is a myth that violence has always been a part of American life. In the early years of the country, nine Americans out of ten did not feel that they needed a gun to protect themselves. Second, guns were expensive. A gun would cost a farmer a whole year's income (*Economist,* 1999).

76 Why did more Americans own guns after the Civil War? There was one reason: money. When the war started, the Union government owned 327,000 muskets and rifles and the Confederate government owned 150,000. By the end of the war, the Union army had given out 4 million weapons to its soldiers. Of course it also trained those soldiers to shoot. The Union army had 1.5 million soldiers and
80 the Confederate army had 1 million. When the war was over and the soldiers went home, the army let them keep their guns. Now there were many more Americans with guns they got for free (Bellesiles, 1999).

The war also made guns less expensive. In the few years of the war, gun manufacturers made more guns to supply the war than they had made in the
85 entire history of the country (Economist, 1999). The gun manufacturers had to learn how to mass produce guns to supply the army with so many guns so quickly, which meant that not only did they have many more factories but that the guns were much cheaper. When the government stopped buying guns for the war, the manufacturers had to sell more guns or close down the new factories, but they
90 were saved because the war had created many new customers who owned guns and had learned to shoot in the war.

So you can see that it is a myth that guns have always been a part of American life and that without people owning guns America would not have been able to protect its freedom. Gun supporters say people buy guns to protect
95 themselves, but according to the statistics the only people likely to be shot by their guns are themselves or a member of their family. People say they buy guns to defend America's freedom, but who do they think they will defend it from? Those who believe in the myth of a nation of Minutemen may be sincere, but all they guard is the profits of the gun manufacturers who have blood on their hands.

Works Cited

Bellesiles, Michael. "The Origins of Gun Culture in the United States, 1760-1865." *Journal of American History.* 83 (1966): 425–455.

Guns in America   Page 4

Bellesiles, Michael. "Gun Laws in Early America." *Law and History Review*. 16 (1998): 567–589.

Bellesiles, Michael. *Lethal Imagination.* New York University Press: 1999.

Davidson, Osha Gray.*Under Fire.* University of Iowa Press: 1998.

Dykstra, Richard. *The Cattle Towns.* Knopf: 1968.

Economist Staff, "Guns in America." *Economist.* July 3, 1999.

National Rifle Association *NRA-ILA Research & Information Page.* The National Rifle Association Institute for Legislative Action. http://www.nraila.org/research/.

CHAPTER 5 IN A NUTSHELL

About Your Argument . . .

You rest claims on reasons, and you usually base reasons not directly on evidence but on reports of it. You can't base reasons on the evidence itself because it is almost always somewhere else in time or place, always "outside" your argument. When you report evidence that you yourself observed or that someone else has reported, you must report it accurately and cite your sources, so that readers can check it for themselves.

Since readers usually need more than one reason before they will agree to a claim, don't be satisfied with only one.

Except for the simplest, most obvious cases, don't cite reports of evidence without also stating a reason that connects those reports to the claim. Reasons not only support claims, they also interpret evidence. The reason should tell readers what to see in the evidence that is relevant to your claim.

. . . and About Writing It

When you have multiple reasons, select an order that helps readers:

- If reasons are parallel, order them on the basis of strength, acceptability, complexity, or familiarity.
- If your reasons are linked, decide whether you want them to follow an external process or the internal steps of your reasoning.

Make a plan to gather your evidence. Think about these questions:

- What kind of evidence do your readers expect you to report?
- Will the cost of searching for specific evidence be greater than the benefit of finding it?

- Where are you most likely to find the evidence you need—libraries? the Internet? personal interview? observation?

Once you begin accumulating evidence, evaluate your progress:

- Start by sampling the evidence to see if there will be enough.
- Periodically take stock of the evidence as it mounts.
- Start to plan and even draft before you have all your evidence.

Keep a balance between reasons and reports of evidence:

- Beware the argument that is made up mostly of quotations or data.
- Conversely, be certain that you have at least tried to find evidence for every reason.

CHAPTER 6

Reporting Evidence

In this chapter, we discuss different kinds of evidence, with a special focus on how to evaluate what you have and decide what more you need.

You take a big step toward making good arguments when you realize two things:

- Careful readers distinguish reasons from evidence and reports of evidence.
- They judge your arguments as stronger and your ethos more credible when you support reasons with reports of evidence that you gathered from reliable sources.

But we mislead ourselves when we speak of "gathering" evidence, as if it were scattered around, waiting to be picked up. Getting evidence is closer to a hunt. Colomb spent five years, on and off, hunting for the address of a doctor who practiced in London at the end of the seventeenth century (it turned up in a box of books in a library basement). You probably can't spend weeks, much less months or years, hunting data for your arguments, but you'll still need to do some sleuthing to meet your burden of evidence. (In this chapter, we will use the shorter term *evidence* to refer to both the evidence itself and your reports of it. When we have to distinguish between reports of evidence and the evidence "itself," we will. Until then, assume that *evidence* means a report of it.)

When you do find evidence, you'll find it difficult to question it as closely as your readers will, because they will think of objections to it that you won't. Or they are likely to think of other evidence that you did not even find. Or they may not think that it is as relevant to your reasons as you do: It is a sad but true comment on the human mind that we all tend to seize on evidence that confirms what we want to believe; and worse, we ignore, reject, or even distort evidence that contradicts it. So to meet your burden of evidence, you have to see it from your readers' point of view to anticipate the questions they may ask.

Weighing Your Burden of Evidence

You know you have met your burden of evidence when readers don't ask for more. But you can't judge when you have enough simply by adding it up. Readers will want more and better evidence when you ask them to accept a claim that seems surprising or unlikely or that has significant consequences. You have to judge each case individually, but here are three questions to help you decide what evidence you need and how good it has to be:

1. **How closely must you match the disciplinary expectations of your readers?** Your first question must be about the kind of evidence your readers will accept *as* evidence, particularly if they expect you to write as a member of their academic or professional community. You have to present the kind of evidence *they* count as evidence and to report it in ways they judge appropriate to their community. An environmental science teacher will expect you to draw toxicology data from technical reports, not from the local newspaper; a history teacher will expect you to work with primary documents, not secondary accounts of them. Disciplines vary too much for us to give any general rule other than this: When you write in a new community, ask an experienced member to show you what counts as evidence.

   You also have to match the kind of evidence you report to the kind of problem you address. In an argument about binge drinking, for example, you would need one kind of evidence to argue that it is caused by the psychology of late adolescence and another by our culture of addiction. The problem is that each new argument presents new demands that you have to puzzle out case-by-case.

2. **How strongly will readers resist your claim?** The more readers resist a claim, the more evidence they want. Assume that your readers will resist most and so want more evidence when you ask them to

   • accept a claim that contradicts what they deeply believe;

   • do something that costs them time or effort;

   • do or think something that creates new problems, such as the loss of something they like, the disapproval of others, etc.

In these situations, their feelings matter as much as your logic. For example, suppose you found evidence that an international political figure and author knowingly included false stories in a book that made her famous. Her political opponents will snap up any evidence against her, while her admirers will demand more and better evidence before they agree that she is a fraud, because in accepting that claim, they would have to give up more than a belief. (See the case of Rigoberta Menchú in Project 10 on p. 167.)

3. **How fully do you want your readers to accept your claim?** If you ask readers to accept a strong claim wholeheartedly, they will expect your best reports of the best evidence. But they may be satisfied with less evidence if you ask them for less—only to approve or endorse a claim, or to understand and respect your reasons for making it. If Harry asks the dean to form a committee to study the need for longer library hours to accommodate students with day jobs, the dean might want more than anecdotal evidence about dissatisfied students. But she may be receptive to a few good stories if Harry only wants her to believe that students have a reasonable complaint.

Above all, don't rely on evidence only from personal experience—the striking event, the memorable person, that one great class in philosophy that made you think that philosophy classes in general must be great. It is only one point of data among the many that readers expect you to report. Sometimes we have no alternative but to build an argument out of personal experiences because it's all we have and those experiences are so vivid that they fill up the mental space we reserve for evidence. Other times we use easily remembered anecdotes because we get lazy and they are ready to hand. Under any circumstances, while reports of personal experiences can enliven an argument, alone they rarely convince thoughtful readers of a contestable claim. A "for instance" is not proof.

The Four Maxims of Quality

Once you think you have sufficient evidence of the right kind to satisfy readers, you have to evaluate its quality, but again from their point of view. Readers judge evidence by four criteria: (1) accuracy, (2) precision, (3) representativeness, and (4) reliability. How severely they apply them depends on how much they have at stake in agreeing to your claim. For instance, if a researcher claims that Alzheimer victims improve when they take some natural herb, researchers dubious about such cures will demand to know precisely what counts as "improve" and how it was measured. On the other hand, those with a family member suffering from Alzheimer's are likely to accept a lower threshold of evidence, and the producers of the herb a lower one yet. Imagine your readers asking these questions about your evidence:

1. **Is your report of evidence accurate?** This is the prime maxim. Get one fact wrong and readers may distrust not just everything else you say— but you, as well.

2. **Is your report of evidence precise enough?** It is 100 percent accurate to say that the population of Ohio is between a million and a billion, but not precise enough for most purposes. What counts as precise, though, differs by both use and field. A physicist measures the life of a particle in millionths of a second; a paleontologist might be happy to date the appearance of a new species give or take half a million years. Reports of evidence can also be too precise. A historian might date the moment the Soviet Union was ready to collapse in a range of weeks or months but would seem foolhardy to place it at "2:11 PM on August 18, 1991, because it was at that moment that Gorbachev . . . "

3. **Is the evidence you report representative?** This also depends on your kind of problem. If you generalize about how people get off welfare, you need a huge sample to cover all the reasons they were on it. But if you are studying a new chemical element, you can make big generalizations from tiny samples. Human populations vary a lot; samples of a chemical element little or not at all.

4. **Are your reports of evidence from reliable sources?** The problem of reliable sources turns on four issues. The first variable is **competence.** Will your readers think that your source is competent to judge the quality of evidence it reports? Readers will be at least suspicious of data that you pull from the Web site of someone neither you nor they have ever heard of. But even expert credentials do not ensure competence: Linus Pauling won a Nobel Prize in chemistry, but he was judged to be a flake when he moved out of his field to tout vitamin C as a cure for most ills known to medicine.

   The second variable is **freedom from bias.** Will your readers be confident that however expert your sources are, they are not tainted by self-interest? Not long ago, a government review of research into the safety of silicone breast implants was almost dismissed as wholly discredited when it was discovered that just one of the scientists on the panel had received research funds from a company making the implants. Even if that scientist had been utterly objective, the critics were right to charge that the mere appearance of a conflict of interest was enough to undermine the image of integrity of the whole panel. The best sources of evidence are those who have something to lose in offering it. A gun manufacturer who testifies that trigger locks are needed to make guns safer is more credible than a gun dealer who says they wouldn't help.

   The third variable is, for the lack of better term, **"pecking order."** Like it or not, readers are more likely to trust evidence you gather from people with good reputations, strong credentials, important positions, and name recognition. For instance, Jane Goodall is perhaps the most respected primatologist in the world. If the topic is chimps and apes, when Jane Goodall talks, people listen. But she started out as an unknown, trusted by hardly anyone, until she was endorsed by the famous anthropologist, Louis Leakey.

A fourth variable is **level of source.** *Primary sources* are those closest to the evidence itself. If you are studying texts, primary sources are the original books, letters, diaries, and so on. If you are studying physical phenomena, primary sources are the reports of those who directly observed, collected, and reported the evidence "itself." Use primary sources when you can: for textual evidence, a recent edition by a reputable publisher; for physical evidence, the original article (not just the abstract or, worse, someone's report of it). Be aware that some journals have better reputations for publishing sound research than others. Find out which journals are most (and least) respected before you cite evidence from one.

If you can't find primary sources, look for *secondary sources*—scholarly journals and books that report on primary sources. If you can't find secondary sources, you have to rely on *tertiary sources* that report work found in secondary sources. Tertiary sources include textbooks, articles in encyclopedias, and mass publications like the *Reader's Digest.* If these are the only sources available, so be it, but never assume that all readers will accept them as authoritative. They know that a report of a report of a report is too far from the evidence itself to be trusted.

IN THE READINGS . . .

Evidence, Ethos, and Credibility

It can be tricky deciding what readers will count as acceptable evidence, and how their decision affects your credibility. In "Purging Bingeing" (p. 418), Ed Carson argues that bingeing is not the problem many say it is. He questions the credibility of those who say it is a problem by questioning one use of unrepresentative evidence:

So last year, when the Center on Addiction and Substance Abuse at Columbia University (CASA) claimed the percentage of college women drinking to get drunk had more than tripled during the previous 15 years, the news media were quick to hype the finding that drinking on campus had reached "epidemic proportions." But as Kathy McNamara-Meis revealed in the Winter 1995 *Forbes MediaCritic,* CASA's conclusions were based on a misleading comparison of results from a 1977 survey of all college women and a 1992 survey of freshman women. Since freshmen drink more than any other class, such a comparison would suggest an increase in drunkenness even if nothing had changed.

In response, Carson offers not a report of evidence but a report of a claim by someone presented as an authority by virtue of the credentials cited:

In fact, says David Hanson, a professor of sociology at the State University of New York at Potsdam who has studied alcohol use on campus for more than 20 years, "the evidence shows that the actual trend is as flat as your little sister's chest."

If Carson is right that the CASA based its claim on unrepresentative evidence, does that disprove its claims that bingeing is on the rise? How credible does Carson's authority seem? Do you judge his credibility and ethos differently because he chose to quote that distasteful metaphor?

Representing Evidence

We've emphasized that what you present as evidence is not the evidence itself, but reports of it, because whoever reports evidence always shapes it to suit her own goals and interests. So when you gather and report evidence from the reports of others, you have to be aware that your source has already shaped it, and that you will again. Even when you report your own observations of the evidence "itself," you cannot avoid giving it some "spin." To report evidence responsibly, you have to understand its different kinds, what each kind is good for, how it is predictably distorted, and what are the best ways of presenting it.

Reports of Memories

As you look at these words, you feel the heft of this book, the texture of its pages. You can close the book and hear it snap; you can sniff it, even nibble at a page to taste it. Your senses are reporting evidence from "out there," evidence that supports your belief that you exist and so does this book. But put the book down for a moment and look away. [_____] The instant you did that, the self-evidence of this book vanished, leaving you with nothing but mental traces—a lingering taste, perhaps; a visual or tactile memory. At that point, your memory was only *reporting* the evidence that your senses reported a moment before. Your memory of the book was at that moment already a report of a report.

Memories are the least reliable evidence you can report, and yet they are the kind of evidence we are most likely to trust, especially recent ones, because they seem to represent our "direct" experience, the evidence of our senses. But when we store a memory of an event, we impose on it a form that makes it easy to recall. In so doing, we eliminate certain details that don't fit, enhance others that do, and in some cases invent elements to make the memory more shapely. Then when we tell a story based on our already storylike memory, we shape our told story still more, adding and deleting details, re-organizing them to make a "better" story. And that told-story in turn reshapes our memory into something more shapely and coherent yet, which is the basis for an even more shapely retold-story.

In short, be cautious about using memories (your own or those of others) as a reliable report of evidence. If you have a story based on eyewitness testimony, always try to corroborate it with other evidence: other memories, if that's all you can get, but other kinds of evidence if possible.

Never Trust Eye-Witnesses

In one study showing that memory is unreliable, people recalling a videotape of a car accident estimated the speed of the cars differently, depending on whether they were asked how fast the cars were going when they *bumped* or *smashed* into each other. They even "remembered" different amounts of broken glass, even though the videotape showed none at all!

Source: Elizabeth F. Loftus and John C. Palmer. "Reconstruction of Automobile Destruction: An Example of the Interaction Between Language and Memory." *Journal of Verbal Learning and Verbal Behavior* 13 (1974), pp. 585–589.

Anecdotes

As unreliable as memories are, anecdotes based on them are even less reliable because an anecdote is a short-short story that imposes on memory a story-like structure. Illustrative anecdotes have considerable persuasive power, especially when used to help readers grasp "objective" numerical data. When we see pallid statistical data enlivened by a vivid anecdote, the numbers take on the quality of evidence from "out there" because we seem to experience what they represent in our mind's eye.

Compare these:

> Fifty-three percent of Americans over the age of 65 have an annual income above $30,000, but 15 percent have incomes of less than $7,000 a year.

> Around 9 A.M., the cabin attendant on TWA flight 1643 to San Francisco asked Oliver and Sarah Peters whether they wanted the western omelet or the fruit plate for breakfast. Recently retired, they were on their way to visit their children and grandchildren in California, happy to be escaping the below-zero windchill in Chicago. At about the same time, 85-year-old Amanda Wilson was sitting at her kitchen table, staring at two five-dollar bills, a quarter, and a dime, trying to figure out one more time how to get through the next two weeks on 85¢ a day. She lives on $565 a month Social Security, most of which goes for heat, light, and rent on her one-room apartment.

The single sentence offers what most people would take to be a report of evidence, but the longer, detailed passage feels more vivid, because as we read it, we seem to see for ourselves what the generalization hides. Some might complain that the anecdote is unrepresentative and therefore unfair. Even so, it elicits a stronger emotional response than numbers do, and it is that kind of strong response that makes stories, anecdotes, examples, and illustrations such powerful reports of evidence. It is also what makes them potentially deceptive.

Photographs, Recordings, and Drawings

"Ocular proof" is compelling, because it makes us feel we are experiencing what really happened. We might even think that recordings are more reliable than memories. Like stories, they bring data to life by letting us experience them more directly than through words. For example, NATO attacked Serbia for many reasons, but it was visual images of suffering refugees and massacred civilians that made vivid President Clinton's abstract claims about moral imperatives.

As we all know, however, images and recordings of all kinds can be fabricated so convincingly that even experts can't distinguish fakes from the real thing. (Always distrust images you find on the Web.) But even when they are not doctored, images and recordings reshape what they record. That's why you must tell your readers who took the pictures or recorded video or audiotape that you offer as evidence, and under what circumstances.

Quantitative Data

For some readers, numbers are more compelling than stories or images, partly because they seem to report evidence most objectively, partly because they are recorded by exacting types like scientists and accountants. If any evidence feels as though it is "out there" in the world, it is what we can count, and what we can count we can represent as cold, objective numbers.

But of course numbers, just like any other form of evidence, are shaped by the aims and interests of those who record them. When the counters gather data for an argument about the safety of air bags, the counters have to decide what to count—traffic fatalities, serious injuries (what counts as serious?), people brought to hospitals, those who make insurance claims, etc. They also have to decide how to organize the numbers—total fatalities, fatalities per year, fatalities per thousand, fatalities per miles driven, fatalities per trip, etc., each of which affects the impact that the numbers have on readers.

For example, imagine you are deciding whether to invest in one of two companies, Abco or Zorax. Look at the three ways shown here to represent the same "facts." Which way of representing the data helps you make the best decision?

Table 1

| | 1996 | | 1997 | |
	Gross Income	Net Income	Gross Income	Net Income
Abco	$145,979,000	$32,473,000	$164,892,000	$32,526,000
Zorax	134,670,000	25,467,000	136,798,000	39,769,000

Figure 6.1

Cost Ratio

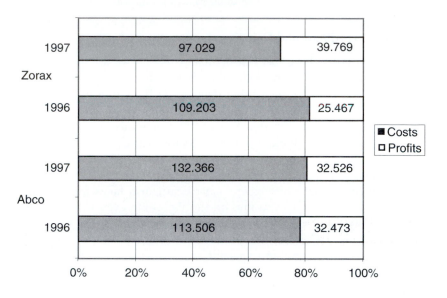

Figure 6.2

Income and Profits

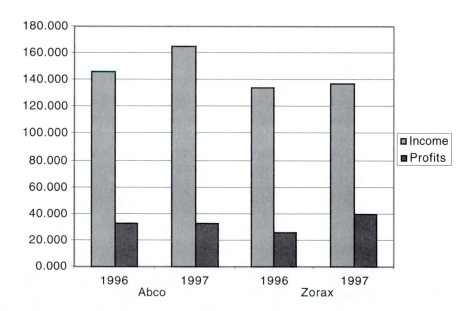

We could also represent these data in words, but words spin the data even more than pictures do. How attractive are Zorax and Abco in these two accounts?

> Zorax improved its net profits in 1997 from 1996 by more than 50 percent despite relatively level sales. In contrast, Abco failed to increase its net profits significantly despite substantially higher sales.

> In comparison to Zorax's increased sales and profits, Abco increased its profits and significantly increased its gross 1997 income over 1996.

We might think that the table is the most "objective," but that very objectivity is a rhetorical choice. We see in these reports of evidence the same "facts," but we are affected by them in different ways. How do you decide what kind of evidence to use? That depends on the kind of evidence your readers expect.

Reports from Authorities

Some students think they offer evidence when they quote an authority. But what they usually offer is only that authority's report of evidence, or more often, just a reason offered in a more authoritative voice. For example, Mai might think she is supporting her claim with a quotation, but here she only restates it:

> Teachers who read their teaching evaluations are more likely to improve their teaching than those who do not. According to J. Wills, for example, teachers who study their evaluations "profit from their openness to criticism" (*The Art of Teaching*, 330).

Wills may be right that the teachers profit from openness to criticism, but the quoted words of that claim are evidence only that Wills thinks so. Despite her misleading use of "for example," Mai simply restates in Wills's words what she already offered as a claim in the previous sentence. She could strengthen her own claim if she reported not just Wills's claim but his support for it as well:

> There is good reason to believe that teaching evaluations can lead to improved teaching. _{claim} According to J. Wills, teachers who study their evaluations "profit from an openness to criticism." _{reported reason} He studied 200 teachers who spent at least an hour reviewing their evaluations. The next term, they achieved 15 percent higher evaluations than those who circulated teaching evaluations but did not read them (*The Art of Teaching*, 330-35). _{reported evidence}

When you quote authorities, you do two useful things:

- If your authority really is an authority, you make your own position more credible.
- If your authority gathered the evidence you report, you bring readers as close to that evidence as they can get, short of reading the authority itself.

You enhance your own credibility when you show that an authority agrees with you, but that's all you do. You still have to show that the authority has based her reasons on sound evidence.

Evidence as Negotiated Agreement

When readers accept reports of evidence as evidence, they have tacitly agreed not to question it further. For example, imagine having this exchange with Sam:

Sam: Why don't you take a course in statistics? ~claim~

You: Why should I?

Sam: Employers are looking for people who can crunch numbers. ~reason~

If you believe that Sam is reliable, you might accept what he says without asking for the evidence behind his reason. It doesn't matter whether his statement is *really* a reason or *really* evidence. All Sam cares about is whether you *take* what he says as reliable and sufficient grounds for his claim.

But suppose you don't quite trust him, so you ask what he bases his reason on:

Sam: Employers are looking for people who can crunch numbers. ~reason~

You: Why do you think that? What do you base that on?

Sam: Business magazines say that personnel directors can't find liberal arts grads who can deal with numerical data. ~reported evidence~

Sam's response looks like reported evidence. But if you still have doubts, you might *treat* what he says not as a report of evidence, but only as one more subordinate reason, still in need of its own evidence.

Sam: Business magazines say that personnel directors can't find liberal arts grads who can deal with numerical data. ~reason~

You: Which ones say that?

Sam: I've researched this. *Business Today* says, "According to 100 personnel directors from Fortune 500 companies, companies can't find enough liberal arts grads who can deal with complex numerical data." ~quoted primary evidence~

You could question even that, asking

You: Well, have you seen the actual survey?

(At that point, of course, Sam is probably thinking he made a mistake offering you advice in the first place.)

In the first exchange, you accepted as a basis for Sam's claim a reason that you agreed to treat as a fact. But in the longer exchanges, you and Sam negotiated what you would agree to count as a reliable report of evidence. Sam may have offered what he thought was evidence, but you kept treating it as just one more reason. If he finally read you the words on the page and you rejected them too, the negotiation would end, because Sam would have nowhere to go from there.

Here's our point: In every argument, you and your partner have to agree on what to count as a reliable report of evidence before you can agree or disagree about reasons and claims. You may offer each other what you think is evidence, but you must be ready for someone to treat your statement not as evidence, but as just another reason still in need of its own support.

Radical Skepticism

When we start treating concepts like *evidence, reports of evidence,* and *reasons* as matters of agreement, we seem close to giving up on the metaphor of a "sound foundation" of objective evidence. And in fact, we do. Some philosophers, however, believe that if we accept as evidence anything less than utterly certain, objective fact, we surrender to hopeless relativity and subvert not just the quest for truth, but the very idea that it exists. How can we be sure of anything if we define evidence only as what we agree to?

But this definition of evidence is not threatening if we agree never to ignore sound arguments based on the best reports of the best evidence available. We could, for example, agree that the world is flat, and base our claim on the evidence of our senses. But to keep believing that, we would have to ignore reports of other intractable, undeniably better evidence that should lead us to believe that the world is round. That makes "truth" less a matter of capricious agreement and more a matter of thoughtful inquiry and argument.

To be sure, if readers want to be difficult, they can stubbornly refuse to agree to *any* evidence. It's a standard trick for derailing arguments. Not too long ago, for example, some critics charged that New Jersey state police stopped African-American drivers almost five times as often as they did whites. In a debate on that issue, one person kept questioning the data because, as he said, "everyone knows you can twist statistics to mean anything you want." In so doing, he refused to engage in a good faith argument because he denied even the possibility of reliable evidence.

So what do you say to someone who never accepts anything as uncontested but just keeps saying, *What is that based on? Can you show me more?* You can say nothing. Such a person has refused your offer to engage in a collaborative search for the truth.

Questions Have to Stop Somewhere

There is a story told by the anthropologist Clifford Geertz of an Englishman in India, who, upon being told that the world rests on the back of an elephant, asked "On what does the elephant stand?" "On the back of a turtle," he was told. "And on what does the turtle stand?" he asked. "On the back of another turtle." "And on what" the Englishman asked again, "does *that* turtle stand?" "Ah, Sahib," replied the Indian, "after that, it is turtles all the way down!"

> Arguments are a bit like that. Our claim is that the world rests on the elephants of our reasons; each elephant/reason stands on the back of a turtle of evidence. But when someone asks what that turtle rests on, we realize that our argument is potentially turtles all the way down. We can only hope that at some point readers stop asking about the next one.

WRITING PROCESS 6
Evidence

Thinking-Reading-Talking

Use Sources to Learn What Kind of Evidence Readers Trust

As you move through your academic career, you will read arguments in different fields. Note the kind of evidence they offer: Is it quantitative data? quotations? field observations? anecdotes? memory? Note also whether sources explain how the evidence was collected. Use what you find to guide you in making your own arguments, with this qualification: Teachers will usually want more evidence from you than they do from their colleagues, not (just) because they don't trust you, but because they want to see how you think.

Preparing and Planning

Taking Notes

When you assemble an argument based on sources, your most important preparation is taking notes. Unlike the writing you do when you talk back to your readings, you have to record accurately what you may need later. When you take notes, keep several things in mind:

Notes from Written Sources

• Record all bibliographic information:

> For a book, record the full title, author, and publication date, plus the name of the publisher and city. If you photocopy the title page, write down the year (from the copyright page, which is on the back side of the title page). Include the library call number: you may need your source again.

For a journal article, record the author, full title, volume number, and page numbers. Record the library call number of the journal.

For an Internet source, record the URL (Uniform Resource Locator) and any information you can find about the author of the text and the date it was posted and last changed.

- Summarize and paraphrase when the information is important, but its particular form of expression is not.

- Quote the exact words when they are striking or complex. If the passage or data table is long, photocopy it.

In your notes, always distinguish what you have quoted directly from what you summarize or paraphrase, and without fail distinguish what you paraphrase from your own thinking. (Use different colored ink or cards; on a computer, different fonts.) A week later, it's easy to think that what you took as notes are your own ideas, even your own words, when in fact they belong to someone else.

- Record the context.

Note whether the quote is a main point, a minor aside, a concession, etc. It is unfair to your source and reader to treat what a writer says in passing as something she would stand behind.

A technical note: When working with an Internet source, open a word-processing file at the same time. Rather than paraphrase or retype, cut and paste key information into the word-processing file. Be sure to add all relevant bibliographical information.

Notes from Interviews

- Record all identifying information—including the exact spelling of your source's name. Record the date and place of the interview.

- Tape-record the interview if you can. If you can't, try to get the exact words. If you transcribe from a tape recorder, edit out the *umm's* and *you know's,* but don't change anything else to make it sound better.

- Prepare your questions and bring them to the interview. Don't read them like a script, but use them to avoid wasting the time of whomever you are interviewing. Before you leave, glance over your questions to see if you have missed any important ones.

Notes from Observation

- Record the date and place of the observations and any relevant circumstantial detail before you start. If the location is relevant, sketch a map.

- Record data precisely. If you record quantitative data, create a data table or chart before you start.

Drafting

Quoting and Paraphrasing

When you report evidence, you have to quote directly, paraphrase, or summarize. The difference is not one of degree:

- When you quote directly, you reproduce the original text word-for-word, punctuation-for-punctuation.
- When you paraphrase, you substitute your words for the authors' in order to make a statement clearer or better fit its context. A paraphrase is usually shorter than the original, but it need not be.
- When you summarize, you reword and condense the original text to much less than its original length. When you do that, no one should be able to say, *"This sentence matches the one on page X."*

Paraphrasing or Summarizing in Disciplines that Do Not Focus on Words but on Data

In the natural sciences and the "harder" social sciences, writers draw on sources for one or more of three reasons:

- to review previous work in the common ground,
- to acknowledge alternative positions, or
- to use the source's findings (main claim) or data to support their own claims and reasons.

In these cases, readers care more about results than the exact words reporting them, so writers seldom quote sources directly; instead, they paraphrase or summarize.

When you paraphrase a source, cite the source as your field expects you to (citation forms vary from field to field). Include the author's name in your paraphrase if the source is important; otherwise, put the name in a citation:

> Several processes have been suggested as causes of the associative-priming effect. For instance, in their seminal study Meyer and Schvaneveldt (1971, p. 232) suggested two, *automatic (attention-free) spreading activation* in long-term memory and *location-shifting*. Neely (1976) similarly distinguished between a process of automatic-spreading activation in memory and a process that depletes the resources of the attentional mechanism. More recently, a further associative-priming process has been studied (de Groot, 1984).

The writer thought that Meyer and Schvaneveldt as well as Neely were important enough to name in her sentences, but cited de Groot only as a minor reference.

Quoting in Disciplines that Do Focus on Words

In the humanities, writers both quote and paraphrase. Use direct quotations to do the following:

- Cite the work of others as primary evidence.
- Focus on the specific words of a source because

    they have been important in other arguments,

    they are especially vivid or significant,

    you want to focus on exactly how a source says something,

    you want to state the source's case fairly before disputing it.

Paraphrase or summarize on these occasions:

- when you are more interested in the substance of reasons and evidence than in how they are expressed, and
- when you can say the same thing yourself more clearly.

Don't quote just because it's easier or because you don't trust yourself to report a source fairly.

Integrating Quotations into Your Sentences

When you offer quotations as evidence you must follow certain conventions. Those conventions differ in different fields, but here are some common ones:

- Introduce a quotation with a colon or an introductory phrase.

    Plumber describes the accident that took Princess Diana's life in terms that reflect the cost of too little government regulation: "People like Diana believe they are immune from ordinary dangers and so don't bother with things like seat-belts. But everyone who died was not belted, and the one who survived was" (343).

- Weave the quotation into your own sentence (be sure the quotation fits into the grammar of your part of the sentence):

    Plumber speaks in terms that remind us of the cost of too little government regulation when he points out that "everyone who died [in that crash] was not belted, and the one survivor was" (343).

(Note that when this writer changed the original, she used square brackets to indicate the change.)

Set off in an indented "block quote" quotations of three or more lines:

> After Oldenberg's balloon crashed into the ocean on his fifth failed attempt to circumnavigate the globe, his wife began to suspect there was more to his obsession than the "desire to achieve." She thought she found an answer in evolutionary biology:
>
> > The brain of the human male evolved under circumstances where caution was essential because risk was ever-present. When civilization

reduced the risk, men began to feel that their natural, evolved impulse toward caution made them weak and unmanly. When men create for themselves situations of extreme risk, it's not the risk they crave but a good reason to exercise their caution. (Idlewild, 135)

Avoiding Inadvertent Plagiarism

Don't paraphrase a source so closely that you seem to follow the source word for word, even though the actual words differ. For example, the following would be a plagiarizing paraphrase of this paragraph:

> If you paraphrase, avoid language so similar to the source that your words correspond to its words, despite the fact that the words differ. For instance, this plagiarizes what you just read.

To avoid inadvertently plagiarizing, read the original; sit back and think what it means; then express it in your own words without looking back. You are too close to the original if you can run your finger along a paraphrase and recognize the same sequence of concepts (not words). The following would not be plagiarism of this paragraph:

> Williams and Colomb suggest that to keep from plagiarizing, digest the meaning of a passage, summarize it in your own words, then compare the sequence of ideas in your summary with the source. (Colomb and Williams, 164).

Our advice applies to most fields in the humanities, but unspoken rules differ in different fields. In the law, for example, writers report a judge's ruling using the same words without quotation marks. In some social sciences, researchers often paraphrase the main finding of an experiment quite closely. Find and follow the practice in your particular field.

Revising

Assess Your Dependence on Quotations and Data

Inexperienced writers run opposing risks:

- They assemble a paper out of one quotation after another, quilting them into a pastiche with a little of their own work.
- They construct an argument out of opinion unsupported by evidence.

To diagnose whether you have done either, highlight every quotation and statement of data:

- If you highlight more than two-thirds of your paper, you may have a data dump.
- If you highlight less than one-third, you may not have enough evidence to support your reasons.

Working Collaboratively

Share Plans and Resources

Of all the jobs in assembling an argument, gathering evidence is one that your teacher may be happiest to see you share. If your teacher approves, work with others to formulate a plan for gathering evidence. As you all search for evidence, you are likely to find evidence helpful to one another.

Test Each Other's Drafts

Since evidence is what readers do not question at the time, your colleagues can help you anticipate what readers will accept. Once you have a draft, try this:

- Ask two colleagues to highlight the most and least reliable reports of evidence in your paper. If they disagree, ask them to explain.
- Ask other members of the group to evaluate how well your reports of evidence meet the four maxims of quality (pp. 150-52).

When someone questions a report of evidence as not close enough to a primary or secondary source, you must accept that judgment as appropriate for that reader. If that person is responding in good faith, there is no point debating whether he or she should have questions. If several colleagues have questions, assume your readers will too.

INQUIRIES

Reflections

1. How many removes from "the evidence itself" are the following?

   Fourteen notices of office hours posted in Blaine Hall were as follows: 3 hours: 1; 2 hours: 2; 1 hour: 9; 30 minutes: 2.

   Faculty in Blaine Hall keep inadequate office hours.

   The average number of office hours per week that faculty in Blaine Hall keep is about one.

2. Invent three or four plausible scenarios in which others will feel you are being rude to ask them to justify a report of evidence they have just offered. What makes your question impolite?

3. In the early history of science, an experimenter invited other scientists to witness an experiment so that they could testify to the accuracy of the data gathered. Would it seem reasonable today for a scientist to insist on watching data being collected before she accepted it as sound? Why not? How then do we today get "testimony" concerning the reliability of reports of research?

4. Should reproductions count as primary evidence? How about a video-tape of an event? An audiotape of a speech? A photograph? Would you trust a tape or photo more or less if you knew the person who offered it were technologically naïve? What if that person were a technological whiz? Why should that matter? Would it help to have witnesses who could testify about the circumstances in which the tape or photo was produced?

5. Are there situations in our everyday lives when we expect each other to be as hard-nosed about evidence as juries and scientists should be? Are there situations when we should not be hard-nosed about seeing the evidence for ourselves? How do you distinguish the two kinds of situations?

6. Some people think that just as there is no disputing taste, it is pointless to argue about values. Others say that we can argue about values, but that we have to use a different kind of evidence. Consider an argument about disputed values, such as whether it is morally wrong to help someone with a terminal illness commit suicide. What would count as evidence supporting reasons for or against such a position? What sources would be more authoritative than others? How do they derive their authority? Is there in fact a difference in the kind of evidence we use in arguments about values? Is there a difference in how we use it?

Task

7. Return to the old papers that we asked you to work on. Highlight in a dark color reports of evidence that you think no reader would have questioned. Then highlight in a lighter color reports of evidence that some readers might have. How "weighty" is the evidence in your argument? If you have highlighted more than two-thirds of your paper, it is probably too weighty. What would you add: more reasons, warrants, acknowledgments and responses? If, you have highlighted less than one-fourth of your paper, it is not weighty enough. How easily could you get more evidence?

Projects

8. Analyze a magazine ad as an argument. (Select one that's half a page or larger.) Assume that the main claim is an unexpressed *Therefore you should buy this product.* What does the ad offer as reasons for buying the product? What does it offer as a report of the evidence? If it is a picture, how did the ad "spin" that report?

9. Look at the advertising in four or five magazines that appeal to people with different demographic profiles. For example, a teen magazine, a techie magazine, an intellectual magazine, a sports magazine, a woman's magazine, etc. How do they differ in the ways advertisers try to get their

particular readers to buy products? Do the ads in the same publication use similar kinds of reasons and evidence? Do ads for similar products use similar kinds of evidence even for different readers?

10. A recent book that uses stories as evidence is *I, Rigoberta Menchú,* a searing account of atrocities allegedly committed by the Guatemalan army. Written by Rigoberta Menchú Tum, the human rights activist and winner of the Nobel Peace Prize, the book has become highly controversial required reading on hundreds of campuses because it sparks a debate over the "higher value" of falsehood over truth. The controversy began when prestigious schools like Stanford required the book in general education courses, in some cases replacing writers like Shakespeare. Then in 1998, David Stoll, a specialist in Mayan history, showed that Menchú had fabricated some of her most sensational stories:

   • She described herself as a child working in near-slave conditions, unable to speak Spanish until adulthood, but she had actually attended Catholic boarding schools.

   • She describes acts of violence as though she witnessed them; in fact, she was away at school most of the time.

   • She says she watched the Guatemalan military burn her brother alive, but she wasn't there when it happened and the military probably did not do it.

   • She says another brother starved to death, but she had no such brother.

   • She says that her family lands were confiscated by wealthy landowners; in fact, they were lost to her father's in-laws.

   Menchú at first denied that she had committed "purposeful inaccuracies," adding, "I didn't find anything in these reports that changes the fact that my people are dead. And that is my truth" (*New York Times,* January 21, 1999). Later, she admitted some inaccuracies, but has yet to recant her story.

   Her critics were severe: one nominated her for the "Nobel Prize for Lying." Most of her supporters echoed her defense that she told a "larger truth." Some attacked Stoll for valuing mere fact over a "higher" truth. Others suggested that facts don't even matter: "Menchú made it clear from the outset that [she] had a political purpose, . . . to expose the atrocities committed by the Guatemalan army. This was not the fruit of some judicial investigation striving to be fair" (*Guardian,* December 16, 1998). But even before Stoll had exposed her, her admirers had argued that an oppressed person has an authenticity that lets her speak for all her people; that what matters is not truth, but personal, ethical, and economic motives that break the "silence of the oppressed."

Suppose that Menchú's critics are right: What she says she saw, she did not. In fact, some of the things she said happened never happened at all. But also suppose that in a sense she is right: things like those she described did happen to people like her and her family. Should she have described her work as a work of fiction? Would it have had the same impact? Would it have been effective to add incidents that happened to others without pretending they happened to her? List reasons for accepting or rejecting her "larger truth" defense. Which weigh more with you?

11. Given what you learned about lying in the readings, do you think Rigoberta Menchú lied? If so, was it an acceptable lie? List your reasons for saying so. What general principle (warrant) would you offer to explain why you make that judgment?

12. The Greek philosopher Aristotle argued that fiction describes events more truthfully than a history. A history, he said, has to stick to the facts, whereas fiction can describe things more plausibly—as they should have occurred, not just as they happened to. Can you think of a way to defend Menchú's book based on Aristotle's idea of truthfulness? Sketch the major steps in such an argument. Would *you* accept such a defense?

WRITING PROJECTS 6
Project 6.1

Context.   It is an old belief that "factual" or "scientific" truth (the kind we establish by arguments based on evidence) is not the only truth. But in recent years, some postmodern theorists have argued that it should not be the only kind of truth we accept in fields such as law or history. It is an act of political oppression, they say, to require just the facts.

Scenario.   In 1999, six Nobel Peace Prize winners gathered for a conference on the future of human rights and social justice. The event was such a success that several colleges in your state are jointly sponsoring a similar conference at the state capitol. Among the speakers will be Rigoberta Menchú, but local political groups are trying to get her removed from the conference because of the controversy over her book (see Inquiry 10). As the student representative from your school on the organizing committee, you have been appointed to the subcommittee assigned to respond to those who oppose Menchú's participation.

Task 1.   Your subcommittee has asked you to write a brief summary of the controversy. (You can find a list of articles, including abstracts, in the newspaper databases available in most libraries.) Be sure not to represent the controversy as a simple for-or-against debate.

Task 2.   The subcommittee has decided to respond to what it sees as an unfairly one-sided presentation of the issue by the opponents. Your assignment is to draft an essay describing the controversy, which will be published in the student newspapers of all participating colleges. Above all, the committee wants you to represent the different positions fairly, including their support for their claims.

Task 3.   The subcommittee wants to make the entire Menchú episode a learning experience for those who attend the conference. It will include in the conference program a collection of essays on the issue of factual evidence versus larger truths. Your assignment is to write an essay taking a stand on the issue. Since the subcommittee wants these essays to be models of fair argument, be sure that your argument acknowledges the strengths of the other positions.

Project 6R

Scenario.   Your teacher has made it clear that he will focus on the quality of the evidence in your research paper.

Task.   For each report of evidence, summarize why you think it is (1) accurate, (2) precise, (3) representative, and (4) reliable.

SAMPLE ESSAY

Task 1.   Return to your marked-up pages evaluating the evidence in "Guns in America" (Chapter 5, p. 142). Select the four most important items of evidence. Evaluate each in terms of the four maxims of quality (pp. 150-52).

Task 2.   Compare the evidence offered in support of the first major reason, "guns were not popular in America until after the Civil War," with the evidence offered in support of the second "the reasons people began to buy guns had more to do with money than with patriotism." Which evidence is stronger? Why? Should the writer have downplayed the reason with the weaker evidence? Why or why not? What other options might the writer have for acknowledging this disparity in the evidence?

Task 3.   Here again is the introduction to "Guns in America." Identify its elements by picking out the common ground, destabilizing condition, cost or consequences, and solution or promise of solution.

Guns in America

1   If you listen to the NRA, owning a gun is the ultimate symbol of American freedom and democracy. So most people believe them when they say that gun ownership has been a part of America since the Revolution and that it is a violation of
basic American beliefs when the government tries to take away the people's guns.
5 But this is just propaganda. The claim that for our forefathers owning guns was a
patriotic duty is erroneous. History shows that guns were not popular in America

until after the Civil War, and that the reasons people began to buy guns had more to do with money than with patriotism. People should not be duped into thinking that supporting gun control laws is unpatriotic or un-American.

Now read this revised introduction with the new title, "The Minuteman Myth: The True Story of Guns in America." Identify its elements by picking out the common ground, destabilizing condition, cost or consequences, and solution or promise of solution.

The Minuteman Myth: The True Story of Guns in America

1   When the English colonists sailed to America, they brought to this continent many ideas that made America what it is today: religious freedom, dedication to liberty, and the belief that people should govern themselves. Did they also bring over the American love of guns? One of the first laws passed in Jamestown,
5   Virginia, required every man to own a gun for defending the settlement. By the Revolution, most of the colonies had laws requiring citizens to own guns (Davidson, 1998), and after the Revolution, since the federal government had no army, local governments were required to have a militia made up of gun-owning citizens (*Economist,* 1999). Also, the Bill of Rights included the idea that the
10   safety of the country depended on people owning guns: "A well-regulated militia being necessary to the security of a free State, the right of the people to keep and bear Arms shall not be infringed."

Today the government passes laws, not to require citizens to own guns, but to restrict them from owning guns the government thinks are dangerous, such as
15   assault rifles. Supporters of gun control say we need laws because of all the crazies and criminals who get their hands on guns: Lee Harvey Oswald, John Hinkley, the Columbine killers, drug pushers, and many others. Opponents of gun control like the NRA try to offset this by talking about gun-owning American heroes from history, such as the Minutemen of the Revolution and Daniel Boone
20   (NRA, 1999). They say that even if bad people get guns, good people need them too for the same reason that the colonists and the other historical heroes needed them, namely to defend themselves and their families. Besides, owning a gun is presented as the ultimate symbol of American freedom and democracy. So most people believe them when they say that gun ownership has been a part of
25   America since the Revolution and that it is a violation of basic American beliefs when the government tries to take away the people's guns.

But this is just propaganda. People should not be duped into thinking that supporting gun control laws is unpatriotic or un-American. The gun control opponents' claim about Americans always owning guns because we believed that
30   owning guns was a patriotic duty is erroneous. History shows that guns were not popular in America until after the Civil War, and that the reasons people began to buy guns had more to do with money than with patriotism.

1. Which introduction makes the writer seem more knowledgeable? More evenhanded?
2. How does the inclusion of evidence affect your response to the "Minuteman" introduction?
3. How does the new title better prepare readers for the rest of the essay?
4. How does the expanded common ground better prepare readers?
5. How do the new title and expanded common ground change your perception of the writer's ethos?

CHAPTER 6 IN A NUTSHELL

About Your Argument . . .

No skill is more useful than distinguishing reasons, evidence, and reports of evidence *from your reader's point of view.* You need more and better evidence when you want readers to change important beliefs, to do something costly or difficult, or to accept a solution that may create new problems. Your biggest challenge will be to find enough evidence to satisfy your readers, because we all tend to be satisfied with less evidence than our readers want.

Once you think you have enough evidence, evaluate it: Is it accurate, precise, representative, and reliable? Then be aware of the kind of evidence you are offering and question it in ways appropriate to its kind:

- Memories are always unreliable, because they are shaped by what we want to believe and by our inclination to turn them into a good story.
- Photographs and recordings are never objective. Even when they haven't been doctored, they depict just a slice of what they seem to represent.
- Quantitative data can be represented in many different ways, and each way gives it a "spin."
- Reports from authorities may be evidence only of what they believe. Distinguish what they offer as reasons from the evidence they report.

Remember that you ask readers to accept reports of evidence in lieu of the evidence itself, so they must be confident that you report it accurately. Along with warrants, evidence is one of the two anchors that readers must agree on before you can even make an argument.

. . . and About Writing It

When you gather and use quotations, think about readers: Are they likely to value the exact words of your sources or will they be satisfied with paraphrases? In general, those in the humanities are more likely to value the exact words; those in other fields will accept close paraphrases, when the data are from observation and are quantifiable rather than verbal.

When you copy notes into your argument, be aware of how easy it is to forget that what you copy is not your own words, but those of your sources, so scrupulously distinguish in your notes between your own words and those from a source. If you are using a computer to record quotations, use a distinctive font. If you write them out, do so on different colored cards or in different colored ink—whatever will help you distinguish your own words from those of your sources.

CHAPTER 7

Warranting Claims and Reasons

In this chapter we address the difficult task of deciding whether you have connected reasons and claims soundly. Even when reasons are true and based on reliable evidence, readers have to believe that each reason is relevant to the claim it supports. When that relevance is in question, you show it through warrants.

Once readers see why your problem matters to them, they look for reasons that support your solution and for the evidence on which you base those reasons. If readers don't find them, they won't find your argument. But even if they do, they may still reject your claim if they do not see why your reasons should *count* as reasons. If readers might question their relevance, you have to offer one more element of argument to convince them that your reasoning is sound.

For example, suppose someone opposed a needle-exchange program for drug addicts with this argument:

> This needle-exchange program makes the drug problem worse, ₍claim₎ because it causes people to use more drugs. ₍reason₎

To back up that reason, the program's critics would have to offer data showing that those who participate in the program *in fact* use more drugs than they did before, specifically because of the needle-exchange program. That would be an argument built around a claim supported by a reason based on (reported) evidence.

But suppose those criticizing the program made this argument:

> Since the program is making drug use safer, ₍reason₎ it will encourage more people to use drugs. ₍claim₎

In that case, no one would ask for evidence about the added safety of the needle exchanges because that's a given. But they might charge that while the reason is true—the program does make drug use safer—the claim just doesn't follow from that reason: *Why do you think making needles safer to use encourages drug use? It just doesn't follow!* What they ask for is not evidence about the *particular* needle exchange program, but a *general* principle that covers *all* such programs:

> Whenever you make risky behavior safer, you encourage more people to engage in it. _{warrant} Since this program makes drug use safer, _{reason} it will encourage more people to use drugs. _{claim}

That kind of argument relieves those making it of the need to provide *any evidence at all* about this particular needle-exchange program, because they believe in a general principle that (if true) lets them make their claim about *all* such programs.

That general principle is a **warrant.** It states more than a static belief about a particular needle-exchange program or even about needle-exchange programs in general. That warrant tells us how to think about a vast number of other programs intended to reduce the cost of many other forms of risky behavior, from the distribution of condoms in schools to federally subsidized hurricane insurance for those who build houses on ocean fronts. Claims, reasons, and reports of evidence constitute the core of your argument, but warrants are the glue that binds them together. And when you are putting together your arguments, warrants tell you how to assemble the core; they tell readers what reasons go with what claims.

How Warrants Express Assumptions

Consider this exchange:

> Harry: Princess Diana's death was not a huge tragedy _{claim} because her image was created by press agents and the media. _{reason}
>
> Maude: Her image was certainly a media creation, but why does that mean her death was not tragic?

A question like that asks us to think not about the facts but about our reasoning.

> Harry: True, her death was sad, but you don't have a real tragedy when a person who dies young is not really a substantial person, but just the image of one. _{warrant} Di was entirely a media creation with little substance, _{reason} so her death was not really a tragedy. _{claim}

Maude asked Harry not about his facts, whether Princess Di was or was not a media creation, but about his reasoning. In return, Harry offered Maude not more facts about Princess Di, but a warrant, a general principle applying to *any* such person. That warrant explains why he thinks his reason is relevant to his claim. If Maude accepts the warrant and reason, she must accept the claim.

At first glance warrants might seem not much different from reasons, and to be sure, it's easy to confuse them. Consider this argument:

Though Franklin Roosevelt would not appear in public in his wheelchair or be photographed in it, his federal monument should depict him in his chair. _{claim} He overcame a great disability to become a great leader, _{statement of support 1} and a great leader should be remembered as much for the challenges he overcame as for his achievements. _{statement of support 2}

The two supporting statements both feel like reasons. In fact, in ordinary conversation, we might call both of them reasons:

The Federal monument dedicated to Franklin Roosevelt should depict him in his wheelchair. _{claim} *The first reason* is that he overcame a great disability to become a great leader. _{statement of support 1} *The second reason* is that a great leader should be remembered as much for the challenges he overcame as for his achievements. _{statement of support 2}

But those two statements support the claim in such different ways that we have to use different terms for them if we want to understand how arguments work.

- The first statement refers specifically to Roosevelt and to Roosevelt alone. It is a *specific* reason to support the *specific* claim that a *specific* monument should depict Roosevelt in his wheelchair.

- The second statement has nothing specifically to do with Roosevelt or his particular monument. It is a *general* principle stating that we should remember *any* great leader for overcoming a challenge *of any kind.* If we believe that Roosevelt was a great leader who overcame great obstacles, then he's covered by that generalization, a generalization we call a warrant.

Warrants vs. Reasons

In ordinary talk, it does no harm to call a warrant a reason. Warrants are, after all, reasons for connecting a reason and a claim. One student called warrants *extended reasons.* And in fact, that captures what a warrant does: it "extends" over a reason and claim, holding them together. Other students have asked us, *Doesn't a warrant just say the same thing as the reason and claim, but in a different way?* In a way, it does. A warrant covers the same conceptual territory as the reason and claim it connects. But a warrant covers a much larger territory as well, one with an indefinite number of other reasons and claims, most of which have not yet been thought of: not only leaders and challenges we know of, but countless others we don't.

What Warrants Look Like and How They Work

Warrants come in all shapes and sizes, but they always have two parts. One names a general circumstance:

Someone is a media creation with no substance.

The second states a general inference based on that first circumstance:

> If so, that person's death might be sad, but it is no tragedy.

Put together, the two parts constitute a warrant that explicitly states a general principle of reasoning:

> When someone is a media creation with no substance, that person's death might be sad, but it is no tragedy.

When we state warrants in these two parts, we state a condition and something we can infer from it. We can state their relationship explicitly:

> **When** a dog scratches a lot, _{Part1} it may have fleas. _{Part2}

> **If** a person has cold hands, _{Part1} that person has a warm heart. _{Part2}

We can also state the parts of those warrants without explicit connecting words:

> Scratching dogs _{Part1} may have fleas. _{Part2}

> Cold hands, _{Part1} warm heart. _{Part2}

There is no one right way to state a warrant, but for our purposes we will state them in the same way every time, not because that's how you should too, but because it is the clearest way for us to explain them. We will follow this formula:

> Whenever X, Y.

Sometimes, other introductory words work better: *if, when, if and only if*. But *whenever* is especially useful because it encourages us to consider how widely the warrant actually applies. *Whenever* implies that a warrant is true under all circumstances, unless it is explicitly qualified (as this sentence/warrant illustrates).

Warrants are most familiar to us as proverbs:

> When the cat's away the mice will play.

Schematically, we can represent that warrant like this:

> Authority absent   —[we infer]→   those under that authority will slack off.

If you believe that *general* principle, then you can link a *specific* instance of authority being absent to a *specific* instance of someone's slacking off. Schematically, the link looks like this:

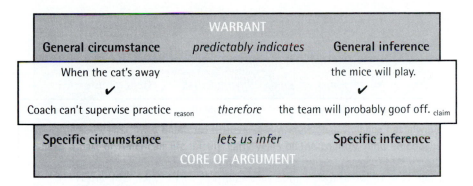

The check marks indicate that we think the specific circumstance and inference qualify as good examples of the general circumstance and inference. (We'll see cases where they don't.) We can reverse the order, if we choose:

WARRANT		
General inference	*predictably follows from*	General circumstance
The mice will play		while the cat's away.
✔		✔
The team will probably goof off _{claim}	*because*	coach can't supervise practice. _{reason}
Specific inference	*follows from*	Specific circumstance
CORE OF ARGUMENT		

The more assumptions, beliefs, and values you share with readers, the fewer warrants you need to state. In fact, if you are on culturally intimate terms with your readers, they may feel you are talking down to them if you state what they think should go without saying (imagine someone who keeps repeating proverbs). But when the experiences and values of your readers differ from yours, you usually have to state your important assumptions, values, and definitions explicitly as warrants.

More important, if you think your readers might reject your warrants, you then have to treat them as claims that you must support with their own reasons and evidence. It is another way you "thicken" your argument. For example, here is an argument that some people accept:

> The lyrics of gangsta rap are so degrading _{reason} that they should be banned from radio and TV. _{claim}

Here is a general warrant that links that specific reason to that specific claim:

> Degrading language should be barred from public airwaves. _{warrant}

We can rephrase that warrant into our standard form, *Whenever X, Y:*

WARRANT		
General circumstance	*predictably indicates*	**General inference**
Whenever language is degrading, ✔		it should be banned from public airwaves. ✔
Some rap lyrics are degrading _{reason} *therefore* they should be banned from radio. _{claim}		
Specific circumstance	*lets us infer*	**Specific inference**
CORE OF ARGUMENT		

If you accept the warrant and reason, then you must accept the claim.

Warrants as Expressions of Cultural Codes

Warrants can help us understand why intercultural communication is so difficult. In multicultural situations, we often wonder how others can fail to reach a conclusion that seems natural to us. The problem is that while the processes of everyone's thinking are alike, different communities start from different assumptions. Those assumptions are not just static beliefs, but dynamic principles that tell us how to reason about specific facts.

For example, suppose we say of a child *She really stands above the crowd because she thinks for herself.* We might then conclude, *She'll probably become an influential person,* because we have an assumption that we state as a warrant something like this:

When a person stands out, that person is likely to influence others.

But the Japanese have a proverb that warns people not to stand out:

The nail that sticks up gets hammered down.

That means that when someone stands out from the crowd, that person will be—rightly—forced to conform. So we have the same fact, a child standing out from the rest, but different communities draw different inferences from it because they reason from different assumptions. Such differences cause many cultural conflicts.

How Warrants Fail

In a sense, it's easy to argue over evidence. It's just there or it's not. But it is more challenging to make an argument about warrants, because readers can question your warrants for four reasons.

- Readers may not see your warrant.
- They may think it is not true.
- They may think your warrant does not "cover" your reason or your claim.
- The warrant may not be appropriate to your specific readers.

What Is Your Warrant?

A warrant can fail if it is left unexpressed and readers cannot imagine it. Consider this little argument:

> Our school needs more writing tutors _{claim} because we are unsure our educa-tion is worth our rising tuition costs. _{reason 1} Tuition has gone up faster than inflation. _{reason 2} In 1997, inflation was 2.4%, but tuition rose 5.1%; in 1998, inflation was 2.1%, but tuition rose 6.7%. _{report of evidence}

The dean might respond:

> You're right that tuition has gone up faster than inflation. You may even be right that we need more writing tutors. But why do you think we need them *because* you are unsure you are getting your money's worth? Why does your reason—you're not sure you're getting your money's worth—*have anything to do with* your claim—that we need more tutors?

That is a hard question. The dean is saying not that she rejects either the reason or the claim, but that she can't even imagine a warrant that could link them.

WARRANT		
General circumstance	*predictably indicates*	**General inference**
???????????????		???????????????.
✔		✔
Not sure getting money's worth _{reason}	*therefore*	need writing tutors. _{claim}
Specific circumstance	*lets us infer*	**Specific inference**
CORE OF ARGUMENT		

So the first way a warrant can fail is that readers can't even imagine it.

If you can't quickly think of a warrant that connects your reason to your claim, your readers probably can't either. So you'll need to find one to state explicitly. Start by replacing the specific terms in your reason and claim with general ones:

Specific	We are not sure we are getting our **money's worth** from our **tuition**, so we need **more writing tutors**.
General	We are not sure we are getting a **value** in return for our **cost**, so we are entitled to **more services**.

Then rephrase the general version with a *whenever:*

> Whenever we are uncertain that we are getting a value in return for our cost, we are entitled to more services.

You can decide whether your readers will accept a warrant only after you can state it for yourself. That one seems dubious.

Is Your Warrant True?

A warrant fails when readers see it, but reject it as untrue. Recall the argument about gangsta rap:

> The lyrics of gangsta rap are vulgar _{reason} so they should be banned from radio and TV. _{claim} Whenever language is degrading, it should not be allowed to circulate in public. _{warrant}

Someone might respond with a warrant that overturns that one:

> I can't agree, because whenever we express our ideas, the Constitution bars anyone from interfering with that right. _{competing warrant} So even though you might not like the lyrics in gangsta rap, they have the same constitutional protection as any expression of ideas.

Or that person might also respond not with a competing warrant but with a counter-example that implies the original warrant is not true:

> I can't agree. According to the Supreme Court, the First Amendment protects sexually explicit movies that are degrading to women. _{counter-example} So even though you may not like the degrading language in gangsta rap, it has the same constitutional protection.

If the counter-example is relevant, it contradicts the original warrant and implies a competing one.

Schematically, the counterargument looks like this:

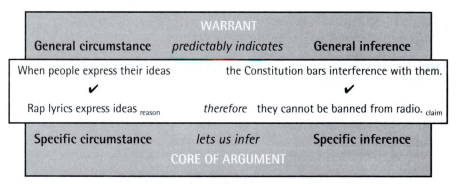

Now the question of whether such lyrics should be banned turns into a question of which warrant is more relevant or basic to our beliefs. To settle that, the person maing the argument would have to treat those dueling warrants as claims needing their own reasons, evidence, and yet more warrants.

We might also accept some warrants as true *in general,* but not when people try to use them to justify extreme cases. What about the following argument?

I helped you wash your car, _{reason} so you should help me paint my house. _{claim} After all, one good turn deserves another. _{warrant}

If your friend did help you wash your car, you might feel you owed him something, but maybe not as much as he asks:

> Yes, you did help me wash my car, and yes, in general one good turn deserves another, but only when the magnitude of the returned favor is proportional to the original one.

In other words, the warrant is generally true, but it has limitations. And once you think of one limitation, you can think of more:

> . . . and so long as I am capable of doing it, and so long as the favor is requested reasonably close to the first good turn, and so long as . . .

When you state a warrant like *One good turn deserves another,* you rarely, if ever, add the obvious limitations: *Of course you can do only what you are able to; of course you expect that a returned favor won't be asked for thirty years later.* All that goes without saying, so you don't say it. What's tricky about using warrants is not just that we usually take them for granted; even when we do state them, we also take for granted their default limitations.

Does Your Warrant Actually Apply to the Reason and Claim?

This next problem with warrants is the most difficult to grasp. Consider this argument:

> I helped you wash your car, _{reason} so you should help me cheat on my test. _{claim} After all, one good turn deserves another. _{warrant}

Represented graphically, it look likes this:

WARRANT		
General circumstance	*predictably indicates*	**General inference**
When someone does you a good turn		you should do one in return.
✔		?
I helped you wash your car _{reason}	*therefore*	you should help me cheat on my test. _{claim}
Specific circumstance	*lets us infer*	**Specific inference**
	CORE OF ARGUMENT	

The warrant is true. So if your friend did in fact help you wash your car, how could you refuse to help him cheat? You might say,

> True, one good turn deserves another, but in this case, helping you cheat on a test *does not count as* a legitimate example of "a good turn." In fact, it would be a bad turn.

The warrant just does not apply to the claim, because the claim is not a legitimate example of the warrant.

This point is complicated, so here is another example:

Tarik: You should buy a handgun. _{claim}

Leah: Why is that?

Tarik: The crime rate is up. _{reason}

Leah: Why should the fact that crime is up mean I should buy a handgun?

Tarik: When your personal security is threatened, you should take reasonable precautions to protect yourself. _{warrant}

Leah: I agree that when we are threatened we should take reasonable precautions to protect ourselves, and maybe the crime rate is up. But first, the crime rate being up *does not count for me as* an instance of my security being threatened, and second, even if it did, buying a handgun *would not count for me as* a reasonable precaution.

Leah is saying that for her neither Tarik's reason nor his claim *count as* an example of being threatened or taking reasonable precautions. Schematically, it looks like this:

WARRANT		
General circumstance	*predictably indicates*	**General inference**
When your personal security is threatened		you should take reasonable precautions to protect yourself.
X		X
The crime rate is up _{reason}	*therefore*	you should buy a handgun. _{claim}
Specific circumstance	*lets us infer*	**Specific inference**
CORE OF ARGUMENT		

It might seem that warrants are too abstract, too general for us to feel strongly about them. But we do. You use warrants to express your deepest values. You use them as certain truths to drive home a point. When you are asked to change such beliefs, you have to change who you are. It is far easier to change the facts we believe than to change something as entrenched as our values and definitions.

Is Your Warrant Appropriate to Your Readers' Community?

Warrants can fail in one more way, having less to do with truth or reasoning, than with their appropriateness to particular readers. We all (or at least most of us) accept some warrants:

When people tell many lies, we eventually distrust everything they say.

Other warrants reflect the beliefs of different historical communities. Here are two that mark an important change from one period in history to another. The first guided the reasoning in most of the world, until 600 or so years ago.

> When evidence contradicts traditional beliefs and authorities, ignore the evidence.

The second replaced it in the reasoning of many European thinkers; it characterizes what some call the modern skeptical mind:

> When evidence contradicts a traditional belief or authority, question the belief or authority.

There are also beliefs that most of us share, but not all other societies do:

> When an action is protected by a Constitution, government may not interfere with it.

As communities become smaller, they share increasingly specialized warrants. Here's one shared by only a few specialists:

> When creatures engage in complex behavior they have not learned, that behavior is probably innate.

Every "community of discourse" is defined by its deep beliefs and assumptions that members express as warrants. That's why those who live in different communities differ on more than just the "facts" they happen to believe. It's why they can agree on the facts but still disagree. For example, first-year law students often have a hard time "thinking like a lawyer." Like most of us, they hold beliefs based on common sense, some of which they have to unlearn. We can state one of those common sense beliefs as a warrant:

> When someone does another an injustice, courts should correct it.

Seems reasonable. But part of the painful education of law students is learning that such warrants do not always apply in the community of lawyers and judges, because other warrants may trump them. For example,

> When people fail to meet legal obligations, even inadvertently, they must suffer the consequences.

More specifically,

> When old people forget to pay their real estate taxes, others can buy their house for a few dollars and evict them.

That warrant leads to common sense injustice, but if buyers obey the law, the house is theirs. Against their most decent instincts, law students have to learn that justice is not what most of us think it should be, but what the rules of law say it shall be.

Those new to a field often find its arguments baffling, because professionals writing to professionals leave only fleeting glimpses of their assumptions, enough for experts, but not for newcomers. None of us can avoid moments in our education when we feel baffled because those at home in a community have not made clear the foundations of their reasoning. We learn those unstated ways of reasoning only from experience.

Information Overload?

If you are reacting as did many students who tried out this book before it was published, you may be feeling overwhelmed with detail. We've given you a lot to think about and, what's even harder, to put into practice. So don't be discouraged if you are feeling like the student who e-mailed us this question:

> Why am I feeling less in control of making arguments as I read more about them? I feel like I'm writing worse, not better.

What we told him may encourage you:

> Some researchers tested new medical students to learn how well they could read X-rays for lung cancer. They found something odd. New med students quickly learned to do it pretty well, but as they gained more experience, they got worse. Then they got better at it again. The researchers concluded that at first, medical students saw exactly what they were told to see. But as they learned more about lungs, chests, and everything else that casts an X-ray shadow, they got confused: The more they learned, the less able they were to sort it out. But once they did learn to sort it out, they could see what was relevant and got better at it again.

That's probably what's making you feel less in control. You have more to think about than you did a few weeks ago. But it's not just that: you are probably also setting higher demands on yourself, because you see more clearly what you must do. So as paradoxical as it may seem, your temporary confusion is a sign of progress. Or as the saying goes, if you're not confused, you haven't been paying attention.

Review: A Test Case

Warrants are as hard to explain as they are to understand, so here is a review. (If you think you understand warrants, you can skip to p. 187.)

> Phil: A lot of people condemn gangsta rap but I think it should be accepted as legitimate artistic expression _{claim} because it reflects the experience of many who listen to it. _{reason}

> Mary: It may reflect the experience of many who listen to it. But why does that count as a reason for accepting it as legitimate artistic expression?

1. What is your warrant?
Mary can't imagine a warrant that would link the reason and claim, so she asks Phil to explain his reasoning by stating the principle that warrants him to connect his particular reason to his particular claim. He might say this:

When an artistic work reflects the experiences of those who enjoy it, it should not be condemned.

Now that Mary knows the warrant, she might ask three more questions.

2. Is your warrant true?

Mary might say of Phil's warrant, *That's just not so.* If she does disagree, then Phil has to treat his warrant as a subclaim inside his larger argument, and so support it with its own reasons, evidence, acknowledgments, and even its own higher warrants. Mary, however, might think that while the warrant is true *in general,* it does not apply to *all* artistic expression, such as anti-Semitic art or music. Mary can express her exception in a variety of ways. She might say this:

> Such music should be condemned if it degrades human dignity. When art degrades human dignity, it should not be accepted. _{counter warrant}

She has offered a counterwarrant of her own that she thinks trumps Phil's warrant. If Phil anticipates that objection, then he has to make an argument that Mary should accept even racist lyrics as legitimate artistic expression, thereby thickening his argument yet again.

3. Are your specific reasons and claims legitimate examples of your warrant?

Here it gets tricky, because you have to analyze whether the reason counts as a good example of the reason side of the warrant, and then whether the claim counts as a good example of the claim side of the warrant.

3.1. Does your reason match your warrant?

Will a reader think that the specific circumstance counts as a good example of the general circumstance side of the warrant? That is, does the warrant "cover" the reason?

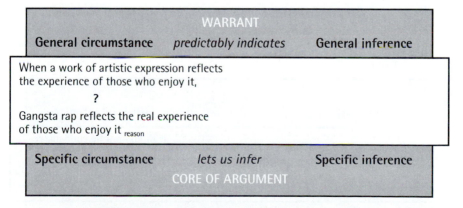

Mary might accept the first half of Phil's warrant as true—we should not ban artistic expression that reflects the experiences of those who enjoy it, even when it degrades others. But she might still argue that gangsta rap *does not qualify* as artistic expression, and therefore Phil's warrant does not cover his reason.

In other words, before Mary can accept Phil's reason as relevant to his claim, she must agree that it is a good example of the general circumstance described in the reason side of the warrant. But if she thinks that the reason side of the warrant does not "cover" the reason, then Phil has to make an argument that gangsta rap is in fact an example of artistic expression.

On the other hand, Phil might decide that he can't make that argument to Mary's satisfaction. If so, he could try to revise his warrant to accommodate his reason:

WARRANT		
General circumstance	*predictably indicates*	**General inference**
When a **popular** form of expression reflects the experience of those who enjoy it,		it should not be condemned.
?		
Gangsta rap reflects the real experience of those who enjoy it _reason_	**so**	it should be accepted as a legitimate form of artistic expression. _claim_
Specific circumstance	*lets us infer*	**Specific inference**
CORE OF ARGUMENT		

Now the warrant fits the reason (if we believe gangsta rap is a popular form of expression), but is this warrant still true? Mary might defend serious artistic expression from censorship but not what she considers to be merely popular drivel. (We said this was not easy.)

3.2 Does your claim match your warrant?

Let's assume that Mary finally accepts Phil's warrant and reason. She *still* might reject his argument if she thinks his *claim* does not match his warrant:

WARRANT		
General circumstance	*predictably indicates*	**General inference**
		it should not be condemned.
		?
		it should be accepted as a legitimate form of artistic expression. _claim_
Specific circumstance	*lets us infer*	**Specific inference**
CORE OF ARGUMENT		

> She might argue that *accepting* lyrics is not an example of *not condemning* them. If she does, Phil will have to change his claim or the claim side of his warrant, or argue that accepting is an example of not condemning.

Now we see why complex issues are so hard to resolve. Those with different values, assumptions, and definitions keep asking one question after another, objecting to the truth of a warrant or its fit to a reason or claim. You can also see why it is important to think about readers. If you imagine their objections, you can anticipate them. You can't answer them all, but if you acknowledge a few important ones, you encourage readers to see you as more thoughtful than most writers.

You probably are now asking the next question: *OK, I see how important warrants are, but how and when do I use them?* We'll address that question in the Writing Process section at the end of this chapter.

EXAMPLE

The History of a Warrant

> *In this passage, Suzanna Sherry explains the history of a cherished, but contested warrant: our constitutional guarantee of free speech. She shows how the Supreme Court expanded that warrant by narrowing one of its exceptions: the warrant now covers more kinds of supposedly dangerous speech because the court changed the "dangerous speech exception" to cover fewer instances.*

Legislatures have . . . frequently attempted to restrict speech because they believed it to be dangerous. Just before the Civil War, many southern states put abolitionists in prison for publishing their views. During World War I, the government jailed bolshevist sympathizers . . . because they urged men to resist the draft. The McCarthy era saw nationwide crackdowns on anyone with leftist beliefs . . . And during the war in Vietnam, the government tried to prevent publication of the infamous Pentagon Papers.

The justification for these limits on speech is always the same: Especially in times of crisis, we cannot allow speech that will incite lawlessness or endanger lives. It was not until the 1960s that the courts began to reject that justification [that is, that warrant]. Recognizing that all speech is an incitement designed to persuade the listener to action, the Supreme Court, in 1969, specified very narrow circumstances under which a speaker can be liable for the harm that results from his speech: only when the speech is intended to produce, and is likely to produce, imminent lawless action. In other words, we can blame the speaker for the actions of others only when "the evil apprehended is so imminent that it may befall before there is an opportunity for full discussion." Why? Because to do otherwise is to forge a link between speech and action—a link that might be found in any unpleasant speech.

Source: Suzanna Sherry, "I Hate What They Say, but I Won't Stop Them," *Washington Post,* February 14, 1999.

WRITING PROCESS 7
Warrants

Preparing and Planning

Identify Your Key Assumptions

When you plan an argument, think not just about what you intend to say but about what you think usually goes without saying that you might have to say anyway: *What do I believe that my readers must also believe (but may not) before they will think that my reasons are relevant to my claims?* You will find this the hardest question to answer, because we all take our deepest beliefs for granted, rarely questioning them from someone else's point of view.

Suppose you want to argue that the drinking age should be lowered to eighteen because eighteen-year-olds are subject to the draft: What general principle must your readers *already* believe before they will accept that argument? Is it one of the ones in Pamela White's column ("Drinking," p. 423)?

> When you're old enough to gamble, vote, marry, or die for your country, you're old enough to drink.

But is that true? Why do you think so? Maybe because you believe a more general warrant:

> When a person is old enough to assume basic civic responsibilities, then that person is old enough to engage in all adult activities.

But is that true? Why do you think so?

Before they agree that eighteen-year-olds should be allowed to drink, some readers would also have to hold other beliefs that have nothing directly to do with drinking in particular:

> When we determine maturity of judgment, we cannot decide on the basis of age alone.

> When you want to prevent bad consequences of overindulging in an activity, you should not ban the activity but try to prevent excess.

> When we criminalize behavior that many people approve of, you do not prevent that behavior, you just make it more attractive.

None of those beliefs has anything directly to do with drinking, but if you favor drinking by eighteen-year-olds, they are assumptions that you have to hope your readers would at least not reject out of hand. You must also think about their limitations: Are those principles true under any and all circumstances?

You might finally decide not to state any of these warrants explicitly in your argument, but you benefit from the discipline of trying to think what they are.

Locate Your Warrants Where They Will Do the Most Good

Warrants are such tricky elements of an argument that it is hard to offer good generalizations about where to put them, but here are two:

1. Lay out important warrants before you offer specific claims and reasons, and if necessary, make an argument supporting them.

   For example, suppose you were arguing that schools should teach not facts, but skills. Rather than jumping straight into the reasons and evidence, you might want to lay down some general principles that you intend to reason from:

   > When we educate young people in a democracy, our first job is to encourage them to become productive citizens who can make good decisions necessary to live in a dynamic and changing democratic system. _{warrant} [Add several sentences supporting this assertion.] Given that responsibility, _{reason} our schools should focus not on transmitting mere facts, but on developing children's ability to analyze those facts critically. _{claim}

2. State warrants that readers are unlikely to contest as a logical flourish after you've offered a specific claim and supporting reasons, adding the warrant almost as a punch line that leaves readers with a sense that the conclusion was inevitable.

   > It is no longer possible to be objective about Senator Z's private behavior. _{claim} There are just too many reports of questionable circumstances to think that he is innocent of everything he's been charged with. _{reason} After all, where there's smoke, there's fire. _{warrant}

Use Analogies as Surrogate Warrants

You can imply a warrant using analogies. This claim is based on a warrant,

> Don't be too worried if you begin to feel less in control of making arguments as this book goes on. When people learn a difficult skill requiring complex knowledge, they almost always perform worse when they first gain the knowledge but improve as they gain experience. _{warrant} So you'll have a period of confusion before you fully master the craft of argument. _{claim}

We can base the same claim on an analogy:

> Don't be too worried if you begin to feel less in control of making arguments as this book goes on. Just as those medical students had to get worse at reading X-rays before they became experts, so you'll have a period of confusion before you fully master the craft of argument. _{analogy}

The analogy implies that an unstated warrant covers both cases and connects a claim known to be true (the "just as" part) to a claim in question (the "so" part).

Readers judge analogies almost as they do warrants. To accept the analogy, they must first believe that your point of comparison (the "just as" part) is true—med students do in fact read X-rays worse as they first gain experience but then get better. Second, they must believe that your analogy matches the claim and reason you are trying to connect—that *getting worse at reading X-rays* matches *being confused about arguments* and that *becoming expert at reading X-rays* matches *mastering the craft of argument.*

Use analogies

- when you think readers will respond better to a vivid statement of a concrete example than to a general statement of a principle;
- when you can't think of a way to state the warrant convincingly;
- when you have stated several warrants and don't want to overdo it.

Avoid analogies

- when readers might question your comparison;
- when readers might not see how the comparison applies to the reason and claim you want to connect;
- when readers might infer a warrant different from yours.

You can gain the benefits of an analogy but avoid its risks, if you state both the warrant and the analogy:

> Don't be too worried if you begin to feel less in control of making arguments as this book goes on. When people learn a difficult skill requiring complex knowledge, they perform worse as they first gain the knowledge, but improve as they gain experience. _{warrant} Just as those medical students had to get worse at reading X-rays before they became experts, so you'll have a period of confusion before you fully master the craft of argument.
>
> analogy

EXAMPLE

Analogy

In this passage, the movie critic Michael Medved uses analogy to defend a proposal to require age identification before young people can see movies rated PG-13 and R.

Skeptics raise substantive objections to nearly all the current reform proposals. In today's multiplexes, a resourceful kid might easily buy a ticket to "Tarzan," but then quietly slip into the theater that's showing "The Matrix." Serious new policies might also give rise to a flourishing new market for fake ID's. Meanwhile, the "forbidden fruit" effect may well kick in. By making adult material more difficult to see, we may succeed only in making it seem more alluring and desirable.

Such arguments might also be deployed, however, against long-standing age-based restrictions on the purchase of tobacco and alcohol. Yet no one doubts that these restrictions reduce the levels of youthful indulgence. We don't let twelve-year-olds legally buy cigarettes even though some of them are wily enough to circumvent the rules.

Source: Michael Medved, "Hollywood Murdered Innocence," *Wall Street Journal,* June 16, 1999.

Working Collaboratively

Most of the people we know share most of our beliefs and values, so we seldom think about warrants at all. That's why even experienced writers struggle to know which warrants their readers need to see. This is another instance where a group can help by offering an outside point of view. As you read one another's drafts, look for places where the logic seems a bit off:

- You can't think of anything in particular to disagree with, but you just don't like the argument. It doesn't seem to "hang together."
- You don't agree with the claim, but you can't put your finger on anything in the argument that explains why. The reasons offered just don't seem like good ones.

These are often signs that you want the writer to state an explicit warrant.

If the group is tough-minded about pursuing such points of uncertainty, it will force you to explain your logic by stating your warrants.

INQUIRIES

Reflections

1. Any warrant can be made broader or narrower. Here is a fairly broad one:

   When a form of expression encourages brutality, it must be rejected as a legitimate form of artistic expression.

   You can broaden this warrant by replacing "form of expression" with the more general "symbolic behavior" or narrow it with "song lyrics." When you change its range, do you change the conditions under which it is true?

2. Suppose you offered this objection to the claim that gangsta rap should be accepted as legitimate art:

   Ordinarily we should accept legitimate artistic expression enjoyed by those who create it, but not when it encourages brutal behavior. In other words, when a form of expression encourages brutality, it should be condemned under any and all circumstances.

Someone responds,

What about "Onward Christian Soldiers, onward as to war"? Do you condemn that hymn?

Where do you go from there?

3. Is it possible for two people to agree that some reason supports some claim, even though they are relying on completely different warrants? For example, here's a reason and claim that two people might agree on:

Grades should be assigned on a curve ₍claim₎ because then we would know who are the most deserving students. ₍reason₎

But here are two different warrants that would "cover" that claim and reason:

When society wants to identify its future elite, it should do so in a way that makes sharp distinctions in quality of performance.

Whenever you want to make teachers objectively identify the hardest-working students, you should force them to rely on the statistically sound assignment of grades.

Imagine two people who accepted the claim, but each on the basis of a different warrant. Would they stop agreeing if they learned about the other's warrant? In other words, are some agreements too shallow to survive shared knowledge?

4. Suppose two people agree to the following:

Whenever you want to make teachers objectively identify the hardest-working students, you should force them to rely on statistically sound assignment of grades. ₍warrant₎ Grades should therefore be assigned on a curve. ₍claim₎

Can we conclude that the two people have deeper agreement because they agree on a shared warrant? Suppose they had these two reasons:

We need to prevent teachers from judging students on superficial matters of personality, ₍reason₎ so grades should be assigned on a curve. ₍claim₎

We need to make sure teachers identify students who do not work hard, ₍reason₎ so grades should be assigned on a curve. ₍claim₎

Both reasons would count as good examples of the reason side of the warrant. But do these two people really agree? Would they feel that they agreed? Maybe when we agree, we don't agree as much as we think. Are there times when we should be satisfied with superficial agreement? Are there times when we should not?

5. We have discussed warrants as if they were explicitly stated or implicitly left unstated, but always "there" in some sense, if not on paper, then in our minds. But when you connect a reason to a claim but don't state the warrant that connects them, must there always be a warrant "in the back of your mind"? In other words, when people connect reasons to claims,

do they always have a warrant available to justify the connection? Or do they just connect a reason to a claim because nothing seems to contradict it? How would we find out?

Tasks

6. Here is a middle-sized warrant that many people believe:

   When a tourist encounters a local custom characteristic of the country she visits, she should participate in that custom.

   That warrant might remind you of the proverb, *When in Rome, do as the Romans do.* Is the proverb broader or narrower than its explicit statement as a warrant? Select two more proverbs that express principles you believe. Restate them as middle-sized warrants like the one above. Then make each broader and narrower. Do you still accept the principle after you broadened it? If not, why not? If so, broaden it again. Do you accept it now?

7. The warrant about good turns is one that we might describe as signaling obligation: "When X is the case, we should do Y." Here are some popular proverbs. Turn them into "When, then" warrants, then decide what kind of relationship they signal. Is it cause-effect, effect-cause, appearance-reality, etc.?

   > Where there's smoke there's fire.
   > One rotten apple spoils the barrel.
   > You can't tell a book by its cover.
   > Look before you leap.
   > If you've seen one, you've seen them all.

   What sorts of limitations apply to these?

Project

8. From a dictionary of proverbs, select a dozen or so that you find odd, puzzling, untrue. For each one, try to construct a little story in which someone follows the proverb. For example,

   Alana wanted to go dancing on Saturday with her friend Tanya, who already had a date. So Tanya tells Alana, "There's a guy in my chem lab this afternoon who would love to go with you. Want me to talk to him?" "Maybe," says Alana, "but first I want to come by the lab." "Why?" asks Tanya. Replies Alana, "Look before you leap."

   Do you find it hard to invent stories in which people would follow a puzzling or untrue proverb? What does that tell you about your ability to understand the warrants of others? Can you imagine yourself acting in the way the characters in your stories do? What does that tell you about your ability to accept the warrants of others?

WRITING PROJECTS 7
Project 7.1

Context.   Proverbs offer insights into different cultures. For example, here is a Japanese saying we mentioned earlier:

> The nail that sticks up gets hammered down.

This means that if you are different from everyone else, you will be forced into conformity, and (according to Japanese thinking) that is a good thing. Here is another Japanese proverb:

> If you love your child, send him on a journey.

That means that if you want your child to become part of the larger community, send him out on his own where he will be cared for by strangers and learn the ways of the community. Are there corresponding proverbs in English? If not, what does that mean?

Task.   This project will require collaborative activity. It will lead, not to a paper but to more informal writing. Spend some time with students from other cultures, asking them for proverbs in their culture. Distinguish those that have parallels in English from those that do not. Then read some proverbs in English to those foreign students and ask if they have any parallels. The group should then share its findings. Once you see the similarities and differences, try to imagine some situations where we and someone from another culture would reason about a circumstance differently.

Here are some English proverbs you might read to people from other cultures. Notice that all of these have to do with different attitudes toward being cautious versus being bold.

> The early bird gets the worm.
> Nothing ventured nothing gained.
> A rolling stone gathers no moss.
> Look before you leap.
> Don't count your chickens before they're hatched.
> Strike while the iron is hot.
> Once burned, twice shy.
> Better safe than sorry.
> He who hesitates is lost.
> No guts, no glory.
> A bird in the hand is worth two in the bush.

Do *not* assume that there are no differences between cultures if every proverb you hear corresponds to one in English and if every proverb you offer corresponds to one in that other language. It probably means that you haven't found unique ones yet.

Project 7R

Scenario.   You have worked on this project so long that you fear you cannot see your draft from your reader's point of view.

Task.   Complete your first draft. For each major reason in each major section, list the warrants that connect it to the main claim. Also list the warrants that connect it to its own reasons and evidence. State them using the formula, *Whenever X, then Y.* Use the following list to test your draft:

- Are the warrants true? Do they apply? Do they need to be qualified?
- Will readers need you actually to state them in your text?
- Will readers accept them, or must you include an argument to support them?

CHAPTER 7 IN A NUTSHELL

About Your Argument . . .

Warrants are difficult to understand, so if you are not entirely certain about them, don't feel that you are alone. Even those who study argumentation have had a hard time understanding how they work. A warrant is a general state-ment that explicitly or implicitly relates a set of general conditions to a set of general consequences. We've expressed warrants in this explicit way:

> When children have been influenced by violent movies, TV, and computer games, they behave in violent ways.

But that can be expressed in a less explicit way:

> Violent movies, TV, and computer games cause violent children.

However we express a warrant, it serves to link a reason to a claim:

> More children are playing Mortal Kombat than ever before. $_{reason}$ We will see more children attacking other children. $_{claim}$

If we believe the warrant and the reason, we have to believe the claim.

. . . and About Writing It

You can have problems with warrants in four ways:

- Readers may not see your warrant.
- They may think it is not true.
- They may think the warrant does not "cover" the reason or the claim.
- The warrant may not be appropriate to your audience.

When you address highly contested issues, step back and ask yourself what you think your readers must believe *in general* about your issue *before* they will accept your specific reasons as relevant to your specific claims. If you think that your readers do not share those warrants, then you have to make those warrants the center of their own argument as claims that need their own reasons, evidence, and warrants.

CHAPTER 8

Acknowledgments and Responses

In this chapter we discuss the kinds of questions, reservations, and objections that readers are likely to raise about your argument. We show you how to anticipate them and decide which to acknowledge and how to respond to them. We conclude with a glossary of terms that you can use to acknowledge and respond to alternative points of view.

You can build complex arguments out of answers to the first four of our five questions:

What are you **claiming?**

What are your **reasons?**

What is your **evidence?**

How do your **warrants** connect your reasons to your claims?

But when an issue is contestable, an argument—and the person making it—can seem arrogant, arbitrary, or generally indifferent to readers by failing to imagine and acknowledge the fifth question they are likely to ask:

But what about these alternatives, reservations, and objections? How would you respond to someone who said . . . ?

It can be hard to answer questions like that, because our emotions get in the way of acknowledging that we might be, if not wrong, then at least not completely right. Our impulse is to be defensive, to fire back (another argument-as-warfare metaphor), demolishing (again) our adversaries (and yet again). But when you can imagine and then calmly answer such questions, not just once but throughout an argument, you deepen and broaden it and project a judicious and thoughtful ethos, something that eventually takes on an independent existence as your reputation.

The Importance of Other Viewpoints

When we say, *There are two sides to every question,* we underestimate the complexity of most contestable issues. The sides are more often three or four. And they contest not just claims, but what counts as reasons, evidence, applicable warrants, even the existence of a problem at all. How many sides are there on the question of whether Congress should apologize for slavery? How many different ways do we judge the quality of American education?

In conversation, those who offer endless alternatives and objections seem willfully obstructive—and sometimes they are. But in arguments about serious issues, you serve others badly if, to avoid seeming obstructive, you offer only mindless agreement or, worse, silent dissent. All parties to an argument have a duty to air alternatives and to raise objections in a spirit not of contention but of collaboration, to create the most thoughtful argument possible.

When you argue in writing, though, without a living voice to ask you those questions, you must imagine them on your readers' behalf. Some inexperienced writers think that they undermine their position if they acknowledge any strength in an alternative argument or any uncertainty in their own. The truth is the opposite. Readers distrust those who lack the ability—or confidence—to acknowledge that others might think differently. But that means you first have to imagine their views.

You also have to be able to deal with those views fairly. Unfortunately, most people find it hard to deal with disagreement. The two of us sometimes do: The first time we shared a draft of this book with students, we had a hard time being patient with one who objected over and over that he had learned on his debate team never to acknowledge the strengths in an opponent's argument.

Regardless of age, education, intelligence, and even experience, we all can succumb to the most common flaw in human thinking: We hold tight to our own views, seeking only evidence that supports our claim, ignoring contradictory evidence, or twisting what we do find to support our views. We don't do it knowingly. It's just what we are all are inclined to do.

You can compensate for that bias if you acknowledge alternatives. Imagine a skeptical but helpful friend questioning every part of your argument. Your friend might think that your claims, reasons, evidence, or warrants are just wrong, or he might think they are right, but offer an alternative argument, or even an alternative way to frame the problem. To help you imagine that friend, we offer a checklist of questions in the next two sections.

Questioning Your Problem and Its Solution

At the most general level, readers question how you frame your problem and solution, even whether there's a problem at all. Recall the conversation about students as customers among Sue, Ann, and Raj (p. 31). If Sue raised with her dean the issue of the lack of convenient office hours, the dean might ask some blunt questions (most questioners would be more tactful):

1. **What makes you think there is a problem?** *How many students in fact can't see their instructors when they have to?*

2. **Why have you posed the problem that way rather than another way?** *Could the problem be not office hours but the willingness of students to make an effort to see teachers?*

3. **Exactly what kind of solution are you asking me to accept?** *How should we treat you like customers? What exactly does that mean? What should we do?*

4. **Have you considered limits on your claim?** *Are you saying that every instructor in every department keeps too few office hours? Most? Some?*

5. **Why do you think your solution is better than the alternatives?** *What's wrong with the student as client model?*

Most important, though, are the two obstacles that every solution to a pragmatic problem must overcome:

6. **How do you know your solution won't cost more to implement than the problem costs?** *To treat you like customers, we will have to retrain everyone, which will take resources away from current programs.*

7. **How do you know your solution won't create new and more costly problems?** *If we treat you like customers, we will erode the teacher-student relationship that a sound education depends on.*

Questioning Your Support

After your readers question your problem and solution, they are likely to question its support. They will probably start by questioning whether you have enough evidence. Imagine the dean responding to Sue's charges:

1. **Your evidence is not sufficient.** *You gathered office hours from a single floor in one building. That can't be more than twenty offices. That's not enough to take your claims seriously.*

Next are questions about the quality of her (reports of) evidence:

2. **Your evidence is not accurate.** *I looked at those offices, and you counted three faculty who are on leave.*

3. **Your evidence is not precise.** *You said faculty average "about" an office hour a week. What's the exact figure? Are they all about the same or do most faculty keep more with only a few keeping much less?*

4. **Your evidence is not representative.** *You looked at offices all from the same department. What about other departments?*

5. **Your evidence is not authoritative.** *How do you know the posted hours are the only times teachers see students? Have you asked the teachers?*

Finally, there are the possible objections we reviewed in Chapter 7 concerning warrants:

6. **Your warrant is not true.** *You say someone who pays money for something is a customer. Why should I believe that?*

7. **Your warrant is too sweeping.** *You say that anyone who pays money for something is a customer, but that's not so. Employers pay employees.*

8. **Your warrant does not apply.** *What students pay for is nothing like what a customer buys. An education is not a refrigerator, so paying tuition is not like buying a refrigerator.*

9. **Your warrant is inappropriate.** *The idea of applying the principle of buying and selling in higher education is simply unacceptable.*

We have phrased these responses as bluntly as we could, not to make Sue's dean seem antagonistic, but to encourage you to be honest with yourself. Readers may not put questions this way face-to-face, but they are likely to ask them at least this directly in the privacy of their minds. In whatever spirit they ask them, though, they are meeting a responsibility that participants in an argument must accept: the duty to engage actively to find the best solution to a problem.

Questioning Your Consistency

Readers will look for one other weakness in your argument—that you contradict yourself:

> Senator, how can you condemn me for accepting contributions from the National Rifle Association when you accept contributions from the Ban Handguns Alliance?

> How can you say that children's moral growth is harmed by sexually explicit movies when you also say that it is not harmed by violence on TV?

Readers will think you contradict yourself when you seem to apply a warrant selectively, using the warrant when it suits your purposes and ignoring it when it does not. For example, if you claim that children are harmed by sex in the movies, readers will infer that the claim is based on a general principle of reasoning something like this:

> Whenever children experience vivid representations of a form of behavior that is glorified, they are more likely to approve of and imitate that behavior.

But that warrant does not give us a basis for distinguishing between sex in the movies and violence on TV. If we believe one is harmful, then we must believe that the other is as well—unless you can show that a more narrow warrant applies. In this case, you might argue that older children are *more* influenced by representations of sex than of violence because their awakening sexuality makes them more attuned to matters of sex. But, of course, you would have to state that narrow warrant explicitly and, since it is not obvious, make an argument to show that it is true.

If a critic can show that what you claim in one case contradicts what you claim in another, you will seem to be guilty of intellectual inconsistency—a profoundly damaging charge, especially when the inconsistency seems to serve your own interests.

- In a pragmatic argument about what to do, you seem *unfair* when you expect others to follow a principle you do not follow yourself.

- In a conceptual argument about what to believe, you seem *intellectually dishonest* when you apply a principle selectively to achieve the results you want.

So in planning your argument, ask whether your readers can apply the principle behind in the case at hand to all similar cases. If not, you have to formulate a more narrow principle that distinguishes your case from the others. Since readers will assume that your principles of reasoning are relatively general ones, you have to state that narrow principle as an explicit warrant and then consider whether you have to make an argument to support it.

By now, you have seen a lot of questions, too many to keep them all in mind. So we've summarized them in the checklist beginning on page 000. When you prepare your arguments, skim the questions, and if one strikes a chord, imagine a reader asking it, then acknowledge and respond to it.

EXAMPLE

How to Use a Response to Restate Your Argument

The excerpt below is from an argument claiming that majors should be abolished because students do not benefit from specialized studies and need more general education. In it, the writer acknowledges and responds to possible objections while simultaneously restating not only the gist of his main claim but also its support. Here, in outline, are the steps he follows:

1. He imagines that those who raise the objection already accept one major part of his claim, *Students need more general education*, thus reinforcing it.

2. He states the objection as an alternative solution, but one that partially agrees with his proposed action: *Majors should be, not abolished, but reduced.*

3. In response to that alternative, he indirectly restates the remaining part of his claim: *Specialization does not benefit students.*

4. Then, to support that response/claim, he restates his three reasons why specialization is not a benefit.

5. Finally, he acknowledges a qualification to his claim, *Some students might benefit from specialization,* but then restates his claim again, *Other students should not be forced to specialize.*

Here's the passage:

Another objection I anticipate [to my argument that majors should be abolished] is from people who would agree that the basic liberal arts learning students get today is inadequate, and who would buy into the idea of an expanded general education program _{restatement of part of main claim} · · · [but would still argue for] a minimally sized major. Students could have the best of both worlds: the advantages of specialism along with the advantages of generalism. _{of alternative solution}

Certainly a curriculum like this would be preferable to what we have now; more, it would be a great improvement. _{benefits of alternative solution} But there is still a difficulty. It is still assumed that having a specialization, regardless of its size, is truly an advantage for students. And that is precisely what I am throwing into question. _{response / restatement of part of main claim} I have suggested that there is no more rigor in forcing the mind toward the greater depth of a major than there is in forcing it toward the lesser but significant depths of several different fields. _{restatement of reason 1 supporting response /main claim} And I have suggested that the way in which a major fine-tunes the mind may end up as a limitation more than an asset—inclining a student to see things from the narrows of one perspective alone. _{restatement of reason 2} Add to this the fact that many students' interests aren't strongly enough defined to make a commitment to a major, and the fact that many others don't need one for the vocational preparation they desire since they will be getting that in graduate school. _{restatement of reason 3} These are all telling reasons for questioning the practice of requiring students to have a major, and together they form a powerful and sensible rationale.

All of this isn't to say that no student should have a major. _{of limitation} But it is to say that we should not require it of all students. _{restatement of main claim} Those in fields like engineering and architecture, those who have an obvious and strong inclinations in other fields, should take majors . . . [But] for other students, there is no good reason for forcing them to specialize.

Responses as Subordinate Arguments

The more you acknowledge and respond to questions, reservations, and alternative views, the more you create an argument that readers judge thoughtful and complex, especially if you support your responses with additional reasons and evidence. By so doing, you enhance your credibility, a crucial component in creating your ethos. For example, here is a piece of an argument claiming that a university should invest more time and money in course evaluations beyond simple in-class surveys:

> . . . Faculty can continue to improve their teaching if they get as much information as we can give them about student responses to their teaching.
>
> Some students may ask "If faculty aren't interested enough to improve their teaching on their own, why would they respond to our criticisms?" _{acknowledgment of objection} We think that view is cynical and that most teachers do care about our education. _{partial rebuttal of objection} But even if they have a point, _{partial concession to objection} the new information we propose to gather will include more than just student gripes. Once the information is part of the record, teachers will not ignore it. _{response/claim} This happens in many professions. When doctors, airlines, or car manufacturers learn about problems with their products or services, they try to improve. _{reason} For example, when data about the quality of the university hospital were made public, hospital officials tried to do better because they were concerned about loss of business. Now the hospital advertises its standings in surveys on TV. _{report of evidence} When the shortcomings of a profession become public, they take action to improve. _{warrant}

This writer explicitly acknowledges an objection that she imagines her colleagues might have, conceding they might be partly right. But she then responds to that objection with reasons, evidence, and a warrant to show why it would not apply in this case.

The writer might anticipate, however, that her readers will in turn question her response to their questions. For example, she might imagine that her most cynical readers would object to the comparison between teachers and airlines:

> But teachers are not like airlines; they have tenure and can't be fired, and colleges are not out to make money, so your analogy doesn't hold.

If she imagines that objection, she must respond to it with yet another argument:

> Of course, tenured professors differ from doctors and airlines because they don't need the approval of customers to stay in business. _{acknowledgment of limitation} But most professors are responsible professionals who understand that colleges have to attract students. _{response/claim} Even state universities depend on tuition, especially higher out-of-state tuition. _{reason} Last year, out-of-state students saved us from a deficit that threatened faculty raises. _{report of evidence} Students have many choices and can shop around. _{reason} When they research schools, they consider the quality of teaching in deciding where to go. _{warrant}

We can imagine someone criticizing that response too, but at some point enough is enough. Life and papers are too short to answer every objection. But you don't have to answer every one to show you have been thoughtful enough to consider some.

What if you can't answer a question? Our recommendation may seem naïve, but it is realistic: If you believe your argument has flaws but none so serious as to defeat it, concede them. Then assert that the balance of your argument compensates for its imperfections:

> We must admit that not every teacher will take these evaluations seriously. But even so, if we can get a substantial number to . . .

Conceding what cannot be denied is how thoughtful arguers respond to legitimate uncertainty.

Nothing reveals more clearly the kind of mind you have, indeed the kind of *person* you are, than your ability to imagine and then respond to alternatives, objections, and reservations. Few of us do that well. But when you do, not only does your argument gain credibility. So do you.

IN THE READINGS . . .

Acknowledgments and Combativeness

We have emphasized the value of thinking of argument not as combat but as collaboration, and we have shown you how to respond to questions your readers will ask so that you can create a collaborative relationship with them. But you won't find much of that in one of the most entertaining readings, Camille Paglia's "Wisdom in a Bottle" (p. 426). In this ultra-hip article from the ultra-hip on-line journal *Salon,* Paglia reinforces her reputation as a pugnacious gadfly, responding to the question of binge drinking by redefining the problem: *It's not binge drinking that's the problem—it's the banality and mediocrity of American higher education.*

Nowhere does she acknowledge views other than her own, much less respond to them. But she does characterize those who disagree. Would they accept her characterizations as fair? Would she want them too? If there is such a thing as combative argument for the fun and sport of it, this is an example. But would Paglia's opponents share her fun? Would her article persuade them to redefine the problem? Do you think she cares? A final point: Notice that the question from "Shaken, not Stirred" begins with an acknowledgment and response. Does that give her or him an ethos different from Paglia's? Why or why not?

WRITING PROCESS 8
Acknowledgment and Responses

Thinking-Reading-Talking

Use Acknowledgments to Understand Context

When you read an argument in a new field, you may not see what is at stake in every part of it. But you can infer some of that from the common ground, especially if the writer reviews research leading to her question. You can find more context in the objections and alternatives that she acknowledges and responds to. She defines the limits of debate in her field in what she acknowledges or dismisses and defines what she thinks is relevant to her position in what she concedes or responds to at length.

Preparing and Planning

Collect Alternatives as You Read

When it is hard to imagine alternatives, start by making a master list of pros and cons. Keep it handy and add to it, especially the cons, as you prepare your argument. Don't forget to look for help in your sources.

- Take notes on positions your sources respond to. If you disagree with the source, those objections may support your own position and give you a lead on further reading. If you agree with your source, you can acknowledge and respond to some of those same alternatives and objections (after you look at them for yourself, of course).

- Don't record only claims that support your position; also record those that contradict it. Include in your notes the reasons and evidence offered to support the claim: If you decide to acknowledge and respond to it, you will need a full argument to respond well.

- When you collect evidence to support your reasons, keep track of what might limit or contradict them. You may decide not to acknowledge those reservations, but they might help you imagine others.

Add Acknowledgments to Your Post-Draft Outline

When you sketch an outline, focus first not on the alternatives or objections you intend to acknowledge, but on your own argument. You invite writer's block if before you start drafting you try to think about every objection a reader might have. Think about alternatives, questions and objections after you have a draft of your own core argument. Then work through your outline point by point, imagining questions readers might raise:

- List objections, but don't immobilize yourself by thinking you have to respond to all of them.

- Respond to two or three important ones. Readers don't expect more, and you don't want to raise so many alternatives that they swamp your position.

Include even objections that you think might not occur to readers. They don't want to follow you down every blind alley, but they benefit when you share significant but ultimately rejected alternatives. They will also like your candor.

We know this advice seems disingenuous—being candid about failures as a rhetorical strategy. Nevertheless, readers judge your ethos by how open you are to alternatives, and they will know that only if you show them what you considered.

Locate Acknowledgments and Responses Where They Will Occur to Readers

Once you identify alternatives to acknowledge, think of a response, outline it, and decide where to put it. Acknowledge alternatives early if they are well established and relate to your whole argument:

- If your whole argument directly counters another, acknowledge that other argument in your introduction and early in your paper.

- If an alternative bears on the whole argument but is one you want to drop quickly, acknowledge it in the common ground of your introduction:

  Many teachers believe that the most important skill they can teach is the ability to solve problems. _{acknowledgment / common ground} But as important as that skill is, it is less important than the ability to discover, then articulate a problem clearly. As Einstein said, "A problem well put is half solved." _{response / destabilizing condition}

- Acknowledge an alternative right after your introduction, as background, if it bears on the whole argument but will occur to readers only after they understand your problem and have a sense of its solution:

  . . . The most valuable skill for students is the ability to discover and then articulate problems clearly. _{claim} The issue of problem formulation, however, has received little attention from teachers. Their traditional focus has been on teaching students to analyze problems in order to . . . _{acknowledgment}

- Respond to incidental alternatives where they are relevant.

  There is a Web site that rates colleges based on students' reports of their experience. That may not be a reliable source, _{acknowledgment} but it is one that students check. _{response/claim} For example, . . .

Building a Whole Argument Around Alternatives

If you know that readers will think of more than one alternative to your solution, organize your argument by sequentially eliminating alternatives, leaving your solution as the last one standing.

  How then should we respond to global warming? It has been suggested that we just ignore it. [explanation] But that won't work because . . .
  It has also been suggested that we exploit it by adapting our lives and especially our agriculture to warmer conditions. [explanation] But that won't work either because . . .
  At the other extreme, some have argued that we should totally restructure our society, ending all atmosphere emissions immediately. [explanation] But that idea is as bad as those who reject the reality of global warming because . . .
  None of these responses addresses the problem in a responsible way. The only reasonable way to deal with global warming is to . . .

Drafting

The Vocabulary of Acknowledgment and Response

Writers fail to acknowledge and respond to alternatives usually for three reasons. First, they cannot imagine them. Second, even when they do, they think that by acknowledging them, they weaken their argument. But a third reason is more mundane and more easily solved: They lack the expressions that experienced writers use to introduce alternatives and responses.

We offer here that lexicon of words and phrases. To be sure (there is one of them right there), your first efforts may feel clumsy (*may* is common in acknowledgments), _{acknowledgment} *but* (a response usually begins with *but* or *however*) as you use them, they will come to seem more natural. _{response/claim}

Acknowledging

When you respond to an anticipated question or objection, decide how much weight to give it by gauging how seriously your readers take it. You can mention and dismiss it, or raise it and address it at length. We order these expressions roughly in that order, from most dismissive to most respectful.

1. You can downplay an objection or alternative by summarizing it briefly in a short phrase introduced with *despite, regardless of,* or *notwithstanding:*

   Despite Congress' claims that it wants to cut taxes, _{acknowledgment} the public believes that . . . _{response}

   Regardless of problems in Hong Kong, _{acknowledgment} Southeast Asia remains a strong . . . _{response}

   Notwithstanding declining crime rates, _{acknowledgment} there is still a need for vigorous enforcement of . . . _{response}

   You can use *although,* and *while,* and *even though* in the same way:

   Although Congress claims it wants to cut taxes, _{acknowledgment} the public believes that . . . _{response}

   While there are problems in Hong Kong, _{acknowledgment Southeast} Asia remains a strong . . . _{response}

   Even though crime has declined, _{acknowledgment} there is still a need for vigorous enforcement of . . . _{response}

2. You can indirectly signal an objection or alternative with a *seem* or *appear,* along with some other qualifying conditioning verb or adverb, such as *plausibly, justifiably, reasonably, accurately, understandably, surprisingly, foolishly,* or even *certainly.*

   In his letters, Lincoln expresses what *seems* to be depression. _{acknowledgment} But those who observed him . . . _{response}

Smith's data *appear* to support these claims. _{acknowledgment} However, on closer examination . . . _{response}

This proposal *may* have some merit, _{acknowledgment} but we . . . _{response}

Liberals have made a *plausible* case that the arts ought to be supported by taxes. _{acknowledgment} But they ignore the moral objections of . . . _{response}

3. You can acknowledge alternatives by attributing them to unnamed sources or to no source at all. This kind of acknowledgment gives a little weight to the possible objection. In these examples, brackets and slashes indicate choices:

    It is easy to [*think / imagine / say / claim / argue*] that taxes should . . .

    There is [*another / alternative / possible / standard*] [*explanation / line of argument / account / possibility*].

    Some evidence [*might / may / can / could / would / does*] [*suggest / indicate / point to / lead some to think*] that we should . . .

4. You can acknowledge an alternative by attributing it to a more or less specific source. This construction gives more weight to the position you acknowledge:

    There are some [*many / few*] who [*might / may / could / would*] [*say / think / argue / claim / charge / object*] that Cuba is not . . .

    [*Most / Many / Some / A few*] knowledgeable college administrators [*say / think / argue / claim / charge / object*] that researchers . . .

    One advocate of collaboration, Ken Bruffee, [*says / thinks / argues / claims / charges / objects*] that students . . .

5. You can acknowledge an alternative in your own voice or with a passive verb or concessive adverb. You concede the alternative has some validity, but by changing the words, you can qualify how much validity you acknowledge.

    I [*understand / know / realize / appreciate*] that liberals believe in . . .

    It is [*true / possible / likely / certain*] that no good evidence proves that coffee causes cancer . . .

    It [*must / should / can*] be [*admitted / acknowledged / noted / conceded*] that no good evidence proves that coffee causes cancer . . .

    [*Granted / admittedly / true / to be sure / certainly / of course*], Adams admitted . . .

    We [*could / can / might / may / would*] [*say / argue / claim / think*] that spending on the arts supports pornographic . . .

    We have to [*consider / raise*] the [*question / possibility / probability*] that further study [*could / might / will*] show crime has not . . .

We cannot [*overlook/ ignore / dismiss / reject*] the fact that Cuba was . . .

What X [*says / states / writes / claims / asserts / argues / suggests / shows*] may [*be true / has merit / make sense / be a good point*]: Perhaps Lincoln did suffer . . .

Responding

You signal a response with *but, however,* or *on the other hand.* Remember that after you state your response, readers may expect reasons and evidence supporting it, because they will take it to be a claim needing its own argument. You can respond in ways that range from tactfully indirect to blunt.

1. You can state that *you* don't entirely understand:

   But I do not quite understand . . . / I find it difficult to see how . . . / It is not clear to me that . . .

2. Or you can state that there are unsettled issues:

   But there are other issues . . . / There remains the problem of . . .

3. You can respond more bluntly by claiming the acknowledged position is irrelevant or unreliable:

   But as insightful as that point may be, it [*ignores / is irrelevant to / does not bear on / was formulated for other situations than*] the issue at hand.

   But the evidence is [*unreliable / shaky / thin / not the best available*].

   But the argument is [*untenable / wrong / weak / confused / simplistic*].

   But that view [*overlooks / ignores / misses*] key factors . . .

   But that position is based on [*unreliable / faulty / weak / confused*] [*reasoning / thinking / evidence*].

Working Collaboratively

It is hard to imagine alternatives on your own, but you can help one another do that by asking tough questions. For each argument you review, find enough weak points and strong alternatives to make the argument seem questionable. Of course, your real aim is to identify just the two or three key alternatives or objections that each writer should acknowledge. Try this in a spirit of goodwill (someone should record what follows):

- Ask the writer of the argument to raise the most severe objections.
- Have each person in turn add objections.
- When the group runs out of ideas, rank the objections from most to least serious and alternatives from most to least viable.

From these two ranked lists, each writer can decide what to acknowledge.

If the group has trouble getting into the spirit of this game, run down the following list of questions and comments. Remember to smile when you offer them.

Problem

1. This is not a problem. Everyone knows that . . .
2. The real problem is not this, but the fact that . . .

Solution

1. I can think of three exceptions to your claim: first . . . , second . . . , and third, . . .
2. I can think of two better solutions/answers: first . . . , and second. . . .
3. This solution will cost too much. It will cost . . .
4. This solution will create several new and bigger problems: first, it will . . .

Reasons

1. I can think of two reasons not to accept your claim: first . . .
2. I can think of three exceptions to your reason: first . . .
3. Why haven't you included this other reason?

Evidence

1. There is better evidence. Why didn't you include it?
2. That evidence is from an untrustworthy source. Why do you believe it?
3. That evidence is not entirely representative. Why should we trust it?
4. That evidence is vague/imprecise. What makes it good enough for the purpose?
5. I doubt your evidence is accurate. How do you know it is?

Warrants

1. You seem to assume that when X is true we can infer Y, but I think that when X is true we must infer Z.
2. That reason/claim does not seem to be a good example of the reason/claim side of the warrant.
3. I can think of three exceptions to that warrant: first . . .

INQUIRIES

Reflections

1. In most academic and professional situations, we make arguments stronger by acknowledging their limitations. But different standards apply in some professional situations—a lawyer defending a client in

court, for example. Can you think of other circumstances in which you should not acknowledge any weakness in your argument? How do those circumstances differ from those that you normally find in academic and professional arguments?

2. Suppose that just before you turn in a paper for a class, you discover an objection to your argument that substantially weakens it. You cannot think how to counter the objection. In fact, you now think your argument is wrong. What should you do? This question is both ethical and practical. Are you ethically obligated to reveal this objection? Why or why not? Practically speaking, would it be wise to tell your teacher that you recognized the objection, but too late to do anything about it? Or should you just keep quiet and hope for the best? Which response do you think will project the best ethos?

Tasks

3. In Chapter 6 we asked you to highlight the evidence in some old papers. Return to those marked-up copies and question the evidence in as many ways as seem appropriate. Do you see weaknesses in your argument now that you did not see then? How would you acknowledge and respond to them?
4. Look at the editorial and op-ed pages of your local newspaper. Identify all the acknowledgments and responses. Which pieces use them best? Do those acknowledgments make those arguments persuasive? Do the same with some TV talk shows. Do the participants acknowledge and respond to other points of view as often? If not, why not?

Projects

5. Spend an hour or so with the editorial and op-ed page of your local newspaper. Formulate reasonable questions for all elements of the arguments. Then sketch how you would answer those questions if you were the author.
6. Return to the old papers you used for Task #3. Add more acknowledgments and responses than you really need, then eliminate those that add little to the persuasiveness of your argument. How far short of this optimum did your original paper fall?

WRITING PROJECTS 8
Project 8.1

Context.   Pamela White's column, "'Drinking Age Has Simply Got to Go,' Say Campus Riots," appeared in several student newspapers. As you can see, the last paragraph suggests that her college student readers do not just believe something, but act on their beliefs by writing letters urging state legislators to abolish the drinking age.

Scenario and Task.   Choose one:

A. The Greek Council has voted to encourage students to write letters about lowering the drinking age on the basis of the argument in this article. You have been chosen to compose a model letter for others to use in writing theirs.

B. You are a member of a student political organization that wants students to write letters about lowering the drinking age, but thinks there are better arguments than those in the article. You have been chosen to develop that better argument and compose a model letter.

C. You are a member of a student organization that opposes lowering the drinking age. You have been chosen to make the argument and compose a model letter .

Project 8.2

Return to any of the papers you wrote in the first weeks of the class. Revise its scenario so that before your readers encounter your argument they believe a position different from the one you have argued. Rewrite the paper, adding acknowledgments and responses supported by subordinate arguments.

Project 8R

Scenario.   Your teacher has asked the class to review each other's drafts before presenting them.

Task.   Find one or two people who will review your draft not to make editorial suggestions but to share their responses: *Where are they confused? Where do they want more evidence? More reliable evidence? Where do they have objections or want to add important qualifications?* If they are confused about your logic, add warrants. If they want more or better evidence, add it. If you can't, acknowledge the problem and respond as best you can. If they raise objections or qualifications, acknowledge and respond to them. Using those responses, produce a final draft. Be sure, as a last step, to revise your prose in accord with the procedures in Writing Processes 12 and 13.

CHAPTER 8 IN A NUTSHELL
About Your Argument . . .

You communicate the quality of your thinking by how candidly you acknowledge and respond to views different from yours. Admittedly, nothing is harder than finding those views and then acknowledging them, so you need a list of questions to ask yourself on behalf of your readers. Anticipate questions and objections about two aspects of your argument:

- Readers question the quality of your claims, reasons, evidence, or warrants. They assert that you are just wrong.
- They find nothing wrong with your argument per se, but think of alternative claims, reasons, and evidence, even ways to frame the issue.

Readers question how you frame the problem and express your claim:

1. Why do you think your problem is a serious one?
2. Why did you pose the problem this way rather than that?
3. Exactly what claim are you are asking me to accept?
4. Have you considered these limits and exceptions to your claim?
5. Why do you think your solution is better than an alternative one?
6. How do you know your solution won't cost more than the problem?
7. How do you know your solution won't create new problems?

Readers also question evidence: They question whether it is sufficient, accurate, precise, representative and authoritative. They might also question whether your warrants are true, too broad, applicable to your reasons and claims, or inappropriate for your readers.

. . . and About Writing It

When you acknowledge and respond to an imagined objection or question, you can follow a well-established formula:

- Begin with a phrase such as *To be sure, Admittedly, Some have claimed,* etc.
- Follow with *but, however, on the other hand,* etc., and go on with the response.

When you respond to these kinds of objections and alternatives, you have an opportunity to thicken your argument by supporting your response with reasons, evidence, warrants, and yet more acknowledgments and responses to your response.

Checklists for Planning and Revising

We have recommended that when you make an argument you ask yourself and your readers many questions. But if you are new to writing arguments, their number may overwhelm you. (You'll find more than ninety in the complete list below.) Not even the most experienced writers can hold them all in mind, much less systematically answer them. As you gain experience, however, you'll find that you won't need to think about them all, because you'll answer most of them without having to ask them. But since even the most experienced writers need help to see their work objectively, we include here four check lists for looking at various aspects of your paper. The first three you can run through quickly. The last is a complete list for when you have time to revise more carefully. At the end, you'll find a step-by-step procedure for storyboarding a long paper.

A Checklist for Evaluating Discussion/Paper Questions

This short checklist will help you find good questions that you can raise in class or use to formulate a conceptual problem for a paper. If you answer "No" to the first five questions, you may have to find a new topic for your argument.

1. Do you care about answering the question you have posed?
2. Will anyone else care about hearing your answer?
3. Can you imagine finding an answer?
4. Can you imagine evidence that would support your answer?
5. Can you imagine finding that evidence?

If you answer "Yes" to these next questions, you may also have to find a new topic.

6. Can you answer the question in just a few words?
7. Does the question call for a simple yes-no answer?
8. Is it a question of fact that a reader could answer just by looking something up?
9. Will your readers accept your answer without asking for reasons and evidence?
10. If they disagree, will they think the answer is just a matter of opinion?

A Quick Checklist for Argument

This checklist will help you analyze the structure of your argument as you plan and as you revise. If you are checking a draft, you don't have to copy from it word-for-word: a brief paraphrase will do. But do write complete sentences, not just topics or phrases.

1. Do your reasons/subclaims "add up" to a strong case for the main claim?
2. Can you think of any other reasons that support the main claim? If so, add them.
3. Are the reasons/subclaims in the best order? If not, reorder them.
4. Will readers recognize the principle of order for your reasons/subclaims? If not, add a transitional word or phrase to signal that order.
5. Does the evidence under each reason/subclaim in fact support it?
6. Is there enough evidence for each reason/subclaim?
7. Is there other evidence that would support a reason/subclaim?

Once you answer those questions and fill in missing information, use the diagram on the following page to guide further drafting and revising.

Ten Steps to a Coherent Paper

This checklist will help you predict whether your readers will judge your argument to be coherent. Use it for drafts that are close to finished. A "No" answer to any of the questions suggests that you have to do some revising.

1. Draw a line between the introduction and the body and between the body and conclusion.
   - Does the body begin with a new paragraph?
   - Does the conclusion begin with a new paragraph?
2. In your introduction, underline the sentences that state the problem or question.
   - Have you told your readers why it should matter to them?
   - If not, will they think it matters for the same reason you do?
3. Box the sentence that states the main point of the paper.
   - Does it respond directly to the problem or question?
   - Does it make an arguable claim?
   - Is it at or near the end of the introduction? If not, is it in the conclusion?
   - If the point is in the conclusion, do the last sentences of the introduction announce the key terms that appear in it?
   - If your main point is stated in both your introduction and conclusion, are the two statements similar?

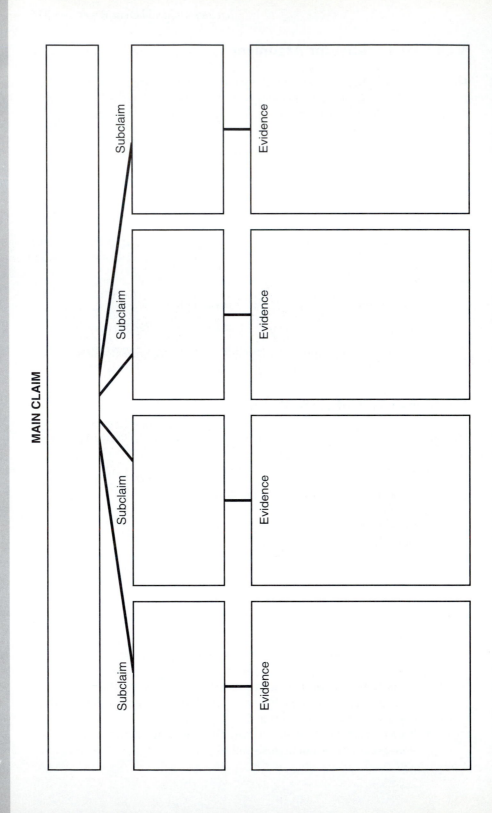

MAIN CLAIM

Subclaim

Subclaim

Subclaim

Subclaim

Evidence

Evidence

Evidence

Evidence

- If they are similar, is the one in the conclusion more specific, more informative?

4. Circle the key words in the last two sentences of the introduction and the most important sentence in your conclusion. Then circle those same words throughout the paper. Then bracket words that refer to roughly the same concepts as the circled words or to concepts that are clearly related to them.
    - Are there three or more circled or bracketed words per paragraph?

5. Circle key words in the title.
    - Are the words that you circled the same ones that you circled in the introduction and conclusion?
    - Are they words that did not appear in your written assignment?

6. Draw a line between each major section of your paper. Box the sentence that states its main point.
    - Does it make an arguable claim?
    - Is it a reason supporting the main point/claim?
    - Do most of the main points appear at the beginning of their sections?
    - Now if you can, do the same thing for each paragraph.

7. Look at the beginning words of each section.
    - Do they begin with words that signal why the paragraphs come in the order they do, words such as *first, second; on the other hand, however; therefore, in conclusion,* and so on?

8. For each paragraph, underline every sentence that reports evidence supporting the point/claim of the paragraph.
    - Have you underlined at least half of the paragraph?

9. Underline the first half of the first sentence in each paragraph.
    - Do the words you have underlined refer back to something already mentioned earlier in the essay?

10. Underline the first six words in each sentence.
    - Do they refer to information that would be familiar to readers, or at least would not surprise them? Are they words that are mentioned earlier in the essay, obviously connected to a concept mentioned earlier, or related to concepts that readers are likely to have in mind? (For more on this issue, see chapter 12.)

A Complete List of Questions

This checklist will help you keep track of all the questions you might ask about your argument. The questions are in categories organized top down, from the most general questions about your readers and problem to the details of sentences. We have marked the most important questions with a star (★), the more important ones with an arrow (↩). If you can't cover every question, review the marked ones, and if you're *really* pressed for time, focus on the starred ones.

1. Preliminary Questions About Your Audience

★ 1. What are the general values of your readers? Liberal? Conservative? Middle of the road? Religious? Secular? Do their values reflect their race? Ethnicity? Marital status? Economic level? Profession? Expertise?

↩ 2. What kind of arguments do your readers prefer? From lots of individual bits of evidence to a generalization? From settled principles and warrants to deductions from them? Will they expect to see the kind of argument that is common in their field of expertise?

↩ 3. What kind of evidence do they prefer? Hard statistical evidence? Field observation? Personal experience? Quotes from authorities? Primary reports of evidence? Anecdotes?

4. How much time do they have for your argument? Will they want a summary of it up front, or will they patiently read through it all?

2. Questions About Your Particular Problem

★1. What kind of problem are you addressing, pragmatic or conceptual? Do you want your readers simply to believe something? Or do you want them to act, or at least support an action?

↩ 2. What costs or benefits are at stake *for your readers* in your problem? Would they agree?

3. Have your readers tried to solve this problem? Do they think they have already solved it? How committed are they to a different solution? If so, what is at stake for them in giving up their solution in favor of yours?

4. What level of agreement are you seeking: Understanding? Respect? Approval? Endorsement? Wholehearted assent?

3. Questions About Your Solution/Claim

★ 1. Is your claim significant enough to make an argument about? Is it contestable? Is it capable of being proved wrong?

↩ 2. If your claim solves a pragmatic problem, will the solution cost less than the problem does? Will it create a bigger problem than the one it solves? Can it be implemented? Why is it better than alternative solutions?

↩ 3. Is your claim sufficiently rich in concepts to anticipate the key concepts in your argument?

4. Is it appropriately complex? Does it open with clauses introduced with *although, if,* or *when*? Does it close with clauses introduced with *because*? Would a shorter, simpler claim be more effective?

5. Is it appropriately hedged? Are there limiting conditions? Exceptions?

6. Is your solution feasible? Ethical? Prudent?

7. If your claim solves a conceptual problem, could other facts, concepts, theories, etc., contradict it?

4. Questions About Your Title

★ 1. Does your title include key words from your main claim? Are there words that someone who knew the assignment would not predict?

2. Have you taken advantage of using a two-line title?

5. Questions About Your Introduction

★ 1. If your problem is pragmatic, have you stated the destabilizing condition clearly? Have you clearly stated the costs and/or benefits from the point of view of your readers?

↩ 2. If your problem is conceptual, have you stated clearly what is not known or not well enough understood? Have you stated the consequences in a way that shows they are more significant than the destabilizing condition?

↩ 3. Where have you located your main claim/solution? If it is in both the introduction and conclusion, do both statements harmonize? If you state it for the first time in the conclusion, did you end the introduction with language that introduces the key concepts you develop in the rest of the argument and repeat in the claim at the end?

↩ 4. Can your reader plainly see where you have ended your introduction and where you begin the body of your argument?

5. Can you find common ground to establish a context for your problem? Does it introduce key concepts about the problem?

6. Would you improve your introduction by adding a prelude, a pithy quotation, an interesting fact, or a brief anecdote that encapsulates the problem? Would a prelude suit the kind of argument you make?

6. Questions About Your Conclusion

★ 1. Have you stated your claim/solution in your conclusion?

2. Have you suggested why it is significant? Have you suggested what is still unknown, uncertain, left to be done?

3. Would you improve your conclusion by adding a coda? Would a coda suit the kind of argument you make?

7. Questions About the Body of Your Argument

★ 1. Why have you ordered the parts of your argument as you have?

☞ 2. If you have divided your argument into two or more parallel parts, can you explain their order? Is it clear to your reader? Have you introduced each part with words that signal the order?

☞ 3. If you have divided your argument into two or more sequential parts, have you ordered them from the beginning of the process to its end or from the end back to the beginning? Is that order clear to your reader?

☞ 4. Can you pick out in the body of your argument key words that you use in your title, at the end of your introduction, and in your conclusion?

5. Have you avoided laying out your argument as a history of your thinking or as a summary of your sources? Have you avoided dividing it into blocks organized around the things given to you by your topic rather than around ideas or qualities *you* discovered and choose to discuss?

6. Have you avoided opening the body of your argument with a long summary of background?

8. Questions About the Body of Your Sections and Paragraphs

★ 1. Have you organized sections as you organize a whole essay? Does each section open with its own introduction? Do you state the point of the section at the end of its introduction?

☞ 2. Do you state in the introduction to each section the key words you develop in the rest of that section?

3. If a section is longer than a couple of pages, have you concluded each section by restating the claim of the section?

4. Have you organized your longest paragraphs like your sections?

9. Questions About Your Evidence

★ 1. Have you based your reasons on reliable reports of evidence? Are your sources authoritative? Have you cited them?

★ 2. Are you sure your readers will accept what you offer as a report of evidence or will they think it is only another reason?

★ 3. Do you have sufficient evidence? Is your evidence accurate? Precise? Representative? Authoritative?

4. Have you been careful not to paraphrase your sources so closely that you have risked a charge of plagiarism?

5. Have you distinguished between quoting an authority just to paraphrase your claims and reasons and quoting an authority as evidence?

6. Have you introduced complex quantitative evidence and long quotations with a reason that interprets the evidence for the reader?

7. Are you depending too much on your memory for evidence? Are you depending too much on a vivid anecdote?

10. Questions About Your Warrants

★ 1. Have you made explicit what your readers must believe in general before they will consider your particular claims and reasons? Have you taken important definitions, values, assumptions for granted?

☞ 2. Should you treat your warrant as a subordinate claim that you must support in a subordinate argument?

3. Do your warrants actually cover your reasons and claims?

4. Are your warrants appropriately limited and qualified?

5. Are your warrants appropriate to your community of readers?

11. Questions About Acknowledgment and Response

★ 1. Can you imagine your readers' objections and reservations? Can you respond to them? Can you support your response as if it were a subordinate claim in a subordinate argument?

2. Can you imagine a reader offering counter-reasons, counter-evidence, counter-analogies to your own? Can you imagine responding to them?

These next questions refer to issues raised in chapters 9-13.

12. Questions About Your Reasoning

★ 1. Have you avoided becoming fixated on you first hypothesis? Have you kept your mind open to alternative ones? Can you imagine at least one hypothesis as an alternative to your own?

2. If you reasoned deductively, from a warrant and reason to a claim, are you certain of the truth of the warrant? Or have your taken it for granted?

3. If you reasoned inductively, from specifics to a generalization, are you certain that you have observed enough instances to draw a generalization?

13. Questions About Meaning and Definitions

★ 1. If your argument turns on a definition, do you want your readers simply to understand a concept in a new way, or once they understand it, do you want them to do something?

2. Are you obliged to work within the four corners of a technical definition or can you work with a common one? Are you relying on a technical definition when your readers expect a common one (and vice versa)?

3. If you rely on a common definition, can you state the criteria of meaning that best serve your purposes and then match features of the referent to those criteria?

4. If you rely on a common definition, can you describe a model member of a category that your readers will accept and then describe your referent to match that model?

5. Can you shape the criteria of meaning and the features of the referent to match each other?

6. If your problem seems to be a conceptual one, is it possible you are addressing a surrogate problem in place of a pragmatic one?

7. Have you become a prisoner of an authoritative definition, either from a standard dictionary or a specialized source?

14. Questions About Causation

★ 1. If your problem is a pragmatic one, have you focused on those causes that you think you can fix?

★ 2. If your problem is conceptual, have you focused on those causes that are highlighted by the special interests you and your readers bring to the question?

3. Have you avoided the "One True Cause" mentality? Have you considered causes that do not immediately precede the effect? Causes that are absent? Causes that are routine rather than unusual? Causes whose magnitude is less significant than the effect? Causes that do not confirm your assumptions?

4. If your problem is a pragmatic one, have you considered offering all five narratives that explain the causes of an effect? Have you explained the problem? How the solution will work? Why the solution will cost less than the problem? Why it won't create a bigger problem? How you can implement it? Why it is better than alternatives?

5. Have you analyzed your theory of causation using an ANOVA table?

6. Have you considered the possibility of multiple causes? Of mutual feedback of causes?

7. Have you begun your analysis of causes far enough back in the chain of causes and effects? Or too far back?

8. Have you analyzed causes at a level of detail that suits the solution to your problem?

15. Questions About Language

★ 1. Do most of the subjects of your sentences name the main characters in your story? Do your verbs name the specific actions those characters are involved with?

★ 2. Do you begin all of your sentences with information that is familiar to your readers?

★ 3. Are your subjects relatively consistent? Are they the characters most significant to your story?

➷ 4. Do your sentences get to main verbs quickly? Do they have relatively short introductory elements? Relatively short subjects? Few interruptions between subjects and verbs?

➷ 5. Have you eliminated empty words, redundant implications of words? Have you compressed several words into one, when you can?

6. Have you tried to choose words that are specific enough to create an image in the mind's eye of your readers? Have you chosen general words for your warrants and definitions?

7. When you use words that invoke values and evoke feelings, do you do so in the context of an otherwise sound argument? Are you clear why you are using them? What problem do you think you are solving?

8. Have you avoided inappropriately trying to deflect your readers' attention away from flesh and blood characters by reifying abstractions and relying on metaphors?

Storyboarding a Long Paper

We've offered advice about organization in several writing process sections, and that advice should get you through most short papers. But for a longer, more complicated one, you may need help planning and managing all its parts. We recommend that you try a storyboard.

When you create a storyboard, you group related parts of your paper on separate pages, in rough outline form at first, but in greater detail as you develop your argument. A storyboard has all the advantages of an outline, but without the fussiness of indentations, having a "b" for every "a", and getting the numbering right. And unlike an outline, a storyboard reduces the complexity that you have to deal with at one time.

- You isolate the units of your paper so that you can work on each one separately without worrying about how it fits into the whole.
- You see at a glance where you have lots of information and where you have gaps.

A storyboard also helps you *see* a complex argument in its entirety, especially when you lay it out on a table or tape it to a wall.

- You take in the organization at a glance, like a physical structure with layers and sublayers all laid out before you.
- You can easily move pages around to try out different arrangements, seeing the structure of each new arrangement at a glance.
- You can easily add or delete sections.

Some people feel that they think better when they physically move around their storyboard, actually looking at it from different angles to get new perspectives on it. If you are a verbal person, better with words than shapes, think of a storyboard as a flexible, expanded outline. If you are a visual person, think of it as a picture of the structure of your paper. In either case, you'll manage a complex argument better if you use one.

1. Create templates.

To start the process, create template pages for you introduction and conclusion, with a heading for each possible element. Use whole pages.

Introduction/Problem	**Conclusion**
Prelude:	Main claim:
Common ground:	
	Significance of claim:
Destabilizing condition:	
Costs/consequences:	Work still to be done:
Solution:	Coda:

Next, create two kinds of reason templates: one for those reasons that you think you can support only with evidence (you should have few of these) and another for reasons that you have to support with a complete nuclear argument. So depending on how complex the support for your reason will be, create one or the other of the two templates below for each reason.

Reason #_____	**Conclusion**
Main reason:	Main reason claim:
Reports of evidence to support main reason:	Reasons in support of main reason/claim:
	Reports of evidence to support reasons:
	Acknowledgment and response:

Finally, create templates for warrants and their supporting arguments and for acknowledgments and responses and their supporting arguments:

Warrant for Reason #_____	**Acknowledgment and Response for Reason #_____**
Warrant/claim:	Objection/reservation/alternative:
Reasons in support of warrants:	Response/claim:
	Reasons:
Reports of evidence to support reasons:	Reports of evidence:
Acknowledgment and response:	Warrant/acknowledgment and response:

For the reason, warrant, and acknowledgment/response templates, make as many copies as your argument has major reasons. Save the blank template pages on your computer, but you'll start out working with them in hard copy.

2. Fill out the templates.

Fill in as many blanks as you can with what you know right now. At first, you may not have much to add, and some of it may be guesses that you have to confirm later. If you have to do some research to find something to add, do it quickly. Don't wait until the pages are full to go on to the next step.

3. Arrange the templates as they will appear in your paper.

As soon as you have enough to go on, tape the sheets to a wall or lay them out on a table, your bed, or the floor as shown below.

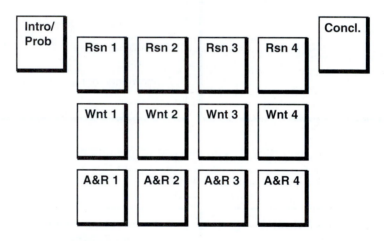

Move the pages around until you feel that you have a workable order. Add ideas as they occur to you.

If the pages get messy with notes, enter them in your computer template and print clean copies on which you can add even more notes. You can also use sticky notes that you can easily add to or delete.

4. Draft, but then revisit your storyboard.

Once you have a workable plan, build your argument piece by piece. As you draft, try different arrangements. From time to time, check the skeleton of your argument by reading straight through the whole *Introduction/Problem* page, the main reasons at the top of the *Reason* pages, and the whole *Conclusion* page. If some sheets remain empty, so be it. They will remind you of opportunities. The point is to decompose your task into parts so that you are not paralyzed by the kind of complexity that even the most experienced writers cannot deal with all at once.

PART 3

Thinking About Thinking in Arguments

In this section, we discuss another set of advanced concepts: the quality of thinking that goes into an intellectually sound argument and how we make that sound thinking apparent to careful readers, especially in arguments that concern words and their meanings or causes and effects. We focus on both the qualities of sound thinking and on the pitfalls that even the most experienced writers sometimes fall into.

- In Chapter 9, we discuss three kinds of thinking: *inductive, deductive,* and what has been called *abductive.* We emphasize the importance of thinking abductively, but also the particular blunders that mindless abductive thinking can lead us into.

- In Chapter 10, we discuss the kind of thinking you have to do when you make arguments that turn on the meanings of particular words, and we show you how to assemble an argument about meaning.

- In Chapter 11, we discuss the kind of thinking you do when you make arguments about causes and their effects, including how to avoid predictable biases in your thinking. We show you what readers look for in arguments about causation and what extra steps you have to take in an argument that holds someone responsible for the consequences of an action.

Thinking About Thinking in Arguments

CHAPTER 9

The Forms of Reasoning

In this chapter, we discuss three kinds of reasoning: inductive, deductive, and abductive. The most common and useful is abductive, a form of problem-solving reasoning in which we propose hypotheses and test them against data, inductively or deductively. We also show you how these kinds of reasoning are commonly distorted by "cognitive biases," predictable habits of thought that keep you from thinking as well as you can. Finally, we offer strategies for avoiding them.

We've told you how to plan and write arguments, but not much about how to think about the thinking that goes into them. In this section, we look more closely at the reasoning that makes an argument sound. If you learn to manage your thinking as you find and evaluate solutions, you can avoid the predictable pitfalls that trap even experienced problem solvers. In the next two chapters, we'll look at the specific kinds of thinking we use to solve problems of meaning and causation. Here, we explain three general forms of reasoning: inductive, deductive, and abductive.

Forms of Reasoning

If you have studied anything about reasoning, you probably know about two kinds: *inductive* and *deductive*. It's a distinction philosophers have made for about 2,500 years, but one that does not reflect how most of us really think. The more common kind of reasoning is called *abductive*. It is the kind of thinking we described earlier: finding and then testing possible solutions to a known problem.

Inductive Reasoning: From Specifics to a Generalization

You reason inductively when you begin with specifics and then draw a general conclusion about them. Imagine that over the years Professor Stein records whether her students wrote papers on a word processor or a typewriter, because she is interested in computer literacy. One day as she looks over her records, she realizes those who used word processors tended to get higher grades. In reaching that conclusion, she reasoned inductively, from a lot of specific data to a general claim that she did not have in mind until the connection occurred to her. That's pure induction: from specifics to a general claim.

Deductive Reasoning: From a Generalization to a Specific Conclusion

We call reasoning *deductive* when we start with a generalization (a warrant), add a somewhat more specific statement (a reason), and then draw a specific conclusion (roughly what we explained in Chapter 7). Imagine that the day after Professor Stein has her inductive insight about grades and word processors, she meets Professor Chen, who says that next year, for the first time, he will require all his students to write on word processors. She then tells him about her insight into grades and computers, causing him to think *If I make my students write on word processors, I'll probably give them higher grades*. He may have reasoned like this:

- A warrant: *According to Stein, when students write on word processors, they tend to get better grades.*
- A reason: *Next year, all of my students will write on word processors.*
- A conclusion: *If Stein is right, I'll probably give higher grades.*

If he did, that's pure deductive reasoning, from a generalization and a reason to a specific conclusion that Professor Chen did not have in mind until he got to it.

Abductive Reasoning: From Problem to Hypothesis to Test to Confirmation

Those examples, however, are misleading. We had to work hard to invent those two stories in which conclusions seemed to jump out of the blue, because we so rarely reason like that. Almost always we reason not because we happen to have a lot of data or a warrant and reason, but because we want to solve a problem. Faced with a problem, we don't randomly collect data, hoping that a solution will jump out of them. Instead, we typically start by coming up with a hunch about a possible solution—call it a probationary *hypothesis*. Then to test that hypothesis, we collect data relevant to the problem, looking for data that support our hypothesis but especially for data that contradict it. If our hunch/hypothesis explains the data better than any competing one, we accept ours as the best available solution to our problem.

For example, imagine that after noticing that most of her students who wrote on computers got better grades than those who didn't, Professor Stein has a hunch that writing on computers could be a *cause* of those better grades. To test that hypothesis, she collects more data about students in other classes and discovers that most of those who wrote on computers also got higher grades.

She might now propose an even bigger hypothesis: She *predicts* that most students get better grades when they write on computers. To support that prediction, she collects yet more data about students from other schools who do and don't write on computers, who write on their own computers or work in computer labs, and so on. Most important, she deliberately tests her hypothesis against competing hypotheses: Maybe students who choose to write on word processors are already better writers or maybe the mere desire to use one indicates greater learning ability. Let's assume her new data support her original hunch: Writing on computers is indeed a significant factor in getting higher grades. She has confirmed her hypothesis abductively: She began with a problem that motivated a hypothesis that she tested against new data.

There is, however, one thing she can never do. She can never *prove* her claim, once and for all. She always knows that tomorrow someone might come up with data that disconfirm her claim. And that's true of every inductive claim: They are only more or less probable. Even if every bird ever seen by the human eye has had feathers, it is only probably true that all birds have feathers, because somewhere there may be a featherless bird. You never know. Biologists once believed that mammals never lay eggs, until someone discovered the platypus.

Real Life Barriers to Thinking Clearly

Sad to say, real thinking is rarely so simple, because all of us have inherited habits of mind that lead our thinking astray, what are called *cognitive biases*. They have little to do with age, intelligence, education, or expertise. There is no cure. All you can do is know them, then be self-critical of your thinking, especially when you face complex issues. These biases undermine abductive, inductive, and deductive reasoning in different ways.

Bias in Abductive Thinking

We've urged you to think abductively, starting with a few tentative hypotheses to guide your thinking toward the solution of a problem. If you start by randomly gathering data, hoping a conclusion will turn up, you depend too much on luck. It would be as if Professor Stein collected data on students who pierced their noses or wore black to see if by chance any of those variables correlated with the quality of their writing. She needed a plausible hypothesis to test before she started gathering her data so that she could know what data to gather. But that's how we fall prey to the most treacherous bias in abductive thinking: We hit on a quick hypothesis, then settle down on it, usually because it serves our purposes or fits our picture of the world. Once we have it, we are anchored to it, even when the best evidence tells us we should let it go. It happens in ways both trivial and significant to just about all of us.

- *A trivial example:* Would you guess the area of France is more or less than two million square miles? OK, now guess the area of Nigeria. Whatever you guess about Nigeria, it will be closer to two million than if we had *first* asked you whether the area of France is more or less than ten million square miles (it is, in fact, 211,207 square miles). In other words, whatever number you hear first anchors your thinking to roughly that number.

- *A more significant example:* When a business starts losing money and frames its problem in terms of production costs, that formulation can exclude consideration of a better solution, like too little advertising.

Even though we need an initial hypothesis to start with, we too often harden our thinking around that first idea. Here are some strategies for avoiding the biases that contribute to anchoring.

Deliberately Seek Disconfirming Evidence

Once a belief is anchored, we are more likely to seek evidence that supports it than evidence that contradicts it. For example, here is a disconcerting finding about the way many doctors diagnose illnesses. When a patient describes symptoms, doctors are likely to make a quick diagnosis, then order tests to see if they are right. If the results of those tests are uncertain, they order more tests that they hope will confirm their diagnosis, and if those don't, yet more. But as studies show, doctors seem not inclined to order tests that would *prove their diagnosis wrong,* even though that would test their judgment more efficiently. They are interested more in proving themselves right than wrong. Once you think you have a good claim, imagine how you would disprove it. No intellectual exercise is more difficult, and more valuable.

What car ads are we most likely to read—for our own car or for another kind? Market studies show that most of us read more ads about our own car because we don't want to see evidence that another car might be better. None of us likes to think we might have bought the wrong car.

Source: Stuart Sutherland. *Irrationality: Why We Don't Think Straight!* New Brunswick, NJ: Rutgers University Press, 1992, p. 141.

Gather and Interpret Evidence Objectively

Even when we try to gather evidence objectively, we tend to reshape it to fit a hypothesis. A good example is reported by Stephen J. Gould in *The Mismeasure of Man* (New York: Norton, 1981.) Samuel Morton, an early nineteenth century scientist with a good reputation for gathering objective data, set out to prove that Caucasians were smarter than other races because they had bigger brains. To measure the size of brains, he filled skulls from different races with mustard seeds, then weighed the seeds, assuming their weight would reflect the volume of the skull and therefore the size of the brain. He found that the seeds that filled Caucasian skulls did weigh significantly more than those from non-Caucasian skulls, so he concluded that Caucasians have larger skulls and therefore larger brains (and therefore greater intelligence).

He later repeated his work with lead shot, because it produced more consistent and reliable measurements. But this time, he found much less variability among the skulls. Did Morton lie about the mustard seed? Apparently not. He had to pack down the light mustard seeds to fill a skull completely, and in so doing he seems to have unconsciously packed down seeds in the skulls of Caucasians more tightly than he did others, thereby increasing their density and total weight, thereby biasing his conclusions in favor of the conclusion he wanted to reach: greater volume for Caucasian skulls.

This bias toward confirmation is what forces researchers to do "double-blind" experiments. When they test a new drug, they do not tell patients whether they are getting the drug or a placebo, because patients sometimes report improvement only because they want a treatment to work. But researchers also have to keep themselves in the dark, because if they knew which patients were getting the drug, they might persuade themselves that those patients had improved. Without such safeguards, none of us can objectively evaluate the evidence we gather.

Don't Dismiss Contrary Evidence

Not only do we tend to gather and interpret evidence in ways that fit our hypothesis; we tend to resist evidence that demonstrably undermines it. For example, researchers assembled two groups of students with opposing views on the death penalty and established how strongly they held their views. Each group then read two articles, one in favor of the death penalty, the other against. We might expect that after reading an article opposing their respective beliefs, both sides would moderate their views and end up closer together. In fact, the opposite occurred. After reading the articles, the two sides were *further* apart than before. Apparently, both sides put more weight on the article that supported their views and rejected the one that refuted them, entrenching themselves in their prior beliefs even more deeply.

How strongly do we hold a belief, even when we have evidence we are wrong? More than we should. Researchers gave students some invented suicide notes, saying that some were fake and some were real. The students were asked to pick out the real ones. As they did so, some students were told they were doing a good job, others that they were not. At the end, the students were told all the notes were fake. Then they were asked how well they thought they would do with a set of real notes. Those who had been told (falsely) that they had one well were far more confident they would do well with real notes that those told (falsely) that they have done badly.

Source: L. Ross, M.R. Lepper, and M. Hubbard. "Perseverance in Self Perception and Social Perception: Biased Attributional Processes in the Debriefing Paradigm". *Journal of Personality and Social Psychology* 32 (1975): 880–92.

This is a hard thought experiment to apply to your own work, but try it: Imagine that you are being paid to *disprove* your own argument. What evidence have you set aside that might help you do that?

Don't Be So Sure of Yourself

Another factor encouraging us to hunker down on a claim is overconfidence. For example, are you an above average, average, or below average driver? More than 90 percent of drivers think they are above average. These same results have been found in a host of other studies: Most of us are certain that we answer questions correctly far more than our actual performance demonstrates. We are chronically loath to question our beliefs because we put more confidence in them than they deserve.

This is not a sign of stupidity or immaturity. If we lightly changed our beliefs at the first hint of contrary evidence, we would fail to see the deeper regularities in our physical and social worlds. We need confidence in our settled beliefs to live settled lives. But the cost of that confidence is becoming so entrenched in a belief that we don't change it when we should. We tend to think hard enough to get by, but no harder. It is behavior that is cost-effective in the short run, which is, after all, where most of us live. In the academic and professional world, however, we are expected to take a longer view. So be modest in your certainty, even when in your heart of hearts you are certain you are right.

The Cautious Language of Good Problem Solvers

A researcher who studied the language of good and bad problem solvers found that the bad problem solvers tend to use words that express certainty and totality: *constantly, every time, all, without exception, absolutely, entirely, completely, totally, unequivocally, undeniably, without question, certainly, solely, only, neither—nor, must, have to.* Good problem solvers more often use words that express uncertainty and qualification: *now and then, in general, sometimes, often, ordinarily, a bit, in particular, somewhat, to a degree, perhaps, conceivable, questionable, among other things, on the other hand, may, can.*

Source: From Dietrich Doerner, *The Logic of Failure: Recognizing and Avoiding Error in Complex Situations.* New York: Addison-Wesley Pub., 1997.

Avoiding Bias in Inductive Thinking

Our most common bias in inductive reasoning is jumping to a conclusion from too little evidence. Starting with the hypothesis that global warming is a myth, someone seizes on a record cold January as proof (or a proponent of warming seizes on a record hot August). Readers judge inductive reasoning sound only when they think you have more than enough data. The problem is guessing what readers count as enough, and that depends on both readers and the subject.

Avoiding Bias in Deductive Thinking

The risk in deductive reasoning is that we ignore evidence entirely, because we trust our warrants to explain the case at hand. Recall the argument about DNA evidence proving that someone in Thomas Jefferson's blood line fathered a child by his slave Sally Hemings (p. 74). Some historians tested their hypothesis inductively, looking at a lot of individual bits of evidence:

- Someone in Jefferson's family had fathered a son by Hemings.
- Jefferson took her with him when he went to Paris as ambassador.
- Some contemporaries publicly accused him of having children by Hemings.
- The children in question looked like Jefferson.
- The children were the only slaves Jefferson freed in his lifetime.
- Stories about Hemings and Jefferson were passed down in her family for 200 years.

They concluded inductively that Jefferson had probably fathered at least one child by Hemings. Historians on the other side dismissed that evidence, because they believed in a warrant and reason that made it irrelevant:

> When a person's life is devoted to freedom, equality, and morality, that person's character excludes doing something as immoral as having sex with a slave. _{warrant} Jefferson devoted his life to freedom, equality, and morality, _{reason} so he could not have had sex with Hemings. _{claim/conclusion}

When you reason deductively, guard against overgeneralizing: Think about the limitations and provisos that we usually leave unsaid. For example, the anti-Hemings historians might have to acknowledge that their warrant has limits:

> People do not act against their fundamental character *unless they are under great stress, or they face great temptation, or they are coerced, etc.*

Taking those limits into account, even the staunchest Jeffersonian would have to acknowledge and respond to at least the possibility that he might have been under stress from loneliness and grief after his wife died and that he faced daily temptation with her half-sister, Sally Hemings.

How do you resist these biases? First recognize them, then engage with others to seek out different points of view, in person and in your imagination. Make time to question your claims and encourage that voice in the back (or front) of your mind to keep asking *But what would you say to someone who asked . . . ?*

The Costs of Biased Evidence Gathering

David Irving, a historian of World War II and Nazi Germany, acquired a superb reputation for his ability to find obscure evidence. He has also denied that the

Holocaust happened. When he was called an irresponsible historian, he sued his accuser. After spending millions of dollars on his case, he lost both it and his reputation. Here is what one observer wrote the day after the verdict:

> [Some] otherwise responsible historians [have] made [an argument] to separate a "good" David Irving, the fact gatherer who has been able to unearth vast amounts of original documents and eyewitness testimony . . . from the not-so-good David Irving who may get some of his interpretations wrong. . . . Perhaps the London verdict [against him] might be an occasion for historians who argue that you can defend Mr. Irving by separating "fact gathering" from interpretation to reconsider, [t]o learn the lesson that fact gathering can be prejudiced by what one is looking for—and by what one is not looking for. Can one praise a fact gatherer who somehow has failed to find the facts of mass murder . . . ? . . . Unlike Mr. Irving himself, they are not guilty of Holocaust denial. But in their naivete about the relationship between fact and interpretation, they might fairly be charged with David Irving denial.

Source: Ron Rosenbaum, "The Roots of Holocaust Denial," *The Wall Street Journal,* April 12, 2000.

WRITING PROCESS 9
The Forms of Reasoning

Preparing and Planning

Slow Your Rush to Judgment

As you decide on a solution/claim, guard against leaping to a conclusion:

1. Consider all the solutions you can think of. Pick at least two, preferably three that you test against the evidence, even if only to disprove some of them.
2. Imagine what evidence would disconfirm a hypothesis, then look for it. You'll save time by ruling out a weak hypothesis right from the start.
3. If you can't think of specific disconfirming evidence that you can find quickly, keep an eye out for it as you gather evidence.
4. Gather more evidence than you think you need.
5. Gather evidence objectively. Ask, *What would I see in this evidence if I opposed this solution/claim?*
6. Interpret evidence objectively. Ask, *How would I interpret this evidence if I opposed this solution/claim?*

Follow steps 2–6 even if you begin with a solution/claim that you fully intend to support. You may not change your mind (though you should stay open to that possibility), but you will better anticipate readers' objections.

INQUIRIES

Reflections

1. Think of a public figure you admire—a politician, writer, sports figure, etc. Now suppose you saw seemingly reliable evidence of a flaw in that person's character: he or she embezzled money, gambles uncontrollably, engages in sordid sex, or any other disturbing behavior. What would be your first impulse: To defend the person? To change your opinion? To feel betrayed? To reserve judgment? Which response do you think would be the most rational? Which would be the most common?

2. Imagine the scenario above involving not a public figure but a close friend or family member. Now what would be your first impulse? Would that response be a rational one? Would a rational response be best?

CHAPTER 9 IN A NUTSHELL

About Your Argument . . .

Traditional philosophers identify two kinds of reasoning:

- *Inductive* reasoning, from specifics to a general conclusion about all of them: *Many samples of ocean water are salty, so ocean water must be salty.*

- *Deductive* reasoning, from a general warrant and reason to a specific claim: *Ocean water is always salty; this water is from the ocean, so it must be salty.*

But the more common kind of reasoning is *abductive*, a kind of reasoning that begins with a hypothesis that might explain the data in question and that we then test using whatever reasoning seems appropriate. Abductive reasoning is problem-driven reasoning: Your hypothesis is always the solution to a problem.

Each kind of reasoning is vulnerable to cognitive biases.

- When you think inductively, you risk basing a conclusion on too few instances. You avoid that risk by gathering more evidence than you think you need and by learning something about statistical sampling and analysis.

- When you think deductively, you risk formulaic thinking, applying the equivalent of a rote mental warrant to every situation.

- When you think abductively, you risk fixating on the first hypothesis that springs to mind. Guard against that by holding your earliest hypotheses delicately, by imagining more than one, and by deliberately seeking out evidence that disconfirms your favorite one.

CHAPTER 10

Arguments About Meanings

In this chapter, we discuss some basic issues in thinking about the relationship between words and meanings. We show you how to make an argument based on meanings and to define terms in a way that encourages readers to see things as you want them to.

In most arguments, we address issues involving either words and their meanings or causes and their effects, and sometimes both, because what we think something is usually influences what we think we should do about it. For example, a few years ago some members of Congress thought they knew what to do when they learned that a federal agency, the National Endowment for the Arts, had funded a museum that exhibited photographs by Robert Mapplethorpe, whose images are so sexually explicit that many call them pornographic. The NEA's critics argued that Congress should abolish the NEA because it promoted pornography.

To support their claim, the critics had to make four arguments. Two of them were about words and their meanings:

- What is the meaning of *pornography?*
- What features of Mapplethorpe's images earn them that term?

Two more were about causes and their effects:

- How does the NEA contribute to the dissemination of those images?
- How would closing the NEA combat pornography?

We base many professional and civic arguments on this relationship between what we should *call* something (*It's pornography!*) and what we should *do* about it (*Get rid of whatever promotes it!*). Faced with a problem, we think we can solve it if we can get others to use words in a particular way. For example,

If supporters of civilian militia could convince us that their members are *patriots,* definition they could argue that we should support them as defenders of our freedom. pragmatic argument

238

If someone could convince us that competitive ballroom dancing is a *sport,* _{defi-} _{nition} she could argue that we should make it an Olympic event. _{pragmatic argument}

In the academic world, on the other hand, researchers often make arguments about meanings and definitions not to get us to *do* anything, but to help us *think* about things more clearly. Here is an argument that turns on the definition of *language*:

> The word *language* is often used loosely to mean communicating information through behavior or signs. So it is said that bees use a "language of dancing" to communicate information about the direction of flowers in bloom. But human language is more than that. It communicates not just predictable and narrowly defined bits of information, but desires, feelings, and ideas unique to the moment. _{definition} Language even in that higher sense, however, is not ours alone, because chimpanzees can be taught to do something like it through sign language or by touching symbols on a computer screen. As rudimentary as their communication is, they demonstrate an ability to use language in ways that resemble what we humans do. _{application of definition} Their ability demonstrates intellectual powers so much greater than we give them credit for that we can no longer think of ourselves as cognitively unique in the animal kingdom. _{conceptual argument}

If we accept the claim about what *language* means and agree that what chimps do exemplifies it, then we have reason to accept the claim that we can no longer think of ourselves as unique in the animal kingdom. Those making that argument might also want us to treat chimps differently and thereby solve a pragmatic problem—for instance, whether we should use them in medical experiments. But their basic aim is to solve a conceptual problem—we think we are unique, but that is wrong. Chimps can do what we can do, so we have to rethink our place in the animal kingdom. To do that, the authors make an argument about the meaning of the word *language* and about the consequences of that meaning.

In this chapter, we discuss arguments that focus on words, their meanings, and the consequences of choosing one meaning over another. But first we have to explain some words and meanings of our own.

Some Terminology

To explain how to make arguments about meaning, we'll use six words that you know—*category, term, feature, meaning, criteria,* and *definition*—but we'll start with one that you may not—*referent:*

- We usually use a word or phrase to talk about something—a person, object, event, concept, and so on. It can be either out in the world (the Eiffel Tower) or in our minds (the square root of 5). We'll call the thing we refer to when we use a word its **referent.**

It is easiest to grasp the idea of a referent when we talk about particular things. If someone asked, *When you mentioned* Sue's cat, *what did you refer to?*

you could pick up or point to that specific cat, the referent you had in mind. You would have a harder time showing what referent you had in mind if someone asked, *When you talked about* pet cats, *what did you refer to?* You could only point to lots of individual examples of pet cats. And you would have a harder time yet explaining the referent of *cat* in a sentence like *The cat is a mysterious creature,* because there *cat* refers to the abstract category of cats. So a referent can be an individual thing in the world, a concept that categorizes many things in the world, or an abstract concept that exists chiefly in our minds.

- We group referents into **categories** when we treat them as alike. Categories range from very large to very small: things, creatures, animals, mammals, felines, cats, Persians, Sue's Persian cat.

Some categories seem to match natural things in the world: *trees, dogs, uranium, water* (though philosophers debate whether categories of "natural kinds" really exist in nature). Other categories we create and then impose on the world: *duty, spice, animals bigger than a breadbox,* even the term *category* itself.

- When we talk about categories, we usually name them by **terms**: the terms *animal, mammal, feline, cat* and *Persian* all name both categories and the referents in them. We gain and lose terms all the time: *CD* is a new one; *gramophone* is almost gone. And we invent terms to name categories for which we have no single word: *creatures that fly.*

- When we talk about what distinguishes the referents in one category from those in another, we talk about their **features**. Persian cats are fluffy, have pug noses, and meow normally; Siamese cats are smooth, have pointed noses, and yowl. The problem is that not every member of a category has to share a common feature. The best known example is the category we call *game*. It is hard to see what distinctive feature is shared by chess and playing catch.

- We create and assign **meaning** to a category based on the features that distinguish that category from others, but also on the associations, values, and other ideas we have about it. We then attach some of that meaning to the term. So when we think about the meaning of *cat,* we call up a mixture of words, images, concepts, feelings, and so on. Like categories, meanings do not have sharp boundaries.

- Psychologists argue convincingly that we experience "meaning" more as a holistic entity than as the sum of individual parts. But when we *talk* about a meaning, we have to break it down into elements that we'll call **criteria** of meaning. For example, when someone asks us what the word *friable* means, we say, *It means the quality of something that is sort of dry and crumbly and easily breaks into little pieces.* The criteria for the meaning of *friable* are "dry," "crumbly," "easily breaks into little pieces." Yet the meaning in our heads is probably more all of a piece.

- We create a **definition** when we state in words some criteria of meaning of a term that we attach to a category. Most definitions consist of a term that names a general category that is modified by more terms that narrow it. The definition of *friable* is a quality (general category) of breaking (narrowing term) into crumbly pieces (narrowing term). Each of those words names a criterion of meaning.

To understand arguments about meaning, we have to make three distinctions:

- We make up definitions, but meanings are imposed on us by the way we and others use words.
- Definitions offer only the sketchiest framework of the meaning we attach to a word. Definitions are to meanings as a whistled tune is to a symphony.

Meaning is infinitely more complex than a definition, especially a dictionary definition.

- Most important, definitions never settle whether we should or should not attach some specific term to some specific referent.

Whether we call someone a *patriot* is not determined by its definition or by the "objective" features of a person who might be one. If readers might question you, you'll need an argument, not just a definition, to settle the issue.

We can use this terminology to explain what happens when we invent new terms. For example: A few years ago people noticed that some drivers _{refer-} _{ents} were displaying hostile behavior. _{common feature} They drove aggressively, seemed angry, used hostile language or gestures, and so on. _{common features} When people treated instances of this behavior as in some ways alike, they created a category that had no settled term attached to it. At first, they referred to the category with various terms: *crazy driving, angry behavior behind the wheel* and so on. Eventually one term with a memorable sound stuck to the category, *road rage*. Now when a specific driver cuts us off, yelling and shaking his fist, we can say, *There's another case of road rage*. If someone asks what we mean, we can point to a specific example, describe a typical case, or give a definition: "driving (general category) in ways that seem aggressive, angry, and hostile (narrowing terms)."

If definitions were as clear-cut as this example seems to be, we wouldn't have to make arguments about words or their meanings. But within some general limits, we all use words and define their meanings in different ways at different times for different purposes to solve different problems. And as a consequence, we do not all agree all of the time about what words mean or how we should use them.

For example, you knowingly tell an untruth when you tell your host at a dinner party that a dish you thought was awful tasted great. But would you call that untruth an *out and out lie?* If you told it to comfort someone you cared for, we might call it a *white lie* or maybe a *fib,* but most of us would be reluctant to call it an *outright lie* even though it might "technically" be one. On the other hand, suppose you know that if you say the dish was fine, the cook will prepare it again for his (and your) boss, get fired, and you'll get his job. You said the same words referring to the same referent, but with a different intention. Now do those words constitute a lie? Aren't we more inclined to call that second case a "real" lie?

Meaning is, to mix metaphors, slippery and fuzzy at the same time, and it's that slippery fuzziness that challenges us when we craft arguments about words and their meanings.

Meanings and Problems

As with any argument, you plan one about meaning by asking first why you have to make it: *What problem do I want to solve?* Not only do you have to decide the kind of problem you pose, pragmatic or conceptual, but you must also be sure that your problem is really about meanings. Even experienced writers can get caught up in arguments that seem to be about the meaning of terms but are in fact about larger, more difficult issues.

Does the Meaning at Issue Resolve a Pragmatic or Conceptual Problem?

Decide right away whether your problem is pragmatic or conceptual, because those two kinds of problems require different kinds of arguments.

- In a pragmatic argument, you discuss meaning *so that* readers will understand why an action is necessary. They expect you to go beyond abstract, theoretical definitions to consider their pragmatic consequences.

- In a conceptual argument, you focus on a definition, not for its own sake, but because it helps readers understand something important about a larger issue or question.

For example, when we defined *argument* in Part 1, we wanted to help you write arguments that your readers would accept, or at least respect. If we (which is to say you) succeeded, we (and you) solved a pragmatic problem. So we focused on practical outcomes and ways to reach them. If, however, we had written a scholarly historical analysis of argument, we would have defined it differently, because *argument* has been used in many different ways and our aim would have been to help you understand the concept rather than do something with it.

So your first decision is this: If readers accept your definition, will they only *understand* something better or will they *do* something?

Is the Issue of Meaning a Surrogate for a Larger Problem?

Once you think you know whether your goal is pragmatic or conceptual, do not fool yourself into unknowingly making a *surrogate* argument. An argument about meaning becomes a *surrogate* argument when it stands in for a larger, more difficult one that you may be avoiding. Surrogate arguments can lead you astray in two ways: an apparently conceptual argument about definitions masks an underlying pragmatic problem or an argument about meaning is really an argument about values and feelings.

Don't Confuse Words and Deeds

When your readers disagree about the meaning of a term, don't expect to solve a controversial pragmatic problem by trying to define the term. You or they are likely to fall into a debate about words instead of focusing on the larger issue. Here is an example of what is probably a surrogate argument. It is a debate about whether two people of the same sex can have a ceremony we call a *wedding:*

Thelma: I had an interesting weekend. I went to a wedding for two women friends of my aunt.

Louise: Well, maybe it was a ceremony, but it wasn't a wedding because *wedding* means joining a man and woman in marriage. You can't have a marriage between two women.

Thelma: Who says you can't have a marriage between any two people when they publicly commit themselves to each other? Who says they can't be the same sex?

Louise: Look at how the word's been used for thousands of years. A wedding has always meant the creation of a marriage bond between a man and a woman.

Thelma: Words change their meaning to suit new realities.

Louise: Maybe some do, but you can't invent new meanings just because it suits your purpose. For most people, *wedding* still means a ceremony between a man and a woman. That's just what it means.

Thelma and Louise risk an endless debate over the meaning of *wedding* and *marriage* until they understand and agree on the kind of problem they want to solve. They could be debating a conceptual problem of linguistic change: *Can individuals change the meaning of words when it suits their purposes?* More likely they are really concerned about one or more pragmatic problems that are solved or created by how society uses the terms *wedding and marriage.*

- Thelma may think that using the term *wedding* for same-sex ceremonies solves a pragmatic problem: Same-sex couples like her aunt's friends are often deprived of the social, personal, and economic benefits associated with traditional marriage partnerships. It is for her a problem of social injustice. To solve it, she would put same-sex couples in the same category as different-sex couples, an aim that would be furthered if we agreed to call their ceremony a wedding, and their relationship a marriage.

- Louise may think that using the word *wedding* for same-sex ceremonies creates a different pragmatic problem: If the state condones same-sex relationships, it implicitly condones what she believes is immoral behavior. It is for her a problem of morality. To solve that moral problem, she wants to keep same-sex couples in a different category from different-sex couples, an aim furthered by refusing to call this ceremony a wedding and their relationship a marriage.

If those unstated pragmatic problems are what really motivate Thelma and Louise to argue over the meaning of *wedding* and *marriage* they are locked in an unproductive surrogate argument. So long as they fail to recognize that, they are unlikely to agree about anything. They are defending their positions (that combat metaphor again) not just because of what they think the term *wedding* "really" means, but because of how they think society should treat same-sex couples. That issue cannot be settled by an argument about meaning.

Here's what to watch for: As you plan to make a conceptual argument about meaning, ask whether it is surrogate for a pragmatic one. If you find yourself going round and round about the "real" meaning of a word, step back and look for a pragmatic problem that occasioned the need to define the word in the first place.

If your argument might be surrogate for a larger one, try to define that larger one and confront it directly. If you can't because it is too big or too sensitive, try explicitly addressing the question of meaning not as an unacknowledged surrogate but as an aspect of the larger problem. Otherwise, you trap yourself and your readers in an aimless debate that misses the point.

IN THE READINGS . . .

Definition or Action?

In "Smoking and the Tyranny of Public Health" (p. 431) Jacob Sullum discusses the dangers of surrogate arguments, using the example of obesity, which public health officials define as a "disease" and an "epidemic": "For the most part, Americans are dying of things you can't catch: cancer, heart disease, trauma. Accordingly, the public health establishment is focusing on those causes and factors underlying them. Having vanquished most true epidemics, it has turned its attention to metaphorical epidemics of unhealthy behavior."

Do Definitions Sneak in Values?

A second way you create a surrogate argument is by failing to recognize that what you really want is for your readers to evaluate something as you do, to feel as you do. Consider this exchange:

Maude: I think *Titanic* is a masterpiece of film art _{claim} that movingly
          dramatizes the tragedy of an epic event from an intimately

human point of view, celebrating human courage and self-sacrifice for another. _{reasons}

Harold: I think it is commercial exploitation _{claim} that crassly appeals to our emotions by cynically denigrating the rich as selfish and cowardly and shamelessly flattering the lower classes as selfless and brave, thereby pandering to class resentments for a bigger box office. _{reasons}

Maude and Harold seem to be concerned with a problem of categorization: Which category does *Titanic* fit into, *masterpiece of film art* or *commercial exploitation?* In that case, they could try to agree on criteria for each category, match them to the features of the movie, and agree which it is—perhaps agreeing that it's a bit of both. But their language suggests something is at stake beyond mere categorization. They are using strong words that invoke strong values and strong feelings: *movingly, tragedy, epic, celebrating* vs. *crassly, cynically, shamelessly, pandering.*

If Harold and Maude are talking about *Titanic* to justify their evaluations or vent their feelings (two sides of the same coin), then their argument does not concern what *Titanic* "really" is. And in any event, neither can change how the other feels by arguing over definitions. Suppose Harold carefully matched features of the film to criteria for the category *commercial exploitation,* but Maude still responded, *Of course it's commercial exploitation, but so what? It's still a great movie. I love it.* Harold would have won an empty victory in a battle he was bound to lose (those combat metaphors again).

Here's what to watch for: Don't debate definitions when you want others to like or dislike, approve or disapprove of something. You won't persuade them that someone is thrifty rather than stingy or outspoken rather than opinionated by defining terms. When a term implies approval or disapproval, its meaning includes our evaluation and feeling. We apply the appropriate evaluative term *after* we *already* approve or disapprove.

When you find yourself in an argument that seems to go round and round, step back and ask whether you are having a surrogate argument that you cannot possibly settle until you settle another one.

Meanings and Criteria

How We Argue About Meanings

When you make an argument that turns on meaning, you usually have a relatively straightforward aim: You want readers to think of a referent in a certain way, so you try to persuade them to call it by a certain term. If they do, they put it in a category that leads them to think of it as you want them to. Let's say you want to argue that Mapplethorpe's photographs _{referents} are not *pornography* _{term 1} but are instead *erotic art.* _{term 2} You therefore have to build an argument that does two things:

- You have to give readers reason to accept certain criteria of meaning for your key terms. So your first task is to get them to agree with your definitions of *pornography* and *erotic art*.

- You also have to give them reason to see that features of the referents, the photos, don't match the criteria of *pornography* but do match the criteria of *erotic art*.

You may have a hard time doing that, because meanings are not as fixed and certain as many think, or wish. Some philosophers want to treat categories and their meanings as rigid containers. They claim we can always know whether a particular referent is in or out of a category, because we can know both the fixed and essential criteria that define the category and whether a referent has features that match them.

But as much as those philosophers wish people would use words and meanings in fixed and predictable ways, that's not how we do it in real life, especially in arguments. Categories are not prefabricated containers, and referents are not predetermined to fit into them, the way a round peg fits a round hole. In real life arguments, we squeeze pegs and stretch holes to fit each other.

Do Readers Expect Common or Authorized Meanings?

To determine how much freedom you have to shape meanings, you must decide whether your readers expect you to rely on *common* or on *authorized* meanings and definitions.

- A *common meaning* is our everyday, nontechnical understanding of a word, like our ordinary meaning of *dog*. In casual conversation, most of us think a coyote is a "kind of" dog, and for most of us urban dwellers, so is a wolf. When we see hyenas on TV, a lot of us think of them as really ugly dogs, even though biologically they are more closely related to cats and most closely to the mongoose.

- An *authorized meaning*, on the other hand, is a technical, stipulated, "officially" defined meaning, such as the meaning a biologist would associate with *dog* when writing a scientific article about the evolutionary relationships among dogs, wolves, and coyotes. For a biologist, a hyena is no more a dog than a cat is.

If your readers expect a common meaning, you are freer to shape your definition to achieve your aim, within limits. But if they expect an authorized meaning, they will hold you within its four corners. For example, the Supreme Court has stipulated (authorized) three criteria for the legal definition of *pornography*. Their definition is in *Black's Law Dictionary:*

> Material is pornographic or obscene [1] if the average person, applying contemporary community standards, would find that the work taken as a whole appeals to the prurient interest and [2] if it depicts in a patently offen-

sive way sexual conduct and [3] if the work taken as a whole lacks serious literary, artistic, political, or scientific value. *Miller v. California,* 413 U.S. 15, 24-25, 93 S.Ct. 2607, 2615, 37 L. Ed. 2d 419.

In court, those critics of the National Endowment for the Arts would have to work inside the boundaries of that authorized definition of *pornography* to argue that Mapplethorpe's photos are legally pornographic. But in a speech to the PTA back home, they could rely on common meanings and create their own definition: *His images are pornographic in the way they degrade human dignity by reducing sex to disgusting animal behavior.*

If you write mostly for teachers, you must remember that they work in fields with technical terms that have been debated sometimes for centuries. So you should anticipate that they will expect you to use those terms with their agreed authorized meaning, or if their meanings are disputed, to acknowledge the debate. If you use the term *social class* in a sociology paper, *tragedy* in a drama class, or *inertia* in a physics lab, your readers will expect you to use those terms as authorized by the fields of sociology, literary criticism, and physics.

The problem is that some terms with authorized meanings in one field may have only common ones in others: *tragedy* is a technical term in literary criticism, but is used with its common meaning in sociology: *the tragedy of teen-age suicide.*

Strategies for Using Common Meanings

Even when you have some freedom to shape the meaning and the referent to fit each other, you have to stay within common sense limits. The more readers use a term and the more they know about a referent, the more likely they will accept only definitions and descriptions that match their sense of things. You can call Benedict Arnold a true patriot, but most readers have a definition of *patriot* that won't stretch that far.

How free you are to put the meaning of a term "in play" also depends on how specific it is and how familiar it is to readers. For example, the terms *gun* and *weapon* both have common meanings, but you can do more with the meaning of *weapon* than of *gun.* The common meaning of *gun* is so deeply entrenched in our thinking that it would be rare for someone to say about gun control, *Well, doesn't it all depend on what you mean by* gun? On the other hand, suppose someone says that since you aren't allowed to bring weapons to school, you can't bring a hammer because it could be used as a weapon. At that point, someone is likely to say, *Well, I guess it all depends on what you mean by* weapon. The meaning of *weapon* is open for discussion in a way the meaning of *gun* is not. Common meanings are more in play than technical ones, but some common meanings are more in play than others. Your job is to shape meanings to support your argument.

Here are three strategies for doing that:

Strategy 1: Shape Criteria and Features So They Match Each Other

If you are not bound to authorized criteria, you can shape a referent to fit the meaning *at the same time* you shape the common meaning to fit the referent. It's like shaving a peg to fit a hole at the same time you shave the hole to fit the peg.

For example, imagine someone wants us to reject a Constitutional amendment that criminalizes burning the American flag. To do so, she decides to use the term *patriotic* to describe those who burn the flag to protest immoral actions by our government. She reasons that if she can get people to see flag-burners as patriots, then they may agree that the Constitution should not ban flag-burning but protect it. Since there are no authorized, stipulated criteria for *patriotic,* she has room to develop its common meaning in ways that help her achieve her aim:

> Those who support a Constitutional amendment criminalizing flag burning appeal first to our patriotism. Many of them define *patriotism* as honoring the flag: waving it, saluting it, standing at attention as it passes by. They see the flag as synonymous with our country itself: damage it, and you damage America. _{acknowledgment of alternative definition} But for those who see more deeply, real patriotism is loyalty not to symbols, but to the principles those symbols represent, including the idea that when a government violates them, truly patriotic citizens must protest. Real patriotism calls attention to such wrongs, even if it takes burning the flag to do it. _{criteria for the meaning of patriot} If such symbolic expression is made a crime, _{destabilizing condition of problem} we will threaten our values more than any flag burner could. _{cost of problem} Congress should reject such an amendment. _{solution/claim}

This writer picked out features of flag burners that she thought made them admirable, but *at the same time,* she crafted criteria for the meaning of *patriot* to match their features: *A patriot is someone with the courage to enrage others in order to preserve the highest values of our nation. Flag burners have that courage.*

Her only constraint is how our beliefs limit what criteria we are able to accept. She cannot succeed if we think any civil protest is wrong, even in defense of "the principles this country stands for." So your freedom to shape features and criteria is limited by your readers' ideas of both the term and the referent.

Strategy 2: Match the Referent to a Model

We commonly talk about meaning in terms of discrete criteria, but psychologists have shown that we probably think about most meanings and categories in another way: We compare a referent not to a check-list of criteria but to what we think of holistically as the best or most typical instance of the category (what psychologists call a *prototype* but we call a *model*). It's a bit like showing readers that your peg is so much like a model peg that it obviously fits the hole.

For example, the following passage describes a familiar instance of a patriot, the Minutemen of 1775. If the reader accepts it as typical, the writer can show that a civilian militia member of today matches that historical model:

> Critics of citizen militias forget that it was civilians with their own guns who won our freedoms 200 years ago. The Minutemen of 1775 were patriots who defended their homes and families by grabbing their rifles from over their fire-

places and joining others in common defense against a tyrannical government, ₘₒdₑₗ just as the freedom lover who joins a militia today leaves his home
to prepare to defend our freedoms. ᵣₑfₑᵣₑₙₜ As we honor those patriots who won
our freedom then, so should we respect those who defend it now.

Your readers will accept a meaning based on a model when they accept the
model as typical of the category *and* they think your referent closely resembles
it. (In this case, a reader might question the resemblance if she knows the
historical facts about militias as reported in "Guns in America," p. 143.)

In these arguments, the more vividly you portray both the model and the
referent, the more persuasive your argument. Of course, you still have to use
words, and they all have criteria of meaning. So in a sense, you are still matching features to criteria, but less as a checklist than as a word picture.

Strategy 3: Combine Matching and Modeling

You can always combine feature matching with modeling:

Those who condemn citizen militias as paranoid gun nuts ignore their deep
love for the principles that this country was founded on. ₍ᵣᵢₜₑᵣᵢₒₙ ₁ Civilian militias are ready to join with others to rise up against unjust tyranny, relying on
force, if necessary; ₍ᵣᵢₜₑᵣᵢₒₙ ₂ and they are ready to lay down their lives to
preserve their freedom and yours. ₍ᵣᵢₜₑᵣᵢₒₙ ₃ They are the true patriots of our
time, no different from the Minutemen of 1775, who defended their homes
and families by grabbing their rifles from over their fireplaces and joining
others in common defense against a tyrannical government. ₘₒdₑₗ In the same
way, civilian militia keep their guns ready to resist a tyranny that wants to
deprive us of our freedom to use them. ᵣₑfₑᵣₑₙₜ If we honor the patriots of 1775,
so should we respect those of today. ₍ₗₐᵢₘ

In an argument based on common definitions, don't assume you must defer
to fixed features of referents or fixed criteria of meaning (even if you find them
in a dictionary). But don't assume either that you are completely free to shape
them in whatever way you will: You could call the Oklahoma bomber, Timothy
McVeigh, a patriot, but you'd have to distort both its meaning and his actions
too much for most readers to swallow. Our language imposes limits on meanings that you violate at your peril. But within those limits, you are free to craft
descriptions of referents, criteria of meaning, and models to solve your problem.

Strategies for Using Authorized Meanings

When your readers expect you to use an authorized meaning, you have much
less freedom. You usually have to accept the stipulated criteria and describe the
features of the referent in a way that matches them. For example, the official
diagnostic manual of the American Psychiatric Association breaks the common
term *alcoholism* into several specific conditions and stipulates criteria for them.
The most serious condition is *alcohol dependence*. A person is alcohol dependent if he or she meets at least two of four criteria:

1. *Tolerance*: The body's cells adapt to high levels of alcohol so that it has
   less effect on them.

2. *Dyscontrol* (psychological dependence): The person drinks to relieve bodily or emotional pain, but does not control when, where, or how he or she drinks.

3. *Medical Complications*: The person suffers physical damage from alcohol.

4. *Withdrawal*: When the person abstains from drinking, he or she suffers convulsions, hallucinations, or delirium.

A clinical psychologist arguing in a professional setting must observe that definition, because it is enforced by canons of professional ethics and peer pressure. So if she is making a case that someone is alcohol dependent, she will describe that person in a way that fits the criteria:

> Mr. Jones shows a high tolerance, demonstrating no visible effects until his blood alcohol level reaches .2, twice what should make a man his size intoxicated. Although he has no medical complications, he does exhibit psychological dependence. He begins drinking every morning, usually alone, and continues even after he knows he should stop. Since Mr. Jones drinks every day, we cannot say whether he suffers withdrawal, but it is likely he would if he ever stopped drinking.

When an authority and its backing institution set out criteria of meaning, you have to match the features of the referent to them. It's a one-way fit, a bit like fitting a wooden peg into a rigid, metal hole: though you can't change the hole, you can reshape the peg to fit. But there are limits. You can *shave* the peg, but not change its features altogether.

Don't Rely on Authorized Definitions Unless Your Readers Do

Writers want their words to carry as much weight as possible, so many try to use terms in an authorized sense whenever they can. For example, the terms *tragedy* and *comedy* have common meanings that we use freely in everyday conversation. But over the last 2,500 years or so, literary critics have given them technical definitions. So students in a drama class seem more authoritative when they use those terms in their technical sense. In fact, students who do not know those technical definitions seem ignorant when they use authorized terms with their common sense meanings.

But you also risk confusing readers and damaging your ethos if you overuse authorized definitions. If your readers understand a term in common ways and you try to override their understanding with an authorized, technical meaning, you are likely to lose both their confidence and assent.

For example, medical and environmental scientists have long failed to educate the public about the "true" risks of nuclear waste, toxic dumps, or trace metals in drinking water and fertilizers. Only recently have they realized that they and the public define risk differently. Experts use an authorized, statistical definition of risk roughly like this:

$$\text{Risk} = \text{Probability of occurrence} \times \text{Cost}$$

Roughly translated, the risk that you face equals the probability that something will happen (over a certain period of time at a certain level of exposure) multiplied by the cost (measured by death, injury, or illness). So a scientist might say that your risk of getting cancer from a nearby nuclear power plant is .000001 if you lived for 30 years within two miles of the plant, a risk they would classify as "slight."

For years, risk communication experts could not understand why ordinary folks wouldn't buy their assurances about how safe those plants were. They explained endlessly that we are more likely to get hit by lightning or drown in a bathtub than to get cancer from an atomic power plant, but we still objected to the risk of living next door to one.

It took a long time for social psychologists to puzzle it out, but now they understand that most of us ordinary folks do not define risk statistically (even when we understand the math), but psychologically, in terms of our own common definition. We define risk by summing at least four factors:

1. *Magnitude of the cost.* If the worst happens, will a lot of people be harmed?

Thousands were killed by an accident at a chemical plant in Bhopal, India. The chances of something like that happening again are infinitesimally low, but the potential magnitude of a disaster like that increases our *sense* of risk.

2. *Immediacy of the cost.* If the worst happens, will people be harmed all at once or over a long period of time?

It is statistically certain that we are safer traveling by plane than car, but many of us feel safer driving, because when a plane crashes a lot of people die at once and it gets a lot of publicity, while traffic fatalities are spread out over time, and we usually hear only about local ones.

3. *Control over the risk.* How much control do we have over the risky activity? Does our risk depend on what we do or on what someone else does?

Another reason some of us feel safer driving than flying is that when we drive, we are in control of the car, but someone else flies the plane.

4. *Choice of the risk.* Is the risk one that we *choose* to run?

We are more comfortable with the greater risk of driving than the tiny risk from a chemical plant going up next door, because we can choose to drive but may have no choice about living next to the plant.

There are a few other criteria that we use to define risk, but those are the important ones. Apparently, most of us nonexperts commonly define risk something like this:

> RISK = Magnitude + Immediacy + Lack of control + Lack of choice

So long as risk experts talked to us only in terms of their authorized, statistical definition, they had no chance to persuade the rest of us that trucking atomic waste through town had an "insignificant" risk. But now that they know that they must explain risk using our common definition, they are better able to help us make sound judgments.

Here are two things to watch for:

- When you make an argument for specialized readers using a term that might have a specialized meaning, look it up in a specialized reference work. You would seem foolish writing to experts in risk communication if you did not acknowledge their stipulated, authorized definition.

- But when you write for ordinary readers, do not expect to override their common definitions with authorized ones. You may think that your technical terms carry the authority to persuade your readers, but they rarely do. You have to adapt your terms to their understanding.

Was It Sex? Or Was It Sex?

President Clinton's impeachment turned on whether he lied when he denied having "sexual relations" with Monica Lewinsky. To define that term, he relied on criteria that had been narrowly stipulated by a court for a specific deposition. Within the four corners of that stipulated definition, Clinton arguably did not have sexual relations with Ms. Lewinsky (though she did with him). On the other hand, the rest of us define sex in its common meaning, so regardless of what the court said, they had sex. Those who tried to say they didn't looked silly.

Why Dictionaries Cannot Settle Criteria for Meaning

When we said that no authority stipulates the criteria for the meaning of ordinary words like *patriotism* and *athlete,* some of you surely thought of dictionaries. Even the Supreme Court relies on them to settle disputes over the meaning of a word as simple as *carry.* But as prestigious as dictionaries are, they do not capture the full complexity of any meaning, and few readers let a dictionary definition outweigh their sense of what a word means.

The Role of Criteria in Dictionary Definitions

Consider this conversation between Erin and her friend Ethan:

Erin: If ice dancing is an Olympic sport, and ice dancers are athletes, why shouldn't competitive ballroom dancing also be a sporting event and competitive dancers be considered athletes?

Ethan: I can't buy that. Dancing is entertainment, like the ballet.

Erin: So what? The Olympics are entertainment, and rhythmic gymnastics is like ballet, but it's still considered a sport.

Ethan: You just don't get the real meaning of *sport* and *athlete*. Let's look them up in Webster's.

Ethan would find that those dictionary definitions have two parts:

1. A word or phrase that names a general category (some call it the *genus*).
2. More words or phrases that narrow the general category to a specific one (some call them the terms that define the *species*).

> athlete: a person _{general category} who competes in contests requiring strength, stamina, or physical agility _{specific criteria}

> sport: an athletic activity _{general category} requiring skill or physical prowess _{specific criteria}

Traditional thinkers believe that an adequate definition includes every referent that belongs in the category and none that don't. Unfortunately, if Ethan believes that, he is led to a conclusion as unwelcome as it is logical:

Ethan: Well, it says here that athletes are "persons," and they "compete in contests requiring strength, stamina, or physical agility," so I guess ballroom dancers fit the criteria for athletes. And then it says that a sport is an "activity" that is "athletic," and "requires skill or phys-ical prowess," and competitive dancing sure does that. So I guess you're right: The tango should be an Olympic event.

He has come to a logical but not necessarily sound conclusion because he bases it on an unreliable authority. It's a kind of conclusion few readers willingly accept.

The Limitations of Dictionary Criteria for Common Meanings

Here are two basic facts about dictionary definitions:

- They stipulate just enough criteria to distinguish a word from every other word, *but no more.*

Meanings are infinitely more complex than definitions. A dictionary definition is to meaning as a hand-drawn map is to the place it describes. A lot gets lost.

- They do not help you decide whether a particular referent does or does not belong in the category the term names.

More important, though dictionaries help us distinguish one word from another, they do not help us decide what to call things. When we decide what to call a referent, we use many features that do not appear in dictionaries as criteria for distinguishing the meaning of that word from others. For example, when we decide whether to call an activity a sport, one relevant feature is its history—something no dictionary definition cites. Ice dancing became an

Olympic event in 1976, partly because it was related to figure skating (which was already an Olympic sport), which was linked to speed skating (a model sport). It was a case of people widening a category by focusing on fewer features: If you do something on skates that takes a lot of skill and strength, it's a sport.

Ethan would have seen the limits of dictionaries, had he tested their sparse criteria for *athlete* and *sport* on borderline referents. If an athlete is *anyone* who competes in a contest requiring strength, stamina, *or* physical agility, then Miss America contestants are athletes, because they require stamina and agility. And when they compete in contests, so do violin players, lumber jacks, and even cooks, so they're athletes as well. But that contradicts our common sense *use* of the word *athlete,* a usage probably based more on our mental model of a "real" athlete than on any criteria listed in a dictionary.

The Limitations of Dictionary Criteria for Authorized Meanings

You might think that the shortcomings of standard dictionaries do not afflict recognized authorities such as a law dictionary or other standard reference works in a field. But the criteria stipulated by those authorities ultimately suffer from the same problem that common dictionaries do.

For example, those critics who wanted to shut down the NEA because it supported pornography might have used the authorized criteria for the legal definition of *pornography* as listed in *Black's Law Dictionary:*

- The average person, applying contemporary community standards, would find that the work appeals to the prurient interest.
- It depicts sexual conduct in a patently offensive way.
- It lacks serious literary, artistic, political, or scientific value.

Relying on those criteria, they could make a standard, criteria-matching argument about what is or is not pornographic.

But that is deceptively simple, because those critics would be challenged to define the words naming the criteria. After all, those words have, in turn, their own criteria of meaning. What criteria define the criterion named *prurient?* We could refer again to *Black's Law Dictionary,* where we would find an authorized definition of *prurient:*

> **prurient:** A shameful or morbid interest in nudity, sex, or excretion. . . . having lustful ideas or desires . . . an obsessive interest in immoral and lascivious matters.

But what criteria define the criteria named *shameful, morbid, immoral,* and *lascivious?* Here's *Black's* technical definition of *lascivious:*

> **lascivious:** Tending to excite lust; lewd; indecent; obscene; sexual impurity; tending to deprave the morals in respect to sexual relations; licentious. [cites]. . . . See *lewd; obscene.*

But now what does that criterion *lewd* mean? Here's part of its definition:

lewd: Obscene, lustful, indecent, lascivious, lecherous.

We have a problem: The criteria for *lascivious* tell us to see *lewd,* but the criteria for *lewd* direct us back to *lascivious.*

That's why, ultimately, we cannot mechanically depend on criteria-based arguments of any kind. Legislators and scientists can stipulate criteria for what they mean by *pornography* or *planet,* but that just shifts the question one step down: What words name the criteria, and what criteria define those words? And what criteria define *those* words, and then . . . You get the idea. Most disconcertingly, criteria at some point loop back on themselves: *lascivious* means *lewd,* but *lewd* means *lascivious.* Ultimately, the criteria of the criteria of the criteria depend on our agreeing to criteria *without* an argument to support them.

You might think that this is treacherously uncertain ground on which to build arguments about meaning, but it is just another form of something that we've seen before: our need to agree with readers on uncontested warrants. A definition is a good model of a warrant:

> When a person competes in contests requiring skill, strength, stamina, and physical agility, that person is an athlete.

Erin needs Ethan to accept this warrant/definition without contesting it before he will agree that Erin's reasons support her claim that ballroom dancers are athletes.

Ultimately, definitions depend on agreement, but that's not a problem; it's an opportunity, because it frees us from the shortcomings of *all* dictionary definitions. By defining criteria, we develop our own meanings in a variety of ways. Even the meaning of *pornography* ultimately depends on the criteria for words like *average person, community,* and *serious artistic value,* all terms that depend on common meanings. As we learned from that Indian sage who explained about the world resting on the back of an elephant standing on the back of a turtle (p. 159): after that, it's turtles all the way down. We eventually just have to stop asking about turtles and what they mean, because the meaning of each turtle (criterion) depends on the next one down.

IN THE READINGS . . .

An Argument of Definitions

The argument in Ed Carson's "Purging Bingeing" (p. 418) turns on definitions in three ways:

- The common ground contrasts college students' common definition of bingeing with the authorized one of the "public health establishment."
- The problem is stated as a problem of what to call things: "But this is not a drinking problem; it is a drinking *behavior* problem."

- And his solution rests on his definition of a new term, *responsible drinking.*

To top things off, he ends his essay with a coda based on a joke about the definition of *moderation.*

The Special Demands of Conceptual Arguments

When you address a conceptual problem, you can't measure your success against an external standard of what readers do, the way the critics of Mapplethorpe could evaluate their arguments: They either persuaded others to abolish the NEA or they didn't (and, in fact, they mostly didn't). Instead, you succeed when readers *understand* something larger and more important than just the meaning itself, an outcome harder to measure.

Recall the conceptual definition of *language* on page 239. That account of the meaning of *language* was not part of a plea to treat apes more humanely (though that might have been an outcome) but a means to understand better the relationship between them and us, and then to understand ourselves better.

But because a conceptual argument focuses readers on what they understand, they expect your definitions to be more than just locally useful: Most readers will accept your definition only if it is also coherent with most of what else they know, believe, and value about an issue. Unfortunately, what people know, believe, and value is not always very coherent with itself, which makes that standard notoriously slippery. So when you define terms in a conceptual argument, you must above all observe the rule of consistency: You have to fit your definition to everything your readers believe rather than challenge their basic beliefs head-on.

If you are not immersed in an advanced field of study, these issues of intellectual consistency may seem remote, even hair-splitting. But once you are in a specialized field of study, you'll find that your conceptual arguments will be tested not just by whether a definition you propose makes local sense and solves a local problem, but by whether it is coherent with the whole body of knowledge, principles, facts, and beliefs that constitute your field. Your readers will judge your qualifications to belong to a field based on how well your definitions cohere with that larger whole, and when they don't, by how good a case you make that the definitions have to be changed.

The Pluto Problem

Not much seems at stake in the problem of whether we call Pluto a planet or a big blob of ice, which it resembles more than it does other planets. So it's a purely conceptual question (though see Reflection 3 on p. 261). Yet astronomers have debated whether to go on calling it a *planet*. It is so different from the unambiguous, model planets that if they keep it in the category of planets they cannot make generalizations about "real" planets—about their origin, age, physical features, even the manner of their rotation. Alternatively, astronomers might argue that even though Pluto differs from other planets, it is not *so* different that excluding it is worth the small saving in conceptual consistency. What they decide to call Pluto—a planet, a large asteroid, or an ice blob—depends on *what else* they want to say not just about it but about the other planets as well.

EXAMPLE

A Definition that Challenged Beliefs

When we define terms in a conceptual argument, we normally observe the rule of consistency. Some writers, however, offer definitions so new but so compelling that they change important beliefs. We call them geniuses. Isaac Newton was one: he redefined the term gravity *in ways that revolutionized not only physics but common sense; that is, until Einstein redefined it again. Freud was another. A third was Charles Darwin, whose term* natural selection *challenged common beliefs about science, history, religion, and society—challenges we still debate today. Here Darwin himself explains his term in light of the difficulties it caused. He works hard to make his definition coherent with rather than contradictory to the common meaning of* natural *and* selection. *Note how he tries to "naturalize"* natural selection *by finding familiar analogies that match his criteria. (Note as well his deft use of acknowledgment and response.)*

Several writers have misapprehended or objected to the term *Natural Selection*. Some have even imagined that natural selection induces variability, whereas it implies only the preservation of such variations as arise and are beneficial to the being under its conditions of life. No one objects to agriculturists speaking of the potent effects of man's selection; and in this case the individual differences given by nature, which man for some object selects, must of necessity first occur. Others have objected that the term *selection* implies conscious choice in the animals, which become modified; and it had even been urged that, as plants have no volition, natural selection is not applicable to them! In the literal sense of the word, no doubt, *natural selection* is a false term; but who ever objected to chemists speaking of the elective affinities of the various elements?—and yet an acid cannot strictly be said to elect the base with which it in preference combines. It has been said that I speak of natural selection as an active power of Deity, but who objects to an author speaking of the attraction of gravity as ruling the movements of the planets? Every one knows what is meant and is implied by such metaphorical expressions; and they are almost necessary for brevity. So again it is difficult to avoid personifying the word Nature; but I mean by Nature, only the aggregate action and product of many natural laws, and by laws the sequence of events as ascertained by us. With a little familiarity such superficial objections will be forgotten. (*Origin of Species,* Chapter IV)

WRITING PROCESS 10
Arguments About Meanings

Preparing and Planning

Anticipate Questions About Meaning

No question about an argument is more common than *But what do you mean by*_____*?,* especially about key terms in your main claim that you repeat in the body of your paper. Start by identifying those terms, then imagine readers asking *But doesn't it all depend on what you mean by*_____*?* If your argument does in fact depend on what you mean by_____ then you have to define it with words naming criteria and with examples. *A patriot is someone who . . . , such as . . .*

Pick an Appropriate Strategy for Matching Referents and Meanings

If you decide to assemble an argument about meaning, focus on matching features to criteria (and vice versa), on creating a model to use as a benchmark for your referent, or both. But there are three more strategies you might consider.

Duck the Definition
Do this when you think that your readers may never agree with your definitions. Focus instead on what's at stake and what will solve the problem. For example, some debate whether alcoholism is a disabling illness.

- Alcoholism ~referent 1~ is not a disabling illness, ~category 1~ but rather a weakness of character, ~category 2~ because if alcoholics wanted to recover, they could. ~distinctive feature~

- Alcoholism ~referent 1~ is not a weakness of character, ~category 1~ but a disabling illnesses ~category 2~ similar to depression, ~referent 2~ because it is as difficult to overcome ~distinctive feature~ as many other mental illnesses.

But a conceptual argument about what alcoholism *is* may be a surrogate for the larger pragmatic problem of what we should *do* about it:

- Many who see alcoholism as character flaw believe that if we call it an illness, we undermine personal responsibility by encouraging alcoholics to see themselves as helpless victims. If they can get us to call it a character flaw, then alcoholics are responsible for their own condition.

- Many who think alcoholism is a disabling illness believe we have a human duty to care for those unable to overcome disabling afflictions. If they can get us to call it an illness, then the fault is not in the person but in circumstances.

Those on either side of the issue can endlessly debate criteria for *disabling illness* and *character flaw,* but the more productive strategy might be to ignore definitions and focus instead on what good and bad will actually happen, what costs and benefits will actually follow once we decide that alcoholics do or do not suffer from a disabling illness. This is the problem that got in the way of Thelma and Louise resolving their discussion about *wedding* and *marriage.*

Find Analogies

Analogies are a bit like model matching, but not quite. You compare the referent in question to another one that might not be a model but still clearly falls within the category. But as a point of comparison need not be an ideal instance of the category, just an unambiguous one. Your logic appeals to intellectual consistency:

1. Referent$_1$ is like referent$_2$.
2. Referent$_2$ is a member of category C, which is called by Term T.
3. Therefore, logical consistency requires us to conclude that referent$_1$ should also be called by term T.

For example:

> Alcoholism is as disabling as depression or schizophrenia. $_{analogy}$ If we do not help alcoholics overcome their condition, then do we stop supporting all mental illnesses such as schizophrenia and depression? $_{appeal\ to\ intellectual\ consistency}$ They are obviously the same.

> Alcoholism may be disabling, but it is not a chemical disorder of the brain like depression or schizophrenia. $_{dis\text{-}analogy}$ Many alcoholics have straightened out their lives. People who are depressed or schizophrenic can't do that. $_{appeal\ to\ intellectual\ consistency}$ They are obviously different.

For an analogy to work, you have to persuade readers to agree both that the features shared (or not shared) by the referents are (or are not) relevant features of the category and that they should respect the principle of logical consistency.

Appeal to History

Another appeal to intellectual consistency is to argue that readers should use a word as history has used it; it's the argument Thelma made about *marriage.* There is, for example, a debate about the word *holocaust.* Some Jewish historians want to restrict it to what Nazis did to Jews during World War II. But some African Americans want to use it to refer to the ocean trip from Africa to the Americas, during which countless slaves died; and Cambodians want to use it to refer to what the Khmer Rouge did to millions of their own people. To argue their cases, they can point out that *holocaust* was used as early as 1671 to refer to an immense loss of life from fire, and thereafter to any immense loss of life.

But that wouldn't settle the issue, because a debate about the meaning of the word *holocaust* is almost certainly a surrogate argument.

Developing Models

When you want to build a model of a category, close your dictionary and crank up your imagination. You have to imagine a "real" example of, say, a *patriot,* then use your powers as a storyteller to bring that image to life in a way that matches your referent. The problem is that we all have somewhat different idealized models. So to base an argument about meaning on a model, you have to determine how closely your model resembles that of your readers. To argue that militia members are (or are not) patriots, for example, you'd start by thinking through two questions:

- What image first comes to mind when *you* think of the category *patriotic?* Is it an action, like flag waving and singing the national anthem, or sacrifice, or protesting laws? Or is it a state of mind, an attitude, a feeling?
- What image do you think first comes to your readers' minds when they think of a prototypical example of patriotism? If yours and theirs match, fine; if not, you have a problem. If you don't know, you have to find out.

You should then picture your referent:

- What is your model of a militia member? Is it a potbellied middle-aged gun nut in a camouflage costume running around playing soldier? Or is it a survivalist able to live in the wild while resisting unjust government?
- What do you think your *readers* first think of as a prototypical militia member? If yours and theirs fit, fine. If not, you have a problem. And if you don't know, you have to find out.

Drafting

Redefining Terms

There are modifying words and phrases that give you elbowroom in defining terms and building models. For example, the writer who wanted to call flag-burners *patriots* gave herself some leeway by starting with a standard definition of *patriotism,* waving the flag and so on, then contrasted it with what she called *real* patriotism. When you argue for special criteria, you can get that leeway by characterizing your criteria as defining the *real, true,* or *genuine* thing. When you want to deny someone else's definitions, describe theirs with terms like *broadly, loosely, technically, or strictly speaking; narrowly or broadly defined.*

> Broadly speaking, anyone who loves his country is a patriot, but a *true* patriot is one who . . .

> Technically, risk is a mathematical probability, but it is actually a feeling that . . .

INQUIRIES

Reflections

1. If all art that arouses sexual urges is pornographic, does that mean *erotica* and *pornography* are the same thing? Does it matter? Think in terms of what problem one or the other word might help you solve.

2. Are there meanings for which there are no words? Why? Are there words for which there are no meanings? If not why not?

3. It has been proposed that Pluto not be classified as a planet because it is too small. The discoverer of the planet Pluto comes from the small town of Streator, Illinois. The citizens of Streator are up in arms over that proposal. Is it the case that nothing other than coherence of meaning is at stake in what we call Pluto?

4. For a long time, the diagnostic manual of the American Psychiatric Association categorized homosexuality as a mental illness. Then in 1980, psychiatrists voted to remove it from the list. Were they mistaken before about homosexuality being an illness? Lay out the considerations that a search for an answer would involve. Start, as always, by thinking about the problem. Is the debate really about whether homosexuality is an illness, a choice, or an inherited disposition, or is that just a surrogate argument?

5. Here's another contemporary example of competing definitions: Is nicotine an addictive drug? What are the competing definitions? Is this argument "really" about the definitions? What is actually at stake here? Is this another surrogate argument?

6. You make arguments to get as close to the "truth" as you can. Presumably, that means that when you aim at that goal, you do not lie to each other. In fact, you typically oppose truth and lying. But is that a genuine opposition? Can you not tell the truth but not lie? Can you tell the truth and still lie? Does it matter how you answer these questions?

7. What might be at stake in deciding whether something should be called by the following:

   art vs. craft; pet vs. livestock; athlete vs. competitor; athlete vs. student; sport vs. game; economic stagnation vs. slump vs. recession vs. depression; hate speech vs. free speech; addiction vs. habit; eccentric vs. mentally ill.

8. Read or do Task 9 and Project 13; if you only read them, spend a moment imagining how you would perform them. Did they elicit stronger feelings than other tasks or projects you have tried? If not, do you know people for whom they would? What does that say about the nature of the task? What does it say about what is at stake in the legal names of things?

Tasks

9. In recent years, our society has renamed many things. When the two of us were young, someone in a wheelchair would be called a cripple;

later, *cripple* was replaced by *handicapped,* which has been replaced by *disabled, differently abled,* or *physically challenged.* Although some people complain that we have gone too far and bristle at terms ending in *-challenged* (one of your authors is vertically challenged, the other horizontally), there are often good reasons for proposing such changes. Think of a pair of terms, one that was once common but would now be judged offensive and one that is a politically correct alternative: crippled–disabled, drunk–alcoholic, retarded–mentally challenged, old–elderly, etc. For each term, (1) list your criteria of meaning and (2) sketch a verbal portrait of a model instance of each category. Do your criteria change when the word changes? Does your model? What does this say about the value of changing terms for sensitive categories?

10. The word *marriage* has so many social, religious, and moral connotations that its use in a phrase like *legalizing homosexual marriage* raises endless problems. Is there any difference between calling the event a *wedding* and calling it by some combination of these words?

	celebration		contract		commitment
a	ceremony	of our	covenant	of	bonding
	ritual		pledge		fidelity

That is, how does "a celebration of our covenant of bonding" differ from "wedding," and how does the result of that celebration of a covenant of bonding differ from what we call *marriage?* Create three or four combinations that could serve as a term for the event in which same-sex partners agree to live together in what others call "marriage." The terms should be ones that you think would satisfy those who want to use the term *marriage* but who might be willing to compromise on another, less contentious term. Then imagine the objections of those who would reject your argument.

11. Search the Internet to find Web sites that concern addiction. How many different conditions do people include in the category *addiction?* List five that seem to you either not "real" addictions or borderline cases. What disqualifies or makes them borderline? What does that tell you about how you understand the term? Why do the writers of the sites want to call them addictions?

12. The meanings of some words seem relatively distinct from other words: *triangle* vs. *circle, odd number* vs. *even number,* and so on. The meanings of other words, however are more relativistic. What is the difference between a very high hill and a very low mountain? Between a very narrow road and a very wide path? We sometimes can't sharply distinguish such oppositions out there in the world, but that doesn't mean there are no such things as hills and mountains, roads and paths. Imagine an occasion where you have to decide between calling something an unusually high hill or an unusually small mountain. What is the *first* question you would ask?

Projects

13. This project picks up on Task 9. Pick the term that you think most likely to be accepted by those who want same-sex unions to be legally recognized. Suppose that term has been proposed as the one your state will use for legal purposes, such as qualifying for health benefits, state income taxes, and so on. List reasons for or against the use of that term, including issues such as what it says about the state's attitudes toward its referents. Assume this is for a public argument in which you must avoid offending people unnecessarily. (Don't be deflected to the issue of whether it is *right* to legally recognize same-sex unions. Stay with the question of what to call them.)

14. In 1990, a 22-member panel authorized a new definition of *alcoholism* that they hoped would be (1) scientifically valid, (2) clinically useful, and (3) understandable to the public. Their work was sponsored by the National Council on Alcohol and Drug Dependence and the American Society of Addictive Medicine, an organization dedicated to effective medical and social treatment of those suffering from addictions. They did not aim to change how specialists diagnosed alcoholism, but to give the public signs to watch for so that people could intervene sooner. How do the goals of these organizations influence them to define *alcoholism* differently from that of the APA? What parts of the 1990 definition are most related to the larger goal of securing fair treatment for those who suffer from addictions? Do they make it less objective than the APA definition? Less scientific?

    Here is the NCADD definition, including definitions for each of the major criteria:

    Alcoholism is a primary, chronic disease with genetic, psychosocial, and environmental factors influencing its development and manifestations. The disease is often progressive and fatal. It is characterized by continuous or periodic: impaired control over drinking, preoccupation with the drug alcohol, use of alcohol despite adverse consequences, and distortions in thinking, most notably denial.

    Primary . . . suggests that alcoholism, as an addiction, is not a symptom of an underlying disease state. **Disease** means an involuntary disability. It represents the sum of the abnormal phenomena displayed by a group of individuals. These phenomena are associated with a specified common set of characteristics . . . which place them at a disadvantage. **Often progressive and fatal** means that the disease persists over time and that physical, emotional, and social changes are often cumulative. . . . **Impaired control** means the inability to limit alcohol use or to consistently limit . . . the duration of the episode, the quantity consumed, and/or the behavioral consequences of drinking. **Preoccupation** . . . indicates excessive, focused attention given to the drug alcohol, its effects, and/or its use. The relative value thus assigned to alcohol by the individual often leads to a diversion of energies away from important life concerns. **Adverse consequences** are alcohol-related problems or impairments in such areas as: physical health . . . ; psychological functioning . . . ; interpersonal functioning . . . ;

occupational functioning . . . ; and legal, financial, or spiritual problems. **Denial** is used here . . . broadly to include a range of psychological maneuvers designed to reduce awareness of the fact that alcohol use is the cause of an individual's problems rather than a solution to those problems. Denial becomes an integral part of the disease and a major obstacle to recovery.

Approved by NCADD February 3, 1990, Approved by ASAM Board of Directors February 25, 1990.

CHAPTER 10 IN A NUTSHELL
About Your Argument . . .

We typically make arguments about meaning when we want readers to understand what something is—in pragmatic arguments, because we believe that what it is justifies doing something about it; in conceptual ones, because we believe that understanding what it is helps us understand a larger issue.

An argument about meaning almost always addresses two issues:

• What criteria of meaning define the term in question?

• What features of the referent qualify it to be named by that word?

Your problem is to match the features to the criteria, in one of three ways:

• When you work with an *authorized meaning* whose criteria are stipulated by some authority, you have to accept those criteria and describe the referent so that its features match them. For example, the criteria for *U.S. citizen* are largely (though not entirely) inflexible, so you have little latitude to modify them, only to adapt the features of a referent to match them.

• When you work with criteria of a *common meaning*, you can shape both the criteria and the features of the referent, so long as you remain within what your readers take to be a common sense understanding of the term and the referent. The common meaning of *American* is flexible enough to let you shape it to fit a referent.

• When you work with a *model of a common meaning*, you are free to portray any model that your readers will accept as within the common sense meaning of the term and to describe your referent to fit the model. Readers know many model Americans, and you can choose whichever ones suit your referent and your purposes.

In a pragmatic argument, readers will focus on pragmatic consequences. Whether the Branch Davidians who died at Waco were a religious sect or a cult depends less on abstract ideas about religion than on how we think the government should deal with enclaves of armed followers of messianic leaders. In a conceptual argument, readers will want your definitions to be consistent with everything else they know. Whether Pluto is a planet or an especially large chunk of space rubble depends less on Pluto than on the whole system of understanding and belief about planets and space rubble.

You can go astray in arguments based on meaning in two ways:

• You unknowingly create an argument about meaning as a surrogate for other issues, either a pragmatic problem or a question of values.

You are most likely to fall into a surrogate argument when the larger problem behind the question of meaning involves issues of values and consequences that you would rather not deal with directly.

• You use dictionary definitions as though they carried more authority than they do. A dictionary alone will never settle a question of meaning.

Anticipate the kind of definition your readers expect you to use. If they are experts, use their terms according to the criteria authorized by their field. If, however, you are the expert and writing to those who are not, you cannot assume that your readers will accept your authorized definitions, no matter how much academic or technical weight they carry.

. . . and About Writing It

As you plan your argument, list every key word that you think you will use. If you are confident that your readers understand those words as you do, don't define them, especially not from a dictionary: You'll make yourself seem amateurish. If your readers may not understand those words as you do but won't question your meaning, define them in passing, as we did a few pages ago:

> No question about an argument is more common than *But what do you mean by*_____?, especially about your *key terms,* **those that name the concepts you will mention in your main claim and repeat often in the body of your paper.**

But if you expect readers to disagree about the meaning of your key terms, define them explicitly.

When you make an argument about meaning, state the meaning, describe the referent, and show how they match so that readers accept all three.

• When you argue about an *authorized meaning,*

State your criteria so that readers recognize them as authoritative, stipulated ones. Cite a reference work if you want to be sure that they do.

Describe your referent one feature at a time, so that readers see how each feature fits the stipulated criteria.

If the fit is not obvious, make a small argument to support it.

• When you argue about *common meaning* using *criteria*,

> State your criteria to match features of the referent, but remain within the bounds of readers' common sense understanding.

> If readers might question your criteria or the fit, you can make a small argument to support them.

• When you argue about *common meaning* using a *model*,

> Describe the model so that readers recognize it as typical of their common sense understanding of the term.

> Describe your referent so that it is as close to the model as is consistent with your readers' common sense understanding of it.

> Make an argument supporting it, especially if readers might question the match. But if your readers reject your model, do not try to make an argument that they should accept it: that's not how models work. They are too deeply entrenched in our social and cultural understanding.

CHAPTER 11

Arguments About Causes

In this chapter, we turn to another common basis for arguments: claims that one event or condition causes or will cause another. We discuss the nature of causation, how we decide what causes to focus on, why we think less carefully than we should about some causes, and how you can test your thinking about them. Then we show you how to design arguments about causation.

We spend most of our lives figuring out why things happen as they do, then how to make them happen as we want them to. We tackle problems ranging from the trivial—why the car won't start—to ones whose solutions require complex written arguments: What causes adolescent suicide and how do we prevent it? To understand an issue that complex, readers expect not just a narrative of one event after another implying cause and effect, but reasons to believe that one event in fact causes the next. Then if we're addressing a pragmatic problem, they also want reason to believe that our solution will change things as we say it will.

The Impossible Vastness of Causes

Causation itself seems simple enough. The classic example is a cue stick hitting a billiard ball, causing it to move. To explain the causes of a more complex event like binge drinking, it may seem that we just have to track more balls on a bigger table. But philosophers have shown us how little we understand causation and how often we mislead ourselves and others when we try to explain it.

First, causation is not something that we can see or measure. We say that the cue hitting a ball "causes" it to move, but that is only shorthand for saying that when the stick touches the ball, the ball moves, as we expect it to. What we call causation is only a predictable relationship among two or more events or conditions. Beyond that problem, however, we cannot, even in principle, account for more than a fraction of all the events and conditions that cause the cue to move the ball:

- *Every cause is part of an endless chain.* The immediate cause of the ball's movement is the cue hitting it, but the cue is caused to move by an arm, which is caused to move by muscles, which are caused to contract by a thought, which . . . How far back must we trace the chain of causes? To an earlier thought? To the beginning of time? We cannot describe them all, so how do we choose where to begin?

- *Every seemingly individual cause consists of countless smaller ones.* Muscle contractions move the arm, but they consist of countless physiological events in countless muscle cells, each of which consists of countless electro-chemical events, each of which . . . We cannot describe them all, so how do we choose how finely to describe them?

- *A cause has an effect only when enabled by countless conditions.* The ball has to be hard enough not to break, the arm strong enough to move the cue, the cue light enough to move. We cannot describe every condition, so how do we choose which ones we should describe?

- *Every cause depends on the absence of disabling conditions.* The arm can move only because it was *not* paralyzed by a stroke a moment before. And what about a plane that did *not* crash into the building, because a part did *not* fail, because . . . ? We cannot describe all the events and conditions that did not happen, so how do we decide which ones to select as significant?

Finding Relevant Causes

Since the causes and conditions that contribute to any effect are so vast that we can never account for them all, we have to select just the relevant ones. We do that in two ways. The first is our unreflective, everyday way of thinking about causes; it takes little effort, but it is typically superficial and simplistic, and often misleading. The other way is more focused, more self-conscious, but in the long run more reliable. Since the first kind of thinking is so pervasive, however, it's useful to know what makes it so unreliable.

Everyday Thinking About Causation

We are easily misled when we think about causes, because, as hundreds of studies have shown, our minds are tuned to focus on the most obvious causes and to ignore others. For example, binge drinking is increasing among college students, causing injury and even death. To solve that problem, we have to change something, but to know what, we first have understand why some students binge and others don't. Two possibilities leap to mind, usually in this order:

- Bingeing is caused by something in a binger's personality: immaturity, insecurity, recklessness.
- Bingeing is caused by something in a binger's social circumstances: bad friends, peer pressure, easy availability of alcohol.

If we knew which was the "real" cause, we could do something about it.

But here are two more possibilities that don't occur to most of us, at least at first:

- Students who are only occasional drinkers underestimate their risk when they consume large amounts of alcohol in a short time.
- Schools fail to educate first-year students about the risks of bingeing.

Most of us don't think of those causes, because we tend to focus on causes that are visibly present at an event, not on ones that are absent and remote. So before you plan an argument about causes, be aware that you too may succumb to five specific "cognitive biases" that undermine sound thinking about causes.

1. **We tend to focus on the event that occurs immediately before an effect.** We call such causes "proximate" or "immediate." For example, someone sinks a two-point basket at the buzzer, winning the game by one point. We are more likely to think that shot won the game than a three-pointer a minute earlier, even though but for the three pointer, the two pointer would have made no difference. When we think about binge drinking, we think first of its immediate causes: Someone binges because it's Friday night, finals just ended, and there's a party going on. We are less inclined to think of a remote cause: The person was not told a year earlier about the risks of drinking. So when you think about causes, consider immediate ones, but deliberately search for more remote ones as well.

2. **We tend to focus on events that occur rather than events that do not.** Imagine you are driving and your passenger asks you to slow down, causing you to catch a red light. You wait for the green, zip through, and get hit by a car running its red light. You might think, *If he hadn't asked me to slow down, I wouldn't have been in the intersection at that moment.* You are less likely to think, *I was in that intersection at that moment because my friend didn't ask me to slow down at the previous light.* We are more likely to see what did happen as a relevant cause than what did not, even though they contributed equally to an outcome. As for why a student binges dangerously, we are not inclined to think first about what does not happen, like a friend's not intervening. When you think about causes, consider what did happen, but think as well about what contributed to an event by virtue of its absence.

3. **We tend to focus on what is surprising and ignore what is routine.** Imagine your teacher always announces a quiz before he gives it. Then

without notice he pops a quiz and you get a zero. You are more likely to think that you got a zero because your teacher *unpredictably* failed to announce the quiz than because you *routinely* did not prepare until warned. Similarly, bartenders serve drinks predictably to those who order them, so we don't identify that as a cause of someone dying from bingeing. On the other hand, imagine that a bar offers a "lucky fan" all the free drinks she can down in five minutes, someone takes the offer, and dies. That offer is unusual, so we'd focus on it as a relevant cause, not on the fact that the bar exists at all. When you think about causes, notice unpredictable, unexpected ones, but think as well about those that are so routine that they seem to fade into the background.

4. **We tend to focus on causes that confirm our assumptions.** Some claim that childhood violence results from the erosion of family values, a cause that they think explains most of the ills of American social life— crime, divorce, drugs, and so on. So when they hear of a child shooting a classmate, they explain it in their standard way: *No family values.* We all tend to find or fit facts to our beliefs rather than change our beliefs to fit the facts. In regard to bingeing, many of us hold assumptions that we can state as one of these two warrants:

   Those who behave self-destructively have a weak character.

   Those who behave self-destructively are victims of bad influences.

   When you think about causes, don't jump to your favorite account. Explore other possibilities, like self-destructive behavior being caused by complex, unpredictable interactions of many factors, including chance.

5. **We look for causes whose magnitude is proportional to their effect.** When a few years ago TWA flight 800 exploded over Long Island, many looked for a cause that would morally and emotionally balance the enormity of the disaster. They rejected as a cause static electricity in a fuel cell, because a random spark seemed too trivial a cause for such an awful effect. So they blamed terrorists or the U.S. military, because only a massively evil cause could balance so massive a tragedy. When you explore an effect as emotionally "big" as a student drinking herself to death, look for causes large enough to bear the blame, like her reckless-ness or the reckless encouragement of friends, but spend some time thinking about little causes that might escape your attention.

The sum of these biases is too often the One True Cause explanation. Those who get stuck on one then tend to formulate a Silver Bullet solution: *If we could just get parents to spend more time with their children, . . .* No one cause is responsible for any event, especially not events important enough to write about.

The Aesthetics of Causation

Here the historian William Manchester explains why people can't accept that Oswald alone shot President Kennedy:

> In the wake of that dreadful Oliver Stone movie [about the assassination], I read that some 70 percent of the American people believed the Kennedy was the victim of a conspiracy. I think I understand why they feel that way. And I think, in a curious way, there is an esthetic principle involved. If you take the murder of six million Jews in Europe and you put that at one end of a scale, at the other end you can put the Nazis, the greatest gang of criminals ever to seize control of a modern government. So there is a rough balance. Greatest crime, greatest criminals.
>
> But if you put the murder of the President of the United States at one end of the scale, and you put Oswald on the other end, it just doesn't balance. And you want to put something on Oswald's side to make it balance. A conspiracy would do that beautifully.

Source: Bob Herbert, "In America: A Historian's View," *New York Times,* June 4, 1997.

Thoughtful Thinking About Causation

The second way of finding relevant causes is harder, but more productive and reliable: We decide which causes are most relevant to solving our problem. So to choose from among the innumerable causes that contribute to the cue's moving the billiard ball, we would have to decide why we need to talk about it at all: If we're talking about how to improve someone's game, we'll look at some causes; if we're explaining the ballistics of round objects, we'll look at others; and if we're addressing the issue of free will, we'll look at others yet.

Of course, we define relevance differently for pragmatic and conceptual problems.

Causation in Pragmatic Problems

In solving a pragmatic problem, we look for those causes that we can change or remove to eliminate the costs that define the problem. We'll call such causes *pragmatically relevant.* For example, when your car won't start, you might first hypothesize that the relevant cause is a dead battery, because that's a cause you can do something about. You might suspect that it's dead because someone left the lights on all night, but while that remote cause might be *conceptually* relevant in helping you understand why the battery is dead, it is irrelevant to solving the immediate problem of starting the car. Use your problem to focus your thinking on those causes most relevant to its solution, specifically on the point in the chain of causes and effects where you—or someone—can intervene to eliminate its costs.

Causation in Conceptual Problems

It's harder to define relevant causes in conceptual problems, because every cause of an event, no matter how small, is potentially relevant to understanding. For example, those trying to end the troubles in Northern Ireland have a pragmatic problem: Where do they intervene in the chain of causes and effects that lead Catholics and Protestants to attack each other? But a historian trying to solve the conceptual problem of explaining the causes would in theory have to consider every one that has ever contributed to the current conflict, including centuries of conflict over religion, politics, economics, ethnicity, and social class. And there is no limit to how finely he could decompose those causes into constituent ones. Even a fleeting thought in someone's mind a century ago could be relevant to an event today. When understanding is at stake, everything is potentially relevant.

So how can we know where to start? That decision is made for us, if we bring to a conceptual problem personal interests that focus us on some causes and exclude others. A historian trained as an economist, for example, is more likely to study how religion affects income than how it affects attitudes toward violence, because she is trained to look at causes rooted in economics.

That explains why those new to a field of study often struggle to find conceptual problems to write about. They typically do not yet have interests that incline them to look at some issues and ignore others. With no special interest to focus their attention, they feel overwhelmed by the possibilities. It is a problem only experience can solve.

Analyzing Causation Systematically

Once you identify causes you think might be relevant to your problem, you must then evaluate them to be sure they are in fact causes. When you do advanced work, you will learn how to evaluate causes in the specific ways appropriate to your field. In a first-year writing course, however, you evaluate causes more informally, but that doesn't mean superficially. You can show that your proposed solution really solves a problem only when you can demonstrate what causes it. To do that, you can use two principles formulated by a nineteenth century philosopher, John Stuart Mill. These principles will not help you discover possible causes, but they will help you demonstrate that those you propose are worth your readers' attention.

1. The Principle of Similarity and Difference

When researchers try to decide whether a proposed cause is a plausible candidate to explain an effect, they try to determine whether the cause "correlates" with the effect in numerous cases: Does the effect usually occur when the proposed cause is present? And does it usually not occur when that cause is absent?

For example, when researchers study why some first-year students get better grades in writing classes, they try to discover factors shared by students who do well (their similarity) that are not shared with those who do worse (their difference). They might show that those who do better compose on computers (the similarity). But they would have to show as well that those who do less well do not compose on computers (the difference).

To use this principle of similarity and difference systematically, some researchers use a 2 × 2 grid because it forces them to consider all combinations of effects and causes, both present and absent. It looks like this:

	Effect occurs	Effect does not occur
Cause present	?%	?%
Cause absent	?%	?%

Down the left, you list a proposed cause as present and absent (you can also use + and − signs); across the top, you list whether a proposed effect does or does not occur. In the boxes, you put the *percentages* (not raw numbers) of the correlations (the percentages in the horizontal rows must add up to 100). (Social scientists call this an analysis of variation, or ANOVA, for short.)

Let's imagine a simple case: An astronomer wants to prove that massive objects bend light. He assembles his data and finds this:

	Light bends	Light does not bend
+ Massive object	100%	0%
− Massive object	0%	100%

According to these data, light bends only when an object is present, never when an object is absent. The researcher can therefore tentatively conclude that massive objects cause light to bend (unless bent light causes the presence of an object or a third cause both bends light and causes the object's presence, both unlikely).

Natural scientists expect such unambiguous results, but social scientists rarely do. They usually have to settle for "more or less." For example, those looking at writing by first-year students might find these numbers:

	Upper half of class	Lower half of class
Use computers	72.1%	27.9%
Do not use computers	34.5%	65.5%

The correlation is not perfect, but students who compose on computers are twice as likely to be in the upper half of their group than those who do not.

The more the numbers differ vertically, the more likely you've found a causal relationship. But if the numbers are close vertically, as in the next table, you can claim a relationship only if you have counted very large numbers of students.

	Upper half of class	Lower half of class
Use computers	72.1%	27.9%
Do not use computers	55.5%	44.5%

What we should count as a significant difference takes complex statistical computations, but ones that everyone who expects to make a living in the twenty-first century ought to learn, along with many other statistical and probabilistic ways of thinking.

Whenever percentages are other than 100% (as they almost always are), it is important to understand that the cause you have tested cannot be a sufficient cause, able to bring about the effect in question by itself. For example, suppose some students who use computers are in the lower half of their class and some who do not are in the upper half. If so, we have to assume that causes other than computers are at work in determining who ends up where. As we said before, complex social events rarely have just a single cause.

2. The Principle of Covariation

Researchers are most confident about causal relationships when the magnitude of a possible cause correlates with the magnitude of a proposed effect. For example: *If students compose on computers for many years, do they write better than those who write on computers for fewer years?* If so, then the use of computers is a plausible cause of better writing. To test for covariation we add additional cells for different magnitudes:

Computer use	Upper third	Middle third	Bottom third
6 years	62.2%	21.9%	15.9%
4 years	41.3%	39.0%	19.7%
2 years	32.5%	45.6%	21.9%
0 years	25.3%	32.8%	41.9%

Results are rarely so neat, but it's what researchers hope for.

You don't need a lot of data to use an ANOVA table. In fact, you don't need any at all if you use it just to force yourself to think in ways you might not otherwise. For example, some think that those who are attracted to risk taking tend to binge more than those who are not. We might imagine this table:

	+ Binge	– Binge
Attracted to risk	?%	?%
Not attracted to risk	?%	?%

Simply imagining this table forces us to speculate about how many people who are attracted to risk don't binge and how many who are not do. If we cannot imagine a 100% correlation between bingeing and risk taking, then we know bingeing is too complicated for this One-True-Cause explanation.

But sometimes, there is one true cause. In one case, Sherlock Holmes noticed that a dog did not bark when the person who committed a crime must have walked by it. What Holmes found significant was the *not* barking. In effect, Holmes created a mental ANOVA table like this:

	+ Bark	– Bark
Stranger walks by	100%	0%
Master walks by	0%	100%

He concluded that since the dog did not bark, his master committed the crime.

Four Cautions About Using the Principles

1. **Imagine causes to test.** These principles help you test causes but do not help you find ones to test. If all your hypotheses are wrong, these tests show you only that—a useful result, but not always one to celebrate. Years ago, for example, malaria was a mystery until someone thought to investigate mosquitoes. Today researchers face the same problem with Alzheimer's. They have tested every possible cause they can think of, but all have failed the tests.

2. **Create contrasting groups.** Once you hypothesize a cause, you have to create groups to fit an ANOVA table, one group exposed to a possible cause, the other not. Some researchers can directly create those groups, as when a biologist plants two fields of corn and treats one with a new fertilizer. Often, though, researchers have to assemble contrasting groups by retrospective statistical sampling. That's how smoking was discovered as a cause of cancer. The problem is that retrospectively created groups can always differ in some unexpected way that turns out to be crucial. In fact, cigarette manufacturers once argued that the urge

to smoke and cancer were both the effect of some as yet undiscovered cause.

3. **Be wary of oversimplification.** When we find that an effect covaries with a suspected cause, we tend to think *Aha, I've figured it out. We can get students to write better if we get them to compose on computers.* But complex effects have complex causes. Maybe students who compose on computers come from wealthy neighborhoods with better schools. And be aware that you may be reversing cause and effect. Maybe those who write better choose to write on computers because they can compose faster.

4. **Don't ignore interactions.** Even when you think you have found a cause, consider the complex ways that causes interact:

   • *Shared cause:* Sometimes two *effects* correlate not because one causes the other, but because both are caused by a third thing: Unemployment and crime correlate, but both may be effects caused by long-term poverty.

   • *Mutual cause:* Some causes and effects influence each other. Poverty correlates with bad education, bad education with crime, and crime with poverty, but they probably all have mutual effects.

   • *Compounded effects:* A recent study reported that the mentally ill are no more likely to commit a crime than well people, while drug addicts are four times as likely. But when the mentally ill are on drugs, they are seven times more likely to commit a crime. The interaction of separate causes may result in more than the sum of their individual effects.

Causation and Personal Responsibility

We've stressed how important it is to evaluate cause and effect objectively. But in one circumstance, we cannot avoid a subjective element: when we can solve a problem only by getting readers to hold a person or institution responsible for actions that led to an effect. When we want to hold someone responsible for something, we think about causation in ways very different from those who engage in scholarly, "objective" research.

Who's Responsible

A few years ago, some preschool children on an outing at a riverfront park fell in the water when they let go of the hand-line that their teachers used to keep them together, but they were saved by a bystander who jumped in after them. Everyone agreed on the facts, but made different claims about how to assign responsibility for both the accident and the rescue:

   • The media made the teachers the responsible cause, because they didn't watch the kids as they should have.

- The children's lawyers blamed the Park Department, because it hadn't built a protective railing along the river.

As to the responsibility for saving the kids,

- The mayor and the media praised the rescuer for his heroism.
- The Red Cross praised its own life-saving course, which the hero had taken.
- A psychologist said that hero's actions were caused by an instinct to aid the helpless, reinforced by cultural training from TV, movies, and books.

We can explain two of the claims about responsibility in fairly simple-minded ways:

- The teachers caused the accident, because they were there, and they obviously did not do something they were expected to do: They did not watch the children.
- The person who jumped in was the cause of their surviving, because they would have drowned but for his immediate and extraordinary action.

Even though the next two explanations seem a bit of a stretch, they solved the problems of those who proposed them:

- The lawyers for the children had a problem of finding someone to sue. Those missing railings pointed to a solution: The lawyers named the city as a cause of the accident because they failed to build railings along the wharf (and had deeper pockets than the teachers).
- The Red Cross solved its problem of gaining publicity for its programs by saying it was a cause of the rescue, remote to be sure, but nevertheless relevant because but for its course, the hero might not have jumped in.

But what do we make of the psychologist who, far from praising the hero, suggested that he was compelled to jump in by cultural conditioning? And why didn't anyone focus on other obvious causes?

- No one held the children or their parents responsible, even though the children let go of the ropes and their parents sent them to that school.
- Nor did anyone give credit for the rescue to the bystander who threw a rope in the water and pulled the rescuer ashore.
- Nor did anyone name gravity as the cause, even though but for it, no one would fall into anything.

No one thought of those as responsible causes, even though they played a role in the event, because they did not meet our criteria for deciding who should be praised or blamed.

Five Criteria for Assigning Responsibility

When we want to name someone as a *responsible* cause, we reason differently from the way we do about a problem involving "pure" causation. After we determine what events and actions actually caused the outcome, we have to identify the persons or institutions we will hold responsible. To do that, we try to infer a person's state of mind:

1. Did the person *choose* to perform an action that led to the effect in question? Or did forces external to that person force him to act?
2. Could the person *foresee* the consequences of the action, including its risks?
3. Were the person's *motives* selfish or unselfish, pure or corrupt?

Then we ask two more questions about external circumstances:

4. How commonly do most people in similar circumstances act in that way?
5. Did circumstances create an obstacle to the action or enable it?

Those criteria suggest why people assigned responsibility for the riverfront accident as they did:

- Though the children were the immediate cause of their accident, no one held them responsible because they could not foresee the consequences of letting go of the rope.
- Nor did anyone assign responsibility to their parents, because they could not have foreseen that the teachers would be inattentive.
- Everyone held the teachers responsible because they should have foreseen the consequences of not paying attention to the children.
- The lawyers held the city responsible because it should have foreseen the risks of not having railings along the river, and nothing prevented them from doing so.
- The media praised the hero because he seemed to perform his action freely, foreseeing the risk, and because it's unlikely that everyone would have done the same.
- The Red Cross made itself responsible, because it did something that few other agencies do—train people in life saving.

But the psychologist didn't seem to make the hero "responsible" at all. He seemed to say that the hero acted impulsively, without conscious choice, not foreseeing any risk. And that's why his explanation seems so odd. Instead of framing the problem as one of assigning responsibility in order to praise, as others did, he framed it as a problem in the social sciences, as a purely conceptual problem: What causes people to act impulsively? For him, the problem was not responsibility, but pure causation.

When we think about a problem of pure causation, we try to put aside our subjectivity in order to find objective evidence of those causes that help us solve our problem. But when we have a problem involving personal responsibility, we can solve it only by inferring thoughts, feelings, and motivations. In that subjective calculation, however, lies yet another cognitive bias that psychologists call the "fundamental attribution bias," caused by our own subjective involvement in solving the problem of determining responsibility.

The Fundamental Attribution Bias

In explaining why people act as they do in order to know whether to hold them responsible for the outcome of an action, we typically attribute their action either to their external circumstances or to their internal state. Why did Mark McGuire and Sammy Sosa hit so many home runs? If we want to praise them, we treat the problem as one of personal responsibility and attribute their achievement to talent and hard work. If we don't, we treat it as a problem of pure causation and attribute it to their circumstances: they faced weaker pitchers because the league has diluted player quality by expanding.

But we don't choose between circumstances and personality objectively. As many studies have shown, in attributing the cause of a person's actions, we are all biased toward attributing it to her internal motives and dispositions, causing us systematically and predictably to undervalue the force of external circumstances. But that tendency is either reinforced or moderated by certain variables in our own mental and psychological state. We'll discuss only four: (1) knowledge, (2) personal investment, (3) ideology and politics, and (4) culture.

Knowledge

The more we know about the circumstances of an event, the more likely we are to attribute the cause of a person's action to external circumstances. Those who know many gays and lesbians, for example, more often attribute their orientation to circumstances beyond anyone's control—usually genetic predisposition; those who know few are more likely to attribute it to choice. It's a consistent (but by no means universal) pattern of causal attribution.

So if you are judging a situation about which you know relatively little, be aware that you are likely to overvalue motives and character and undervalue circumstances. And if your readers know more than you do, keep in mind that they will be inclined to assign responsibility more to external circumstances than to someone's internal disposition.

Personal Investment

A second variable concerns how we feel about the person and the results of her actions. For example, when someone we like does something we admire, we tend to attribute her achievement to her intelligence, hard work, and so on. If she wins an award, we say she earned it. But if she loses, we say circumstances conspired against her. On the other hand, if someone we dislike wins, we attribute her success to luck or other circumstances. But if she fails, we attribute it to personal weakness.

It's a familiar behavior. To his supporters, President Clinton was responsible for the good things that happened in his administration, but was a victim of circumstances in regard to the bad. To his detractors, he was not responsible for any of the good but was responsible for all the bad. We don't all make decisions along these lines all the time; it is only a tendency. But it's a tendency worth reflecting on when you make arguments about praise and blame. So when you feel personally invested in someone, either positively or negatively, be aware that your judgments about personal responsibility may be biased. And depending on your readers, you may be working against their judgmental grain.

Ideology and Politics

Another factor is our politics (though it may also be that our politics results from how we tend to assign responsibility). Where stereotypical liberals argue, *Circumstances deprive those on welfare of opportunities to escape poverty,* stereotypical conservatives argue, *They lack the determination to hold a job.* Liberals justify gun control by arguing, *Our high murder rate is due to the easy availability of guns,* while conservatives respond, *Guns don't kill. People do.* But we can't draw this distinction too broadly: When there was a controversy in Los Angeles over racial profiling by police, liberals who distrust police attributed it to their racist disposition, while conservatives who trust police attributed it to the dangerous circumstances of urban life (an example of personal investment trumping politics).

Explain or Judge?

In a 1999 interview, Hillary Clinton suggested that a factor in her husband's infidelity was conflict in his childhood. Critics instantly charged that she was trying to relieve him of responsibility for his actions. Here is one commentator on that issue:

[There is a] tendency of modern Americans to either misunderstand or fail to recognize the distinction between *explaining* a person's or group's actions and *justifying* them.... [I]t is the one error committed by both conservatives and liberals, although usually for opposing reasons. Conservative Americans are so committed to the principle of personal responsibility that they either deny or are hostile to any explanation of human action in sociological or psychological terms, fearing—incorrectly—that this implies people are not answerable for their actions. Many liberals fall in the opposite trap: an oversocialized view of people, so sensitive to the social forces conditioning us that they are unable or unwilling to hold those who fail responsible for their actions. What each side misses is that it is possible to both explain a person and hold that person responsible for his or her actions. The failure to make this distinction between explanation and justification bedevils human relationships and public policy.

Source: Orlando Patterson, "The Lost Distinction Between 'Explain' and 'Justify,'" *New York Times,* August 8, 1999.

Culture

The deepest influences on our habits of thought regarding responsibility may be cultural. Anthropologists commonly point out that unlike other world cultures, Westerners in general and Americans in particular are inclined to believe that people personally control their actions. In contrast, researchers have found that in many Asian cultures people judge personal actions less in terms of individual choice and more as controlled by social contexts. This is the deepest bias of all. So should you ever find yourself making an argument with someone from a culture very different from yours, keep in mind that your differences may run much deeper than the particular issue you are addressing.

Blame in Two Cultures

A study comparing Japanese and American newspaper reports of financial scandals found that American writers tended to focus more than twice as often on the motives of individuals involved in the scandals. Japanese newspapers tended to focus on circumstances:

> One [*New York Times*] article described Mozer as "Salomon's [a financial firm] errant cowboy": who "attacked his work as aggressively as he hit tennis balls." Another implied Hamanaka's lack of shrewdness in stating that he "was known more for the volume of his trades than his aptness." Whereas the lack of organizational controls was a minor theme of Americans in the *NYT,* it was a major theme of Japanese reporters . . . [They] commented that "somebody in Sumitomo [a financial firm] should have recognized the fictitious trading since documents are checked every day," and that Daiwa [another firm] "is embarrassed that its internal controls and procedures were not sufficient to prevent the case."

Source: Tanya Morris et al. "Culture and the Construal of Agency: Attribution to Individual Versus Group Dispositions." *Journal of Personality and Social Psychology* (1999).

As you reason about why people act as they do, particularly to praise or blame, be aware that we all tend more to assign cause to intentions, character, and motives rather than to circumstances and external forces. Even more important, no matter how you explain a person's actions, consider how *your readers* are likely to reason about the issue. How much do they know? What do they have at stake? How does their ideology or culture incline them to reason about the event in question?

Above all, if you attribute the cause of an effect *entirely* to someone's motives or *entirely* to his circumstances, reflect for a moment whether you made that judgment on the merits of the case or on your predispositions. Imagine readers asking either of two questions:

> Are you saying this person was *entirely* responsible for his actions, that circumstances played no role at all?

Are you saying this person was *entirely* a victim of circumstances, that he bears no responsibility at all for his actions?

Careful readers are suspicious of explanations that are that simplistic, but especially when they exclude circumstances as a relevant cause.

WRITING PROCESS 11
Arguments About Causes

Preparing and Planning

Five Narratives Supporting Solutions to a Pragmatic Problem

As you outline an argument addressing a pragmatic problem, you have to plan not just one narrative about causes and effects, but at least two and perhaps up to five. The first two are the stories of the problem and its solution.

- **Narrative 1: What causes this problem?** Readers trust a solution only when they know the story of the causes and effects constituting the problem (imagine each step expanded as a claim at the heart of its own argument):

  Administrators don't know about new research in evaluating teaching, cause 1 . . . so they use flawed evaluations. effect 1/cause 2 . . . As a result, they don't know why students don't learn effectively, effect 2/cause 3 . . . and that causes students to be frustrated and unhappy. effect 3/cause 4

- **Narrative 2: How will the action you propose solve the problem?** When you propose a solution, you must construct another narrative. This one is about the future, how intervening in the chain of causes and effects will eliminate the cost of the problem (each of these steps would also be fleshed out):

  We can improve teaching by creating a better teaching evaluation form. cause 1 . . . to help teachers better understand what confuses their students and how to avoid doing so, effect 1/cause 2 . . . making their students happier with their education. effect 2/elimination of cost

Even if readers accept your account of the problem and entertain your solution, you may have to construct three more narratives to respond to their objections and reservations. These narratives would all be about the future.

- **Narrative 3: How will your solution be implemented?** If readers might think your solution is not feasible, you have to respond to their doubts by creating a narrative explaining how it can be implemented:

To create a new teaching evaluation, the administration can appoint a student committee to develop it, _{step 1} . . . and then with the help of consultants _{step 2} show faculty how to use and learn from it. _{step 3}

- **Narrative 4: Will your solution cost more than the problem?** If readers might worry that your solution will cost more than the problem, then you have to respond by telling another story assuring them that it will not:

Creating a new evaluation may require resources, _{acknowledgment} · · · but the benefits will outweigh the costs. _{response} First, we are likely to attract more students as we become known for good teaching _{reason 1} · · · Second, · · · _{narrative of costs and benefits} Some fear that teachers might feel coerced into grading more leniently or giving less work. _{acknowledgment} But that risk is slight . . . _{response}

- **Narrative 5: Why is your solution better than the alternatives?** Every problem has more than one solution, so you may have to show that yours is best, that it complements others, or at least that it does not contradict them:

Some have claimed that instead of revising the evaluations, we institute seminars for faculty. True, such seminars would be a valuable resource, _{acknowledgment} but if we must choose between them and new teaching evaluations, the evaluations would be a better choice. _{response/claim} First, the cost of bringing in outside consultants will exceed the cost of revising the evaluations _{reason 1} . . . Second, it will be hard to offer seminars to every faculty member _{reason 2.} . . . third, seminars are a one-time event; better teaching evaluations will occur every semester _{reason 3} · · ·

When you compare solutions, avoid an *either-or* argument.

We can improve teaching in lots of ways, including *both* seminars and better evaluations.

A Default Plan for Pragmatic Arguments

Those five narratives provide a default plan for a cause-effect argument about a pragmatic problem:

1. What causes this problem?
2. How will the action you propose cause the problem to go away?
3. How will your solution be implemented?
4. How do you know your solution will not cost more than the problem?
5. Why is your solution better than alternatives, or at least complement them?

In your final draft, of course, you might decide that you need to mix-and-match these parts or even drop some altogether.

Once you have a plan, you have to make three more decisions:

- How far back on the causal chain do you start? Do your readers need to know the remote causes of bingeing?

- How much detail do they need? Must they understand the minute psychological processes that compel people to binge?

- How much must you "thicken" your narrative by arguing that event A in fact causes B? How do you know that in fact some people binge from insecurity?

Where Do You Start Narrating the Problem?

We can't give you a rule for where to start in the chain of causes and effects. With pragmatic problems, readers need enough context to understand the causes you finally focus on, so start your narrative at least a step or two before the point where you propose intervening with a solution:

> For more than 200 years, college life has been so associated with drunken parties that getting drunk is now a tradition. _{remote cause} Of course, many students began drinking in high school, often with at least their parents' tacit approval. _{middle cause} But they lose even that loose supervision just when they join a community that seems to invite them to get drunk. _{near cause} So when sitting with a case or fifth in a dorm room or frat house, they risk drinking to the point of injury or even death. In those circumstances, the weak constraints colleges put on them will be less useful than the ones they put on themselves. We might avoid the worst effects of drinking by educating students about its risks from the moment they set foot on campus. _{claim/solution}

Avoid going so far back that the history becomes irrelevant. We usually go deeper into the history of a conceptual problem: Someone studying student drinking not to control it but only to understand it might recount its centuries-long European tradition, Prohibition in the 1920s, and so on. Historical narratives are a sign of scholarly diligence.

How Much Detail Do Readers Need?

Once you decide where to start the story of your problem, you have to decide how much detail readers need to understand it. We can't give you a pat answer, because it again depends on the nature of your problem and its solution. Readers need enough detail to understand your problem and to be confident that you do too. For example, in addressing the problem of helping students avoid certain anxieties in their first year of college, a writer might offer this as part of an argument for expanding orientation for first-year students:

> Orientation for first-year students should be expanded from one week to two to help students understand better what lies ahead. _{claim} Too many freshmen become anxious and frustrated during their first semester _{cause/effect} because they misunderstand what teachers expect of them.

_{cause/effect}. They think that they will succeed in college if they just do what they did in high school. _{cause} After all, high school is the only model of education we know, and few of our teachers told us what to expect here.

But that account is so general that it is hard to grasp the logic of its implied causes and effects. The writer could craft a more detailed chain:

> Orientation for first-year students should be expanded to two weeks to help students understand better what lies ahead. _{claim} Many students become anxious and frustrated during their first semester _{cause/effect} because they misunderstand what teachers expect of them. _{cause/effect} For example, most teachers want us to think and write critically about what we've read, but many first-year students think teachers just want them to report it back accurately. So they summarize their readings and their notes, but get poor grades for doing so. _{cause/effect} This happens most often with students who succeeded in high school by reporting back what they heard in class. _{cause/effect} After all, that's what many of our high school teachers told us to do, and no one warned us that our task in college would be different. _{cause}

If readers needed more help, that chain could be broken into yet finer sequences.

Inexperienced students tend to be too general rather than too specific, so as a rule of thumb, create a narrative more detailed than you think it has to be.

How Much Explanation Do You Need?

If you could offer a narrative that exactly suited your readers, they would need nothing more. But more likely, they look for reasons to believe that one event does not just follow another, but is caused by it. If so, you have to weave explanations into your narrative that explicitly establish causal relationships that a simple narrative only implies. You do that with analogies, warrants, and explicit analysis.

Analogies
Use an analogy when the cause and effect in question is so much like another case that readers will quickly infer the same cause-effect relationship:

> Starting college is like moving to a new town or taking a new job. It takes a while to get comfortable.

Analogies are useful in arguments about the future, because the only way we can predict it is by recalling the past. Analogies suggest that a proposed solution is so like another that worked before that it will work now.

> We can rid our dormitories of alcohol as effectively as we did drugs with a zero-tolerance policy. Before we instituted our current policy, we did not enforce rules against drugs for fear of violating student privacy. But once we decided to suspend anyone caught using drugs, and some were, drug use virtually disappeared. _{analogy} A zero-tolerance policy can end alcohol use in the same way. _{claim}

The problem is, history is full of counter-analogies:

We tried national Prohibition in the 1920s, but that just made alcohol more attractive and drove it underground. If we ban alcohol from university property, the same thing will happen again. _{counter-analogy}

EXAMPLE

Analogy and Causation

You've seen a part of this passage in Chapter 9 (p. 190). In this part, the movie critic Michael Medved responds to those who deny that violent entertainment causes violence in society.

Although hundreds of studies demonstrate a link between brutal media imagery and brutal behavior, skeptics argue that this reflects the tastes of violent kids rather than the influence of violent entertainment. Hollywood's most nimble apologists never tire of pointing out that our prisons are full of cold-blooded murderers who never saw "The Basketball Diaries," whereas the overwhelming majority of children who regularly enjoy brutal movies or video games will never shoot their classmates.

Yet these reassuring arguments amount to very little, for one can say similar things about cigarettes: some people who never smoke get lung cancer, and most people who smoke never get lung cancer. But so what? Smoking still enormously increases your likelihood of getting sick. By the same token, you prove nothing with the undeniable observation that most consumers can view even the most disturbing and irresponsible products of our pop culture without discernible harm.

Consider the logic behind TV advertising: A commercial's failure to sell everybody doesn't mean it fails to sell anybody. If a Lexus ad inspires even one in a thousand viewers to take a test drive, it has dramatically improved the fortunes of the car marker. And if one of a thousand kids who watch intense violence on TV or at the movies were to try out that violence in real life, then it dramatically changes America.

Source: Michael Medved, "Hollywood Murdered Innocence," *Wall Street Journal,* June 16, 1999.

Warrants

Behind every analogy is an implicit warrant. When you articulate a warrant, you make explicit the principle that lets us analogize one cause and effect relationship to another:

Everyone feels lost when they enter a new community whose expectations seem baffling. _{warrant} So when you start your first year here, _{cause} you will feel bewildered. _{effect}

But we rely on warrants at the risk of making doctrinaire claims. When you take a fresh look at the cause and effect relationship, do not rely on your stock warrants. Analyze your issue as a new problem.

Analysis
You analyze cause and effect when you run through Mill's questions (pp. 272-76).

- When a cause occurs, does the effect usually occur?
- When a cause is absent, is the effect usually absent?
- Does the magnitude of an effect usually vary with the magnitude of its cause?

> We can see the contrast between students from high schools that emphasize discussion and critical writing as opposed to rote learning. Almost 90 percent of their graduates report that they feel comfortable in our first-year classes, while almost 60% of first-year students from schools that emphasize rote learning report anxiety, confusion, and frustration.

Here is how you weave these explanations into your narrative:

> Orientation for first-year students should be expanded to two weeks to help students understand better what lies ahead. _{claim} **Everyone feels lost when they enter a new community whose expectations seem baffling.** _{warrant} **It's like moving to a new town or taking a new job. It takes a while to get comfortable.** _{analogy} In the same way, students become anxious and frustrated during their first semester here _{claim/effect} because they don't know what teachers expect of them. _{cause/effect} For example, most teachers want them to think and write critically about what they've read, but many first years think teachers just want them to report it back accurately. _{cause} And so they only summarize their readings and their notes. _{effect} This happens most often with students who succeeded in high school by reporting back what they heard in class. _{cause/effect} After all, that's all that many of their high school teachers expected of us, and too few warned us about that our task in college would be quite different. _{cause} **We can see the contrast in students from high schools that emphasize discussion and critical writing as opposed to rote learning. Almost 90 percent of their graduates report that they feel comfortable in our first-year classes, while almost 60% of first-year students from schools that emphasize rote learning report anxiety, confusion, and frustration.** _{analysis}

Planning an Argument Assigning Personal Responsibility

To argue that someone is responsible for an action, use the same devices you use to make any argument about causation: narratives, analogies, warrants, and Millsian analyses. But in an argument about personal responsibility, not only must you establish causation, you must also address the criteria for assigning responsibility.

Establish Causation and the Need to Assign Responsibility

1. Did the person actually cause what you claim she did?

Ordinarily, this is not an issue. If you claim that your school has failed to educate students about the risks of bingeing, readers are unlikely to wonder whether you've missed something. On the other hand, this question is crucial in matters such as who committed a crime.

2. Was the intended outcome good (or bad)?

If someone saves a drowning child, the outcome is self-evidently good. But if the person jumped in to save a child's doll, the child might be grateful, but few adults would praise an action for a purpose so trivial. It may seem obvious to you that an action had an effect worthy of praise or blame, but do readers judge it as you do? In this matter, readers want details. It does little good to praise someone because she "helped many people."

Address the Five Criteria for Assigning Responsibility
What was the person's state of mind?

1. Did she freely choose to perform the action?
2. Could she foresee its risks and consequences?
3. Were her motives pure?

These three questions require detailed answers. To praise a heroic action, for example, you have to show that the person chose to act (she didn't act impulsively or wasn't forced at gun point), that she intended to achieve the outcome and knew the risks (she wasn't drunk or too excited to know what she was doing), and that she didn't do what she did out of pure self-interest (just to get a reward).

You may also have to answer questions about the context and circumstances.

4. Was her action out of the ordinary? Would most people have chosen *not* to do it?
5. Was her action aided or hindered by the physical circumstances?

If most of us would not risk our lives to rescue someone in a river, then the few who do deserve our praise—more if they leap unaided into a swift and dangerous current, less if they wade into placid waters with a life preserver. The more extraordinary and difficult the action, the stronger our judgment of the person responsible for it. Conversely, if most of us would wade into a shallow pool to save a drowning child, then the few who don't deserve our blame. The less extraordinary and difficult the action, the stronger our blame of the person who does not do it.

In answering all of these questions, details matter, so make your narrative more specific than you think your readers need.

Drafting

Careful readers know that every effect has multiple causes that interact in unpredictable ways, and rarely will you have all the evidence you need to make a claim with 100 percent confidence. So you must state your claims cautiously and modestly. You can express causality with high confidence or extreme diffidence. These phrases move from absolute certainty to relative uncertainty:

> X *causes* Y, is *a cause of* Y, *contributes* to Y, *correlates* with Y, *is implicated in* Y, *is a factor in* Y, *is linked to* Y, *is associated with* Y

You can make the truth of a claim stronger or weaker by using verbs that modulate how certain you are of that causal relationship. Compare the certainty in these two:

> We have *proved / established / shown / argued* that X causes Y.

> Evidence *indicates / suggests / implies* that Y correlates with X.

And you can make those statements more or less certain with *may / might / could be / seems / appears:*

> *Some* evidence *appears* to *indicate* that Y *may correlate* with X.

This is another example of the Goldilocks Rule—not too certain, not too cautious, but just right. As a general principle, though, lean toward diffidence.

When praising and blaming, you need language that implies knowledge, intention, and responsibility.

knowledge:	*know(ingly), recognize, realize, aware, foresee.*
intention:	*intend, intentional(ly), deliberate(ly), purpose(fully), in order to, so that.*
responsibility:	*responsible(ity), answerable, should have, could have.*

Be aware of the ambiguity of *why* and *because:* They both fail to make the crucial difference between *What caused X to . . . ,* a question that encourages you to focus on external circumstances, and *What reasons did X have for . . . ,* a question that encourages you to focus on intentions.

INQUIRIES

Reflections

1. Here is a quotation from the last few pages of Leo Tolstoy's novel *War and Peace,* written about a 130 years ago. Tolstoy was trying to explain free will versus determinism. Does this have any relevance to anything discussed here?

   > [T]o imagine the action of a man entirely subject to the law of inevitability without any freedom, you must assume the knowledge of an infinite number of space relations, an infinitely long period of time, and an infinite series of causes. To imagine a man perfectly free and not subject to the law of inevitability, you must imagine him all alone, beyond space, beyond time, and free from dependence on cause.

   Tolstoy, of course, knew that neither was possible. Now what?

2. Here are two stories about AIDS. Why does the second continue to circulate widely even though no evidence supports it?

   a. A virus randomly mutated in an African primate that by chance bit someone who happened to be sexually active and traveled widely enough to infect others, who unwittingly went on to infect more, eventually creating the world-wide epidemic of AIDS.

   b. A CIA lab created a virus as a weapon. As the end of the Cold War approached, they decided to use it to wipe out homosexuals and drug users, and eventually African-Americans. They enlisted drug dealers to create an epidemic of addiction to get people to infect themselves. Once this is exposed, the CIA will be revealed for the evil force it is.

3. When Princess Diana was killed in that automobile accident, just about everyone focused on the drunk driver or on the paparazzi chasing her as the cause. A few pointed out she was not wearing a seat belt and that the person in the front seat who was wearing one survived, so it was her failure to buckle-up that killed her. But after a day or two, most commentators stopped saying that, and focused on the driver and the paparazzi. Why did so few mention her not buckling up as a plausible cause of her death?

4. Imagine everyone wears seat belts all the time. How would that have changed how we understand the cause of Diana's death? Would it ever be imaginable that seat belts would make as interesting a causal story as drinking?

5. Imagine this: Every day for a month, you try to start your car; it doesn't start. You look under the hood. Someone has detached the battery wire. Then one day the car starts: the person didn't detach the wire. Do you say that the cause of the car starting was that the person did *not* detach the wire? Or try this: A school crossing guard does not show up one morning, and a child is hit by a car. Do you say that one of the causes of the child's being hit was that the guard did not show up? Now suppose there was never a guard at that crossing. Does that change your account of causation? Why?

Task

6. When you fill in the details of your narrative of a problem or its solution, you do more than help your readers. You also test your own reasoning. Reread the two stories about the origin of AIDS above in inquiry 2. Make each story more detailed by filling in possible causes for each step in the narrative. Is one story easier to fill in than the other? Does one become less plausible the more you fill it in?

CHAPTER 11 IN A NUTSHELL
About Your Argument . . .

Every event has countless causes. When you make an argument about causes, you have to decide which ones to single out as relevant to your argument. A cause is *pragmatically relevant* if, by fixing it, you solve the problem. A cause is *conceptually relevant* if it allows you to understand an event in light of some special interest you and your readers bring to the question.

When you think about causes, you have to guard against biases we all share:

1. We tend to focus on causes that occur just before an effect.
2. We tend to focus on present rather than absent causes.
3. We tend to focus on unpredictable and unexpected causes.
4. We tend to prefer causes that confirm our assumptions.
5. We tend to prefer causes whose magnitude is proportional to their effect.

You guard against these biases by considering as many causes as you can identify, especially those that most of us tend to miss: what we don't think of because it's absent or too routine to notice.

When you tell the story of the problem, you have to decide how far back in the chain of causes to begin. For a pragmatic problem, you should go just far enough back to give your readers a sense of the context for your solution; for a conceptual one, you should go deeper into its history since readers generally want to see more causes when you ask them to understand a question rather than approve a solution.

Use an ANOVA table to help you test your reasoning. Label each row down by the presence or absence of a possible cause. Label each column across by the presence or absence of an effect. You can claim a plausible cause when you find a significant correlation between the possible cause and the effect, specifically if

- the effect usually occurs when the cause is present, and
- the effect usually does not occur when the cause is absent.

The greater the difference between the percentage of times when the effect is present and when it's absent, the more significant the correlation and the more confidently you can claim a plausible cause.

. . . and About Writing It

When you plan a cause and effect argument about a pragmatic problem, you may have to include up to five stories that answer these five questions:

1. What causes this problem?
2. How will the action you propose cause the problem to go away?
3. How will your solution be implemented?
4. How do you know your solution will not cost more than the problem?
5. Why is your solution at least not contradictory to the alternatives, and maybe even better than them?

In a pragmatic problem start your narrative of causes and effects a bit before the point where you propose intervening to eliminate its cost. In a conceptual problem, begin a bit further back in history. Decompose your narrative into finer detail than you think you have to, because we all tend to be too general rather than too specific. Flesh out your narrative with explanations that show that a cause in fact produces its effect. Use analogies, warrants, and Millsian analyses.

PART 4

The Languages of Argument

Once you generate ideas, collect evidence, and arrange the elements of your argument to suit your readers' needs, you will have invested lots of time thinking, reading, and writing. At that point, some writers think that all they have to do is write up a draft, spell-check it, and print it out. It is tempting to treat this last stage as a routine chore, but if you do, you pass up a significant opportunity, because words do more than just make good ideas visible. Choosing and revising them is also an act of discovery and creativity.

- In Chapter 12, we discuss how language affects what readers understand and remember. We also explore how your language can influence how readers feel about your argument, its subject matter, and even about you.

- In Chapter 13, we explore certain structures of language entrenched so deeply in our reasoning that they are almost indistinguishable from it. They can shape our thinking in ways that we are unaware of.

CHAPTER 12

Clear Language

In this chapter, we discuss the process of writing clear sentences: why readers judge clarity as they do, how you can recognize unclear writing and how to revise it. We also discuss two other qualities of prose that readers value: concision and vividness. Concise writing uses the fewest words necessary. Vivid writing gives readers an image of what they are reading about. Those qualities also raise the issue of the place of feelings in a persuasive argument.

You can convince readers to accept your claims only if they recognize the parts of your argument and see how they add up to a coherent whole. But if they first have to slog through one confusing sentence after another, they may never grasp your argument well enough to judge it fairly. And even if they do, they are unlikely to be well disposed toward it or you. Imagine that you had to read forty pages of prose like this:

> 1a. The Federalists' argument that destabilization of government was the result of popular democracy was based on their belief in the tendency of self-interested groups toward sacrificing the common good in favor of their own narrow objectives.

You would feel friendlier toward the writer if those forty pages were closer to this:

> 1b. The Federalists argued that popular democracy destabilized government because they believed that self-interested groups tend to sacrifice the common good for their own narrow objectives.

In fact, write prose like (1a) and you risk not just your readers' good will, but their willingness to read at all.

So once you have drafted your argument, you still have to be sure it is as clearly written as its substance allows. But in making that judgment, you face two problems:

- When you reread your own prose, you always understand it more easily than your readers will, because you remember too well what you meant when you wrote it.
- Even when you do recognize what needs revising, you might not know how to change it.

In the first part of this chapter, we show you how to do two things:

- Identify sentences that may make readers struggle, even when they seem clear to you.
- Revise them so that readers understand them as easily and quickly as the ideas they express allow.

Clarity and Your Ethos

Some students think their writing style is merely cosmetic: *What's important is not my words but my ideas.* But that assumes readers will struggle through difficult prose to find your ideas. In fact, few readers have the time or patience. It is a mistake to assume that they won't care about the words you choose, because many readers believe that the quality of your writing reflects the quality of your mind. So if they think you write unclearly, they may question how clearly you think. For example, here's what one reviewer said of a book on teaching apes how to talk:

> This is fascinating stuff, but it is amazing how quickly the momentum is lost when the authors begin expounding in science-speak. You're just getting into the mind of the ape . . . when the mind of the cognitive psychologist feels compelled to elaborate: "It was expected that if apes do have language, its presence would be revealed by the animals' innate syntactical competence, a putatively genetically determined ability to order the symbols in multi-word utterances." . . . [T]here are times when the more the authors explain, the less we understand. Apes certainly seem capable of using language to communicate. Whether scientists are remains doubtful.

Source: Douglas Chadwick, *New York Times Book Review*, December 11, 1994

Your style significantly shapes your ethos. In fact, clarity is itself an element of persuasion, because it projects a voice of candor: *I am being straight with you, no tricks, no hiding behind fancy language.* Clarity can't replace logic, but it gives readers some cause to trust you.

Some Principles of Clear and Direct Writing

We talk about style as being clear or unclear, simple or complex, but when we use those terms, we say only how sentences make us feel as we read them. We say a sentence is confusing when *we* feel confused; unclear when *we* feel uncertain about what it means; convoluted when *we* feel lost in its twists and turns.

Such terms, however, don't help us know what makes us feel that way. To diagnose and revise your prose, you have to look not for those qualities, but for the specific sentence structures that make readers use terms like *clear* or *convoluted, dense* or *direct.* In the principles we offer, we focus on what it is *on the page* that makes readers struggle.

To help you identify and revise sentences likely to give readers difficulty, we'll give you six easy principles. To use them you have to know a few common grammatical terms you've probably heard before. Three important ones are *subject, verb,* and *noun.* It helps to know a few others: *object, preposition, active, passive, phrase, main clause,* and *subordinate clause.* If you haven't thought about those terms in a while, you can review them at the end of this chapter. We also use a technical term you probably don't know, but we'll define it when we need it. Take these principles not as ironclad rules that you impose on every sentence you write, but rather as tools for predicting how most readers will judge your sentences and for revising those you think readers might find difficult.

- **Principle 1: Use subjects to name your main characters**.

Readers understand sentences most easily when they see in the simple subjects of verbs the most important characters you write about. By character we mean not just people but whatever is so distinct in your readers' minds that they can understand a story about it. As we shall see, you can tell clear stories about abstract ideas, so long as they are familiar to readers. But readers judge characters to be clearest when they are people or concrete objects that can be named in a word or two.

For example, look again at the two examples you read above. We have picked out the one-word simple subjects (*italicized*) inside the whole subjects (<u>underlined</u>):

1a. <u>The Federalists' *argument* that destabilization of government was the result of popular democracy</u> was based on their belief in the tendency of self-interested groups toward sacrificing the common good for their own narrow objectives.

1b. <u>The *Federalists*</u> argued that <u>popular *democracy*</u> destabilized government, because <u>*they*</u> believed that <u>self-interested *groups*</u> tend to sacrifice the common good for their narrow objectives.

In (1a) the simple subject, *argument,* is an abstract noun inside a long, abstract phrase constituting the whole subject:

WHOLE SUBJECT	VERB
The Federalists' *argument* that destabilization of government was the result of popular democracy	was based . . .

Moreover, inside that long abstract subject is another abstract subject:

WHOLE SUBJECT	VERB
destabilization of government	was . . .

In contrast, look at the whole subjects of (1b):

WHOLE SUBJECT	VERB
The *Federalists*	argued . . .
popular democracy	destabilized . . .
they	believed . . .
self-interested groups	sacrificed . . .

The whole subjects in (1b) are short and specific. Three name people (*Federalists, they, self-interested groups*) and the fourth a familiar concept (*democracy*). That's the main reason why most of us find (1b) easier to read. So the first principle of a clear style is this:

Keep your subjects short and concrete, preferably human actors.

But now we have to add a qualification: Sometimes we want to tell stories not about flesh-and-blood characters but about abstractions. Look at the whole subjects of the following sentences (whole subjects are underlined; simple subjects are italicized):

Few *aspects* of human behavior have been so difficult to explain as rational thinking. *Rationality* depends on a range of short-term behaviors, such as not jumping to a hasty conclusion or action, having the patience to gather evidence, and the ability to bring together evidence and reasons in support of claims. But perhaps the *hallmark* of human rationality is the capacity to think about thinking, to reason about reasoning, to reflect on the quality of the thinking that assembles those reasons and claims into an argument.

The subjects of those sentences are all abstractions:

WHOLE SUBJECT	VERB
Few *aspects* of human behavior	have been . . .
Rationality	depends . . .
the *hallmark* of human rationality	is . . .

In that passage we see no human characters, but those abstract characters are so familiar to readers who have thought about this issue that the terms *human behavior* and *rationality* seem almost as distinct as people who behave and think. Moreover, even though those subjects are abstract, the longest is only five words long.

To decide whether the subjects of your sentences will be clear to your readers, you have to look at them from their point of view. Don't make anything the subject of a sentence if it might seem to readers like an amorphous blob, especially a long amorphous blob such as *the Federalists' argument that destabilization of government was the result of popular democracy.* Few readers can hold a subject that long in mind, much less see it as a clear and distinct "thing."

You can usually revise such sentences by recasting them around flesh-and-blood characters. If you thought readers might find abstractions like *rationality* and *behavior* difficult, you could revise to make their subjects flesh-and-blood characters:

> <u>Psychologists</u> have found it difficult to explain what <u>we</u> do when <u>we</u> behave rationally. <u>We</u> think rationally when, in the short run, <u>we</u> do not jump to hasty conclusions, but instead patiently gather evidence, and bring evidence and reasons together to support claims. But <u>we</u> are perhaps most rational when <u>we</u> reason about our reasoning, when <u>we</u> reflect on how well <u>we</u> thought when <u>we</u> assembled our reasons and claims into an argument.

You can't always revise stories about abstractions around flesh-and-blood characters, but to the degree you can, readers will judge your prose to be clearer and more vivid. You may, however, feel that flesh-and-blood characters make your sentences seem simplistic, especially when your readers are specialists in a field. If so, use technical terms as characters in the subjects of your sentences, but only if your readers are familiar with them.

- **Principle 2: Use verbs, not nouns, to name the actions associated with the characters.**

Once readers get past a short, concise subject, they look for a verb that expresses a specific action. When they find one, they are more likely to judge your prose to be readable and lively. Compare the verbs (boldfaced) in the two passages about the Federalists:

1a. The Federalists' argument that destabilization of government **was** the result of popular democracy **was based** on their belief in the tendency of self-interested groups toward sacrificing the common good for their narrow objectives.

1b. The Federalists **argued** that popular democracy **destabilized** government, because they **believed** that self-interested groups **tend** to **sacrifice** the common good for their narrow objectives.

The only verbs in (1a) are empty: *was* and *was based.* They express no action at all. The verbs in (1b) name actions: *argue, destabilize, believe, tend, sacrifice.*

But if the actions in (1a) are not in verbs, where are they? They are in abstract nouns (boldfaced):

1a. The Federalists' **argument** that **destabilization** of government *was* the result of popular democracy *was based* on their **belief** in the **tendency** of self-interested groups toward **sacrificing** the common good for their narrow objectives.

There is a technical term for these action nouns derived from verbs: It is *nominalization*. (When you nominalize the verb *nominalize,* you get the nominalization *nominalization.*) Nothing more characterizes what feels like highly professional abstract prose than lots of these abstract nominalizations, especially in the subjects of sentences. When you use nominalizations, not only do you have to use weaker verbs instead of the stronger verbs you could have used, but you also have to add lots of prepositions that you don't need when you use the stronger verbs:

1a. The Federalists' argument that destabilization **of** government would be the result **of** popular democracy was based **on** their belief **in** the tendency **of** self-interested groups **toward** sacrificing the common good **for** their narrow objectives.

So here is the second principle of clear prose:

Make your verbs communicate distinct actions; do not bury actions in abstract nominalizations.

We can join these two principles: Match key elements in your sentences—subjects and verbs—to key elements in your story—characters and actions.

SUBJECT	VERB
CHARACTER	ACTION

Taken together, these two principles explain why we judge some sentences as unclear and abstract, others as clear and concrete. When we see characters in concise subjects and actions as verbs right after them, we more easily "image" what we read. The more easily we image the story of a sentence, the more likely we judge that sentence to be clear.

• **Principle 3: Get to verbs quickly.**

Contrast the following sentences (whole subjects are underlined; simple subjects are italicized; main verbs are boldfaced):

2a. *Parents* who believe that school uniforms would solve most of the discipline problems in our schools **argue** in favor of them, but many other parents who fear that government already intrudes too much into our private lives **object.**

2b. Some *parents* **argue** that *school uniforms* would solve most of the discipline problems in our schools, but many *others* **object** because *they* fear that *government* already intrudes too much into our private lives.

In both sentences, the simple subjects are human characters, *parents* and *others,* but is it fair to say that most of us probably prefer (2b)? In (2a), you have to read 17 words to get to the verb in the first clause, *argue,* and 16 more to get to the verb in the second, *object.* In (2b), you have to read only two words before you get to the main verb in each clause:

2b. <u>Some parents</u> **argue** . . . but <u>many others</u> **object** . . .

This principle of getting to a verb quickly implies three subordinate ones:

- **Principle 3A: Avoid long introductory elements that delay a reader from getting to a subject.**

Compare these sentences (the introductory elements are italicized):

3a. *In view of recent research on higher education indicating at least one change in their major on the part of most undergraduate students,* <u>first-year students</u> **should be** 100 percent certain about the program of studies they want to pursue before they load up their schedule with requirements for a particular program.

3b. *According to recent research on higher education,* <u>most students</u> **change** their majors at least once during their undergraduate careers, so <u>first-year students</u> **should be** 100 percent certain about the program of studies they want to pursue before they load up their schedule with requirements for a particular program.

3c. <u>Recent research on higher education</u> **indicates** that most students change their majors at least once during their undergraduate careers, so <u>first-year students</u> **should be** 100 percent certain about their program of studies before they load up their schedule with requirements for a particular program.

Most readers find (3a) less clear than (3b) or (3c). In (3a) we must work through a twenty three-word introductory phrase before we get to the main subject and verb, *first-year students* **should be.** In (3b) we have to work through only a seven-word introductory phrase, and in (3c) we start directly with the subjects of both clauses.

- **Principle 3B: Keep whole subjects short.**

Once we get to a subject, we want to get to a verb. This principle connects to our first one, to make subjects clearly defined characters, because distinct characters usually have short names. Compare these:

4a. <u>A social *system* that fails to create a legal environment in which foreign investors can rely on the rule of law and on the strict enforcement of contracts</u> _{subject} **will** not **thrive.**

4b. *If a social system fails to create a legal environment in which foreign investors can rely on the rule of law and on the strict enforcement of contracts,* _{subordinate clause} <u>that *system*</u> **will** not **thrive.**

4c. <u>A social *system*</u> **will** not **thrive** *if it fails to create an environment in which foreign investors can rely on the rule of law and on the strict enforcement of contracts.* _{subordinate clause}

In (4a), we see where the whole subject starts: right at the beginning of the sentence; but we can't see at a glance where it stops, because it is so long. In (4b) we quickly identify a shorter subject and the verb in a fairly long subordinate clause. And in (4c) the main subject and verb are short and right at the beginning of the sentence: <u>A social *system*</u> **will** not **thrive** . . .

- **Principle 3C: Avoid interrupting subjects and verbs with long phrases and clauses.**

Compare this pair of sentences:

5a. <u>Some scientists</u>>*because they write in a style that is so impersonal and objective,*< **do** not **communicate** with lay people easily.

5b. <u>Some scientists</u> >< **do** not **communicate** with lay people easily, *because they write in a style that is so impersonal and objective.*

We easily see where the subject of (5a), *some scientists,* starts and stops, but just when we expect a verb, we hit that long interrupting *because*-clause. When we don't see a verb right after a subject, we are likely to judge the sentence to be more difficult than it has to be. You can shift an interrupting element to the end or beginning of its sentence, depending on where it fits better.

The sum of these three subprinciples is this:

Help readers get through a short subject to its verb quickly. If you can, put long and complicated elements after the verb.

- **Principle 4: Begin sentences with information that is familiar to your readers.**

This principle has the same effect as the first three, but depends less on the grammar of a sentence than on the psychology of its reader: We read more easily when early in a sentence we deal with information that is easy and familiar before we have to deal with information that is new and complex. Compare:

6a. Particular ideas toward the beginning of sentences define what sentences are "about." The cumulative effect of a series of repeated subjects indicates what a passage is about, so our sense of coherence depends on subjects of sentences. Moving through a paragraph from a consistent point of view occurs when a series of subjects seems to constitute a coherent sequence. A seeming absence of context for sentences is one consequence of making random shifts in subjects. Feelings of dislocation, disorientation, and lack of focus occur when that happens.

6b. As we read, we depend on the subject of a sentence to focus our attention on a particular idea that tells us what that sentence is "about." In a series of sentences, we depend on repeated subjects to cumulatively tell us the topic of a whole passage. If we feel that a series of subjects is coherent, then we feel we are moving through a paragraph from a coherent point of view. But if we feel its subjects shift randomly, then we have to begin each sentence out of context, from no coherent point of view. When that happens, we feel dislocated, disoriented, out of focus.

Most of us have a problem with (6a) that we do not have in (6b). As we start each sentence in (6a), we have to deal not just with long abstract subjects, but with information that *to us* is newer and less familiar than the information at the ends of those sentences:

6a. <u>Particular ideas toward the beginning of sentences</u> . . .

<u>The cumulative effect of a series of subjects</u> . . .

. . . <u>our sense of coherence</u> . . .

<u>Moving through a paragraph from a consistent point of view</u> . . .

<u>A seeming absence of context for sentences</u> . . .

<u>Feelings of dislocation, disorientation, and lack of focus</u> . . .

In (6a), we begin each sentence in strange territory, with no sense of how it connects to what we just read. In (6b), however, we begin each sentence with information that seems more familiar and is therefore easier to grasp:

6b. As <u>we</u> read, <u>we</u> depend on . . .

In a series of sentences, <u>we</u> depend on . . .

If <u>we</u> feel that <u>a series of subjects</u> . . .

But if <u>we</u> feel <u>its subjects</u> . . .

Then <u>we</u> have to begin . . .

When <u>that</u> happens, <u>we</u> feel . . .

From this principle of how to begin a sentence, we can infer another about how to end it.

- **Principle 5: Put at the end of a sentence long and complex units of information containing unfamiliar technical terms.**

And from principles (4) and (5), we can infer a sixth.

- **Principle 6: Keep your subjects consistent. Avoid beginning several sentences in a row with unrelated subjects.**

In (6a), we sense no consistency in its subjects. When sentences in a series all begin differently, we are likely to judge the passage to be unfocused, disjointed, even disorganized. In (6b), the subjects are more consistent. As a result, we read (6b) more easily. In short,

Don't vary your subjects; focus them on a limited set of characters.

Here are the six principles again:

1. Name the main characters in your story in the subjects of sentences.
2. Express their actions not as abstract nouns but as verbs.
3. Get to the main verb quickly.

   a. Avoid long introductory elements.

   b. Avoid long subjects.

   c. Avoid interrupting subjects and verbs.
4. Begin sentences with information that is familiar to readers.
5. Push to the end information that is newer, more complex, and therefore more difficult to understand.
6. Begin sentences consistently. Focus your subjects on familiar characters.

You may have to use difficult language when the substance of your ideas demands it. But you can avoid making readers work harder than they should if you help them get up a head of steam at the beginning of a sentence so that they can deal with newer and more complex information toward the end.

The Ethics of Deliberate Complexity

Some writers deny that clarity is as valuable as we have claimed. In fact, some write complex prose deliberately, thinking either that their ideas demand it or that complexity makes them sound impressive, and what sounds impressive must be persuasive. Occasionally, complex ideas do require complex sentences. And sometimes naïve readers are impressed by fancy language. But more often, complex prose is a product of self-indulgence, or at least indifference to readers. Some writers even claim that we benefit from the struggle to decipher their complex prose, because the struggle makes us think harder. They're wrong about that. All the research into reading indicates that when readers have to struggle with a complex style, they understand not more, but less.

Concision and Vividness

Readers judge sentences to be clear when they see short, specific subjects followed by verbs expressing important actions. But they look for more. Compare the subjects and verbs of these two passages (we underline subjects, boldface verbs):

> The consensus of our national belief **is** the right and freedom to engage in practices reflecting the inheritance of our different cultural and historical backgrounds. Allowing widows to end their lives as sometimes happens in certain parts of the world **must** obviously **be made** illegal and forbidden by law, but there should **be** allowances for things like female head coverings in educational settings. But there **is** a degree of uncertainty and unease in regard

to cultural practices and traditions such as the binding force of an arranged future marriage between those not yet old or mature enough to take responsibility for the consequences of their decisions.

We generally **believe** that <u>Americans</u> **should be** free to practice the cultural traditions of their parents. Though <u>we</u> **forbid** a widow from throwing herself onto her husband's burning funeral pyre, as <u>Indian women</u> **are** sometimes **coerced** to do, <u>we</u> **allow** Islamic girls to wear head scarves in public school. But about some cases <u>we</u> **are** less certain: **Must** <u>a court</u> **recognize** as binding a <u>contract</u> arranging a future marriage of two eight-year-olds?

The first feels indirect and complex; the second more straightforward, partly because it has shorter, clearer, and more familiar subjects. But the second has another virtue: It also seems "sharper." It lets us better "see" what the words refer to, and if we can vividly see their referents in our mind's eye, we are likely to respond more strongly.

You create that kind of more vivid prose in two ways:

- Express ideas in the fewest words your readers need.
- Use words that let readers see in their minds' eye what those words refer to.

Do that, and your readers will read your argument faster, understand it better, and remember it longer. Use more words than you need, especially abstract words, and readers are likely to judge your argument to be vague, fuzzy, foggy, muddy—pick your metaphor.

In the rest of this chapter, we look at how to write a prose style that is not just clear, but memorable and even moving because it is vividly concise.

How to Be Concise

It is easy to tell you to be concise, but doing it is hard, because editing for concision is labor-intensive and requires a big vocabulary. But if close editing takes time, it pays off—first for your readers, because you make their task easier, and second for you, because readers are always grateful when you save them time and effort. We would give you rules to make editing easier if we could, but we can't. About the best we can do is show you some kinds of wordiness to look for and some ways to cut through it. No shortcuts here.

Repetition and Clutter

Prose is wordy when it says the same thing twice, uses words with little meaning, or explicitly says what readers can easily infer. For example, this first passage combines both useless repetition and empty words; the revision neither:

Various improvements in productivity basically depend first and foremost on certain fundamental factors that generally involve psychology more than any kind of particular technology.

Productivity rises when we improve not just machines but the minds of those who operate them.

Here are some typical examples of empty words:

certain	various	particular	specific	given	individual
really	basically	generally	virtually	actually	

Some typical examples of redundant pairs:

full and complete	hope and trust	any and all
true and accurate	each and every	basic and fundamental
hopes and desires	first and foremost	various and sundry

Decomposed Meaning

You most commonly befog a concept when you spread a meaning you can express in one word over several. When you read a word in context—*I'd like you to meet my* **brother**—the word *brother* seems to invoke in your mind a unified, holistic concept. But as we saw in Chapter 10, we can think of the meaning of *brother* as a cluster of criteria (*human, male, descended from the same parents*). But if someone said, *I want you to meet someone who is male and descended from my parents,* you might know what that person meant, but judge him to be a bit odd.

That's a silly example, but we read that kind of writing every day:

> You did not read through what you wrote paying close enough attention to finding and correcting errors.

instead of,

> You did not edit carefully.

That longer sentence breaks ideas into pieces by naming their separate criteria of meaning, smearing it across many words. The shorter sentence uses a single word, which is almost always more vivid:

read through . . . errors	→	edit
paying close attention	→	carefully

Your problem in writing concisely is not just knowing when to replace a phrase with a word, but knowing that word.

Implied Meaning

Another kind of wordiness states what other words imply. Compare:

> Imagine someone trying to learn the rules and strategy for playing the game of chess.

> Imagine learning chess.

Learn implies *try, strategy* implies *play, game* implies *play, chess* implies *game,* and *game* implies *rules and strategy.* So if we cut what readers can infer, we get something both more concise and more vivid:

Imagine ~~someone trying to~~ learn[ing] ~~the rules and the strategy for playing the game of~~ chess.

Do not, however, confuse concision with merely fewer words. Compare these:

Write directly.

Make important characters subjects and make their verbs specific actions.

The first is shorter than the second, but less vivid, because it is so general; it omits information that a reader must know.

How to Be Vivid

Once you've squeezed the wordiness out of your prose, you still have to be sure that the words on the page convey not just the meanings you intend, but the nuances of tone that support them, even the feelings that you want to evoke. Words differ along so many stylistic scales that it is hard to list them all. Here are some general categories:

- **Slang vs. informal vs. formal** (*wheels* vs. *car* vs. *automobile*):

  When a fruitcake shows up in an ER too whigged out to think straight, the doc has to make the call whether to shoot him up with downers.

  When someone comes to an emergency room unable to think rationally, the doctor must decide whether to calm him with drugs.

  When a mentally incompetent individual presents in an emergency room, the attending physician must determine whether to sedate him with tranquilizing medication.

- **Neutral vs. emotional** (*pregnancy termination* vs. *abortion* vs. *infanticide*):

  Lowering taxes will raise net income.

  If we could cut back on what the tax man sucks out of our paychecks every week, we could keep more of the money we sweat for every day.

- **Native vs. borrowed** (*speed* vs. *velocity*):

  You have to show guts when the times call for it.

  It is necessary to demonstrate courage when the occasion demands it.

- **Common vs. scientific** (*belly button* vs. *navel*):

  As you go higher, the air thins out.

  As altitude increases, the atmosphere attenuates.

- **General vs. specific (*livestock* vs. *pig*):**

  A good worker plans carefully in order to do the job right the first time.

  A master carpenter measures twice to cut once.

These criteria often correlate: When a word is formal, like *abdomen,* it is likely to be less common, borrowed, learned in tone, and less vivid and distinct, evoking less emotion than words like *belly* or *gut,* which are informal, likely to be native, more common, more vivid, and more emotionally evocative.

These choices affect not just how we read, but how we judge a writer's ethos. Those three ways of describing a patient in an emergency room say something different about the writer and how she relates to readers—intimately, informally, or formally:

When a fruitcake shows up in an ER too whigged out to think straight . . .

When someone comes to an emergency room unable to think rationally . . .

When a mentally incompetent individual presents in an emergency room . . .

It's hard to offer any big generalizations here. The best advice is to choose the middle way most of the time, because that lets you set a neutral background for the stronger impact of a formal or informal word.

Abstract Versus Concrete

Of these distinctions, the most important to a vivid style is between words that evoke no image and those that do. The more easily we can image what the word refers to, the more vivid the style and the more we respond in a visceral way. Contrast these:

When someone needs emergency care, but acts so irrationally that he cannot legally consent to treatment, only the attending physician can decide whether to give that person medication without his permission before beginning treatment.

When 16-year-old Alex White staggered into the Fairview Hospital Emergency room, raving about demons under his shirt and gushing blood where he had slashed his belly with a hunting knife, trauma physician Amanda Lee's first job was to stop the bleeding. But when White grabbed a nurse by her hair and threw her to the floor, screaming that she was the Whore of Babylon, Lee had to decide at that instant whether to inject him with the tranquilizer thorazine before asking him to sign her hospital's two-page single-spaced permission form. Ohio law and hospital rules require every physician to ask for permission before administering drugs, but White was screaming too loud to hear anything, much less a request that he read and then sign on the dotted line. So as would any physician in that situation, Lee decided to tranquilize White without asking for his permission.

That second version is longer than the first, but more vivid, evoking more feeling. Which is better? That depends on what the writer intends. If the writer wants to evoke feeling, then she uses vividly specific language. If she wants to avoid those emotions, she chooses more general words.

What a reader can image, of course, depends partly on what he knows—say *drag racing* to Colomb and up jump lots of vivid images. But for him to evoke those images in people who don't call the LaPlace Dragway home, he would have to use words more specific: *Sixteen-year-old Colomb burning rubber down a deserted Claiborne Avenue at 3 A.M. on a Sunday morning in a supercharged '57 Bel Aire, hubcap to hubcap with Don Debarbaris' four barrel GTO.*

Most of us, though, most of the time, prefer more rather than less vivid writing, because we read it faster, understand it better, and remember it longer. So what we lose in economy measured by number of words, we gain in efficiency measured by effect. And of course, a writer can combine them:

> When someone needs emergency care, but acts so irrationally that he cannot legally consent to treatment, . . . For example, when on the night of May 13, 1998, 16-year-old Alex White staggered into the Fairview Hospital Emergency room raving . . .

The System of Imageable Words

There is, however, more to being vivid than just being specific, because not all kinds of specificity are equal. For example, what image comes to mind when you read the word *life?* Not much, certainly no image most of us would have in common; we get no distinct image even from the more specific word *vegetation*. Now imagine a *pine tree.* For most of us, that term evokes a distinct image with a more distinct feeling. But now imagine a *Joshua tree:* Unless you know desert vegetation, this even more specific term probably blocks your imagination more than it helps it. In other words, as words become more specific, at some point they evoke in us a clear image, but when they get still more specific, we can't imagine the image unless we happen to know the specific referent.

Speakers of every language seem to organize their vocabulary in that systematic way, on a scale from more general to more specific, with a break point between words that call up no shared distinct image and words that do. In the array below, the break point is shaded:

life	thing	stuff	nourishment	utility
creature	object	merchandise	food	transportation
animal	device	household goods	produce	conveyance
livestock	tool	furniture	fruit	vehicle
horse	hammer	table	apple	motorcycle
palomino	ballpean	Federal dropleaf	Fuji	Harley

Words like *horse, hammer, table, apple* and *motorcycle* refer to things at what psychologists call the *basic level of categorization.* This is the only level at which most of us share similar mental images. Above the basic level (*livestock, tool,* etc.), we conjure up images randomly. Below the basic level, we create more specific images only if we happen to know what a ballpean or Fuji looks like. For the rest of us, a Fuji is just another apple, nothing more.

Most of us prefer prose that evokes images at the basic level because we understand and remember that kind of writing most easily. As writers, though, we see images in our prose more distinctly than our readers do, because we know our subject too well (recall Colomb's response to *drag racing*). If you write about a *creature's right to be free from cruel treatment,* you may have in your mind's eye the image of a little bunny writhing from the burning chemicals dripped into its trusting, black button eyes. But your readers will share that image only if you give it to them.

For example, instead of using general words like *crime* and *firearm,* try words that represent kinds of crime and kinds of weapons a reader can image:

> Recently, crimes involving the use of inexpensive firearms have decreased.

> Compared to a few years ago, a person is less likely to be a crime victim from someone with a cheap handgun.

> Compared to 1995, you are half as likely to mugged by someone shoving a fifty dollar Saturday night special in your face.

We picture the second more readily than the first, and the third more than the second, and as we image more readily, we respond more viscerally.

Desirable Generality

Sometimes, though, you don't want that kind of specificity, especially if you want to develop general claims or avoid evoking emotions:

> We the People of the United States, in Order to form a more perfect Union, establish Justice, insure domestic Tranquillity, provide for the common defense, promote the general Welfare, and secure the Blessings of Liberty to ourselves and our Posterity, do ordain and establish this Constitution for the United States of America.

We do not improve that passage by making it more specific:

> We over-21 property-owning white men of the thirteen States signing this document, to create a nation that is free from the tyranny of King George and the pain and poverty that such tyranny creates, to establish a system whereby white men are treated fairly by the Courts, to insure that people in every town, city, and state do not fight with one another, to provide for soldiers and sailors who will defend our borders, . . .

We also need general language to express general warrants. Here's a good example in another of our historical documents:

> . . . whenever any Form of government becomes destructive of these ends, it is the Right of the People to alter or to abolish it, and to institute new Government, laying its foundation on such principles and organizing its powers in such form, as to them shall seem most likely to effect their Safety and Happiness.

That principle of democratic governance resonates today because it is general enough to cover not just this country more than two centuries ago, but all countries at all times. It would have been a mistake for the drafters of the Declaration of Independence to have written this:

> . . . since King George III and his Parliament have taken away our right to be free to do what makes us happy, like making money, we have the right to revolt and create a new country . . .

That sentence is so specific that it expresses too much emotion and no universal truth. In the early part of the Declaration, the Founders wanted to assert, coolly, the philosophical principles (their warrants) that justify self-governance. Later in the Declaration, however, they wrote more vividly and thereby evoked more emotion when they described King George's crimes against the colonies:

> He has excited domestic insurrections amongst us, and has endeavoured to bring on the inhabitants of our frontiers, the merciless Indian Savages, whose known rule of warfare, is an undistinguished destruction of all ages, sexes and conditions.

By cataloguing King George's crimes in more specific language, Jefferson intended to evoke emotion. This more general version would have done that less well:

> He has caused us problems by helping indigenous peoples act against us.

As always, we aim at the Goldilocks Rule: not too general, not too specific, but just right. What is just right is hard to gauge, but you might hold these two principles in mind:

- When you offer examples, evidence, and illustrations, your readers are likely to prefer language that is concrete, distinct, and vivid.
- When you state general principles, values, and assumptions, readers are likely to sense the power of those statements if you express them in general language.

Keep in mind, though, that all of us are more likely to be too general than too specific, because generalities require little hard thought. But hard thinking is a quality of all arguments worth making, so thinking hard about your language is a way to think better about your argument.

WRITING PROCESS 12
Clear Language

Thinking-Reading-Talking

The Language of Judging Prose

We usually become aware of someone's prose style only when we have to slow down to understand it, particularly when we read about topics we don't know well. When that happens to you, you might think you don't know enough to understand or maybe you're just not smart enough. We have all occasionally felt that way. And sometimes we're right, but more likely the problem is in what we are reading. So the next time you struggle to get through a difficult passage, spend a moment thinking about who's lacking, you or the writer.

Start by describing how you feel about what you've read. We use many metaphors to describe prose, but most of them come from just four areas:

1. Some metaphors suggest movement along a path: You *follow* prose when it keeps you *on track* so that you see *where you are going, step-by-step*. It *carries you along* without making you *stop* to figure out *where you are*. But when prose *loses* you, you *wander* into *blind alleys*.

When you describe a passage with language like *getting lost,* the passage may be disorganized or lack a clearly stated point in its introduction. Go to the conclusion and look for a point there. If you find one, reread the passage with it in mind.

2. Some metaphors focus on *flowing* along that path: When a passage does not *flow* it is *choppy,* or *disjointed*. You have to *labor* through it, because it feels *stilted* and *awkward,* rather than *skimming* through it *effortlessly*.

When a passage makes you feel like that, it probably suffers from an "old-new" problem. Check how the sentences begin: Does each begin with a different subject or with information that seems unrelated to the one before? If so, you can blame the writer, *unless* she is aiming at knowledgeable readers, for whom all of her information is familiar.

3. Other metaphors suggest vision: You *see* what a writer means when his prose is *clear* and *transparent*. It feels *vivid, distinct,* and *sharply focused*. Or it is so *obscure, vague, fuzzy,* or *opaque,* that it leaves you *in the dark*.

When you use words suggesting darkness, the problem may be sentences full of technical terms, nominalizations, and other abstractions, especially in subjects. You test for that by looking at the first seven or eight words of every sentence in the passage.

4. Other metaphors suggest visual simplicity and complexity: Prose is *plain, simple, direct,* and *straightforward* or *convoluted, tangled,* and *complex*.

When you use those last three words, the problem is probably long sentences with many qualifying phrases and clauses. Prose like that is sometimes supposed to reflect a mind at work, starting, stopping to backtrack or qualify, starting again. If we have the time and the writer has an interesting mind, we enjoy that kind of prose. If not, we don't.

A key variable in these judgments is how much knowledge we bring to what we read. The more we know of a subject, the less likely we notice its style. And that's why you are your own worst editor: You know too much about what you write to read it as your readers will.

Jargon Watch

Even book reviewers complain about academic jargon. Here a *New York Times* book reviewer complains about an impenetrable style. Notice the visual metaphors he uses to describe what he has to read:

> Mr. Rabinow, a professor of anthropology at the University of California at Berkeley, tells the story of the collapse of an agreement between a French institute and an American company to collaborate on genetic research [which reveals some deep beliefs about French attitudes toward the body.] . . . [His] telling of this story is brilliant but unkempt, penetrating and impenetrable at the same time. . . . [His] writing is turgid and stilted, or so it will seem to people unaccustomed to the language and the in-group devices of the American Anthropological Association. . . . [His] main idea here threatens to become lost in a fog of highfalutin lingo, but occasionally it emerges sufficiently into the clear to be understood by mere mortals. . . . It is too bad that he chose to tell this very modern tale from within a closed professional world that keeps the rest of us on the outside looking in.

Source: Richard Bernstein, *New York Times*, October 13, 1999.

If a *New York Times* reviewer has to struggle to understand, the problem is not his but the writer's. Don't be reluctant to make the same judgment about what you read.

Revising

You can use the principles of a clear style to diagnose and revise your prose. Start with passages where you struggled to express yourself or were uncertain about your meaning. In moments like that we all tend to fall into confusing prose. Then look at the rest of your argument. Follow these steps.

Diagnose Your Style

Start by underlining (or just skimming) the first seven or eight words in each sentence (ignore short introductory phrases, especially when they refer to previous sentences). Consider revising if you see these characteristics:

- The subject is an abstraction with lots of phrases attached.
- By the eighth or ninth word, you see no verb, or if you do, it is not specific.
- Those first seven or eight words express information that a reader would not remember from previous sentences or have reason to expect.
- Most important, several sentences in a row keep changing subjects so that you see no consistent set of characters or concepts in those first few words.

For example, in the first eight words in the sentences in this passage, notice how long it takes to get to the verb in the main clause:

> <u>Attempts</u> at explanations for increases in voter participation in recent elections **came** from several candidates. <u>A general *cynicism* about honesty in government</u> **was** a common claim of some conservative politicians. But <u>the public's greater *interest* in their private affairs than in national public affairs</u> **is** also a possible reason for the drop in voting.

In the first sentence, the character *voter* appears *in* the subject, but not *as* the subject, and the whole subjects are long and complex, and connected to verbs that express no specific actions: *came, was, is.* It is a passage begging for revision.

Revise Your Sentences

1. Start by finding important characters. In the above passage, they seem to be *voters, candidates,* and *conservative politicians.*

2. Identify the key actions they perform. Voters *participate (less), are cynical,* and *are not interested;* candidates *attempt* and *explain;* conservative politicians *claim.*

3. Now revise the sentences so that most (not necessarily all) begin with important characters as subjects and are immediately followed by key actions in verbs.

   > <u>Several candidates</u> **tried to explain** why <u>fewer people</u> **voted** in recent elections. <u>Some conservative politicians</u> **claimed** that <u>voters</u> **were** generally cynical about honesty in government. But perhaps so <u>few</u> **voted** because <u>they</u> **were** more interested in their private affairs than in national public affairs.

4. Your diagnosis might turn up a long introductory phrase.

   > *Despite their role in creating a sense of loyalty among students and alumni and generating financial resources that support minor sports, on balance* <u>major intercollegiate sports</u> damage the aims of higher education

If so, you can revise it in either of two ways:

- Make the phrase an independent clause:

  > <u>Major intercollegiate sports</u> **may create** a sense of loyalty among students and alumni and generate financial resources that support minor sports, but on balance <u>they</u> **damage** the aims of higher education.

- Make the phrase a subordinate clause. Move it after the main clause, if it communicates new information. If it is old information, try to shorten it.

  > On balance, <u>major intercollegiate sports</u> **damage** the aims of higher education, *even though* <u>they</u> create a sense of loyalty among students and alumni and generate financial resources that support minor sports.

  > *Although* <u>major intercollegiate sports</u> create loyalty and generate financial resources, on balance <u>they</u> **damage** the aims of higher education.

Your diagnosis might turn up a long whole subject whose simple subject is a flesh-and-blood character.

> <u>Athletes who receive special academic consideration because their time is taken up with training and competition</u> are not necessarily academically ill-prepared for the rigors of a high-quality education.

If so, you can revise it in either of two ways:

- Turn the subject into an introductory subordinate clause, but make the simple subject its whole subject, if you can:

> *Although* <u>athletes</u> **might receive** special academic consideration because their time is taken up with training and competition, <u>*they*</u> **are** not necessarily academically ill-prepared for the rigors of a high-quality education.

- Or turn the subject into its own main clause:

> <u>Some athletes</u> **may receive** special academic consideration because their time is taken up with training and competition, but <u>they</u> **are** not necessarily academically ill-prepared for the rigors of a high-quality education.

Your diagnosis might turn up an interrupting element:

> <u>Major intercollegiate sports,</u> *because they undermine the intellectual integrity that higher education is supposed to support by lowering standards for athletes,* **should be abolished.** That kind of erosion will inevitably lead to . . .

If so, move that element either to the beginning or end of its sentence, depending on whether it connects more closely to the preceding or following one.

> <u>Major intercollegiate sports</u> **should be abolished,** *because they undermine the intellectual integrity that higher education is supposed to support by lowering standards for athletes.* That kind of erosion will inevitably lead to . . .

A last word on active and passive verbs: If you remember any advice about writing at all, it is probably to avoid writing in the passive voice. Generally, that's good advice, but often not. For example, after the first sentence in this next passage, imagine active and passive verb sentences:

> Some astonishing questions about the nature of the universe have been raised by scientists investigating black holes in space. <u>The collapse of a dead star into a point perhaps no larger than a marble</u> **creates** _{active verb} a black hole. So much matter compressed into so little space changes the fabric of space around it in surprising ways.

> Some astonishing questions about the nature of the universe have been raised by scientists investigating black holes in space. <u>A black hole</u> **is created** _{passive verb} by the collapse of a dead star into a point perhaps no larger than a marble. So much matter compressed into so little space changes the fabric of space around it in surprising ways.

In that context, the passive verb would be the better choice for two reasons:

- The subject of the active verb is long and abstract: *The collapse of a dead star into a point perhaps no larger than a marble.* But the subject of the passive verb is short, simple, and easily grasped: *A black hole.*

- The passive verb puts into the subject something we just read about in the previous sentence:

> . . . exploring **black holes in space. A black hole** is created by . . .

We don't advise you to write in the passive voice, but nor do we tell you always to avoid it. You *choose* the active or passive, depending on what you want as the subject of the sentence. That's what the passive is for.

Here is a last ~~very useful~~ and ~~important~~ principle of ~~careful~~ editing that you can ~~always~~ rely on: Draw a line through ~~every single~~ adjective that appears before a noun and ~~all~~ adverbs, regardless of where they appear. Then of each, ask whether you ~~really~~ need it. You will ~~probably~~ keep some, but you can ~~certainly~~ get rid of a ~~great~~ many. To be ~~really~~ vivid and concise, write ~~deliberately~~ in ~~specific~~ nouns and verbs, not adjectives and adverbs.

INQUIRIES

Reflections

1. We have tried to persuade you that the best style is, as a rule, the clearest style, but some have claimed that the plain style is deceptive. They argue that complex facts are never as simple as a plain style makes them seem. Clarity itself is a trick to fool readers into accepting simplistic versions of the truth. Can you think of instances when someone might use plain speaking as a trick? How about advertisers? Politicians? Can you think of instances when someone (lawyers? experts?) might use complex language as a trick? Is any style inherently more "honest" or "sincere" than another?

2. Academic writing is rarely vivid, for reasons you can imagine. But why do so many people write so blandly, even after they leave school? For example, here is an excerpt from a report written by a swine veterinarian (that is, a pig doctor) to an operations manager (farmer) with little formal education (schooling). In person, this woman's talk is as salty as any, but notice how fuzzy her language gets when she writes. (Incidentally, "PRRS"—pronounced *purrs*—is a pig's version of a cold, and a "gilt" is a young female pig, terms familiar to her readers.)

   Of greatest urgency and most immediate concern in your ongoing project for enhancing productivity, especially as measured in market weight, is to limit the effects of PRRS on the rate of growth. Elimination of the virus is impractical chiefly in terms of ROI (return on investment), although reduction is a goal worth consideration. Most efficient, however, is to maintain growth rates after infection. Limiting gilt acquisition and proper acclimation are the most efficient additional steps, although the current program of vaccination will have to be maintained.

She could have written something like this:

If you want to market larger pigs, you must limit the effects of PRRS on their growth. Although you'd have to spend too much to eliminate the virus entirely, you can take steps to reduce it. Most important is to maintain growth rates after your pigs are infected. To do that, continue to vaccinate pigs as you do now. The best thing to do is limit the number of gilts you buy and to acclimate those you do.

Or this:

To sell fat pigs, don't let PRRS stunt their growth. It costs too much to get rid of the virus, but you can keep sick pigs growing if you keep vaccinating them, don't buy more gilts than you need, and don't mix them with others until you've exposed them to the virus.

Can you think of any reasons why the vet would write in such a fuzzy, academic style? Are any of them good reasons? Between the second and third version, which do you think would be more appropriate? Why?

Tasks

3. For a week, note the style of what you read. Copy passages that seem particularly easy or hard to read, particularly well or poorly written. Can you identify features *on the page* that make those pages seem better or worse? Try revising the ones you find difficult.

4. Select a passage from a past paper in which your language is bland, pallid, or otherwise undistinctive. Rewrite it to be as vivid as you can. Use words that are specific, imageable, slangy, emotional, and so on. Have you improved it?

GUIDE TO TERMS
Clear Language

To understand how readers will judge your prose, you have to know how sentences work, and to do that you need to know a few terms: *noun, subject, verb, main/independent clause, subordinate/dependent clause, active* and *passive*. The clause is the basic unit of understanding how we read, so we'll start there.

Clauses and Phrases

A clause is a subject and verb and whatever attaches to them. These are clauses, because they have both a subject (underlined) and a verb (boldfaced):

dogs **bark**

the analysis of style **depends** on knowing how to tell a good story

once you **have understood** subjects and verbs

although few of us **write** a clear first draft

These are not clauses because they do not have both a subject and verb:

| a basic unit of style | subjects and verbs | is the sentence |
| the sentence | write a clear first draft | few of us |

Those units are phrases, sequences of words that "hang together" as a unit. A phrase consists of a "head" word (a noun, verb, adjective, or adverb) with words and phrases attached to it. For example, here is a noun phrase composed of a noun with an adjective phrase attached to it and an adverb phrase attached to that:

NOUN PHRASE:	a very easily identifiable **style**
ADJECTIVE PHRASE:	very easily *identifiable*
ADVERBIAL PHRASE:	very <u>easily</u>

On the other hand, these are not phrases, because they don't hang together:

| basic unit of | subjects and | is the |
| to tell a good | a clear first | of style depends on |

Independent Versus Dependent Clauses

We have to distinguish two kinds of clauses: dependent and independent. (Some teachers use the terms *subordinate* and *main*.)

Independent Clauses

By definition, an independent clause doesn't depend on anything else and so can be a free-standing sentence. These are independent clauses with subjects underlined and verbs boldfaced:

> <u>The basic unit of style</u> **is** the sentence.
>
> <u>You</u> **should understand** subjects and verbs.
>
> And <u>readers</u> **look** for subjects to understand what a sentence is about.

You do not begin independent clauses with subordinating conjunctions such as *because, if, when,* and so on. But contrary to what some say, you can begin them with a coordinating conjunction: *and, or, but, yet, so, for.*

Dependent Clauses

As the term suggests, a dependent clause depends on something else. You can usually identify it by an introductory word signaling its dependency. We will examine three kinds of dependent clauses: (1) adverb clauses, (2) adjective clauses, and (3) noun clauses.

Adverb Clauses

Adverb clauses indicate time, place, manner, cause, condition, and so on: they almost always begin with an adverbial conjunction such as *because, if, when, although, before, as, since,* and *unless.* We italicize the words that signal dependency, underline subjects, and boldface verbs:

> *because* <u>readers</u> **look** first for the subject of your sentence

> *if* <u>you</u> **want** to write clearly

> *unless* <u>your argument</u> **addresses** a conceptual problem

Most adverbial clauses can be moved around:

> *Because readers look first for the subject of a sentence,* <u>the best editors</u> **start** revising by looking at subjects.

> The <u>best editors</u> **start** revising by looking at subjects *because readers look first for the subject of your sentence.*

> The <u>best editors,</u> *because readers look first for the subject of your sentence,* **start** revising by looking at subjects.

When you punctuate an adverbial clause as a separate sentence, you create what writing teachers call a *fragment:*

> The best editors start revising by looking at subjects. Because readers look first for the subject of your sentence. _{fragment}

Adjective Clauses

Adjective clauses modify nouns. They usually begin with a relative pronoun such as *who, whom, whose, which, that,* and *where.*

> a book _{noun} <u>*that*</u> **is** hard to read _{adjective clause}

> a point in the story _{noun} *where* <u>the reader</u> **will stop** _{adjective clause}

Relative clauses usually occur right after the noun they modify, but there are exceptions:

> <u>Some people</u> *who don't deserve to succeed* **do**.

> <u>Some people</u> **succeed** *who don't deserve to*.

When you punctuate an adjective clause as a separate sentence, you create what writing teachers call a *fragment:*

> Before we could repair the engine, we had to drill out some bolts. Which were so rusted that they were frozen onto the frame. _{fragment}

Noun Clauses

Noun clauses can be subjects or objects. They typically begin with the same words that adjective clauses do: *who, what, which, that, where.*

> [<u>*That your argument* **will fail**</u>] _{noun clause} **is** always possible.

> <u>Your reader</u> **wants** to know [*why* <u>you</u> **have raised** the problem]. _{noun clause}

Subjects and Verbs

It is hard to define subjects and verbs separately, because each defines the other. There can be no subject without a verb or verb without at least an implied subject (as in commands: *Stop!*).

Verbs

You may remember being told that a verb is an "action" word. That definition works in this sentence:

> <u>He</u> **revised** his prose carefully.

The verb is an action. But that definition doesn't work for this sentence:

> <u>His revision of his prose</u> **was** careful.

The verb is *was,* but the real action is in the subject, *revision.*
    Though we can't define a verb easily, we can tell you how to identify one: A verb is the word whose ending you change when you change past to present, present to future, future to past, etc. Do that in a two-step process:

1. Decide whether the sentence refers to the past, the present, or the future. For example, this sentence refers to a past action:

    Studies of the problem **were** conducted by the staff.

2. Change the time, in this case from past to present:

    Studies of the problem **are being** conducted by the staff.

The words you change are verbs (ignore words like *today, tomorrow,* etc.).
    For our purposes, we also count as verbs what follows the word *to:*

> The need <u>to</u> **review** the program **caused** us <u>to</u> **hire** more staff.

We call these "infinitives."

Subjects

You may also recall being told that the subject of a sentence is the "doer" of the action expressed by the verb. A lot of sentences are like that:

> <u>We</u> **made** mistakes when <u>we</u> **tried** to **explain** why <u>the project</u> **failed.**

But that definition of subject as "doer" doesn't work with a sentence like this:

> <u>Our explanation of the failure of the project</u> **had** mistakes in it.

In the first sentence, the subjects are *we* and *the project,* and they both seem to do things: *make mistakes, try to explain,* and *fail.* In the second, the subject consists of a series of actions: *explanation of the failure.* The verb, *had,* refers to no action at all.

We have asked you to identify two kinds of subjects, what we have called the *simple* subject and *whole* subject.

Simple Subjects

The simple subject is just the word or words that the verb agrees with in number:

> Our *need* to work toward compromise on these problems **was** obvious.

> The *answers* offered in response to the question **were** not responsive.

> *A problem and its solution* **are** at the heart of every argument.

Whole Subjects

The whole subject is the simple subject and everything attached to it:

> <u>Our *need* to work toward compromise on these problems</u> **was** obvious.

Here's a way to identify whole subjects and simple subjects:

1. Locate the verb as described earlier:

   > Our need to work toward compromise on these problems **was** obvious.

2. Turn the sentence into a question by putting *who* or *what* before the verb:

   > What **was** obvious?

The most complete answer is the whole subject:

> <u>Our need to work toward compromise on these problems</u> **was** obvious.

The shortest possible answer is the simple subject:

> (Our) <u>need</u> **was** obvious.

Active and Passive Voice

Grammatically, we define "active" and "passive" by three criteria:

1. The subject of an active sentence feels like a "doer" doing something to the object of the verb:

   > <u>The collapse of a dead star</u> _{subject} **creates** _{verb} a black hole. _{object}

   The subject of a passive sentence, on the other hand, is the object toward which the action is directed:

   > <u>A black hole in space</u> _{subject} **is created** by . . .

2. The passive verb always has a form of *be* in front of it and is in its past participle form: **is created.**

3. The active verb has an object: .... **creates** *a black hole.* A passive verb, on the other hand, may (or may not) be followed by a prepositional phrase beginning with *by* naming the doer of the action expressed by the verb: **is created** *by* the collapse of a dead star.

When you look for passive verbs, you have to distinguish what is technically passive from what only *feels* passive. This sentence is passive in the technical, grammatical sense:

Poor people **are** often **deprived** of food.

This next sentence is not passive in that grammatical sense, but it certainly feels passive because its subject is a nominalization:

Deprivation of food often **afflicts** poor people.

Nouns, Adjectives, and Adverbs

Nouns

You may recall being told that a noun refers to a person, place, or thing. To make that definition work, though, we'd have to group under "thing" anything that we already know is a noun. In this next sentence, the nouns are boldfaced:

The **success** of the **program** was hampered by an endless **series** of **problems** whose **solutions** were wholly beyond our **ability** to implement.

We call the boldfaced words *things* not because they are like rocks, chairs, and cars, but because we know they're nouns and we think of nouns as things. A simpler definition is anything that fits this frame:

(The) _____ is good.

To grasp how we judge prose, we must distinguish three kinds of nouns:

1. Nouns that are concrete: *chair, book, person, car, tree, door, sky, stairs.*
2. Nouns that are intrinsically nouns, but abstract: *law, series, motion, strategy, vision, effort, shape.*
3. Nouns that are abstract because they are derived from verbs or adjectives: *movement, investigation, resemblance, responsibility, equivalence.*

The technical term for a noun derived from a verb or adjective is *nominalization.* When you nominalize *nominalize* you create the nominalization *nominalization.*

Adjectives

You can identify most adjectives by trying them out in this frame:

That is very _____.

Some adjectives like *additional* and *molecular* don't fit, but it's a handy guide. Like verbs, adjectives can be nominalized: *intelligent* → *intelligence*.

Adverbs

Some adverbs are derived from adjectives: *careful* → *carefully*. Others are intrinsically adverbs: *often, very, rather,* and so on. They modify verbs, adjectives, and other adverbs.

CHAPTER 12 IN A NUTSHELL
About Your Prose . . .

Once you draft your argument, you face a problem when you revise its style. Since you read into it what you want it to mean, you cannot read your own prose as your readers will. To overcome that obstacle, you need an objective way to diagnose your prose so that you can sidestep your too good understanding of it. Here are six principles to take not as ironclad rules, but as advice about how most sentences should work:

1. Make your main characters the subjects of verbs. If they are abstractions, be sure that they are terms familiar to your readers.
2. Use verbs, not nouns, to express the important action.
3. Get to the verb in the main clause quickly:

    Avoid long introductory phrases.

    Keep whole subjects short.

    Don't interrupt subject-verb connections with long phrases or clauses.

4. Begin your sentences with information that seems familiar *to your readers*.
5. End sentences with information that seems new to them.
6. Keep your subjects consistent by using as subjects your most familiar characters. Avoid beginning successive sentences with unrelated subjects.

In addition to writing sentences with distinct subjects and verbs, work to write prose that is more rather than less vivid. You do that in three ways:

- Avoid using words that add little or nothing to your ideas, such as *very, basically, really,* and so on.
- Avoid decomposing a meaning that can be expressed in a single word into several words.
- Avoid stating what a word implies.

You are likely to write more vividly if you choose words that are common and down to earth: *belly button* versus *navel*. Some writers, such as newspaper editorial writers, rarely use either slang or more formal words, sticking to a middle style. Other writers use a lot of slang and no formal words; still others—scientists, for example—use no slang and all formal words. And some good writers include an occasional formal or slang expressions to give their prose a little kick.

Another way to create a vivid style is to choose a word that conjures up an image in the mind of your readers. Just about every word is on a scale of more or less generality/specificity. But for many scales, there is a breakpoint where one word creates no particular image in our minds, but the next more specific one does: *object - weapon - gun - pistol - Glock 19*. We might have a vague image associated with *gun,* but *pistol* has a more distinct one.

On the other hand, some arguments need some prose that is general and abstract enough to avoid evoking feelings or to assert general philosophical principles, to lay down warrants and assumptions that govern specific cases.

. . . and About Revising It

Diagnose your prose: Underline the first seven or eight words in each major clause (ignore short introductory phrases and clauses, especially when they refer to previous sentences). Consider revising if you see these characteristics:

- Subjects are not a specific character named in a short phrase.
- By the eighth or ninth word, you don't see a verb.
- Those first seven or eight words express new information.
- Several sentences in a row keep changing subjects.

Revise like this:

1. Start by finding the important characters.
2. Identify the key actions they perform.
3. Revise so that most of your sentences begin with important characters as subjects and are immediately followed by key actions in verbs.

When you see a long introductory phrase, rewrite it into a sentence or clause of its own.

When you identify a long subject, consider these revisions:

1. Revise it into an introductory subordinate clause.
2. Revise it into a sentence of its own.

When you identify a long interrupting element between the subject and verb, move it to the beginning or end of its sentence, depending on whether it connects more closely to the preceding sentence or to the one that follows.

CHAPTER 13

The Overt and Covert Force of Language

In this chapter, we discuss how language invokes values and thereby feelings. We show you some of the subtle ways that writers use language to shape belief: how they use characters to influence who or what readers see as responsible for events, and how metaphors shape the unspoken story readers find in prose.

In Chapter 12, we looked at clarity, concision, and vividness, qualities that help us not only understand an argument, but respond to it with both thought and feeling (the distinction is less sharp than most of us think). But the force of language goes beyond clarity and vividness. In this chapter, we look at how words shape belief in ways that are both obvious and subtle, sometimes marginally dishonest. We do this not to show you how to use language dishonestly, but to make you aware of its power to lead and mislead.

Invoking Values, Evoking Feeling

Value-Laden Words

We shape responses most blatantly by using words that play on readers' values, thereby evoking positive or negative feelings. If we oppose a cut in the income tax, for example, we might claim that the cut will

> stuff the wallets of those fat cat rich who already hoard most of our nation's wealth.

But if we support the cut, we might argue that it will

> restore to American workers some of their hard-earned wages that the IRS sucks out of our paychecks every month.

Both descriptions are vivid, but they invite us to respond to different values in *stuff the wallets, fat cat rich,* and *hoard our wealth* versus *restore to American workers, hard-earned wages,* and *IRS sucks out* (not to mention the more subtle **those** rich versus **our** *paychecks*).

We see value-laden language most clearly in politics and advertising. Ads depend on a covert argument whose rarely expressed main claim is obvious enough: *Buy this product.* For example, notice the language of this ad for Lady Foot Locker, in a fashion magazine for older teens and young adults:

> Sure, working out's all fabulous the first month or so. And then somehow, the treadmill is about as appealing as that ex-boyfriend of yours with the color coordination issues. Luckily, new Nike Tuned Air (with the perfect combination of cushioning and stability) can help you fall in love with your workout all over again. Which is more than we can say for your ex.

Lady Foot Locker wants readers to imagine the tedium of working out when they read *the treadmill is about as appealing as that ex-boyfriend of yours with the color coordination issues.* But that language relies on values shared by only some women. How would readers of a woman's body-building magazine respond?

Values in Academic Writing

In academic writing, you will rarely see words as value-laden as *swell the wallets of those fat cat rich who already hoard most of our nation's wealth.* Language like that in a political science paper would damage your credibility. Academic readers expect you to project an *ethos* of cool distance. That does not mean you eliminate all signs of value in your writing. (You couldn't if you tried.) You might, for example, write in a political science paper how the tax cut would *augment the personal wealth of those who already control most of the nation's resources.* That kind of language reflects values but does not seem crudely emotional.

You Can't Avoid Values

Some argue that we betray the spirit of fair, rational argument when we use value-laden language of any kind, because it "slants" or "biases" our argument. We should appeal, they claim, not to our readers' warmest feelings but to their coolest logic. Following that principle, both sides in the tax cut debate could describe it in terms emptied of emotion:

> The tax reduction will augment the economic resources of those with the highest incomes.

> The tax cut will raise net earned income for everyone.

But even when you drain language of emotion, you still project values. Cool language projects the value of dispassionate objectivity. Moreover, when you avoid words that express values, you betray not only yourself, but your readers, because they have a right to know where you stand. How would you feel if after listening to an apparently disinterested argument about flawed statistics used to support gun control laws, you learned the speaker worked for the National Rifle Association?

In fact, we so often get caught up in debates over names because what we call something invokes values and thereby evokes feelings: *abortion* versus *murder; fetus* versus *baby; reproductive rights* versus *rights of the unborn; pro-choice* versus *pro-life.* The Supreme Court will eventually have to decide an issue in which the values invoked by words matter. The contending parties frame the issue in many different ways:

The right to die.

The right to assisted suicide.

The right to determine the time and manner of one's death.

The right to hasten certain death in a humane and dignified manner.

The right to be free of government interference in ending pain.

The right to bodily privacy.

The duty of the state to protect the helpless.

The duty of the state to prevent physicians from killing their patients.

Each of these ways of framing the issue reflects values that those on the other side of the question must work to overcome. In such exchanges, those with the power to frame the question enjoy an advantage, because it imposes on others the burden of denying values that the words seem to make self-evident. It is easy to say that there is no "right" way to phrase an issue, but there is also no way to avoid framing every issue in *some* way. None of the parties to an issue can escape a commitment to values by using general or scientific language, because the generality of the language itself implies the value of objectivity.

How Values Reflect and Create Multiple Perspectives

Those different ways of framing the issue just mentioned don't set up polar oppositions, the way words like *big* and *small* or *rich* and *poor* do. We usually use such opposites to refer to substantially different things: what is big is not little, who is rich is not poor. In contrast, all those ways of posing the issue of assisted suicide refer to the *same* action, but from a different framework of values.

That's why two people can look at exactly the same thing, but disagree about how to describe it:

Lee is a reckless daydreamer! No, he is a daring visionary!

Jones is a chauvinist reactionary! No, he is a patriotic conservative!

We could probably agree that if Jones is anything like a left-wing, flag-burning radical, he cannot arguably be a chauvinist reactionary, because we could probably agree on basic criteria that distinguish them. But how do we decide whether Jones is a chauvinist reactionary or a patriotic conservative? We agree that he waves the flag, speaks proudly about his country, votes to cut taxes and increase military spending, is against gun control and for prayer in the schools, and supports a constitutional amendment banning flag burning. But does that make him a chauvinist or a patriot? A conservative or a reactionary? Is it a matter of degree? Does he wave the flag too much? Talk too boastfully about his country? But what counts as "too much"? In cases like this, we can't rely on common criteria of meaning.

We have to go back to first principles. What problem occasions the need to decide what Jones is? What he "is" depends less on what he objectively *is* than on what we think is at stake in *calling* him by one or the other term (review p. 242). If we think we solve the problem by getting people to think well of him, then we call him *a patriotic conservative;* if we think we solve it by getting people to think badly of him, we call him *a chauvinist reactionary.* We cannot choose between such terms by checking their criteria against Jones' features. We decide first what problem we want to solve, *then* pick the words that support the solution. In matters like this, the debate over what to call Jones is probably a surrogate argument for a larger issue (see pp. 242-45).

The Unethical Use of Value-Laden Words

It is fair to use value-laden words to elicit feeling, so long as your argument is otherwise sound. In fact, for some matters you would be wrong not to enlist your readers' emotional commitment. Those debating the assisted suicide issue are right to appeal to our deepest feelings, given what's at stake, but not if they substitute an appeal to feelings for a sound argument.

We should condemn as ethically contemptible those who cynically use words to appeal to feelings alone. In the election of 1996, for example, a political consultant circulated a list of words that he urged his clients to use:

- To incite animosity toward their opponents, they were told to call them *liberals* and *liars,* to say they were *extreme, radical, wasteful, corrupt,* and *hypocritical* and to refer to themselves as *pioneers* with *vision,* as *fair* and *moral,* dedicated to principles of *truth* and *courage.*

- To exploit voters' common decency, they were advised to talk about their own *pride,* their *families, common sense,* and *duty,* and to accuse others of *betraying* the *common good* by their *greed* and even *treason.*

Those words convey more than different shades of meaning, because we can find in them different criteria to match to features of referents. We know the meaning of *courage* and *treason,* and we know that the difference is more than just political "spin."

When politicians of any party use language that cynically, they undermine the foundations of democratic discourse, not just because they substitute feeling for thinking, but because they teach us to distrust all political discourse. As bad money drives out good, cynical language drives out thoughtful argument.

How Emotional Language Can Undermine Sound Thinking

Even when you back up value-laden language with what you think is a sound argument, you can undermine sound reasoning when your words evoke feelings that overwhelm it.

Polarizing Choices

If you characterize your views as *sincere, normal,* and *reasoned,* you risk implying that others must be *cynical, abnormal,* and *irrational,* thereby demonizing them. If your reader is not *pro-choice,* then she must be *anti-choice;* if not *pro-life,* then *anti-life.* Politicians, in particular, are fond of polarizing: If you are not conservative, then you must be a liberal. If you are not tough on drugs, then you must be weak on them. Polarizing language excludes complexity, middle ground, or possibilities beyond just two. Few of us are purely kind or cruel, generous or selfish, normal or abnormal; we are all one and the other at different times, and most of the time somewhere in between.

Polarizing language is most corrosive to sound thinking when it leads us to reason in what are called *disjunctive syllogisms:*

> You must be either a conservative or a liberal.
>
> You are not conservative?
>
> Therefore, you must be a liberal.

> The answer to the drug problem is either punishment or treatment.
>
> You think that more treatment programs are the answer?
>
> Therefore, you must not favor tough drug laws.

In both examples, the reasoning is formally valid but substantively false, because it offers readers simplistic mutually exclusive alternatives:

- Maybe both choices are right. Maybe we need both tougher laws and new drug treatment programs.
- Maybe both are right along with a third choice. Maybe we need both of those and more diplomatic negotiations with drug-producing countries.
- Maybe both choices are partly right and partly wrong. Maybe we need somewhat tougher laws and a few new drug treatment programs.
- Maybe both are wrong and some third choice is right. Maybe all we need is more education.
- Maybe we need some combination of everything.

Reality is almost always more complex than *either-or* language allows. You owe your readers a duty not only to avoid making things more complex than they have to be, but also, as Einstein once said, no simpler than they really are.

Respecting Differences of Degree

Here is how a prominent evolutionary biologist explains our need to find opposing features that definitively distinguish us from apes:

> We have generally tried to unite our intellectual duty to accept the established fact of evolutionary continuity with our continuing psychological need to see ourselves as separate and superior, by invoking one of our worst and oldest mental habits: dichotomization, or division into two opposite categories, usually with attributions of value expressed as good and bad or higher and lower. We therefore try to define a "golden barrier," a firm criterion to mark an unbridgeable gap between the mentality and behavior of humans and all other creatures. We may have evolved from them, but at some point in our advance, we crossed a Rubicon that brooks no passage by any other species.... The basic formulation of them vs. us, and the resulting search for a "golden barrier," represents a deep fallacy of human thought. We need not fear Darwin's correct conclusion that we differ from other animals only in degree. A sufficient difference in quantity translates into what we call a difference in quality *ipso facto*. A frozen pond is not the same object as a boiling pool—and New York City does not represent a mere extension of the tree nests [of chimpanzees in their native habitat] at Gombé.

> Source: Stephen Jay Gould, "The Human Difference," *New York Times,* July 2, 1999.

Alienating Thoughtful Readers

In addition to your ethical duty to avoid polarizing language, you also have a more pragmatic reason: No matter how persuasive you think strong language sounds, it is likely to alienate thoughtful, well-informed readers, because it seems to discredit any way of looking at an issue other than your own. To be sure, when you use moderate, nuanced language, you risk being called wishy-washy by those who take a with-us-or-against-us attitude. And in some cases, nuanced language is wrong. Many people couldn't believe that Hitler was as thoroughly evil as he turned out to be. Except for that kind of rare case, however, you do well to err on the side of moderation, because nuanced language encourages nuanced thinking, in both writer and reader.

Emotional Language and Ethos

Here a reviewer complains that a writer of an otherwise good book loses credibility from extreme language:

[The author] makes his claims about Allied capabilities [to destroy German concentration camps during World War II] mostly persuasive, but does so in a style as dogmatic and vindictive as that of some of the "myth" purveyors he condemns. . . . Such invective detracts from his weighty evidence and illustrates a disturbing trend: some scholars shout as if engaged in "McLaughlin Group" combat or the exposé culture of the tabloids. Gray academic prose presents its own problems, and [the author] is not the first on this subject to shout. But his tone can cheapen his valuable scholarship.

Source: Ann Finkbeiner, *New York Times Book Review,* October 12, 1999.

The reviewer doesn't criticize the author's facts or judgment, but his words.

Subjects and Point of View

In Chapter 12, we showed you that what readers take away from sentences is a story—not the words themselves but images, scenes, a mental scenario. That's why the most readable prose is storylike: The key elements of a story—characters and actions—match the key elements of sentences—subjects and verbs. But storytelling offers you other opportunities as well, not just to be clear, but to shape how readers understand and judge.

Manipulating Subjects to Assign Responsibility

We don't exaggerate much when we say that every sentence you write forces you to decide first who or what to make its subject. You can't even plan a sentence until you know how it begins, who or what will be its central character. But more than that, when you choose to make one character rather than another the subject of a sentence, you impose on your readers a point of view toward the story the sentence tells. For example, compare these pairs of sentences; both sentences in each pair arguably refer to the same state of affairs in the world.

1a. Smith obtained stolen goods from Jones.
1b. Jones provided stolen goods to Smith.

2a. I have proved with this evidence that Jones sold stolen goods to Smith.
2b. This evidence proves that Smith bought stolen goods from Jones.

3a. We learn from history that we need free speech to strengthen democracy.
3b. History teaches us that a democracy grows strong from free speech.

4a. Susan McDougal defrauded the bank in the Whitewater affair by using a document prepared by Hillary Rodham Clinton.
4b. Hillary Rodham Clinton prepared the document used by Susan McDougal to defraud the bank in the Whitewater affair.

If the first sentence in each pair is true, then arguably so is the second, but we respond to them differently because each assigns responsibility to a different character, thereby imposing on us different points of view about the source of the action.

We cannot, however, choose who to make the subject just by looking at who did what out in the world. We might think that subjects are somehow in the nature of things "doers" of actions:

The dog **chased** the cat for a while before <u>he</u> finally **caught** her.

In that world, the dog did something to a cat; so it seems natural to make it the subject of *chase* and *caught*. But events do not determine subjects. We can *choose* to make the cat the center of attention:

The cat **ran away** from the dog until <u>it</u> finally **got caught.**

By reshaping that sentence around the cat, we change which character seems both the center of events and the center of our attention.

That story, of course, is a trivial one. Here is one more consequential:

Reporters grilled the mayor until they finally got the answer they wanted: Companies owned by friends who got contracts with the city gave his campaign $100,000 in contributions.

The mayor got a grilling from reporters until he finally told them what he had tried not to reveal: He had taken $100,000 in campaign contributions from friends whose companies got contracts with the city.

The first sentence focuses on the press; the second on the mayor. Which is "truer?" Wrong question: if one is true, so arguably is the other. The right question is which better serves the interests of the writer. Who does the writer want us to focus on as the main character, the mayor or the press?

Such choices matter, because we tend to remember best the character that appears most often in subjects, and we tend to assign to that character most responsibility for what happened. So by managing—or manipulating—the subjects of sentences, deft writers can induce us to make judgments about things without explicitly knowing that we have, much less why.

But to manage subjects, you have to manage verbs. The easiest way to change subjects is to shift between active and passive verbs.

My friend **taught** me Spanish.

<u>I</u> **was taught** Spanish by my friend.

<u>We</u> **recorded** the fluid velocity at thirty-second intervals.

The fluid velocity **was recorded** at thirty-second intervals.

Those of you in technical fields will write many sentences like that last one, because technical writers usually tell stories about things like velocity or fluids rather than about those who measure them.

Another, more subtle technique is to find verbs that tell roughly the same story, but from different points of view:

<u>My friend</u> **taught** me Spanish.

<u>I</u> **learned** Spanish from my friend.

<u>George</u> **bought** a handgun from Fred.

<u>Fred</u> **sold** a handgun to George.

Sometimes, we have to think harder to find alternatives:

<u>The New York Yankees</u> **are losing** fans to the Mets.

<u>The New York Mets</u> **are attracting** fans from the Yankees.

<u>Fans</u> **are moving** from the Yankees to the Mets.

All three sentences arguably refer to the same action "out there," but they encourage us to see who is responsible for that action in different ways.

Displacing Attribution

In Chapter 12 we saw how we displace judgments about style from our impressions to the sentence that causes them:

This was hard to understand.— I worked hard to understand this.

But we displace judgments about many other qualities as well:

You are aloof.— I don't feel close to you.

That light is too bright.— When I look at that light, my eyes hurt.

What seems to be about the world is actually about how we feel about it.

As simple as this point seems, behind it are some vexing philosophical issues. In some cases, it is not at all clear where to locate a quality like *sweet, loud, heavy,* and so on—in the object or in the perceiver? Contrast these five pairs of sentences: the (a) sentences focus on the object judged, the (b) on the person judging:

1a. The sun is hot today.
1b. When I was out in the sun today, I felt hot.

2a. Vinegar tastes sour.
2b. When I taste vinegar, I get a sharp taste in my mouth.

3a. Killing children is evil.
3b. I condemn the killing of children.

4a. Expensive wine is a waste of money.
4b. When I buy expensive wine, I waste my money.

5a. Homosexuality is immoral.
5b. I reject homosexuality for moral reasons.

If someone makes these (b) statements sincerely, then for that person each is "true." But would they be true if uttered by everyone who reads them? To determine that, we have to substitute a *you* for *I*. For most of us the first three might be true.

    1c. You agree that if you were in the sun today, you would feel hot.

    2c. You agree that when you sip vinegar, you get a sharp taste.

    3c. You agree that you condemn the killing of children on moral grounds.

But the next two are more problematic:

    4c. You agree that when you buy expensive wine, you waste money.

    5c. You agree that you reject homosexuality for moral reasons.

Though (4b) and (5b) might be true for the writer, (4c) and (5c) are by no means universally true for every reader.

This issue of where qualities reside—in the referent or in our judgment of it—has been debated for millennia, so we will not even try to scratch its surface. Whatever philosophers decide, you can *choose* to write a sentence that locates the quality in the thing (vinegar is sharp) or in a person's experience of it (I get a sharp taste from vinegar). It's worth a minute to think through such sentences, because when you attribute qualities to a thing, you may be referring to everyone's experience, or only to your own.

Treating Means as Agents

Another way to move responsibility from flesh-and-blood actors to things and concepts is just this side of metaphor:

You can't buy happiness with money.   ➔   Money can't buy happiness.

You can conquer all with love.   ➔   Love conquers all.

The English language lets us make that kind of transformation systematically:

A does B to C by means of D		D does B to C
You cut yourself with the knife.	➔	The knife cut you.
You can't buy happiness with money.	➔	Money can't buy happiness.
We can conquer all with love.	➔	Love conquers all.

As common and as innocuous as this stylistic device seems, people fight over it. We've all seen or heard the slogan on this bumper sticker:

Guns don't kill, people do.

Those who oppose gun control focus on the agents of shootings—people; those who support it focus on the means—guns. Thus we have a battle over two forms of the "same" concept, one a transformation of the other:

A does B to C by means of D		D does B to C
People kill people with guns.	➔	Guns kill people.

This pattern also lets a writer attribute a claim to an objective-seeming source :

We **have proved** that teachers need a raise by these data.

➔ These data **have proved** that teachers need a raise.

In their study, Smith and Yang **found** evidence from which they concluded that those who smoke become prematurely senile.

➔ A recent study (Smith and Yang, 1997) **found** evidence pointing to the conclusion that smoking causes premature senility.

➔ Evidence from a recent study (Smith and Yang, 1997) points to the conclusion that smoking causes premature senility.

Those sentences refer to the same "fact," but each slants who or what is responsible for it.

To be sure, on most occasions, you do little harm when you speak of studies and evidence proving, showing, or suggesting. Readers know what you mean. But think twice when you read such sentences, because they urge you to ignore an important variable: the human judgment behind them.

Reifying Abstractions

Another way to shift responsibility takes us into the realm of metaphor. One way we make metaphors is by writing about an abstraction as if it were a human agent:

Life will find a way.

Nature always tells us when she thinks we have violated her laws.

Duty requires us to sacrifice.

We turn *Nature* into a person by making it the subject of verbs implying human action, such as *tell* and *think*. The technical term for doing that is *reification;* we also call it *personifying* or *anthropomorphizing,* which means to treat something not human as if it were.

Sometimes we reify abstractions to deflect readers from a human cause:

Science **has** the power to reveal nature's laws, but it **cannot define** our values; only religious faith **can guide** us down the moral path.

When we think about science and religion, we typically prefer not to focus on the fact that both are constructed through human action. So few writers would revise that sentence into this:

> <u>Scientists</u> have the power to reveal the patterns in the natural world, but <u>they</u> cannot define our values; only <u>religious leaders</u> can guide us down the moral path.

More commonly, however, we reify abstractions not to hide human agency but to express matters too complex for readers to picture easily. If we say,

> <u>Your ethical responsibility</u> **demands** that you resign.

we are not deflecting attention from some obvious agent:

> <u>People</u> **will think** you are unethical if you do not resign.

Instead, by reifying abstractions, we describe a situation in which there are no specific agents as if there were. Similarly, when the scientist in the movie *Jurassic Park* warns that the cloned dinosaurs will reproduce despite the efforts to prevent it, he says,

> <u>Life</u> **will find** a way.

He is not hiding a human agent, but using the reified abstraction to describe a situation without one.

By no means is reification always dishonest or unethical. Indeed, in our most revered political document, the drafters of the Declaration of Independence made several abstractions seem to be human agents. Here are just two, with our translations:

> **Original**: . . . <u>a decent respect</u> to the opinions of mankind **requires** . . .
>
> **Revised**:   If <u>we</u> decently **respect** the opinions of mankind, <u>we</u> **should** . . .

> **Original**: . . . such is now <u>the necessity</u> which **constrains** them . . .
>
> **Revised**:   As a result, <u>we</u> **decided** that <u>we</u> **must** . . .

In that first sentence, the drafters were reaching beyond specifics to generality. In the second, they used a metaphor that made themselves not agents free to act, but an oppressed people forced to act by circumstances and duty: *necessity requires us to act*. These reifications are not just clever wordplay, because the rest of the Declaration is a model of sound argument. The drafters used reifications not for unfair advantage, but to support a larger and more complex argument.

Following Metaphorical Trains of Thought

The most dramatic way we use language to shape belief is by metaphorical scenarios. Metaphors do more than reify a single abstraction. They can create a virtual world in which we can play out many implications, some illuminating, some misleading. If well chosen, metaphors can also imply values that evoke in us feelings that support the writer's aim. The problem is that when we create a metaphor, we risk implying what we ought not.

We earlier discussed two metaphors and some of their consequences: argument as war and communication as shipping a package of meaning. The two metaphors are easy to combine:

> I will *advance* my claims as *forcefully* as I can until you *yield* to the weight of my evidence. But if you can just *see into* my thinking about this, you'll *get the picture.*

In that sentence, we imagine two ways of coming to agreement: We force an idea on a reader, or the reader can look inside the argument to find its meaning.

We can imagine a different model for communication: guiding readers along a path that gets them from here to there:

> I will *lead* you *through* a line of reasoning that together we can *follow* to *reach* agreement.

So what if these metaphors differ? They lead us to see an event in different ways, and those differences may have consequences. For example, what if your reader fails to agree with your argument?

- If argument is war, then you lose the battle because you are not strong enough.

- If communication is a bundle of meaning sent and received, you can blame the reader for unwrapping the package incorrectly.

- If communication is a path down which you lead readers, you must blame yourself for being a bad guide.

A metaphor can also be so vivid that it creates networks of implications that are simply wrong. Consider these metaphors:

- A school official explains why a student was suspended from school for expounding unpopular ideas:

> That kind of hate speech is a *virulence* we had to *stamp out.* We *isolated* the student because his views could have *infected* our community.

Beliefs are not communicable diseases, but the metaphor encourages us to think that it makes sense to quarantine those who might spread unpopular ideas.

- An environmentalist defends those who vandalize logging equipment:

> A living thing has the *right* to protect itself from predators. And if it cannot *defend* itself, then those who love it have a duty to do so. The redwoods cannot *defend* themselves, so we who *love* them must *defend* them and *punish* their *attackers*. That's *nature's law.*

Trees do not have rights; only people do. But if we think in terms of "nature's law," then the metaphors of prosecution, defense, and punishment follow.

- A police officer on the accidental shooting of an innocent person in a drug raid on the wrong apartment:

> The *war* on drugs is no picnic. *Wars* have *casualties,* but that can't stop us from *fighting* an *enemy* that *attacks* innocent children. We cannot *surrender,* to the *tyranny* of heroin and cocaine.

In the heat of battle, armed forces kill innocents, but do we judge police as we do soldiers? In short, metaphors can infiltrate our thinking and shape it in ways that are seriously misleading.

We do not say that you should never use value words, manipulate subjects, reify abstractions, or create metaphors. You cannot think without metaphors. Just be aware of the language you choose, because it can mislead not only your readers, but yourself.

The Use and Abuse of Natural Selection

Scientists have long personified nature. When Darwin called evolution *natural selection,* he helped his readers understand a complex matter through a memorable metaphor: Nature selects those species most fit to survive. He combined an agent his readers knew well, *Mother Nature,* with a process they also knew well, *selective breeding:*

> We have seen that man by selection can produce great results, and can adapt organic beings to his own uses, through the accumulation of slight but useful variations, given to him by the hand of Nature. But Natural Selection . . . is immeasurably superior to man's feeble efforts as the works of Nature are to those of Art. (*Origin of Species,* ch. 2)

When he defended *natural selection* against the charge that he spoke of it "as an active power of Deity," he pointed out that scientists had done the same for centuries: *magnets* **attract** *or* **repel** *one another, gravity* **holds** *the planets in their orbits, water* **finds** *its own level.* He claimed this was a harmless way of talking because "Every one knows what is meant and is implied by such metaphorical expressions" (*Origin,* ch. 4).

Perhaps, but Darwin could not predict how others would use his metaphor. At the end of the nineteenth century John D. Rockefeller used *natural selection* and its rugged cousin, *the survival of the fittest,* to defend brutal business practices:

> The growth of a large business is merely the survival of the fittest. . . . The American Beauty rose can be produced . . . only by sacrificing the early buds which grow up around it. This is not an evil tendency in business. It is merely the working-out of a law of nature and a law of God.

It's a view still current today: "Darwin was right. Only the fittest survive—especially when the creatures involved are graying commodities companies battling in the pits of a downcycle" (Robert Matthews, Susan Warren, and Bernard Wysocki, Jr., *Wall Street Journal,* August 20, 1999).

WRITING PROCESS 13
The Overt and Covert Force of Language

Drafting

When to Think About Values

It is important to pay attention to how your language evokes values and feelings, but *when* you should pay attention depends on how you write.

- If you are a slow drafter, decide before you draft the emotional tone you want your readers to respond to and then watch your words as you draft.
- If you are a fast drafter, look at your words as you revise. Then ask how readers will respond. As you revise, look for opportunities to make your tone more consistent.

Revising

Subjects and Point of View

After you are sure your prose is clear and direct, check whether you have used the subject position to focus readers on those characters that you want them to see as most responsible for the events in your story. Here is a simple test:

1. Pick out the characters that your sentences focus on:

    - Circle or boldface the subject of each main clause and subordinate clauses.
    - If an important character appears in a phrase before the subject, circle or boldface it. For example,

        Thinking about **politicians**, Americans cannot help but be cynical about the future of argument as a tool of democracy.

        Then if you can, revise so that the first character is the subject of the sentence:

        <u>**Politicians**</u> make most Americans cynical about the future of argument as a tool of democracy.

2. Have you picked out a few characters repeated often or many different characters?

    - If you find a few characters, are readers more likely to accept your argument because they think of these as the main characters? If not, revise to focus on those that will support your argument.
    - If you find many characters, would you improve the story by focusing on just one or two? If so, revise to focus on them.

3. Are your characters people or abstractions?

  • If abstractions, are they so familiar to readers that they can build a story around them? If not, revise to focus on people or more familiar abstractions.

INQUIRIES

Reflections

1. Look again at the Lady Foot Locker ad (p. 326). Its appeal to younger women goes beyond its language. It also uses the structure of a problem (and a fairy tale) as part of its pitch. See if you can match each sentence to one step in a problem statement, including common ground and claim/solution. Who is the hero who steps in to solve the reader's problem? Does this structural design appeal to the same values as the language? Would the idea of being saved by a hero be attractive to women who read body-building magazines? Adult singles magazines? Would it appeal to men?

2. Recently, the Heinz company changed its advertising to appeal to teens. After surveying them, its ad agency decided that they would ignore traditional appeals, so it created a TV spot that called Heinz "the rude ketchup" for making people wait and included in its print ads lines like "Will work for food" and "Can't help broccoli." What do these slogans imply about the values that the advertisers are trying to invoke among teens? Are those your values?

3. It is almost always easier to see the emotional charge in the language of those whose opinions we reject than of those with whom we agree. Why is that? What does that tell you about the role of emotion in your relationship to your readers?

Tasks

4. An issue much in the news is the question whether states should fund only public schools or any school parents choose. Proponents call it the "voucher system" or "school choice"; opponents call it "state funding of private schools." List different ways of stating this issue that reflect different stances on the question. (You can use the rights-and-duties pattern of the assisted suicide example, above.) Bring out as many facets of the debate as you can. Here are other issues: homosexual marriage, immigration, affirmative action, metal detectors in schools, school uniforms, requiring people by law to wear seatbelts.

5. Can you write without using metaphors? Is it possible to be entirely literal in every sentence? In a paper for this or another class, find a

passage of at least half a page in which you use no metaphors. Remember that metaphors are part of our everyday vocabulary, so look for covert metaphors that you might not notice in casual reading. If you find a passage without metaphor, add some. If you can't find a passage, pick one and try to rewrite it free of metaphor. Ask a friend to read both passages, with and without metaphors. Which does your friend like better? How do they make you seem as a writer?

6. Science has a reputation for objectivity, but scientists use metaphors when they write. We saw how Darwin treated nature as a human agent in his key term *natural selection,* but that was a long time ago. If you are taking a science class, look through your textbook to see how many metaphors you can find, especially covert metaphors. If you find any, does that mean that the writer is not being objective? Why?

7. In addition to the two refications in the Declaration of Independence we pointed out on page 336, there are a few others. Find them, then decide why the drafters used them.

CHAPTER 13 IN A NUTSHELL

About Your Prose . . .

All words imply values, so you cannot write in a completely value-free way. Your problem is to figure out what values you want to invoke, because values evoke feelings, and feelings are often as powerful an element in an argument as its "pure" logic.

The most difficult issues in framing a question arise not from polar oppositions—tall versus short or rich versus poor—but when you and your readers disagree about a point of view: filthy rich versus wealthy, poor versus impoverished. In such debates, you waste your time if you try to match criteria to features. Instead, you have to think clearly about the problem you are trying to solve. If one term solves the problem better than the other, then that is the term you argue for.

You use value-laden words unethically when you knowingly use them to replace the rational force of an argument, rather than to augment it. You can deflect rational thinking if you let the emotion in your language overpower it. When you use polarizing words, you polarize choices. You force your reader to be with you or against you, rather than somewhere in between, which is where most thoughtful people find themselves. Polarizing language squeezes out nuance, moderation, and complexity.

Every story has more than one character, so you can tell your story from different points of view. You make a character dominate a passage when you make it the subject of all or most of its sentences. Readers then focus on that character as responsible for most of the events in that part of your story.

. . . and About Writing It

- If you are a slow drafter, watch your words as you draft. Decide on an emotional tone before you begin drafting.
- If you are a fast drafter, pay attention to your words later in the revision stage.

You lead readers to focus on a character by working that character into the subjects of sentences. You do that in six ways:

- You can switch between active and passive verbs, which is the simplest way: *I recorded the observations* versus *The observations were recorded.*
- You can find verbs that let you move into the subject the character you want readers to focus on: *I bought a car from you* versus *You sold a car to me.*
- You can displace a feeling onto what makes you feel that way: *I had a hard time solving that problem* versus *That problem is difficult.*
- You can move the instrumentality of an action into a subject: *You can't buy happiness with money* versus *Money can't buy happiness.*
- You can reify abstractions by making them subjects of verbs you usually use with flesh-and-blood characters: *Love conquers all.*
- You can create metaphoric scenarios: *Racism contaminates the thinking of many people.*

APPENDIX 1

Fallacies

Throughout this book we've discussed both how the quality of your thinking contributes to the quality of your argument and, no less important, how the quality of your argument can improve the quality of your thinking. We've shown you how to use the elements of a written argument to guard against common mistakes in reasoning, even to avoid those deep-seated biases that can lead us all astray. When you look for and evaluate reasons, evidence, warrants, and especially acknowledgments and responses in your arguments, you think more systematically and more carefully about the soundness of your claims.

There is, however, another common way to encourage sound thinking, one that is almost 2,500 years old. In this approach, logicians study systematic errors in reasoning that they call *fallacies*. A fallacy is not a false belief, like thinking that the earth is flat. Rather, fallacies are missteps in the *process* of reasoning your way to such a conclusion. By this definition, you can reason validly and conclude that the earth is flat or fallaciously and conclude that it is round.

Over the centuries, logicians have identified scores of these fallacies and given them formidable Latin names such as *post hoc ergo propter hoc, ad verecundiam, non sequitur.* Some of them will always undermine your reasoning, while others do so only in certain circumstances. So we group them into two categories to help you distinguish blunders in reasoning: those that you should always avoid and those that you should question carefully.

Errors in Reasoning

These fallacies are outright errors in getting from a reason to a claim. They can all be explained in terms of "technical" problems in one or more elements of the argument. We'll introduce each of these fallacies as if we're being charged with it, and then add the technical explanation.

1. "But what you said doesn't follow!" (Your reason is irrelevant to your claim.)

Cyberspace will make government irrelevant _{main claim} by making all data instantly available. _{reason 1} Once we can be in contact with everyone else, _{reason 2} artificial national borders will wither away _{claim/reason 3} and government will have nothing to do. _{claim/reason 4}

You might be right, but I can't follow the steps in your chain of reasoning. First, I don't see why making information available faster makes government irrelevant. Second, I don't see how being in contact with everyone will make national borders disappear. And third, I don't see why the lack of borders leaves government nothing to do. Maybe I can see some connection between governments having nothing to do and their being irrelevant, but the steps between are too much of a stretch.

When a claim follows a reason with no a warrant to connect them, we call the claim a *non sequitur,* pronounced "nahn SE-kwi-toor," which means literally *It doesn't follow.* If your readers might think you've committed a *non sequitur,* you have to think about warrants: Do readers share your underlying assumptions, and have you failed to state warrants you should have?

2. "You're arguing in a circle and begging the question!" (Your reasons just restate your claim.)

To ensure our safety, we should be free to carry concealed guns _{claim 1} because we should have the right to carry a weapon to protect ourselves. _{reason 1} When criminals worry that we might have a gun and would use it, _{reason 2} that knowledge will make them realize that we are ready to defend ourselves. _{claim 2} Only when criminals worry about their own safety _{reason 3} will we be able to stop worrying about our own. _{claim 3}

You are reasoning in a circle. You keep saying the same thing—we should be free to do something because we have the right to do it. That makes no sense. Then you say that when criminals know something they know something. That may be true, but it doesn't make sense either.

You argue in a circle when your claim and reason mean the same thing. You can test for circular arguments by switching claims and reasons. If the sentence means the same after the switch, you're arguing in a circle:

To ensure our safety, we should be free to carry concealed guns _{claim} because we need the right to carry one to protect ourselves. _{reason}

We need the right to carry a weapon to protect ourselves _{claim} because we should be free to carry concealed guns to ensure our safety. _{reason}

If you cannot reverse the reason and claim and make sense, your argument is not circular. Compare the last sentence in the example, which does not reason in a circle:

Only when criminals worry about their own safety _{reason} will we be able to stop worrying about our own. _{claim}

Only when we are able to stop worrying about our own safety _{reason} will criminals worry about theirs. _{claim}

If your readers might think you are arguing in a circle, you have think about your claims and reasons. If they are too similar, then you must find better reasons to support your claim.

3. "You're assuming things that we haven't settled!" (Your reason is not supported with evidence or an argument.)

We should reject the mere opinion _{implied claim} of a known liar like Smith. _{reason}

Who says that what Smith says is "mere opinion," and who says he is a "known liar"?

This is cousin to begging the question. It's a little like that nasty question, *When did you stop beating your dog?* It occurs when someone tries to support a claim with statements that assume a judgment or fact that readers do not accept because it has not been proven.

4. "But you can't use the lack of evidence to prove an affirmative claim!" (You rely on a false warrant: When something has not been disproved, we should believe it.)

People who say they have been kidnapped by UFOs should be taken seriously, _{claim} because no one has proved that their stories are false. _{reason}

Hold on! No one has proved that I don't have an oilfield under my back yard, but that doesn't mean that I'm going to start drilling. I don't know something is true because I don't know for sure that it's not.

The technical term for this fallacy is *ad ignorantiam,* pronounced "add ignore-AHN-tee-em." If you make a claim, you bear the burden of offering good *affirmative* reasons for believing it. It is not up to the other person to *disprove* it. Those who make these arguments often say, *Well, if you can't think of a good alternative to my claim, then I must be right.* But a claim is not true simply because no one can think of a good alternative.

A somewhat weaker strategy is to say, *Well, it could be true.* In a sense, anything could be true, even alien abductions. We can leave room for the chance that a claim could be true, but we should file such claims in a corner of our minds reserved for possibilities waiting on evidence.

5. "You can't prove something by claiming that the consequences of not accepting it are intolerable!" (You rely on a false warrant: When it would hurt us not to believe something, we should believe it.)

The Constitution protects our right to privacy, _{claim} because if it did not, then states could regulate our most intimate behavior, including our sexual lives. _{reason} That would be intolerable. _{reason}

You're right; it's intolerable that states should be able to interfere in our private lives. But that's irrelevant to what the Constitution does or doesn't say. As bad as it may seem, the Constitution gives states the power to snoop in our bedrooms.

This fallacy is called *ad baculum,* pronounced "add BAck-yu-lum." It means "with force." Those who argue like this imply that if we do not agree, something bad will happen to us.

Inappropriate Rhetorical Appeals

Unlike fallacies we just discussed, these may or may not be errors, depending on the circumstances of the case. The problem is not that the writer misuses an element of argument but that he relies on a warrant that applies in some cases, but not all. The trick is to know when your readers will accept these appeals and when they will not.

Inappropriate Appeals to Intellectual Consistency

6. "But what you said last month contradicts what you say now!"

You claim that we should evaluate teachers every quarter, because only then will they know whether they are helping us achieve our goals._{acknowledgment} But last month, you argued that teachers should not evaluate students because their tests do not fairly represent your strengths and abilities._{response} How can you say that you should evaluate teachers when you reject their evaluations of you? _{appeal to consistency}

What I say now may not be perfectly consistent with what I said a month ago. But that was a different situation, and the world is too complex for us to be perfectly consistent. That was then; this is now.

This fallacy is called *tu quoque* (pronounced "too kwo-kway"), literally "You too." It is a charge of inconsistency, at worst of dishonesty. But this charge is tricky: It feels legitimate to point out inconsistency—we distrust those who are. But that may have nothing to do with the merits of the case at hand: So what if someone contradicts herself? Regardless of what the writer said before, we have to judge the issue before us on its merits: Should students evaluate teachers? Yet some inconsistencies do undermine an argument. And so strongly do we dislike those who contradict themselves that we reject even a good argument when made by hypocrites. If readers might think that you contradict yourself, you should consider acknowledging the objection and responding with an argument showing why the inconsistency is not fatal.

7. "If you take this one step you will go all the way!"

We can't legalize marijuana for medical purposes _{claim} because if physicians prescribe pot for dying patients, they'll soon prescribe it for people only in pain, then for people who just claim to be in pain. _{reason}

You insult the intelligence of physicians, implying that they don't know the difference between taking this one step and going all the way. It is like claiming that if you drive one mile over the speed limit, you will end up driving 100 miles an hour.

This fallacy is called the *slippery slope* argument. It is a claim that one step must inevitably lead to the next, and the next, and the next. But we know that this is not always true. On the other hand, as every parent knows, there are occasions where a first step does lead to the next:

Daughter: Oh, can't I have one little cookie?

Father: Well, OK, but just one, and just this once!

A particular kind of slippery-slope is called *reductio ad absurdum*—reduction to absurdity, pronounced "ruh-DUK-tee-o add ab-ZERD-um". Instead of claiming that an argument begins a slippery slope, it asserts that it has hit bottom.

> You want students to evaluate their teachers? I suppose you also want the criminally insane to evaluate their psychologists or criminals to evaluate their judges or children to evaluate their parents.

When a critic reduces an argument to an absurd version and then attacks it, we say the critic has built a *straw man*. It is never fair to do that.

Appeals to Inappropriate Perspectives

8. "You offer a false choice between only two alternatives. There are more!"

> It is time to end the debate between "whole word" reading and phonics. The failure of "whole word" pedagogy _{reason,} demands that we return to the time-tested phonics method. _{claim}
>
> *But most good teachers use some of both and a few other ways of teaching as well.*

It is misleading to insist on *either-or* choices when the facts of the matter allow both *more-or-less* or *some-of-both*. In some cases, however, the choice really is between two and only two mutually exclusive alternatives:

> We must decide whether we are going to administer capital punishment or not. It is not fair to sentence people to death and then let them live out their lives as the delays drag on. _{reason} It is not fair to the criminals, who must wait in limbo as their death is postponed; and it is not fair to the families of their victims, who must wait for closure on their grief. _{reason} If we sentence people to death, they should be executed; if they are going to live out their lives in prison, that is the sentence they should receive. _{claim}

As you plan your argument and find yourself arguing for a choice between two exclusive alternatives, stop and think: Could you choose both, or at least some combination? Are there third, fourth, or even fifth choices?

9. "That's just a metaphor! You can't act as though it's literally true."

> Such sick ideas like X can infect those too weak to resist them _{reason} so we must keep people from spreading their ideas by isolating them. _{claim}
>
> *You may be right that the idea may spread, but ideas are not diseases. You can't stop ideas from spreading the way you stop TB.*

It's easy to let metaphors mislead, but the fact is, we can't communicate without them: It's not the metaphoric language itself that's the problem; it's how it's used. So think hard about how far you can push the metaphors you use.

Inappropriate Appeals to Social Solidarity

10. "You're just appealing to the crowd! Why should we go along with everyone else?"

When parents pay for the education of their children, they have the right to decide what should be taught. _{warrant} Most people think creationism should be taught alongside evolution, _{reason} so that's what school systems should teach. _{claim}

That caters to popular ignorance. We don't vote on scientific truth. The only relevant issue is what the facts are. Suppose most parents thought that the earth was flat? Should that be taught?

This fallacy is called *ad populum,* pronounced "add PAH-poo-lum." It means the arguer puts more weight on majority beliefs than on what he thinks is the truth. The basis of an *ad populum* argument is probably our inherited human bias to conform with the thinking of the tribe. But an appeal to popular will is not always a fallacy:

The city council must reject the plan to build a new stadium, _{claim} because the people don't want to pay for it. _{reason} This is a democracy. _{warrant}

If readers might think your appeal to popular opinion is inappropriate, acknowledge and respond to the objection:

The city council must reject the plan to build a new stadium, _{claim} because the people don't want to pay for it. _{reason} We know that the team might move _{acknowledgment} and that some businesses might suffer. _{acknowledgment} But in matters of public spending, the people and not the Chamber of Commerce decides. _{response} This is a democracy. _{warrant}

Your argument will legitimately appeal to the popular will when you can legitimately use this warrant:

When most people believe/decide X, we should accept X.

11. "We don't have to accept your claim just because X says so!"

According to Senator Wise, the predicted rise in atmospheric carbon dioxide will help plant growth, _{reason}because plants take in carbon dioxide and give off oxygen. _{report of evidence} He was born on a farm, _{reason} and he knows plants. _{claimed} _{authority} So we ought not fear green house gases. _{claim}

Senator Wise may be an admirable person, but being born on a farm doesn't make him an expert on atmospheric chemistry.

This fallacy is called *ad verecundiam,* pronounced "add vare-uh-COON-dee-ahm." *Verecundiam* literally means the "modesty" we should exhibit before authority. The psychological basis for this appeal is probably the deference we feel to power and prestige. An appeal to authority goes wrong when the authority has no reason to deserve our trust. The fact that Wise was born on a farm is irrelevant to his standing to make predictions about greenhouse gases.

But the problem is some people are real authorities whose expertise we should respect. So when you want to use an authority, you have to weigh three questions: Is this a case where expertise matters? Is your authority truly an expert in this field? Will your readers be willing to defer ("be modest") in this case?

If readers might question an authority, anticipate their questions. You address the first two by telling them why they should accept your authority as an expert in this case and the third by reporting not just what the authority claims but the reason for claiming it.

> According to Dr. Studious, we would be prudent to stockpile medication in anticipation of a new outbreak of Asian flu. _{claim} As Director of Epidemiology at the National Institute of Health, he was responsible for our being ready for the epidemic of 1987. _{basis of authority} In his research on that and twenty other epidemics, _{basis of authority} he found that the lag between the first cases and an epidemic is about two months. _{reason} Now that the first cases have begun to appear, we know that we have about two months to prepare. _{reason}

12. "You are just engaging in mud-slinging! Unfair personal attacks have nothing to do with the issues."

> Senator Boomer avoided the draft during the Vietnam War, _{reason} so he is disqualified from judging the use of military power. _{claim} No one who shirks his duty can say anything about the service he scorned. _{warrant}

> *Stick to the issue instead of making a personal attack! His actions as a 20-year old are irrelevant to his current analysis of the facts of the matter.*

This fallacy is called *ad hominem,* pronounced "add HA-mi-nim." It literally means "against the person." It is the corollary of a fallacious appeal to authority: Just as we err when we accept an argument because we admire the person making it, so can we err when we reject an argument because it is made by someone we dislike. At times, however, we should question an argument on the basis of who makes it, if that person is regularly dishonest, unreliable, or careless.

A version of this appeal is "guilt by association," which is sometimes fair and sometimes not.

> Professor Hack claims that crime drops when citizens carry concealed weapons. But his research is funded by gun manufacturers, _{reason} and he serves on a committee for the National Rifle Association. _{reason 2} We should look at his research skeptically. _{claim}

If readers might think you are unfairly attacking the person who makes an argument, then you have to acknowledge and respond to their objection:

> . . . We should look at his research skeptically. _{claim} That does not mean his research is necessarily unreliable, _{acknowledgement} but the source of his support gives us reason to look at his methodology carefully. _{response} Even a cautious researcher can be influenced by the interests of those who support his or her work. _{warrant}

13. "Don't give me that sob story. You're just appealing to my pity!"

> Teachers here at State U. are so anxious over rumors about eliminating departments _{reason} that adding a new teaching evaluation form will make them insecure and fearful. _{claim}

> *Our job is to improve teaching. If that makes teachers unhappy, that's too bad. It's irrelevant to creating a sound undergraduate education.*

This technical term for this fallacy is *ad misericordiam,* pronounced "add miz-ÁIR-uh-CORE-dee-um." It asks us to put our sympathies ahead of relevant reasons and evidence. The foundation of such an appeal is our sound intuition that we should respond sympathetically to the suffering of others and act to mitigate it when we can.

Although we can be wrong to put sympathies ahead of our reasons, we can also be right to do so:

> States have released people from institutions for the mentally ill, pushing them onto the streets, where they are homeless and helpless. It is inhuman _{claim} to abandon those who cannot care for themselves to a life of suffering they did not cause and cannot escape. _{reason}

If readers might reject an argument based on sympathy, you have to give them reasons that go beyond it:

> . . . cause and cannot escape. _{reason} We must never put politics and economics above basic human dignity. _{warrant} That's not being a bleeding-heart. _{acknowledgment} If we knowingly refuse to help the helpless, _{reason} we become a morally callous people who will lose all sensitivity to injustice. _{claim}

There are dozens of other so-called "fallacies," but these are the ones most often charged. Be alert to these fallacies in what you read, but their real value is that they help you reflect on your own thinking.

APPENDIX 2

A Quick Guide to Citations

Readers expect you to cite your sources accurately. Since no one can see the "evidence itself," they have to be satisfied with your reports of it. But that means you have to draw your evidence from reliable sources and describe them precisely enough that readers can, if they want, find the source and check the evidence themselves. Some students wonder why their teachers demand that citations precisely follow a set form. When you follow a form that readers can anticipate, they can find your sources most easily.

There are two parts to a complete citation:

- The citation of a source in the body of the paper.

- The list of references at the end of the paper.

There are many forms of citations, but two are most common:

- Modern Language Association (MLA) citations, common in the humanities.

- American Psychological Association (APA) citations, common in the social sciences.

So you should first find out which style your reader expects, MLA or APA. We cannot cover every form of citation or every kind of source, so you should buy a short guide to citation style. You will get plenty of use out of it. Here we will explain the most common kinds of sources in the two most common forms, MLA style and APA style.

MLA Citations

First, we'll discuss listing your references. Then we'll discuss how to cite them in the body of your paper.

Books (Including Collections of Articles)

General Format

The general format is as follows:

> Author. *Title.* Publication information.

> Last-name, First-name, Middle Initial. *Title: Subtitle.* City: Publisher, year.

> Meargham, Paul R. *The History of Wit and Practical Jokes.* Boston: Smith, 1988.

Note that (1) titles must be either underlined or italicized, (2) there is a period after each unit of information, and (3) the second line of the entry is indented.

Special Formats

Multiple Books by the Same Author

- List each book in chronological order, but instead of repeating the author's name, type three dashes and a period.

> Meargham, Paul. *Wit: Its Meaning.* Boston: Smith, 1984.
> ———.*The History of Wit and Practical Jokes.* Boston: Smith, 1988.

Multiple Authors

- For the first author, put the last name first; for remaining authors, start with their first names. Put a comma after each author but the last.

> Meargham, Paul, Harry Winston, and John Holt. *Wit: Its Meaning.* Boston: Smith, 1984.

- For four or more authors, you can give just the first author's name followed by *et al.*

> Meargham, Paul, et al. *Wit: Its Tragic Meaning.* Boston: Smith, 1989.

Multiple Volumes

- When referring to a multivolume work as a whole, indicate the number of volumes after the title (abbreviate *volumes*).

> Meargham, Paul. *Wit: Its Meaning.* 2 vols. Boston: Smith, 1984.

- When referring to a particular volume, indicate which one you are using.

> Meargham, Paul. *Wit: Its Meaning.* Vol. 1. Boston: Smith, 1984.

- When referring to a particular volume in a series, indicate which one you are using and give the title of the series.

> Meargham, Paul. *Wit: Its Meaning.* Vol. 1 of *Wit and History.* 2 vols. Boston: Smith, 1984.

Multiple Editions

- When referring to any edition other than the first, indicate which one after the title but before the volumes (abbreviate *edition*).

Meargham, Paul. *Wit: Its Meaning.* 3rd ed. 2 vols. Boston: Smith, 1984.

Translation

Meargham, Paul. *Wit: Its Meaning.* Trans. George Playe. Boston: Smith, 1984.

Edited Book

Meargham, Paul, ed. *Wit: Its Meaning.* Boston: Smith, 1984.

Individual Item in Edited Collection

Meargham, Paul. "The History of Jokes." *Wit: Its Meaning.* Ed. George Playe. Boston: Smith, 1984. 123–46. [Note: not 123–146]

Individual Item in Reference Work

Meargham, Paul. "The History of Jokes." *Encyclopedia of Humor.* Boston: Smith, 1984.

Articles

General Format

The general format for journal articles has the same general categories as books:

Author. Article Title. Publication information.

Last-name, First-name Middle Initial. "Article Title." *Journal Title* vol. number (year): page numbers.

O'Connell, James. "Wit and War." *Theory of Humor* 21 (1983): 55–60.

Note that article titles are not underlined and that the publication information includes the title of the journal (underlined article or italicized), data on the specific issue, and page numbers for the article.

General Circulation Magazine

O'Connell, James. "Wit and War." *Humor Today* May 1996: 45–66.

If there is no author, start with the article title.

Newspapers

O'Connell, James. "Wit and War." *Tulsa Clarion* 13 June 1983: 1B.

If there is no author, start with the title.

Scholarly Journal

O'Connell, James. "Wit and War." *Theory of Humor* 14 (1997): 335–60.

Special Formats

Journals that Do Not Number Pages Continuously

Most scholarly journals number pages continuously through the year. If you are citing one that starts the pages numbers over with each issue, add the issue number to the volume number.

O'Connell, James. "Wit and War." *Theory of Humor* 14.2 (1997): 33–60.

Reviews

If the article is a review of another work, put the name of the reviewer and the title of the review (if any) first, then the name and title of the work reviewed.

Abbot, Andrew. "I'm Not Laughing." Rev. of *Wit and War* by James O'Connell.
    Theory of Humor 14 (1997): 401–19.

Films

Start with the title (italics or underlined), then name the director, the distributor, and the year of release. You can add other information (such as the screenwriter) between the title and the distributor.

It's a Funny War. Dir. Nate Ruddle. Wri. Francis Kinahan. RKO. 1958.

Television

Include at least the title of the episode, the series title, the network or local station that broadcast it, and the broadcast dates. You can include other information (such as the name of the director or screen writer) after the series title.

"The Last Laugh's on Bart." *The Simpsons.* FOX. May 22, 1996.

On-line Print Sources

If you cite a book or article that was originally printed but you obtained online, add the URL to the end of the citation.

O'Connell, James. "Wit and War." *Theory of Humor* 14.2 (1997): 33–60.
    <http://www.funnystuff.hope.edu/theory/ wit.html>

Web Pages

Start with the author/owner of the page, if you can find one; otherwise, use the best identifying information you can find. Include the date of the last update, if you can find it, and the URL.

Center for Wartime Humor Home Page. 23 May 1999 <http://warjokes.org>

Citing Sources in the Body of Your Paper

The principle is to let your reader know exactly where to look in your source to find what you refer to. There are three variables you have to consider.

- If you mention your source in your text and your reader unambiguously knows to whom you are referring, you can simply insert a page number in parentheses before the final period:

In arguing that wit is closely allied to tragedy as a way to deflect the experience of pain and death, O'Connell points to the gravedigger scene in *Hamlet* as an example of how wit and humor can relieve the oppressive weight of the unendurable (34).

- If, however, the reader cannot unambiguously find the source, you have to be more explicit. For example, if you include more than one book or article by O'Connell, you have to make clear which work you are drawing from. You do that by inserting a word from the title before the page number:

  In arguing that wit is closely allied to tragedy as a way to deflect the experience of pain and death, O'Connell points to the gravedigger scene in *Hamlet* as an example of how wit and humor can relieve the oppressive weight of the unendurable (*Wit*, 34).

- If you refer to more than one writer in a passage, insert the source's name before the page number (and if necessary, a title):

  In arguing that wit is closely allied to tragedy as a way to deflect the experience of pain and death, O'Connell disagrees with Halliday, who points to the gravedigger scene in *Hamlet* as an example of how wit and humor can relieve the oppressive weight of the unendurable, (O'Connell, *Wit*, 34).

APA Citations

Books (Including Collections of Articles)

General Format

The general format is as follows:

Author (Date). *Title*. Publication information.

Last-name, Initials (date). *Title: subtitle*. City: Publisher.

Meargham, P. (1988). *The history of wit and practical jokes*. Boston: Smith, 1988.

Note that (1) the year of publication is included in parentheses after the author, (2) titles are underlined or italicized, (3) only the first word of a title is capitalized, (4) there is a period after each unit of information, and (5) the second line of the entry is indented.

Special Formats

Multiple Books by the Same Author
- List each book in chronological order. If there is more than one entry for a single year, order them alphabetically and add a letter after the year.

  Meargham, P. (1984). *Wit: its meaning*. Boston: Smith.
  Meargham, P. (1988a). *The history of wit and practical jokes*. Boston: Smith.
  Meargham, P. (1988b). *War jokes*. Boston: Smith.

Multiple Authors

- List all authors last name first followed by initials. Use ampersand (&) in place of *and:*

  Meargham, P., H. Winston, & J. Holt (1984). *Wit: its meaning.* Boston: Smith.

- For six or more authors, you can use just the first author followed by *et al.*

  Meargham, P., et al. (1984). *Wit: its meaning.* Boston: Smith.

Multiple Volumes

- When referring to a multivolume work as a whole, indicate how many volumes in parentheses after the title (abbreviate *volumes*).

  Meargham, P. (1984). *Wit: its meaning.* (Vols. 1–2). Boston: Smith

- When referring to a particular volume, indicate which one you are using.

  Meargham, P. (1984). *Wit: its meaning.* (Vol. 1). Boston: Smith.

- When referring to a particular volume in a series, indicate the title of the series, the volume number, and then the title of the volume.

  Meargham, P. (1984). *Wit and history.* (Vol. 1). *Wit: its meaning.* Boston: Smith.

Multiple Editions

- When referring to any edition other than the first, indicate which one in parentheses after the title (abbreviate *edition*).

  Meargham, P. (1984). *Wit: its meaning.* (3rd ed.). Boston: Smith.

Translation

Meargham, P. (1984). *Wit: its meaning.* (G. Playe, Trans.). Boston: Smith.

Edited Book

Meargham, P. (Ed.) (1984). *Wit: its Meaning.* Boston: Smith.

Individual Item in Edited Collection

Meargham, P. (1984). The history of jokes. In G. Playe (Ed.), *Wit: its meaning* (pp. 125–142). Boston: Smith.

Individual Item in Reference Work

Meargham, P. (1984). The history of jokes. *Encyclopedia of humor* (pp. 173–200). Boston: Smith.

Articles

General Format

The general format has the same general categories as books:

Author. (Date). Article title. Publication information.

Last-name, Initial. (Date). Article title. *Journal title* vol. number, pages.

O'Connell, J. (1983). Wit and war. *Theory of humor* 21, 55–60.

Note that article titles are not underlined and that the publication information includes the title of the journal (underlined or italicized), data on the specific issue, and page numbers for the article.

General Circulation Magazine

O'Connell, J. (1996, May). Wit and war. *Humor today,* pp. 45–66.

If there is no author, start with the title.

Newspapers

O'Connell, J. (1983, June 13). Wit and war. *Tulsa clarion,* p. 1B.

If there is no author, start with the title.

Scholarly Journal

O'Connell, J. (1983). Wit and war. *Theory of humor* 21, 55–60.

Special Formats

Journals that Do Not Number Pages Continuously

Most scholarly journals number pages continuously through the year. If you are citing one that starts the pages numbers over with each issue, add the issue number to the volume number.

O'Connell, J. (1983). Wit and war. *Theory of humor* 14.2, 33–60.

Reviews

If the article is a review of another work, put the name of the reviewer and the title of the review (if any) first, then the name and title of the work reviewed inside square brackets.

Abbot, A. (1977). I'm not laughing. [Rev. of Wit and War by James O'Connell]. *Theory of Humor* 14, 401–19.

Films

Start with the director and anyone else responsible for the film (such as a producer), then the year in parentheses, the title underlined, and the distributor.

Ruddle, N. (Director). (1958) *It's a funny war.* RKO.

Television

Start with the name(s) of the producer, director, or other significant contributors, then the date in parentheses, the title (underlined), and the network or local station that broadcast it.

Kinahan, F. (Writer). (1996, May 22). The last laugh's on bart. *The Simpsons.* FOX.

On-line Print Sources

If you cite a book or article that was originally printed but you obtained on-line, add the date you retrieved it and the URL to the end of the citation:

O'Connell, James. (1997). Wit and war. *Theory of humor* 14.2, 33–60. Retrieved on March 10, 2000 from http://www.funnystuff.hope.edu/theory/wit.html.

Internet and Web Pages

Start with the author/owner of the page, if you can find one; otherwise, use the best identifying information you can find. Include the date of the last update, if you can find it, and the URL:

Center for Wartime Humor Home Page. (1999, May 23). Retrieved from http://warjokes.org.

Citing Sources in the Body of Your Paper

The principle is to let your reader know exactly where to look in your source to find what you refer to. There are three variables you have to consider.

- If you mention your source in your text and your reader unambiguously knows to whom you are referring, you can simply insert the year, followed by "p." or "pp." and page number in parentheses before the final period:

   In arguing that wit is closely allied to tragedy as a way to deflect the experience of pain and death, O'Connell points to the gravedigger scene in *Hamlet* as an example of how wit and humor can relieve the oppressive weight of the unendurable (1992, p. 34).

- If there is more than one publication from the same year, distinguish them with a lowercase letter:

   In arguing that wit is closely allied to tragedy as a way to deflect the experience of pain and death, O'Connell points to the gravedigger scene in *Hamlet* as an example of how wit and humor can relieve the oppressive weight of the unendurable (1992a, pp. 34–39).

- If there is any chance of ambiguity, insert the source's name before the year:

   In arguing that wit is closely allied to tragedy as a way to deflect the experience of pain and death, O'Connell disagrees with Halliday, who points to the gravedigger scene in *Hamlet* as an example of how wit and humor can relieve the oppressive weight of the unendurable, (O'Connell, 1992a 34).

READINGS 1

Attitudes Toward Teaching and Learning

Obstacles to Open Discussion and Critical Thinking
The Grinnell College Study
◆

CAROL TROSSET

*L*ike many institutions, Grinnell College hopes that one benefit of an increasingly diverse student body will be that students talk about their differences
with each other. It sees open discussion of sensitive issues as an important part of
the learning process—both in and out of the classroom. Since the college has made
many attempts to foster a good climate for these discussions, recent reports that a
number of students feel silenced have been disturbing news.

In an attempt to understand this problem, I undertook several semesters of
ethnographic research, focusing on student assumptions about the purposes of
discussion. The attitudes revealed by this study have far-reaching implications,
not just for the discussion of diversity issues but for our educational mission of
fostering critical-thinking skills.

Discussion as Advocacy

We presented approximately 200 students with a list of sensitive diversity-
related issues (such as "whether race is an important difference between
people"); for each, we asked whether it was possible to have a balanced discussion of that issue (involving more than one perspective, with each perspective
receiving about equal support and with people being civil to each other). We
also asked them to explain why they did or did not want to discuss the issue.
The majority of students not only thought that balanced discussion of these
issues was impossible but feared that a single viewpoint would dominate—and
feared reprisal if one spoke against that perspective.

The main reason students gave for wanting to discuss a particular topic
was that they held strong views on the subject and wished to convince others.
Likewise, not having a strong view—or finding an issue difficult—was often
given as a reason for not wanting to discuss a subject. This conflict is reflected
in the following student responses:

- "I want to discuss the causes of sexual orientation because I have strong
  views on this issue."
- "I want to discuss affirmative action because I want to educate people."

CAROL TROSSET *is Director of Institutional Research and Lecturer in Anthropology at Grinnell
College. The author thanks the following people for their contributions to this project: Grinnell's
former President Pamela Ferguson, anthropology Professor Douglas Caulkins, and the students who
conducted the interviews, especially Gabriel Grout, Brandi Petersen, and Neelay Shah. From*
Change, *September/October 1998.*

- "I like discussing gender issues because I feel knowledgeable about them."
- "I'm not sure what multiculturalism is; I don't know much about it, so I don't want to discuss it."
- "I don't want to discuss race because I never know how to approach the subject."
- "In a few cases, people cry sexual misconduct when it isn't, so I don't want to talk about it in those few cases."

Some students are so convinced of advocacy as the point of discussion that they see silence as the only way to avoid it: "I wouldn't want to discuss religion as I don't want to impose my views on others."

A few explicitly generalized this model beyond the treatment of diversity issues, saying, "Ideally, you should talk in order to make the other person realize that what they said was wrong," or, "I don't want to talk about things I'm unsure of."

Only five out of the 200 students in our sample volunteered a different, more exploratory, view of discussion, such as "I want to talk about multicultural education because I'm not sure I know enough about it," and "I want to discuss race, as it would open my mind to things I don't experience myself."

In exploratory discussion, people who are seeking more information and other view-points speak in order to learn about things. This is very different from the advocacy model, in which people who have already made up their minds about an issue speak in order to express their views and convince others.

One of our annual surveys of first-year students found 54 percent preferred to discuss a topic on which they held strong views (over a topic about which they were undecided).

Another survey, with a differently worded question, found the same preference increasing over time, rising from 25 percent of freshmen to over 50 percent of juniors. (The preference declined slightly among seniors, but the sample of seniors was not representative.) There were no ethnic or gender differences correlating with this preference in either survey.

The Search for Consensus

When we asked students why people should talk about their differences, we quite often heard about the desire to reach a consensus:

- "The best thing is when opposing views find some point of agreement."
- "Ideally, people should talk in order to mold all opinions together in a compromise."
- "People should talk in order to achieve a unified world view, the dissolution of the idea of the other, and an awareness of the oneness of all things."

Some students also told us that there's no point talking about something unless people can agree: "Discussing these things is futile; it wears you out. It seems you can never reach a consensus." Despite the discouraged tone of this last comment, many interviewees expressed great optimism about the possibility that people with different views can find common ground.

Some students spoke about issues as if a consensus already existed:

- "I don't want to discuss race because it's not an important difference between people."
- "I don't want to discuss the causes of sexual orientation because this topic is irrelevant to the nature of homosexuality."

Sometimes this assumption was combined with a preference for advocacy. One woman wants to be an advocate representing a consensus she assumes to exist: "I want to discuss sexism due to a personal interest in stating the female experience."

When we asked how likely people were to listen to and think about what someone else said under various conditions, most students said, predictably, that they would be likely to listen to someone with whom they already agreed. A majority also said that they would be unlikely to listen to someone with whom they disagreed. Their reasons included the following:

- "I have a set opinion about the causes of sexual orientation—I wouldn't want to participate in a conversation when other people have disagreeable views, but I would talk with people who have similar opinions."
- "I have strong ideas about what constitutes a multicultural education—I would have difficulty listening to those who disagree."
- A discussion of abortion wouldn't be balanced—I would have a hard time listening to the opposite view."

Most often, it seems, students created artificial consensus groups by only discussing difficult issues when they knew it to be "safe"—that is, in carefully selected groups with homogeneous opinions, as reflected in the following comments:

- "People don't talk about race on this campus—carefully selected company might mean opposing views are not present."
- "It appears that people prefer to interact with others who verify their own views, instead of actively pursuing alternative points of view. This could cause individuals to believe there is widespread support for their own views, when in fact there may not be."

Seventy-five percent of the students we asked said that they would discuss diversity issues with people of the same views or background as themselves, but only 40 percent said they would discuss the same issues with people whose views were unknown to them.

Personal Experience as the (Only) Source of Legitimate Knowledge

As with cases in which they already agreed with a speaker, most students we surveyed said they were very likely to listen to someone they perceived as knowledgeable. Before we interpret this as traditional academic respect or expertise, however, we must examine where students think knowledge comes from.

When we asked 47 students in interviews, "How knowledgeable are you about diversity issues?" most said they were fairly to very knowledgeable. When asked where their knowledge came from, most mentioned more than one source. Forty-three percent of the respondents attributed knowledge to personal experience, and another 35 percent said knowledge came from talking to others about their experiences.

This bias in favor of personalized knowledge as opposed to knowledge accessible to all comers such as that contained in scholarly writings—a kind of knowledge stressed by only six of the 47—is also visible in the distribution of which groups claimed knowledge of which issues. Thus, students of color were more likely than whites to claim to be knowledgeable about race, women were more likely than men to claim knowledge about gender, and homosexuals more likely than heterosexuals to claim knowledge about sexual orientation.

White males in their first two years were the only group likely to say that they had little knowledge of diversity generally. Their claim to know little about gender, "because I have no personal experience," shows that these claims attribute expertise not only to experience, but to a particular kind of experience (that of belonging to a typically less powerful group).

About The Study

Grinnell is a selective, private, residential four-year college located in a small town in central Iowa. Its roughly 1,300 students come from all 50 states and some 40 countries.

This study was conducted primarily using ethnographic interviewing techniques, where individuals not only respond to questions face to face but are asked to explain their thoughts and the meaning of what they say, then to situate these things in their experiences.

Each semester for three years, I trained student interviewers through an anthropological research methods class; they then collected data from their fellow students, while I gathered additional data and guided the project design and analysis.

Several different samples, most comprising about 200 students, contributed to the data presented here. Each sample has good representation with respect to race, gender, and class year.

—Carol Trosset

This valuing of one kind of experience helps to limit what can be said in discussions. For example, the following comments on sexism came from two men and two women:

- "Guys are not able to challenge women's sexist remarks."
- "Women are unlikely to be labeled sexist no matter what they say."
- "I want to discuss gender—it's easy to say, I'm a woman; as a woman . . ."
- "Not being a woman, I don't feel my comments would be seen as valid."

This bias both forces members of less powerful groups into the role of peer instructors, and supports the impression that members of more powerful groups have nothing legitimate to say.

The Right Not to Be Challenged

Not only do people participate in discussion for the purpose of advocating views they already hold, but some of them expect to do so without anyone questioning or challenging their statements. In our most representative interview study, when asked, "As a member of a diverse community, what are your rights?" 15 percent of the sample volunteered the idea that they had the right to think or say whatever they liked without having their views challenged.

Some of the phrases used to express this position include

- "I have the right to present my views without being criticized";
- ". . . to not have people judge my views";
- ". . . to say what I believe and not have anyone tell me I'm wrong";
- ". . . to feel and think anything and not be looked down on";
- ". . . to hold my own beliefs and not feel attacked because of them"; and
- ". . . to speak my mind and not feel inhibited."

The students who claimed the right not to be challenged were nearly all women. Twenty-five percent of the women we interviewed made this claim, compared to only 6 percent of the men. (Other statements in their interviews suggest that most Grinnell men expect their views to be challenged by others.) Equal proportions of whites and students of color made this claim (which was rarely made by international students). Particularly disturbing is the fact that this claim was made evenly across the four class years, suggesting that students who arrive with this assumption do not alter it as a result of what they learn.

Implications

We hear a great deal these days about the pedagogical benefits of discussion. But the assumptions we uncovered—such as the belief that advocacy is the purpose of discussion—illustrate why this method is often not as effective as we'd hope. Cultural attitudes of this sort have a pervasive impact on behavior.

These attitudes affect not only how students discuss things among themselves, but how they hear what professors say and how they read course material.

Many of us as academics share a number of expectations about the dispositions of educated people. These include exploring ideas from a variety of perspectives, learning about things outside one's own experience, evaluating the quality of evidence and arguments, and the capacity to be persuaded of new perspectives when presented with high-quality evidence and argument. In line with this, the fostering of critical-thinking skills appears in the mission statements of our institutions. But our students often do not share this common faculty agenda.

Colleagues in philosophy have told me they see students who think Socrates was a bully. One student even equated Socrates with Rush Limbaugh—this on the grounds that both of them want everyone to agree with them.

A faculty member I encountered at a conference, who clearly valued both diversity and open discussion, also claimed that Socratic academic discourse was a bad model for students. One complication here is the difference between critical and empathic thinking, both of which may be educational goals but which should not be confused with each other.

Some students to whom I presented this research told me, quite articulately, that "your identity comes from what, not how, you think." One, apparently struggling with the need to change his views on certain subjects, said he resolved this by realizing that at his age his identity was still changing. These statements were strikingly different from the typical scholar's identification with how one uses evidence and argument—something that has nothing to do with one's conclusions of the moment, since these will always change in the face of new evidence and better arguments.

Radical Relativism

Developmental and learning-style theorists may take issue with my concerns; it's all a "stage" or just their "style," they say. Their challenges, however, beg the question of how we as teachers are going to accomplish our educational missions, which are centered around the development of critical-thinking skills and which require our students to grow analytically.

What should we do, for example, with a student who says, after reading Malinowski (whose publications were based on four years of detailed field research), we still can't say anything about the Trobrianders because "it's just his opinion"? Traditional relativism, of course, is an important part of anthropology; it is based on the idea that any statement is made from a particular perspective, which must be taken into account when considering its meaning. The radical relativism of students carries this perspective beyond its original intention and argues that, therefore, everything is "just" an opinion and that no comparisons can be made between ideas or perspectives. (Indeed, people taking this position usually argue that any perspective claiming the ability to make comparative judgments is inferior.)

This orientation among students supports their claim that there is no way to learn about something outside one's own experience. This assertion, in effect, denies the methodological basis of most disciplines. It also supports students' idea that people have the right not have their views challenged. Critical thinking itself is devalued here, since the assessment of evidence and logic is seen as just another way of doing things.

Given these orientations, we need to recognize that when we recommend "tolerance" to students, they may not hear the same message we're trying to send. Many of us think of tolerance in terms of civility, of behaving in well-mannered ways toward all members of the community, whether or not we approve of their views or behavior. Many students, on the other hand, think that being tolerant means approving of all ways of being, and believing that all ways are equally valid (except, of course, any position that openly makes value judgments and does not extend equal approval to all).

Being Comfortable

Eighty-four percent of the first-year class we surveyed chose the statement "It is important for the college community to make sure all its members feel comfortable" over the statement "People have to learn to deal with being uncomfortable." Across the student body, it is a common demand that the college as a whole, as well as its individual members, must act to ensure the comfort of all students, especially those who are members of traditionally underrepresented groups. At the same time, people insist that members of traditionally powerful groups (such as heterosexuals) should get comfortable, quickly, with previously unfamiliar groups and lifestyles.

"People are not interested in the sources of discomfort. They just want everyone to get comfortable," one student said. Of course, people should not be made to feel excluded because they belong to a minority group. But the demand for comfort often reaches much farther than this, sometimes to the point of claiming that no persons should have to learn new behaviors or ways of thinking, or indeed to do anything that might make him or her uneasy.

These e-mail messages were sent to colleagues of mine; the students clearly expect that they will be accepted as legitimate excuses:

- "You haven't received my paper because I'm not comfortable with it yet."
- "I'm not coming to class today because I haven't done the reading, and I'm not comfortable asking any of the other students if I can borrow their books."

Exploring new ideas, encountering people with different values, learning a new discipline's way of thinking, and having someone point out a flaw in one's argument—these can be uncomfortable experiences. For some people, simply finding themselves disagreeing with someone else is uncomfortable. Promising our students that we will make them comfortable may simply confirm them in their view that they have the right not to be challenged.

Ironically, typical suggestions for how to foster discussion feed into this attitude. Stressing the importance of making everyone feel "safe" often seems to result in making many people afraid to disagree with anyone, for fear of intimidating or offending them. Perhaps the teacher's solution is not ever more safety and respect (words that can be variously interpreted), but cultivating a more careful distinction between the idea and the person.

Speakers need to remember this distinction when they issue challenges, but those on the receiving end also need to remember it, so as not to overinterpret any conceptual or factual challenge as a threat to identity. With respect to sensitive issues, it might help to encourage everyone to think less, rather than more, about identity; to focus students' attention not on their differences, but on some shared interest or problem-solving task that has the potential to bring them together.

Clearly, many students hold assumptions about discussion that present difficulties for teaching critical thinking. Deeply personal issues are, of course, among the most difficult places for anyone to apply such skills. But the ability to hold just such discussions would be an acid test of whether we have indeed fostered critical thinking in our students.

On the Uses of a Liberal Education

◆

MARK EDMUNDSON AT THE UNIVERSITY OF VIRGINIA

Today is evaluation day in my Freud class, and everything has changed. The class meets twice a week, late in the afternoon, and the clientele, about fifty undergraduates, tends to drag in and slump, looking disconsolate and a little lost, waiting for a jump start. To get the discussion moving, they usually require a joke, an anecdote, an off-the-wall question—When you were a kid, were your Halloween getups ego costumes, id costumes, or superego costumes? This sort of thing. But today, as soon as I flourish the forms, a buzz rises in the room. Today they write their assessment of the course, their assessments of me, and they are without a doubt wide-awake. "What is your evaluation of the instructor?" asks question number eight, entreating them to circle a number between five (excellent) and one (poor, poor). Whatever interpretive subtlety they've acquired during the term is now out the window. Edmundson: one to five, stand and shoot.

And they do. As I retreat through the door—I never stay around for this phase of the ritual—I look over my shoulder and see them toiling away like the devil's auditors. They're pitched into high writing gear, even the ones who struggle to squeeze out their journal entries word by word, stoked on a procedure they have by now supremely mastered. They're playing the informed consumer, letting the provider know where he's come through and where he's not quite up to snuff.

But why am I so distressed, bolting like a refugee out of my own classroom, where I usually hold easy sway? Chances are the evaluations will be much like what they've been in the past—they'll be just fine. It's likely that I'll be commended for being "interesting" (and I am commended, many times over), that I'll be cited for my relaxed and tolerant ways (that happens, too), that my sense of humor and capacity to connect the arcana of the subject matter with current culture will come in for some praise (yup). I've been hassled this term, finishing a manuscript, and so haven't given their journals the attention I should have, and for that I'm called—quite civilly, though—to account. Overall, I get off pretty well.

Yet I have to admit that I do not much like the image of myself that emerges from these forms, the image of knowledgeable, humorous detachment and bland tolerance. I do not like the forms themselves, with their number ratings, reminiscent of the sheets circulated after the TV pilot has just played to its sample audience in Burbank. Most of all I dislike the attitude of calm

---

MARK EDMUNDSON *is a contributing editor of* Harper's Magazine. *He is the author of* Nightmare on Main Street, *a study of the gothic in contemporary culture. From "On the Uses of a Liberal Education," by Mark Edmundson. Copyright 1997 by* Harper's Magazine. All rights reserved. Reproduced from the September issue by special permission.

consumer expertise that pervades the responses. I'm disturbed by the serene belief that my function—and, more important, Freud's, or Shakespeare's, or Blake's—is to divert, entertain, and interest. Observes one respondent, not at all unrepresentative: "Edmundson has done a fantastic job of presenting this difficult, important & controversial material in an enjoyable and approachable way."

Thanks but no thanks. I don't teach to amuse, to divert, or even, for that matter, to be merely interesting. When someone says she "enjoyed" the course—and that word crops up again and again in my evaluations—somewhere at the edge of my immediate complacency I feel encroaching self-dislike. That is not at all what I had in mind. The off-the-wall questions and the sidebar jokes are meant as lead-ins to stronger stuff—in the case of the Freud course, to a complexly tragic view of life. But the affability and the one-liners often seem to be all that land with the students, their journals and evaluations leave me little doubt.

I want some of them to say that they've been changed by the course. I want them to measure themselves against what they've read. It's said that some time ago a Columbia University instructor used to issue a harsh two-part question. One: What book did you most dislike in the course? Two: What intellectual or characterological flaws in you does that dislike point to? The hand that framed that question was surely heavy. But at least it compels one to see intellectual work as a confrontation between two people, student and author, where the stakes matter. Those Columbia students were being asked to relate the quality of an *encounter,* not rate the action as though it had unfolded on the big screen.

Why are my students describing the Oedipus complex and the death drive as being interesting and enjoyable to contemplate? And why am I coming across as an urbane, mildly ironic, endlessly affable guide to this intellectual territory, operating without intensity, generous, funny and loose?

Because that's what works. On evaluation day, I reap the rewards of my partial compliance with the culture of my students and, too, with the culture of the university as it now operates. It's a culture that's gotten little exploration. Current critics tend to think that liberal-arts education is in crisis because universities have been invaded by professors with peculiar ideas: deconstruction, Lacanianism, feminism, queer theory. They believe that genius and tradition are out and the P.C., multiculturalism, and identity politics are in because of an invasion by tribes of tenured radicals, the late millennial equivalents of the Visigoth hoards that cracked Rome's walls.

But mulling over my evaluations and then trying to take a hard, extended look at campus life both here at the University of Virginia and around the country eventually led me to some different conclusions. To me, liberal-arts education is as ineffective as it is now not chiefly because there are a lot of strange theories in the air. (Used well, those theories *can* be illuminating.) Rather, it's that university culture, like American culture writ large, is, to put it crudely, ever more devoted to consumption and entertainment, to the using and using up of goods and images. For someone growing up in America now, there are few available alternatives to the cool consumer worldwide. My students didn't ask for that view, much less create it, but they bring a consumer *weltanschauung* to school, where it exerts a powerful, and largely unacknowledged, influence. If we want to understand current universities, with their multiple woes, we might try leaving the realms of expert debate and fine ideas and turning to the classrooms and campuses, where a new kind of weather is gathering. [. . .]

How did my students reach this peculiar state in which all passion seems to be spent? I think that many of them have imbibed their sense of self from consumer culture in general and from the tube in particular. They're the progeny of 100 cable channels and omnipresent Blockbuster outlets. TV, Marshall McLuhan famously said, is a cool medium. Those who play best on it are low-key and nonassertive; they blend in. Enthusiasm quickly looks absurd. The form of character that's most appealing on TV is calmly self-interested though never greedy, attuned to the conventions, and ironic. Judicious timing is preferred to sudden self-assertion. The TV medium is inhospitable to inspiration, improvisation, failures, slips. All must run perfectly.

Naturally, a cool youth culture is a marketing bonanza for producers of the right products, who do all they can to enlarge that culture and keep it grinding. The Internet, TV, and magazines now teem with what I call persona ads, ads for Nikes and Reeboks and Jeeps and Blazers that don't so much endorse the capacities of the product per se as show you what sort of person you will be once you've acquired it. The Jeep ad that features hip, outdoorsy kids whipping a Frisbee from mountaintop to mountaintop isn't so much about what Jeeps can do as it is about the kind of people who own them. Buy a Jeep and be one of them. The ad is of little consequence in itself, but expand its message exponentially and you have the central thrust of current consumer culture—buy in order to be. [. . .]

What they will not generally do, though, is indict the current system. They won't talk about how the exigencies of capitalism lead to a reserve army of the unemployed and nearly inevitable misery. That would be getting too loud, too brash. For the pervading view is the cool consumer perspective, where passion and strong admiration are forbidden. "To stand in awe of nothing, Numicus, is perhaps the one and only thing that can make a man happy and keep him so," says Horace in the *Epistles,* and I fear that his lines ought to hang as a motto over the university in this era of high consumer capitalism.

It's easy to mount one's high horse and blame the students for this state of affairs. But they didn't create the present culture of consumption. (It was largely my own generation, that of the Sixties, that let the counterculture search for pleasure devolve into a quest for commodities.) And they weren't the ones responsible, when they were six and seven and eight years old, for unplugging the TV set from time to time or for hauling off and kicking a hole through it. It's my generation of parents who sheltered these students, kept them away from the hard knocks of everyday life, making them cautious and overfragile, who demanded that their teachers, from grade school on, flatter them endlessly so that the kids are shocked if their college profs don't reflexively suck up to them.

Of course, the current generational style isn't simply derived from culture and environment. It's also about dollars. Students worry that taking too many chances with their educations will sabotage their future prospects. They're aware of the fact that a drop that looks more and more like one wall of the Grand Canyon separates the top economic tenth from the rest of the population. There's a sentiment currently abroad that if you step aside for a moment, to write, to travel, to fall too hard in love, you might lose position permanently. We may be on a conveyor belt, but it's worse down there one the filth-strewn floor. So don't sound off, don't blow your chances.

But wait. I teach at the famously conservative University of Virginia. Can I extend my view from Charlottesville to encompass the whole country, a whole generation of college students? I can only say that I hear comparable stories about classroom life from colleagues everywhere in America. When I visit other schools to lecture, I see a similar scene unfolding. There are, of course, terrific students everywhere. And they're all the better for the way they've had to strive against the existing conformity. At some of the small liberal-arts colleges, the tradition of strong engagement persists. But overall, the students strike me as being sweet and sad, hovering in a nearly suspended animation.

Too often now the pedagogical challenge is to make a lot from a little. Teaching Wordsworth's "Tintern Abbey," you ask for comments. No one responds. So you call on Stephen. Stephen: "The sound, this poem really flows." You: "Stephen seems interested in the music of the poem. We might extend his comment to ask if the poem's music coheres with its argument. Are they consistent? Or is there an emotional pain submerged here that's contrary to the poem's appealing melody?" All right, it's not usually that bad. But close. One friend describes it as rebound teaching: they proffer a weightless comment, you hit it back for all you're worth, then it comes dribbling out again. Occasionally a professor will try to explain away this intellectual timidity by describing the students as perpetrators of postmodern irony, a highly sophisticated mode. Everything's a slick counterfeit, a simulacrum, so by no means should any phenomenon be taken seriously. But the students don't have the urbane, Oscar Wilde-type demeanor that should go with this view. Oscar was cheerful, funny, confident, strange. (Wilde, mortally ill, living in a Paris flophouse: "My wallpaper and I are fighting a duel to the death. One or the other of us has to go.") This generation's style is considerate, easy to please, and a touch depressed.

Granted, you might say, the kids come to school immersed in a consumer mentality—they're good Americans, after all—but then the university and the professors do everything in their power to fight that dreary mind-set in the interest of higher ideals, right? So it should be. But let us look at what is actually coming to pass.

Over the past few years, the physical layout of my university has been changing. To put it a little indecorously, the place is looking more and more like a retirement spread for the young. Our funds go to construction, into new dorms, into renovating the student union. We have a new aquatics center and ever-improving gyms, stocked with StairMasters and Nautilus machines. Engraved on the wall in the gleaming aquatics building is a line by our founder, Thomas Jefferson, declaring that everyone ought to get about two hours' exercise a day. Clearly even the author of the Declaration of Independence endorses the turning of his university into a sports-and-fitness emporium.

But such improvements shouldn't be surprising. Universities need to attract the best (that is, the smartest *and* the richest) students in order to survive in an ever more competitive market. Schools want kids whose parents can pay the full freight, not the ones who need scholarships or want to bargain down the tuition costs. If the marketing surveys say that the kids require sports centers, then, trustees willing, they shall have them. In fact, as I began looking around, I came to see that more and more of what's going on in the university is customer driven. The consumer pressures that beset me on evaluation day are only a part of an overall trend. [. . .]

How did we reach this point? In part the answer is a matter of demographics and (surprise) of money. Aided by the G.I. bill, the college-going population in America dramatically increased after the Second World War. Then came the baby boomers, and to accommodate them, schools continued to grow. Universities expand easily enough, but with tenure locking faculty in for lifetime jobs, and with the general reluctance of administrators to eliminate their own slots, it's not easy for a university to contract. So after the baby boomers had passed through—like a fat meal digested by a boa constrictor—the colleges turned to energetic promotional strategies to fill the empty chairs. And suddenly college became a buyer's market. What students and their parents wanted had to be taken more and more into account. That usually mean creating more comfortable, less challenging environments, places where almost no one failed, everything was enjoyable, and everyone was nice.

Just as universities must compete with one another for students, so must the individual departments. At a time of rank economic anxiety, the English and history majors have to contend for students against the more success-insuring branches, such as the sciences and the commerce school. In 1968, more than 21 percent of all bachelors' degrees conferred in America were in the humanities; by 1993, that number had fallen to about 13 percent. The humanities now must struggle to attract students, many of whose parents devoutly wish they would study something else.

One of the ways we've tried to stay attractive is by loosening up. We grade much more softly than our colleagues in science. In English, we don't give many Ds, or Cs for that matter. (The rigors of Chem 101 create almost as many English majors per year as do the splendors of Shakespeare.) A professor at Stanford recently explained grade inflation in the humanities by observing that the undergraduates were getting smarter every year; the higher grades simply recorded how much better they were than their predecessors. Sure.

Along with softening the grades, many humanities departments have relaxed major requirements. There are some good reasons for introducing more choice into curricula and requiring fewer standard courses. But the move, like many others in the university now, jibes with a tendency to serve—and not challenge—the students. Students can also float in and out of classes during the first two weeks of each term without making any commitment. The common name for this time span—shopping period—speaks volumes about the consumer mentality that's now in play. Usually, too, the kids can drop courses up until the last month with only an innocuous "W" on their transcripts. Does a course look too challenging? No problem. Take it pass-fail. A happy consumer is, by definition, one with multiple options, one who can always have what he wants. And since a course is something the students and their parents have bought and paid for, why can't they do with it pretty much as they please? [. . .]

It is a surprise, then, that this generation of students—steeped in consumer culture before going off to school, treated as potent customers by the university well before their date of arrival, then pandered to from day one until the morning of the final kiss-off from Kermit or one of his kin—are inclined to see the books they read as a string of entertainments to be placidly enjoyed or languidly cast down? Given the way universities are now administered (which is more and more to say, given the way that they are currently marketed), is it a shock that the kids don't come to school hot to learn, unable to bear their own ignorance? For some measure of self-dislike, or self-discontent—which is much different than simple depression—seems to me to be a prerequisite for getting an education that matters. My students, alas, usually lack the confidence to acknowledge what would be their most precious asset for learning: their ignorance. [. . .]

Then how do those who at least occasionally promote genius and high literary ideals look to current students? How do we appear, those of us who take teaching to be something of a performance art and who imagine that if you give yourself over completely to your subject you'll be rewarded with insight beyond what you individually command?

I'm reminded of an old piece of newsreel footage I saw once. The speaker (perhaps it was Lenin, maybe Trotsky) was haranguing a large crowd. He was expostulating, arm waving, carrying on. Whether it was flawed technology or the man himself, I'm not sure, but the orator looked like an intricate mechanical device that had spring into fast-forward. To my students, who mistrust enthusiasm in every form, that's me when I start riffing about Freud or Blake. But more and more, as my evaluations showed, I've been replacing enthusiasm and intellectual animation with stand-up routines, keeping it all at arm's length, praising under the cover of irony.

It's too bad that the idea of genius has been denigrated so far, because it actually offers a live alternative to the demoralizing culture of hip in which most of my students are mired. By embracing the works and lives of extraordinary people, you can adapt new ideals to revise those that came courtesy of your parents, your neighborhood, your clan—or the tube. The aim of a good liberal-arts education was once, to adapt an observation by the scholar, Walter Jackson Bate, to see that "we need not be the passive victims of what we deterministically call 'circumstances' (social, cultural or reductively psychological-personal), but that by linking ourselves through what Keats calls an 'immortal free-masonry' with the great, we can become freer—freer to be ourselves, to be what we most want and value."

But genius isn't just a personal standard; genius can also have political effect. To me, one of the best things about democratic thinking is the conviction that genius can spring up anywhere. Walt Whitman is born into the working class and thirty-six years later we have a poetic image of America that gives a passionate dimension to the legalistic brilliance of the Constitution. A democracy needs to constantly develop, and to do so it requires the most powerful visionary minds to interpret the present and to propose possible shapes for the future. By continuing to notice and praise genius, we create a culture in which the kind of poetic gamble that Whitman made—a gamble in which failure would have entailed rank humiliation, depression, maybe suicide—still takes place. By rebelling against established ways of seeing and saying things, genius helps us to apprehend how malleable the present is and how promising and fraught with danger is the future. If we teachers do not endorse genius and self-overcoming, can we be surprised when our students find their ideal images in TV's latest persona ads?

A world uninterested in genius is a despondent place; whose sad denizens drift from coffee bar to Prozac dispensary, unfired by ideals, by the glowing image of the self that one might become. As Northrop Frye says in a beautiful and now dramatically unfashionable sentence, "The artist who uses the same energy and genius that Homer and Isaiah had will find that he not only lives in the same palace of art as Homer and Isaiah, but lives in it at the same time." We ought not to deny the existence of such a place simply because we, or those we care for, find the demands it makes intimidating, the rent too high.

What happens if we keep trudging along this bleak course? What happens if our most intelligent students never learn to strive to overcome what they are? What if genius, and the imitation of genius, become silly, outmoded ideas? What you're likely to get are more and more one-dimensional men and women. These will be people who live for easy pleasure, for comfort and prosperity, who think of money first, then second, and third, who hug the status quo; people who believe in God as a sort of insurance policy (cover your bets); people who are never surprised. They will be people so pleased with themselves (when they're not in despair at the general pointlessness of their lives) that they cannot imagine humanity could do better. They'll think it their highest duty to clone themselves as frequently as possible. They'll claim to be happy, and they'll live a long time.

It is probably time now to offer a spate of inspiring solutions. Here ought to come a list of reforms with due notations about a core curriculum and various requirements. What the traditionalists who offer such solutions miss is that no matter what our current students are given to read, many of them will simply translate it into melodramas, with flat characters and predictable morals. (The unabated capitalist culture that conservative critics so often endorse has put students in a position to do little else.) One can't simply wave a curricular wand and reverse acculturation.

Perhaps it would be a good idea to try firing the counselors and sending half the deans back into the classrooms, dismantling the football team and making the stadium into a playground for local kids, emptying the fraternities, and boarding up the student-activities office. Such measures would convey the message that American colleges are not northern outposts of Club Med. A willingness on the part of the faculty to defy student conviction and affront them occasionally—to be usefully offensive—also might not be a bad thing. We professors talk a lot about subversion, which generally means subverting the view of people who never hear us talk or read our work. But to subvert the view of our students, our customers, that would be something else again.

Ultimately, though, it is up to individuals—and individual students in particular—to make their own way against the current sludgy tide. There's still the library, still the museum, there's still the occasional teacher who lives to find things greater than herself to admire. There are still fellow students who have not been cowed. Universities are inefficient, cluttered, archaic places, with many unguarded corners where one can open a book or gaze out onto the larger world and construe it freely. Those who do as much, trusting themselves against the weight of current opinion, will have contributed something to bringing this sad dispensation to an end. As for myself, I'm canning my low-key one-liners; when the kids' TV-based tastes come to the fore, I'll aim and shoot. And when it's time to praise genius, I'll try to do it in the right style, full-out, with faith that finer artistic spirits (maybe not Homer and Isaiah quite, but close, close), still alive somewhere in the ether, will help me out when my invention flags; the students doze, or the dean mutters into the phone. I'm getting back to a more exuberant style, I'll be expostulating and arm waving straight into the millennium, yes I will.

Has Student Consumerism Gone Too Far?

◆

Michael Pernal

There is little doubt that college administrators are changing their methods of dealing with students because of the movement that has come to be known as "student consumerism." As a result of state and federal legislation, court rulings, and voluntary changes on the part of colleges themselves, higher education institutions are now viewed by many as *marketers* of products or services. Students, in turn, have come to be regarded as *purchasers.*

While much has happened to support such a trend, it should be kept in mind that the student consumer phenomenon actually developed as an offshoot of the general consumer movement in the United States. Although a number of similarities exist between the two, there is much about the student-college relationship that is unique to the educational environment. As a result, strict marketplace applications of this relationship occasionally miss the mark.

This article, which acknowledges the fact that many reforms were necessary to protect students from abuses at colleges, will attempt to advance the notion that further development of student-college relationships within the concept of consumerism should be undertaken only after serious study. In short, this article asks the question: Have we gone far enough to protect the interests of our students?

Where We Are Today

Few educators would claim that colleges view their students as they did 20 or 30 years ago. As a result of increasing court suits and legislation, colleges have gradually come to regard students more as adults and less as children who have been placed in the care of deans, administrators, and faculty members. The Educational Amendments of 1976, for example, adopted a federal strategy for student consumerism. Colleges which disburse federal financial aid are now required to provide prospective students, on an annual basis, complete information regarding financial aid programs, application procedures, and conditions of awards (loan requirements, etc.). In addition, institutions of higher education must be prepared to furnish, upon request, placement statistics which indicate, by major or program, the college's record in finding employment for its graduates before students are obligated to contract for loans.

As a result of passage of such legislation and other bills like the Family Educational Rights and Privacy Act of 1974 (the so-called Buckley Amend-

---

The writer is dean *of personnel administration at Eastern Connecticut State College in Willimantic. From* The College Board Review, *Summer 1977.*

ment), the federal government has declared itself to be clearly on the side of the student. While few are prepared to argue that the student consumerism movement has not sprung up for good and valid reasons, concern does exist that institutions of higher education, both traditional and proprietary, will become buried in an avalanche of red tape and mounting expenses if additional public regulations force further adjustments to administrative practices. Many students themselves complain that registration lines have become more cumbersome because of the mountains of paper work and questionnaires that greet them in response to federal and/or state regulations concerning their rights and privileges. Despite significant red tape already caused by federal regulations involved with the Buckley Amendment, Educational Amendments of 1976, Title IX, etc., consumer advocates want colleges and universities to do more. Among the many possibilities suggested as further needs are the following:

- licensing of college recruiters by states or accreditation agencies;
- written contracts between professors and students with respect to course requirements, evaluative procedures and criteria, and grading practices; and
- abolishment of mandatory student activity fees in favor of voluntary fee structures, which permit users to pay and non-users to forgo.

Have We Gone Far Enough?

Despite cries for further action on the part of student consumer advocates, my contention is that we have gone far enough for the present in protecting the rights of students, and that more attention should be paid to measuring the impact of existing safeguards on the colleges' ability to maintain their integrity as educational institutions. It certainly can be argued that students should be protected from colleges that misrepresent programs. In fact, federal dollars can be withheld from institutions which give false or misleading impressions of the success of their graduates, the types of programs offered, the costs involved, etc. Students are also presently accorded avenues on most campuses for exercising their rights to non-discrimination, grievances, privacy, disclosure of records, challenge of information contained in records, and a fair hearing in the case of disciplinary offenses. If the facts be known, many colleges have grown overly sensitive to protecting the rights of their students. While exceptions to this trend are still to be found, a question exists concerning the good that any further pressures on colleges would accomplish.

In particular, recent federal regulations, which were actually implemented to protect students from fly-by-night institutions that promise what they cannot deliver, have had a profound impact on academically oriented institutions (i.e. liberal arts colleges) which profess few vocational implications with respect to their degrees. One major example stemmed from abuses involving the federally insured student loan programs. Certain institutions fleeced the system by encouraging students to use the program to finance tuition and fees only to cease operations leaving students indebted to lending institutions with nothing to show for their investment. Resultant legislation now requires schools to furnish placement data to prospective student borrowers and to give complete breakdowns of academic and/or vocational programs. Few can argue that steps were not necessary to curb such abuses. The question remains, however, whether the safeguards which now exist are sufficient to protect student interest as consumer.

In my opinion, the cause of consumer protection in higher education has reached a point where most of the bases are covered, and time should now be taken to see how well things work before additional steps are taken. It may be possible that further safeguards, well-intended as they may be, could impose unnecessary burdens on institutions without taking into account the fact that colleges and universities do not strictly fall into a seller-consumer framework.

Where the Model Breaks Down

In short, the unique relationship which exists between colleges and students does not adequately lend itself enough to the seller-purchaser model to justify further commitment to the consumer concept which advocates seek. Five of the ways in which application of such a framework breaks down are listed below.

1.The Problem of Performance

In a strict seller-purchaser model, the performance requirement rests clearly with the seller. Consumers who purchase an automobile or television set expect that the machine will render reasonably trouble-free service or they can seek adjustment or replacement. In similar fashion, purchasers of a service such as legal assistance can expect certain actions or performance levels on the part of an attorney. Basically, therefore, the consumer model is premised on a certain degree of passivity on the part of the purchaser. The performance expectation rests clearly with the provider. In the college setting, however, a greater degree of responsibility rests with student consumers to maintain certain performance levels of their own. While students have a right to expect a certain level of performance on the part of the institution, the students cannot escape the fact that certain requirements are expected of them. Thus, a strict consumer framework is not entirely applicable in the college setting, and considerable grey area can exist when students make contentions that they are being shortchanged by poor teaching, administrative procedures, etc.

2. The Degree Is a Dual Creation

In the consumer marketplace, a clear distinction exists between who creates the product or service and who uses that creation. A manufacturer creates a product or service and offers it to individuals for a price. As a general rule, the purchaser has no hand in the creation of the product. Unless the user damages a manufactured product, it does not change as a result of its usage. In contrast, however, the product dispensed by colleges and universities is a mutual creation. Specifically, the college degree or licensing certificate is packaged mutually by the institution and its students. Attainment of a college degree is realized as much by the input of the student (examinations, term papers, lab experiments, class discussion, etc.) as by the role of the various instructors and administrators. As a result, it is difficult to prove that any two B.A. degrees, even if granted by the same institution, are alike. In short, colleges must not be boxed into situations that force them to advertise the value of particular programs with respect to occupational implications. Prospective employers judge the credentials of student applicants as much as, if not more than, the institutions from which they are graduated.

3. There Is No Warranty

In the general marketplace, we can think of a familiar consumer protection that is not accorded college students—the warranty. In actuality, the warranty is a protection more for the *seller* than for the *consumer.* It usually indicates that, after a specified time, the product can fall apart without any obligation forced on its manufacturer. In effect, it is the seller who is protected in the long run. After a brief period, the consumer is left powerless. In the educational setting, the college is not protected by a warranty which indicates that the result of its service need only work for a brief, specified time. Students and the general public expect colleges to provide some sort of preparation for life and tend to hold the failings of colleges accountable for a far longer period than we expect of consumer products in general. In fact, the best an educational institution can hope to do is alter its programs, when funds permit, to reflect a constantly changing occupational marketplace. Consequently, the choice of degree or program of study places as much responsibility on the student to seek information as it does on the institution to provide it.

4. The College Is not Necessarily Selling Anything

There is never any doubt in the general marketplace that the producer is selling either a product or a service. In the academic setting, the notion has arisen that colleges and universities are also placing a commodity on sale. Consumer advocates would have us believe that education is a product that is dispensed, quite simply, for a price. This argument, however, is strained at best. As long as colleges do not make such claims, education cannot be regarded as a commodity since there exists no way to measure the absolute value of a degree or certificate. Such value is dependent on a set of specifications that result from the interplay of individual students with a whole set of instructors, textbooks, outside activities, facilities, and resources. In short, students take what they choose from their educational experiences. Just what is sold can never be defined.

5. The Problem of Profit

A final way in which consumer advocates cannot reconcile the uniqueness of educational institutions centers around the question of profit. In the general community, products and services are offered to the public with the purpose of providing a profit for the producer. With the exception of proprietary institutions, the same condition simply does not hold true for colleges and universities. Consequently, decisions on how much to bill for tuition, room, board, etc. are predicated on providing educational services at the lowest possible cost. The financial records of institutions are usually available to public scrutiny in ways that are not available to the general consumer who has a complaint against a manufacturing company. Thus, the traditional decision made by colleges to bill all students for campus activities is predicated, not on reasons designed to raise income, but on the promise that such activities enhance the educational opportunities of all students, both participants and nonparticipants. While I am certain that abuses exist, it can be said that the profit motive provides a unique distinction which separates educational institutions from strict consumer comparisons.

While the major thrust of the student consumerism movement in higher education has been a much needed phenomenon, the time has come to reassess its impact in light of the nature of educational institutions. If the relationship between college and student is developed further in a strict consumer framework, we risk losing a number of important features of colleges by developing a legalistic orientation designed to satisfy external regulations. As a result, colleges could lose their uniqueness and ability to operate independently in the pursuit of knowledge. In short, the ability of institutions to educate men and women would diminish in such a framework. The pluralism among American colleges and universities would tend to disappear as institutions conform to externally invoked regulations and guidelines.

In conclusion, it is acknowledged that the consumerism movement in higher education continues to serve a useful purpose. Among other things, it has alerted colleges to assess more carefully their roles in society at large. At the same time, it should also be acknowledged that further developments toward consumerism should be advocated only after taking into consideration the perspective that we are dealing with unique institutions which mission is not to sell, but to educate.

The Student as Consumer: The Implications and Limitations of a Metaphor

◆

JILL J. MCMILLAN AND GEORGE CHENEY

The metaphor of "Student as Consumer" appeared upon the social horizon in North America and Western Europe seemingly for all the right reasons: the responsibility of higher education to its public, the attendant accountability, an interest in practical applications of knowledge, and spiraling increases in the cost of going to college. Widespread adoption of the metaphor, however, can produce some negative educational consequences. Drawing upon the literatures of organizational studies, education, communication and rhetoric, we trace the rise of the student consumer metaphor, explore its limitations, and suggest alternatives to its use. Specifically, we argue that this metaphor (a) suggests undue distance between the student and the educational process; (b) highlights the promotional activities of professors and promotes the entertainment mode of classroom learning; (c) inappropriately compartmentalizes the educational experiences as a product rather than a process; and (d) reinforces individualism at the expense of community. We conclude with a consideration of a more embracing model of the learning process which we term "critical engagement."

We rely so heavily on metaphor that we often overlook its powerful and practical role in our discourse. Euphemisms such as the currently popular organizational terms "downsizing" or "rightsizing" become so widely accepted that many users forget the old-fashioned and more brutally direct terms "firing" and "layoffs." And, every organizational member recognizes and has learned to respond appropriately (i.e., in the organizationally expected way) to such potent expressions as "We've got to destroy the competition"; "Her power rose yesterday"; and "This negotiation is just a game." Also metaphors migrate from one domain of human activity to another: for example, "blow-by-blow," "networking," and "dead wood." These and other metaphors can be compelling to users and bearers, not only in the sense of making conversation or written speech more lively, but also in winning an argument or altering a viewpoint (see Lakoff & Johnson, 1980).

JILL J. MCMILLAN *(Ph.D., University of Texas) is an Associate Professor of Speech Communication at Wake Forest University, Winston-Salem, NC 27109. George Cheney (Ph.D., Purdue University) is an Associate Professor in the Department of Communication Studies at University of Montana, Missoula, MT 59812. Earlier drafts of this paper were presented at the annual Macromarketing Conference, Boulder, CO, August 1994, the annual meeting of the International Communication Association, Albuquerque, May 1995, and the annual meeting of the Speech Communication Association. San Antonio, TX, November 1995.* From Communication Education, *January 1996.*

It is now commonplace in the scholarly literature to observe that metaphors and other tropes and figures do more than simply decorate discourse (see Burke, 1945/1969). Still, we often fail to recognize how these compelling metaphors actually contribute to our knowledge of who we are, both individually and collectively. As Bellah, Madsen, Sullivan, Swindler, and Tipton (1991) observe:

> . . . While we in concert with others create institutions, they also create us: they educate us and form us—especially through the socially enacted metaphors they give us, metaphors that provide normative interpretations of situations and actions. (p. 12)

The metaphor of organization as machine, for example, arose early in this century and eventually came to dominate not only theorizing about worklife but also managerial practice. Today, as the century draws to a close, the same metaphor is prevalent in business, government, education, athletics, health care and other institutional contexts. In fact, its implications continue to be far-reaching, especially in terms of how the metaphor casts the role of the individual person, the organizational member.

The initially appealing metaphor of "student as consumer" has found its way into the vocabulary and practice of the educational institution and it suggests questionable practical and social consequences for all constituents. From a Southeastern school system which touts "School work is our work" and plasters stickers to that effect on student lunchboxes to the lofty forum of the American Association of Higher Education (AAHE), the "student as consumer" metaphor increasingly has found traction in public discourse. In fact, for the last few years, the AAHE, itself a prominent force in education and a source of national standards for many in higher education, has virtually adopted the metaphor. In the 1990's, the student/client/consumer metaphor has been especially prevalent as the AAHE has explored assessment of education outcomes. Now, for many, assessment *equals* the specific application of the student/client/consumer metaphor for program evaluation.

We argue in this essay that all of us concerned with education ought to take a closer look at the currently popular model of "student as consumer," a metaphor which appeared in the 1980s seemingly for all the right reasons—responsibility, accountability and practical relevance, to mention a few—but whose popularity and institutionalization threatens to reshape educational philosophy and process in some rather alarming ways. It may seem a bit of a stretch to lay the potential for such drastic organizational restructuring at the feet of one small metaphor. If we believe, however, that we have a certain tendency to *become* what we *say we are,* then perhaps such attribution is not so far-fetched. Our analysis is premised on just such ideas: that language is powerful, both descriptively and prescriptively; that in particular ways it can shape the way we think and act, especially in terms of the application of compelling labels and categories; that it announces what we know and how we know it, often embodying or promoting the taken-for-granted quality of our collective understandings; and that when collectively we come to share a linguistic construction, language shapes our institutions as well—in that the very distinctions and classifications we make come to affect our future thinking and behaviors in much the same way as a rule can come to "rule" its creators (see Douglas, 1986).

To advance our basic argument here, we will explore the limitations of the student-as-consumer metaphor and suggest alternatives to its use. . . .

Limitations of the Student-as-Consumer Metaphor

As is the case with most metaphors, there is nothing inherently wrong with the "student as consumer." With Joan Stark (1977), we believe that educational institutions should be held accountable for the goods and services that they provide: that is, they should be willing to describe their services, announce the price, specify outcomes, participate in assessment, and provide channels for complaints. Like William Massy (1989), we believe that educational institutions should adapt to the needs and interests of their constituencies. In other words, changing social and cultural trends, such as multi-culturalism and affirmative actions, should be assessed and often appropriately assimilated into the academic and social life of the institution. Along with Derek Bok (quoted in McMillen, 1991), we believe that organizations should generate and use their financial resources responsibly. While the lure of television revenues for big-time athletics or the increasing appetite for profits from scientific study may be appealing, educational institutions owe it to their constituencies to preserve their financial as well as their philosophical integrity. Like John Farago (1982), we believe that academics should not cloister themselves away from the activities and concerns of the "real world," from which their student charges come and to which most must return—hopefully with a job. Educational institutions should acknowledge the cold realities of a turbulent job market which may face students and their parents, rather than treating such concerns as superficial and shallow. Finally, we agree with Frank Riessman (1988) that we are obligated to train students "to find and raise their voices" even when what they say is disturbing. In short, our quarrel is not with the positive aspect of accountability and responsiveness that the consumer metaphor highlights; it is rather with those aspects of the educational process which the metaphor obscures or dismisses.

1. The student-as-consumer metaphor suggests undue distance between the student and the educational process. At the same time, the widespread adoption of the metaphor can undermine other organizational relationships: notably, those between faculty and administrators.
There is a rather natural temptation to treat organizations as boxes and their "environments" as everything outside. In fact, the organization-as-container metaphor went unquestioned in the writings of organizational theory until very recently (Cheney & Christensen, in press). However, the container metaphor is

limited in its suggestion that the boundaries of an organization really are fixed and perhaps even impermeable. In fact, the organization's identity, and therefore many of its activities, make sense *only in reference* to a larger environment. This is the case for any type of organization, but it is acutely relevant to *service* organizations such as schools, counseling centers, and advertising firms in which the "client" should be considered both a temporary member of the organization *and* an inhabitant of the larger environment "out there" (see Cheney, Block and Gordon, 1986). Such persons may regard themselves as *de facto* but unpaid (and often *paying*) members of the organization, especially if their association with it spans some months or even some years. In the case of student-clients, their dual status in a university, their ambiguous roles and their goals which are only partially aligned with those of the institution, are misrepresented by the metaphor which portrays students as "customers" alone. In fact, it is important for the advancement of higher education that students fulfill both roles simultaneously.

Because of students' confusing status in the organizational scheme, they are likely to have only partial commitment to the wider goals of the institution. Furthermore, they may shun the role of "co-creators" of the educational experience (Pernal, 1977). Keeping the educational process somewhat at arm's length, students may approach the university as they might a McDonald's drive-through window: selecting an option with little thought to the process that created the Big Mac or the Quarter Pounder. If students internalize the "outsider-consumer" identity, their attitude may tend toward that of a student representative to a recent faculty meeting at the first author's institution. When asked if she had any insights into why students were not signing up for advising appointments, she replied: "They are paying fifteen thousand to go here; they expect to see you whenever they want to." Even if their attitude is less consumer-oriented than that represented above, students may regard their confusing boundary status and temporary tenure as reason enough to withhold participation in the short-term planning of their school, and they and their parents may even become litigious if they believe that they have been victimized by "educational malpractice."

The consumer metaphor can adversely affect other organizational relationships as well: for example, those between administration and faculty. Keat (1990) argues that as the role of the "customer" becomes inflated, a greater degree of managerial interference may be expected. The reason for the increased control is that faculty are not viewed as having a high degree of autonomy in such a system. Thus, the cost-conscious, market-wise college president and administration may become more heavy-handed in surveillance over all aspects of academic life. . . .

2. The student-as-consumer metaphor excessively fosters the self-promotional activities of professors and at the same time promotes the entertainment model of learning.
Professors have recently displayed careerism and professional myopia consistent with the market imperative. A new breed of faculty has been "possessed by

a vertical vision and career opportunities," in which the nebulous contract which is struck with the institution seeks to maximize income and minimize teaching responsibilities (Bledstein, 1976, p. 394). Talk of professors "marketing" themselves as commodities is now common in the academy. In fact, those who reject this strategy are often ridiculed as naïve and unrealistic. Farago (1982), himself an academic, puts the matter even more cynically. He believes that faculty members have historically prostituted themselves for student dollars in order to lead the cloistered life of autonomy and reflection: that our disappointment with our student-consumers is really anger at ourselves for having sold out.

Furthermore, when students are "consumers," teachers become vendors hawking their wares, a role which often frustrates and compromises them. In the age of rampant visual stimulation and sound bites, faculty members often identify more with Laurel and Hardy than with Aristotle or Kant. Neil Postman (1985) is one who has argued persuasively that the educational institution has been profoundly affected by the ascendancy of the televison medium, placing a new premium upon ad hoc, non-sequential learning, simplistic content, and the fast-paced visual stimulation to which television watchers have been acculturated. Postman laments:

> . . . they [students] will have learned that learning is a form of entertainment or, more precisely, that anything worth learning can take the form of entertainment, and ought to. And they will not rebel if their English teacher asks them to learn the eight parts of speech through the medium of rock music. Or if their social studies teacher sings to them the facts about the war of 1812. Or if their physics comes to them on cookies or T-shirts. Indeed, they will expect it. (p. 154)

3. The student-as-consumer metaphor inappropriately compartmentalizes the educational experience as a product as opposed to a process.
Not only does the consumer metaphor divide organizational membership over the matter of basic goals, it tends to recast those goals as well. While classical education sought to prepare an individual for citizenship, contemporary education tends to train for a job (Geiger, 1980). And those of us who have too long played the role of "deep pockets" to our children wonder what can be wrong with such pragmatism. Of course, we want our youth to be prepared for the job market, to be capable of making a good living for themselves and their families. And, we must both recognize and adapt to dramatic and sometimes brutal transformations of the U.S. workplace today (see, e.g., Rifkin, 1995). Increasingly, however, even colleges that espouse liberal learning seem only to be way stations on the way to "the job" (Riesman, 1980, pp. 312-13). In the last twenty years, business and management majors have doubled, mainly at the expense of history, philosophy, and English. In 1992, out of some 1.1 million bachelors' degrees awarded, one-quarter, or 256,000 students received B.A.'s in business and management—compared to 7,500 in philosophy and religion (Staff, 1994, *Chronicle of Higher Education,* p. 31). Jacoby argues, "We

have a zillion students—new crops graduate each year—adept at spreadsheets and risk management and fewer and fewer who know something of the Middle East or even American literature" (1991, p. 291). And what are we giving up by these wholesale defections to the marketplace? Bellah et al. (1991) argue that we are trading in "morally and socially sensitive people capable of responsible interaction" (pp. 177-178) for individuals who regard their brains as mere "commodities" (Harman & Hormann, 1993; Rich, 1979).

Critics denounce the wholesale capitulation of the academy to outside forces as a loss of integrity (Jacoby, 1991). As a result, some argue that we have yielded our "expertise" in favor of student "equality" (for a discussion of the tension between these two values, see Billig, Condor, Edwards, Gane, Middleton, & Radley, 1987). Stanford's William Massy (1989) claims, ". . . tastes have changed: people used to be interested in the classics; now they are interested in making money. . . . We need to provide an interesting menu at the university. . . . If they don't like the menu, we have an obligation of change it" (p. 2). Consistent with this interpretation, many observers suggest that the pendulum moves back and forth: that a renewed interest in a broad liberal-arts education may soon be upon us. In fact, some recent surveys of CEO's show a preference for broadly educated students. Students, however, apparently need more convincing (Butcher, 1990).

In a study of twenty-eight liberal arts institutions, Ragan and McMillan (1989) found that a predominant theme of the public discourse of the schools included equally strong appeals to both a classical and a vocational education. In a sort of "all things to all people" tone, the schools consistently tout their classical roots while promising market skills as well. Ragan and McMillan concluded that these institutions have indeed adapted to the fiercely competitive academic marketplace, while glossing over the fact that the two somewhat contradictory claims which they have woven together so artfully may not always harmoniously coexist in pedagogical practice.

Organizational theorists (e.g., Kaldor, 1971; Stampfl, 1978) warn that disturbing things happen when organizations become too preoccupied with the marketplace: namely, they no longer are able to set their own goals, they cannot capitalize on their own unique strengths, they are unable to predict and to plan, and they may strike dangerous compromises in their own activities in order to serve the whims of the public. In a poignant example, Carnegie-Mellon University's academic units, traditionally called simply "departments," are now commonly referred to as "profit centers." Jacoby (1991) warns that in search of the action, the modern university may have lost its soul (p. 292).

Thus far, we have tended to focus on the implications of the student-as-consumer metaphor for the professor and for the administrator. But, the potential problems with this model become even more apparent when we attend to what it means for the student. For example, those students who have internalized the consumer mentality are usually content to lay back and wait for the "quick information fix" (Martin, 1991, p. 35) which they believe they are due. Adrienne Rich (1979) describes the consumer mentality as one in which students expect to receive an education rather than to claim one: to be "acted upon" rather than to "act" in the pursuit of their educational goal (p. 231). Indeed student . . . "consumers" expect an exchange between the teacher and student which is increasingly monologic and unidirectional; in fact they may demand it. The first author received some criticisms of the portion of a recent course in which students were asked to give class reports. The complaints went something like this: "We didn't sign up to hear what our classmates have to say; we want to hear from you." Of course, the pedagogical sub-text in these comments supports the spoon-feeding approach to learning, the one-way transfer. The position is one of an "academic bystander," waiting to be presented with the most attractive academic option, rather than a co-participant in the transactional enterprise of learning (Pernal, 1977; Rich, 1979).

Riesman (1980) claims that in the numerous interviews which he has done with college students perhaps the most frequent complaint is that they are "bored"—by a professor who speaks in a monotone, reads from ancient lecture notes, and gives examinations that are farcically easy. Rarely do students cite their own inaction or lack of accountability as the problem. . . .

4. The student-as-consumer metaphor reinforces individualism at the expense of community.

Consumerism is self-centered (Lasch, 1979; Levine, 1980; Schmookler, 1993); being "first in line" for The Sale, getting the "best price," receiving "top dollar," "beating out the competition," and "winning the bid." Each of these consumer mantras suggests a zero-sum mentality in which individuals must compete with one another for scarce resources. Indeed, some may argue that consumerism and competition are difficult to disentangle in the happy world of supposedly free enterprise, and that young people must learn both lessons well and without question.

But have we overdone it in the halls of learning where we claim to promote social cohesion and cooperation? Have we taught "getting ahead" so early and so well that subsequent attempts at community have no chance? Alfie Kohn (1986), in his persuasive book, *No Contest: The Case Against Competition,* argues that the message that competition is "appropriate, desirable, required, and even unavoidable is drummed into us from nursery school to graduate school." It is, argues Kohn, "the sub-text of every lesson" (p. 25). And especially in higher education, the connection is drawn by students again and again that it might be nice to cooperate, but that sort of behavior just will not fly in the "real world."[7] Psychologist Elliot Aronson (1976) says that such individualistic notions form early:

> If you are a student who knows the correct answer and the teacher calls on one of the other kids, it is likely that you will sit there hoping and praying that the kid will come up with the wrong answer so that you will have a chance to show the teacher how smart you are. . . . Indeed, [children's] peers are their enemies—to be beaten. (p. 153, p. 206).

Alternatives to the Student-as-Consumer Metaphor

We have sought to demonstrate how the consumer metaphor has come to the academy and has influenced the perceptions and actions of all its constituencies: administration, faculty, students, and community alike. We have applauded the responsiveness and accountability which the metaphor calls for, but have decried its distancing, fracturing effect on organizational actors; its spotlighting of professor's self-promotion and entertainment; its "packaging" of the pedagogical process itself; and its emphasis on "meism" at the expense of the wider social good. At times we have perhaps overstated our case against the student-as-consumer metaphor, but we have done so to make our point clearly and forcefully and in the interest of provoking debate and discussion.

Our answers to the dilemma which we have raised are modest and they are few. They also are confined to what we know best, rhetoric and communication. There seem to be at least three suggestions which make sense, and we direct them to academics and non-academics alike:

1. Be alert to the power of language and deliberate about linguistic choices.

Numerous writers (Beattie, 1987; Fassel, 1990; Schaef, 1987) have suggested that distraction has virtually become an American way of life, and we have learned to do it well—with TV "channel surfing," with alcohol and drugs, with technology, with work, with gambling, and even with more positive things such as health and fitness. When we stop "paying attention," argue Bellah et al. (1991), we diminish our collective intelligence, feeling, and moral sensitivity, and our social institutions become weakened and impoverished. More directly to our point, Schmookler (1993) suggests that we should especially keep a watch out for the "invisible sleight of hand" of the Market, which may appear to give us choices, but which may in fact create a world that we would not opt for if we were truly "free to choose and if we were wise" (p. 13).

Metaphors, too, bear watching and listening. How are they behaving? What might they be hiding? And most-important, do they still mean what we want them to mean? A presumably useful metaphor, such as *Student as Consumer,* when we turn our backs on it, can drag us where we really don't want to go (cf. Wendt, 1994).

2. Strike a good balance: be adaptable, but maintain integrity.

Some interesting voices in this debate are those of the organizational theorists who warn: "We don't care what sort of organization you're running; it will run into trouble if you pay too much attention to *any one* constituency" (see Stampfl, 1978). So while those of us in higher education, in the early days of the metaphor, "attended" as we should have to the interests of our student-customers and their parents and to the community at large, this gaze may now be in danger of becoming a preoccupied "stare." From a rhetorical perspective, this preoccupation with the customer may represent excessive pandering to the audience. Wayne Booth (1972) argues that in any formal communication situation, there ought to be a good balance between the rhetorical concerns of *ethos, pathos* and *logos*. In our application, to overemphasize the customer's wishes of the moment is unduly to privilege *pathos* and thereby assume what Booth calls "the advertiser's stance." (One can, of course, err in a more traditional direction, too, by indulging only the informational content of the message, featuring *logos*, and thus assuming "the pedant's stance." Consider, for example, the image of the classics or the chemistry professor who simply reads from the text, maintaining that "the material speaks for itself.") Offering some examples to illustrate the problem, Booth quips that Winston Churchill would hardly be the historical figure that he is had he offered the British people "peace in our time" with some laughs thrown in because a market analysis had shown that "blood, sweat, and tears" was not playing well to the audience (p.223).

Perhaps the educational institution should take heed. The rhetoric of accommodation to the customer may seem to work well in the short term, but the academy cannot not afford "quick fixes" at the expense of its long-term strength and integrity.

3. Explore alternative ways of expressing who we are and what we do.

When a metaphor becomes inappropriate or counterproductive, argues Turbayne (1970), "we should choose a new one" (p. 65); that is, we should look for different words to talk about who we are and what we do in the academy. Fairclough (1993) argues that today the consumer-driven rhetoric of "promotionalism" emanates from our halls of ivy. DuGay and Salaman (1992) remind us that "for an ideology/discourse to be considered hegemonic, it is not necessary for it to be loved" (p. 630). Rather, argues Leys (1990, p. 127, as quoted in DuGay & Salaman) it is merely necessary that it have no serious rival. Perhaps it is time for those of us who know the academic experience best to submit some serious rivals: some different words, some new metaphors, some creative images.

It has been suggested that we leave the "language of the sovereign consumer" (DuGay & Salaman, 1992), which features such terms as "objectivity," "control," "utility," and "quantity" (Bellah, et al., 1991), for "replacement metaphors." (Ivie, 1987) such as schools as "learning communities" (Gamson & Associates, 1984), as "communities of inquirers" (Peirce, quoted in Bellah, et al., 1991), as "communities of interpreters" (Royce, 1916). Even a move from "customer" to "client" would be helpful for education in that the client is not always right! In that vein, Solow (1993) suggests that educators adopt a relationship to students akin to that of a physical trainer; the teacher's role is to guide and direct the exercise of the muscle of the mind: "Having a good instructor," argues Solow, "is necessary to a successful workout, but the benefit of the session also depends on how hard members [students] work . . . No pain, no gain" (p. 1).

The innovative Marketing Department at Odense University, Denmark, practices what the alternatives above are preaching: In response to their students' challenges to adopt, reflexively, a "pure" (i.e., traditional) marketing orientation, the faculty responds:

> We take to be our mission a product orientation: that is to say, the development and presentation of the highest quality product possible in the study of marketing. We invite you, the student, to learn what we have to offer and to help shape and improve that product. (personal conversations with the second author, 1993)

Thus one academic department seeks to demonstrate the redefinition of a metaphor: to show us that it is indeed possible, through intention and through language, to distribute accountability more equitably across stakeholders in the educational process. (Of course, a product metaphor has its limits, too.)

To those who would promote the student as consumer, we offer the counter-proposal of a model of *critical engagement*. In the past, of course, we were content simply to call students "students." Today, however, the felt need to redefine them is an indication of widespread dissatisfaction with institutions of higher learning, just as it is a diffusion of influence of the sovereign Market. We seek a model that does not distance students from the complete educational process, but one that includes, entices and involves them. At the same time, we need to recognize and preserve the legitimate province of expertise and authority in which faculty members do their work. Students can thus be seen as "collaborators in training," emphasizing that they are co-creators of the educational experience even though they have less experience than their instructors; "citizen-specialists," stressing both the breadth and focus of an individual's education; or "apprentices in learning," suggesting an intimate and multi-faceted relationship between the student and the instructor. Clearly, we need to depart from the old-fashioned model of passive information transmission, in which the student is viewed merely as a receptor and mirror, just as we should avoid the temptation to give students' momentary reactions full governing control of the educational process. The ideal of critical engagement is a classroom of dynamic presentations of important and interesting material, lively discussion and debate, open and constructive criticism, and experiences that not only *connect* with the "real" world but also *transform* perspectives on it. Critical engagement suggests mutual respect between teachers and students, common dedication to the process of learning, and allowance for changes in and re-creating of that process. Critical engagement means that students and teachers are "stakeholders" in education—each with interests, energies and talents to contribute. Students in this way can take a certain kind of "ownership" of learning while respecting the individual and collective wisdom of teachers. Above all and regardless of any terms, metaphors, or images we may settle upon, we should engage students, while preserving their right to critique and shape the very educational process in which they participate.

Notes

[1] As Roderick Hart (1990) observes, it is as if we have admitted a sort of linguistic defeat—that "literal" or prosaic language simply is not equal to the task of expressing our complex thoughts and emotions (p. 219). And so we employ colorful metaphors to decrease the distance between fallible symbols and "what we really mean," recognizing (at least at some level) that all language is metaphorical in that we are forced always to describe one thing in terms of another (See Burke, 1945/1969).

[2–6] . . .

[7] See Deetz (1992, p. 28), for a discussion of the political implications of attributing "realness" to the work world and "abstractness" to the educational one.

References

Aronson, E. (1976). *The social animal.* 2d. Ed. San Francisco: W. H. Freeman.

Associated Press. (1994), September 28). Studies: Tuition rising, and colleges spending more on public relations. *Winston-Salem Journal,* p. 22.

Beattie, M. (1987). *Codependent no more.* New York: Harper and Row.

Bellah, R. N., Madsen, R., Sullivan, W., Swidler, A., and Tipton, S. (1985). *Habits of the heart.* Berkley and Los Angeles University of California Press.

Bellah, R. N., Madsen, R., Sullivan, W., Swidler, A., and Tipton, S. (1991). *The good society.* New York: Knopf.

Berger, P. (1969). *A rumor of angels.* Garden City, NJ: Doubleday.

Bevilacqua, J. (1976). The changing relationship between the university and the student: Implications for the classroom and student personnel work. *Journal of College Student Personnel, 17,* 489–494.

Billig, M., Condor, S., Edwards, D., Gane, M., Middleton, D. & Radley, A. (1987). *Ideological dilemmas: A social psychology of everyday thinking.* London: Sage.

Bledstein, B. J. (1976). *The culture of professionalism.* New York: W. W. Norton and Company, Inc.

Booth, W. (1972). The rhetorical stance. In D. Ehninger (Ed.), *Contemporary Rhetoric* (pp. 218–225). Glenview, IL: Scott Foresman and Company.

Burke, K. (1945/1969). *A grammar of motives.* Berkley, CA: University of California Press.

Butcher, W. C. (1990). Applied humanities. *Vital Speeches of the Day,* 623–625.

Campbell, D. N. (1974). On being number one: Competition in education. *Phi Delta Kappan,* 143–146.

Cheney, G. (in progress). Passion, pressure and paradox: Maintaining humanistic values in a competitive worker-cooperative complex. Unpublished manuscript.

Cheney, G., Block, B., & Gordon, B. (1986). Perceptions of innovativeness and communication about innovations: A study of three types of service organizations. *Communication Quarterly, 34,* 213–230.

Cheney, G., & Christensen, L. T. (in press). Identity at issue: Linkages between "internal" and "external" organizational communication. In F. M. Jablin & Linda L. Putnam (Eds.), *Handbook of Organizational Communication: An Interdisciplinary Approach.* Newbury Park, CA: Sage.

Cherry, M. L., & Miller, M. (1994, February 3). The professor: What it is and what it can be. *Old Gold and Black of Wake Forest University,* p. 8.

Coleman, J. S., & Hoffer, T. (1987). *Public and private high schools: The impact of community.* New York: Basic Books.

Coleman, J. S., Hoffer, T., and Kilgore, S. (1982). *High school achievement: Public, private, and Catholic high schools compared.* New York: Basic Books.

Deetz, S. A. (1992). *Democracy in an age of corporate colonization.* New York: State University of New York Press.

Douglas, M. (1986). *Now institutions think.* Syracuse, NY: Syracuse University Press.

DuGay, P. & Salaman, G. (1992). The cult[ure] of the customer. *Journal of Management Studies, 29,* 615–633.

El-Khawas, E. (1975). Consumerism as an emerging issue for postsecondary education. *Educational Record, 56,* 126–131.

El-Khawas, E. (1976). Clarifying roles and purposes. *New directions for higher education, 13,* 35–48.

El-Khawas, E. (1977, November). Management implications of student consumerism. *NACUBO business officer,* 18–21.

Entman, R. M. & Wildman, S. S. (1992). Reconsidering economic and non-economic perspectives on media policy: Transcending the "marketplace of ideas." *Journal of Communication, 42,* 5–19.

Ewen, S. (1976). *Captains of consciousness: Advertising and the social roots of the consumer culture.* New York: McGraw-Hill.

Fairclough, N. (1993). Critical discourse analysis and the marketization of public discourse: The universities. *Discourse and Society, 4,* 133–168.

Farago, J. M. (1982). When they bought in, did we sell out? *Journal of Higher Education, 53,* 701–715.

Fassel, D. (1990). *Working ourselves to death: The high cost of workaholism and the rewards of recovery.* San Francisco: Harper.

Featherstone, M. (1991). *Consumer culture and postmodernism.* London: Sage Publishers Ltd.

Gamson, Z. F. & Associates. (1984). *Liberating education.* San Francisco: Jossey-Bass.

Geertz, C. (1983). *Local knowledge.* New York: Basic Books.

Geiger, R. (1980). *The college curriculum and the marketplace: Academic discipline and the trend toward vocationalism in the 1970's.* Connecticut: Institute for Social and Policy Studies, Yale University.

Harman, W. & Hormann, J. (1993). The breakdown of the old paradigm. In M. Ray & A. Rinzler (Eds.), *The new paradigm in business* (pp. 16–27). New York: Jeremy P. Tarcher/Perigree.

Hart, R. (1990). *Modern rhetorical criticism.* Glenview, IL: Scott Foresman.

Hyde, M. J. (in press). Human being and the call of technology. In J. Wood & R. Gregg (Eds.), *The future of the field: Communication in the twenty-first century.* Cresskill, NJ: Hampton Press.

Ivie, R. L. (1987). Metaphor and the rhetorical invention of cold war "idealists." *Communication Monographs, 54,* 165–182.

Jacoby, R. (1991, Spring). The greening of the university. *Dissent,* 286–292.

Jung, S. & Hamilton, J. (1977). A student information floor. In J. Stark (Ed.), *The many faces of educational consumerism* (pp. xx–xy). Lexington, MA: D. C. Heath & Company.

Kaldor, A. G. (1971). Imbricative marketing. *Journal of Marketing, 35,* 19–25.

Keat, R. (19990). "Introduction," In Keat, R. and Abercrombie, N. (Eds.), *Enterprise Culture* (pp. 3–10). London: Routledge.

Kohn, A. (1986). *No contest: The case against competition.* Boston: Houghton Mifflin Company.

Lakoff, G. and Johnson, M. (1980). *Metaphors we live by.* Chicago: The University of Chicago Press.

Lasch, C. (1979). *The culture of narcissism.* New York: Warner.

Levine, A. (1980). *When dreams and heroes died.* San Francisco: Jossey-Bass.

Lewis. L. S. and Altbach, P. G. (1994, January–February). The true crisis on campus. *Academe, 24–26.*

Leys, C. (1990). Still a question of hegemony. *New Left Review, 180,* 119–128.

Martin, M. (1991, April). Catering to the consumer. *Wilson Library Bulletin, 34–35, 131.*

Massy, W. (1989, January). Stanford school of education, a supplement of the *Stanford Observer,* p. 2.

McKitterick, J. B. (1958). What's the marketing management concept? In F. M. Bass (Ed.), *The frontiers of marketing thought and science* (pp. 71–82). Chicago: American Marketing Association.

McMillan, J. J. (1987). In search of the organizational persona: A rationale for studying organizations rhetorically. In L. Thayer (Ed.), *Organizations–Communication: Emerging perspectives* (pp. 21–45). Norwood, NJ: Ablex.

McMillen, L. (1991, April 24). Quest for profits may damage basic values of universities, Harvard's Bok warns. *The Chronicle of Higher Education, 37,* A21, A31.

Oxford Dictionary of English Etymology (1966/1979). Oxford, England: Oxford University Press.

Paglia, C. & Postman, N. (1991, March). She wants her T.V.! He wants his book! *Harper's,* 44–55.

Penn, J. R. & Franks, R. G. (1982). Student consumerism in an era of conservative politics. *National Association of Student Personnel Administrators Journal, 19*(3), 28–37.

Pernal, M. (1977, Summer). Has student consumerism gone too far? *College Board Review,* 2–5.

Postman, N. (1985). *Amusing ourselves to death.* New York: Penguin.

Ragan, S. L. & McMillan, J. J. (1989). The marketing of the liberal arts. *Journal of Higher Education, 60,* 682–703.

Rich, A. (1979). Claiming an education. In A. Rich (Ed.), *On lies, secrets, and silence: Selected prose 1966–1978* (pp. 231–235). New York: Norton.

Riesman, D. (1980). *On higher education: The academic enterprise in an era of rising student consumerism.* San Francisco: Jossey-Bass Inc., Publishers.

Riessman, F. (1988). The next stage in education reform: The student as consumer. *Social Policy, 18*(4), 2.

Rifkin, J. (1995). *The end of work.* New York: Tarcher/Putnam.

Royce, J. (1916). *The hope of the great community.* New York: MacMillan.

Schaef, A. W. (1987). *When society becomes an addict.* San Francisco: Harper and Row.

Schmookler, A. B. (1993). *The illusion of choice: how the market economy shapes our destiny.* Albany, NY: State University of New York Press.

Smith, R. C. & Eisenberg, E. M. (1987). Conflict at Disneyland: A root-metaphor analysis. *Communication Monographs, 54,* 367–380.

Solomon, R., & Solomon, J. (1993). *Up the university.* Reading, MA: Addison-Wesley.

Solow, J. (1993, February). Passive vs. active learning. Paper presented at the conference *Learning and Iowa: Transcending tradeoffs between teaching and research,* Iowa City, Iowa.

Staff. (1994). The nation: Students. *The Chronicle of Higher Education, 41,* (1), 31.

Stampfl, R. (1978). Structural constraints, consumerism, and the marketing concept. *Michigan State University Business Topics, 26,* 5–16.

Stark, J. S. (1977). *The many faces of educational consumerism.* Lexington, MA: D. C. Heath and Company.

Turbayne, C. M. (1970). *The myth of the metaphor.* (rev. ed.). Columbia, SC: University of South Carolina Press.

Wendt, R. F. (1994). Learning to "walk the talk": A critical tale of the micropolitics at a total quality university. *Management Communication Quarterly, 8*(1), 5–45.

Customers and Markets

◆

CRAIG SWENSON

Most academic conferences these days include a paper in which the presenter calls on higher education to "respond to the needs of the market" and to "treat students as customers." As you listen, you can sense the hair rising on the backs of professorial necks.

During the coffee break following one such presentation, I overheard two professors conducting a postmortem. To view students as customers, one argued, leads inevitably to pandering. Students don't know what they don't know. That's the teacher's job—to guide them. All this talk about being responsive to the market, the other suggested, is about economics pure and simple. It has little to do with education. "The market," he said, paraphrasing Charles Dickens' famous observation about the law, "is an ass."

It was, frankly, a troubling conversation—one I've thought about many times since. I don't lack some sympathy for the view of these colleagues. A nostalgic part of me wants the campus to be a cloistered walk, a retreat from the market's incessant clamor. Students should come as intent on preparing to make a life as they are to make a living. Corporations should value as "skilled" employees who have drunk deeply from the well of knowledge and have learned to think broadly and critically.

I'm also a realist. Upwards of half our college and university students are now of the age group we used to refer to as nontraditional—of those, four out of five work full-time. Most will tell you they returned to college to better their economic lot in life. It's difficult to argue that these students shouldn't be viewed as intelligent consumers of higher education, even though doing so appeals to traditional, sometimes paternalistic views of the student-faculty relationship.

As adults, they return to school because they choose to, not to satisfy some coming-of-age ritual. Presumably, their greater life experience makes them abler to participate in determining their own educational needs. They've earned that right by virtue of being grown-up.

At a different level, a profound social transformation has accompanied our shift from a manufacturing to an information economy. If society has changed, it seems naïve to expect that its institutions wouldn't adapt and evolve as well. It seems clear, for example, that our economic future requires a workforce whose members have skills that are in many ways quite different from their predecessors.

"Knowledge" workers must be at once technically skilled and broadly educated. If knowledge doubles every seven years, it no longer seems possible

CRAIG SWENSON *is Regional Vice President at the University of Phoenix. From* Change, *September/ October 1998.*

for a person to learn the "body of knowledge" of a discipline. Rather, students will need increasingly to understand the foundation of a subject as well as how to access and how to use new knowledge as it comes available. Should we be surprised to find, then, that preparing adults who already have many of these skills will require us to change some of our own traditional practices? . . .

Customers as Consumers of Products

To the degree—as my coffee-break colleagues noted—that students "don't know what they don't know," it would be improper to allow them to dictate the specifications of the educational product. In the long run, customers would lose respect of an organization or its product if R&D or quality control were put in the hands of amateurs with short-term agendas. That's true of the college curriculum as well. The faculty can never abdicate its responsibility to ensure that what we teach reflects the hierarchy of knowledge in our disciplines.

What customer-driven organizations know, however, is that giving voice and listening to the people you serve is always essential and pays dividends. This is especially true in fields like health care and education, where the end "product" (health, learning) depends on the customer's active participation. In classrooms, for example, it's tempting for professors to assume that they are the ultimate experts on every topic and how it should be learned. With large numbers of adult students in our classrooms, though, it's likely that on any given night someone in class knows more from direct experience about a particular subject than the professor does. At the same time, faculties dismiss at their peril what students know about their own learning styles and needs.

When creating the 777, we might note, Boeing invested heavily in consulting not only with the airlines that would buy the planes, but with passengers who would fly in it. It's difficult to imagine Boeing adopting a customer's product suggestion that would endanger anyone's safety. But the engineers who designed that plan reported surprise at all the things they hadn't thought of. Their willingness to listen resulted in a superior aircraft.

Customers as Consumers of Services

When it comes to viewing customers as consumers of a service, most of us would agree that the customer is at least usually right. That's what each of us feels, isn't it, when we are on the receiving end of a service? We're quick to condemn the discourteous, slow, or unresponsive service we receive at a bank, service station, or department store. Why shouldn't students feel the same way about the services provided by our institutions?

With this distinction in mind, it seems fair to ask what students are entitled to by virtue of being customers of higher education. Further, in what ways are the organizations that employ our graduates also our customers? Here are five ways that colleges and universities can appropriately respond to students and their employers.

1. Create a culture that focuses on student learning instead of teaching.

In college, the motto of my accounting teachers was, "cover the material." I'm not suggesting that they didn't know their stuff—quite contrary. It just seemed that getting through the text by the end of the quarter was the goal—if students learned some accounting along the way, that was nice too.

But whose goal—and what customer was thus served? The goal of postsecondary educators should be that every one of our graduates knows and is able to do what his or her degree implies. Our business, then, is learning—not offering courses or covering the material.

Happily, most college classes are taught by instructors who know their subject matter and have high expectations for student performance. These are necessary but insufficient conditions for learning, however. Students also deserve "rich" learning environments. They deserve teachers who use methods that recognize differences in learning styles, and who understand that students will learn more if they are actively involved in their own learning. Students also deserve the right to learn from one another—a process that requires a teacher who can facilitate the exchange of information, ideas, and expertise. . . .

Our students further deserve answers to their questions, a clear understanding of expectations, rich and ample feedback on their work, real access to their teachers, and a learning environment that encourages them to take the personal risk of challenging, questioning, and exploring without fear of ridicule. What we give, we can then expect in return.

The assumptions upon which a learning culture depends are quite different from those for a culture emphasizing teaching. In the former, the student is at the center; in the latter, the subject matter. When student learning is the focus, the yardstick is not "Did I cover the material?" but "Did they learn what they should have?" A student (or employer) expects this. It is always the student's responsibility to learn, but the good sense of that must be met by teachers who will do everything possible to facilitate it.

2. Accept the responsibility to teach more than the course content.

Numerous studies have identified the skills needed for our students to become productive as knowledge workers. Those skills include the ability to write clearly and persuasively, to articulate and present ideas to others orally, to work capably in group and team settings, and to analyze and think critically about problems. A college education should teach these abilities as well as the subject matter of a field. But the attitude of some college teachers is an adamant, "That's not my job."

It is foolhardy to expect that a lone, required course in writing, public speaking, or critical thinking will be sufficient to develop these competencies. They require a longer term process of development (and practice), which means they have to be the aim of a learning process extending across the curriculum. The objection that "we don't have time" to teach these abilities and the subject matter betrays a poverty of aims and an ignorance of the learning process. Indeed, we can use development of these competencies to teach disciplinary knowledge more effectively; as we do so, students become more involved and effective in their own learning. Because of this link, we don't have time not to teach them.

Some students, especially some of the younger ones, won't welcome these ideas—so much for the customer always being right. Teachers will need to persuade students that these activities will prepare them better for the future. Also, students aren't the only customers here. The organizations that do or will employ them, as well as the larger society, are also customers to whom we must respond and these are the very abilities they demand of our graduates.

3. Involve students in establishing the objectives for their learning.

Regardless of age, all of us are students of subjects about which we are ignorant; we have limited abilities to make decisions about what to learn because we don't know what we don't know. However, if the literature of psychology tells us anything, it is that goal setting and task performance go hand in hand. Simply handing all students the same canned task seldom brings the personal engagement necessary to learning, especially for adults. To maximize that engagement, each student should have a part in setting goals for learning and have a measure of independence and control over the doing of assignments. This doesn't mean that teachers should abdicate their responsibility for creating a coherent curriculum. It does mean that they can't hope to do so alone.

4. Make administrative services available to students at times, in places, and in ways that meet their needs.

Treating students as customers requires support services that are convenient and accessible to them. Many colleges and universities enroll increasing numbers of commuting students, many of whom are working adults. For these students, services offered between 9 a.m. and 5 p.m., Monday through Friday, present real barriers to participation.

Students often report being forced to drop out or to take much longer to graduate than hoped because classes are often available only during "normal" business hours or only during semesters when certain professors are around. They might prefer to buy books on the way home from work or, better still, by phone or on the Internet; they can't afford to take off work to meet with an academic counselor at 10 in the morning. Soon enough, an institution's commuters come to see responses to their needs taking a back seat to those they perceive to be the real customers of the institution—its faculty and administrators.

Having customers implies giving prompt, courteous, and responsive service. It suggests following through on our commitments to them, returning their phone calls, and not making them feel they are bothering us (as in "This would be a great place to work if it weren't for those—ed students"). It requires that we treat them as we expect to be treated when we are on the receiving end of a service.

5. Listen to the corporate customer.

In my interactions with colleagues who've spent most of their adult lives in higher education, I often sense condescension toward people who chose business as a career. Too many professors think they are better and smarter than those who chose the other path—that higher education is a purer, worthier pursuit.

But my executive friends are as bright, capable, well-rounded, and virtuous as my professor friends. As responsible executives, they know what they need in employees and don't think it too much to ask that higher education assume a share of the burden for preparing them. In many cases, they're footing the bill for their employees' education. They've also found educators who are arrogant and unwilling to listen when they try to make this point.

Contrary to academic belief, business people do not want narrowly educated employees. They recognize the value of people who understand more than just their own jobs. And they believe that the practical and the theoretical can indeed be married. Some give and take on both sides, then, could result in real improvement in the product of higher education.

In sum: having "customers" in higher education doesn't mean pandering. It doesn't mean the customer is always right. It doesn't mean we never say no. It does mean treating people with respect. It means listening and adapting. It means balancing the goals of a liberal education with those of a practical education without diminishing the worth of either.

I believe it is possible to treat students and their employers as customers to be responsive to markets without apology. If higher education won't do so, I'm sure others will.

READINGS 2

Bingeing, Risk, and Public Health

Health and Behavioral Consequences of Binge Drinking in College
A National Survey of Students at 140 Campuses

◆

Henry Wechsler, Andrea Davenport, George Dowdall,
Barbara Moeykens, Sonia Castillo

Objective.—To examine the extent of binge drinking by college students and the ensuing health and behavioral problems that binge drinkers create for themselves and others on their campus.

Design.—Self-administered survey mailed to a national representative sample of US 4-year college students.

Setting.—One hundred forty US 4-year colleges in 1993.

Participants.—A total of 17,592 college students.

Main Outcome Measures.—Self-reports of drinking behavior, alcohol-related health problems, and other problems.

Results.—Almost half (44%) of college students responding to the survey were binge drinkers, including almost one fifth (19%) of the students who were frequent binge drinkers. Frequent binge drinkers are more likely to experience serious health and other consequences of their drinking behavior than other students. Almost half (47%) of the frequent binge drinkers experienced five or more different drinking-related problems, including injuries and engaging in unplanned sex, since the beginning of the school year. Most binge drinkers do not consider themselves to be problem drinkers and have not sought treatment for an alcohol problem. Binge drinkers create problems for classmates who are not binge drinkers. Students who are not binge drinkers at schools with higher binge rates were more likely than students at schools with lower binge rates to experience problems such as being pushed, hit, or assaulted or experiencing an unwanted sexual advance.

Conclusions.—Binge drinking is widespread on college campuses. Programs aimed at reducing this problem should focus on frequent binge drinkers, refer them to treatment or educational programs, and emphasize the harm they cause for students who are not binge drinkers.

From Journal of the American Medical Association, *December 7, 1994.*

Heavy episodic or binge drinking poses a danger of serious health and other consequences for alcohol abusers and for others in the immediate environment. Alcohol contributes to the leading causes of accidental death in the United States, such as motor vehicle crashes and falls.[1] Alcohol abuse is seen as contributing to almost half of motor vehicle fatalities, the most important cause of death among young Americans.[2] Unsafe sex—a growing threat with the spread of acquired immunodeficiency syndrome (AIDS) and other sexually transmitted diseases—and unintentional injuries have been associated with alcohol intoxication.[3-5] These findings support the view of college presidents who believe that alcohol abuse is the number 1 problem on campus.[6]

Despite the fact that alcohol is illegal for most undergraduates, alcohol continues to be widely used on most college campuses today. Since the national study of Straus and Bacon in 1949,[7] numerous subsequent surveys have documented the overwhelming use of alcohol by college students and have pointed to problem drinking among this group.[8] Most previous studies of drinking by college students have been conducted on single college campuses and have not used random sampling of students.[9-12] While these studies are in general agreement about the prevalence and consequences of binge drinking, they do not provide a national representative sample of college drinking.

A few large-scale, multicollege surveys have been conducted in recent years. However, these have not selected a representative national sample of colleges, but have used colleges in one state[3] or those participating in a federal program,[5] or have followed a sample of high school seniors through college.[13]

In general, studies of college alcohol use have consistently found higher rates of binge drinking among men than women. However, these studies used the same definition of binge drinking for men and women, without taking into account sex differences in metabolism of ethanol or in body mass.[3,5,9,12,14-17]

The consequences of binge drinking often pose serious risks for drinkers and for others in the college environment. Binge drinking has been associated with unplanned and unsafe sexual activity, physical and sexual assault, unintentional injuries, other criminal violations, interpersonal problems, physical or cognitive impairment, and poor academic performance.[3-6]

This study examines the nature and extent of binge drinking among a representative national sample of students in US 4-year colleges and details the problems such drinking causes for drinkers themselves and for others on their college campus. Binge drinking is defined through a sex-specific measure to take into account sex differences in the dosage effects of ethanol.

Methods

The Colleges

A national sample of 179 colleges was selected from the American Council on Education's list of 4-year colleges and universities accredited by one of the six regional bodies covering the United States. The sample was selected using probability proportionate to enrollment size sampling. All full-time undergraduate students at a university were eligible to be chosen for this study, regardless of the college in which they were enrolled. This sample contained few women-only colleges and few colleges with less than 1000 students. To correct for this problem, an oversample of 15 additional colleges with enrollments of less than 1000 students and 10 all-women's colleges were added to the sample. Nine colleges were subsequently dropped because they were considered inappropriate. These included seminary schools, military schools, and allied health schools.

One hundred forty (72%) of the final sample of 195 colleges agreed to participate. The primary reason stated for nonparticipation by college administrators was inability to provide a random sample of students and their addresses within the time requirements of the study. The 140 participating colleges are located in 40 states and the District of Columbia. They represent a cross-section of US higher education. Two thirds of the colleges sampled are public and one third are private. Approximately two thirds are located in a suburban or urban setting and one third in a small town/rural setting. Four percent are women-only, and 4% are predominantly black institutions.

When the 55 nonparticipating schools were compared with the 140 in the study, the only statistically significant difference found was in terms of enrollment size. Proportionately fewer small colleges (fewer than 1000 students) participated in the study. Since these were oversampled, sufficient numbers are present for statistical analysis.

Sampling Procedures

Colleges were sent a set of specific guidelines for drawing a random sample of students based on the total enrollment of full-time and undergraduates. Depending on enrollment size, every xth student was selected from the student registry using a random starting point. A sample of undergraduate students was provided by each of the 140 participating colleges: 215 students at each of the 127 colleges, and 108 at each of 13 colleges (12 of which were in the oversample). The final student sample included 28,709 students.

The Questionnaire

The 20-page survey instrument asked students a number of questions about their drinking behavior as well as other health issues. Whenever possible, the survey instrument included questions that had been used previously in other national or large-scale epidemiological studies.[13–14] A drink was defined as a 12-oz. (360-mL) can (or bottle) of beer, a 4-oz. (120-mL) glass of wine, a 12-oz. (360-mL) bottle (or can) of wine cooler, or a shot (1.25 oz. (37-mL) of liquor straight or in a mixed drink. The following four questions were used to assess binge drinking: (1) sex; (2) recency of last drink ("never," "not in past year," "within last year but more than 30 days ago," "within 30 days but more than 1 week ago," or "within week"); (3) "Think back over the last two weeks.

How many times have you had five or more drinks in a row?" (The use of this question, without specification of time elapsed in a drinking episode, is consistent with standard practice in recent research on alcohol use among this population.[3,13,18]); and (4) "During the last two weeks, how many times have you had four drinks in a row (but no more than that)(for women)?" Missing responses to any of these four questions excluded the student from the bingeing analyses.

Students were also asked the extent to which they had experienced any of the following 12 problems as a consequence of their drinking since the beginning of the school year: have a hangover; miss a class; get behind in schoolwork; do something you later regretted; forget where you were or what you did; argue with friends; engage in unplanned sexual activity; not use protection when you had sex; damage property; get into trouble with campus or local police; get hurt or injured; or require medical treatment for an alcohol overdose. They were also asked if, since the beginning of the school year, they had experienced any of the following eight problems caused by other students' drinking: been insulted or humiliated; had a serious argument or quarrel; been pushed, hit, or assaulted; had your property damaged; had to "babysit" or take care of another student who drank too much; had your studying or sleep interrupted; experienced an unwanted sexual advance; or had been a victim of sexual assault or date rape.

The Mailing

The initial mailing of questionnaires to students began on February 5, 1993. By the end of March, 87% of the final group of questionnaires had been received, with another 10% in April and 2% in May and June. There are no discernible differences in bingeing rates among questionnaires received in each of the 5 months of the survey. Mailings were modified to take into account spring break. So that students would be responding about their binge drinking behavior during a 2-week time on campus. Responses were voluntary and anonymous. Four separate mailings, usually 10 days apart, were sent at each college: a questionnaire, a reminder postcard, a second questionnaire, and a second reminder postcard. To encourage students to respond, the following cash awards were offered: one $1000 award to a student whose name was drawn from among students responding within 1 week, and one $500 award and ten $100 awards to students selected from all those who responded.

The Response Rate

The questionnaires were mailed to 28,709 students. Overall, 3082 students were eliminated from the sample because of school reports of incorrect addresses, withdrawal from school, or leaves of absence, reducing the sample size to 25,627. A total of 17,592 students returned questionnaires, yielding an overall student response rate of approximately 69%. The response rate is likely to be underestimated since it does not take into account all of the students who may not have received questionnaires. At 104 of the colleges, response rates were between 60% and 80%, and only six colleges had response rates less than

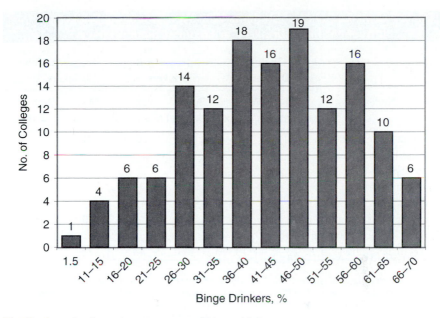

Distribution of colleges by percentage of binge drinkers.

50%. Response rate was not associated with the bingeing rate (i.e., the Pearson correlation coefficient between the binge drinking rate the college and the response rate was 0.06 with a P value of .46).

When responses of early and late responders to the survey were compared, there were no significant differences in the percent of nondrinkers, nonbinge drinkers, and binge drinkers. In the case of 11,557 students who could be classified as early or late responders, there was no significant difference in terms of binge drinking (43% for the early responders vs. 42% for the late responders). An additional short form of the questionnaire was mailed to a segment of students who had failed to return the questionnaire. The rate of binge drinking of these nonresponders did not differ from that of responders to the original student survey.

Data Analysis

All statistical analyses were carried out using the current version of SAS.[19] Comparisons of unweighted and weighted sample results suggested little difference between them, so unweighted results are reported here. Chi-square analyses among students who had a drink in the past year were used to compare nonbinge drinkers, infrequent binge drinkers, and binge drinkers. Binge drinking was defined as the consumption of five or more drinks in a row for men and four or more drinks in a row for women during the 2 weeks prior to the survey. An extensive analysis showed that this sex-specific measure accurately indicates an equivalent likelihood of alcohol-related problems. In this article, the term "binge drinker" is used to refer to students who binged at least

Table 1 Drinking Styles of Students Who Were Nonbinge Drinkers, Infrequent Binge Drinkers, or Frequent Binge Drinkers*

Drinking Styles	Nonbinge Drinkers, %[†]		Infrequent Binge Drinkers, %[∞]		Frequent Binge Drinkers, %[§]	
	Men	Women	Men	Women	Men	Women
	(n = 2539)	(n = 4400)	(n = 1968)	(n = 2130)	(n = 1630)	(n = 1684)
Drank on 10 or more occasions in the past 30 days	3	1	11	6	61	39
Usually binges when drinks	4	4	43	45	83	82
Was drunk three or more times in the past month	2	1	17	13	70	55
Drinks to get drunk[†]	22	18	49	44	73	68

*Chi-square comparisons of students who were nonbinge drinkers, infrequent binge drinkers, and frequent binge drinkers and each of the four drinking styles were significant for men and women separately at $P < .001$. Sample sizes vary slightly for each question because of missing values. Bingeing is defined as four or more drinks for women and five or more drinks for men.

[†]Students who consumed alcohol in the past year, but did not binge.

[∞]Students who binged one or two times in a 2-week period.

[§]Students who binged three or more times in a 2-week period.

Question asked: "On how many occasions have you had a drink of alcohol in the past 30 days?" Response categories were 1 to 2 occasions, 3 to 5 occasions, 10 to 19 occasions, 20 to 39 occasions, and 40 or more occasions.

[†]Says that to get drunk is an important reason for drinking.

once in the previous 2 weeks. Frequent binge drinkers were defined as those who binged three or more times in the past 2 weeks and infrequent binge drinkers as those who binged one or two times in the past 2 weeks. Nonbinge drinkers were those who had consumed alcohol in the past year, but had not binged.

Logistic regression analyses were used to examine how much more likely frequent binge drinkers were to experience an alcohol-related problem or driving behavior compared with nonbinge drinkers, and to compare infrequent binge drinkers with nonbinge drinkers. Odds ratios were adjusted for age, sex, race, marital status, and parents' college education.

In examining secondary binge effects, schools were divided into three groups on the basis of the percentage of students who were binge drinkers at each school. The responses of students who had not binged in the past 2 weeks (including those who had never had a drink) and who resided in dormitories, fraternities, or sororities were compared through χ^2 analyses across the three school types. High-level binge schools (where 51% or more students were binge drinkers) included 44 schools with 6084 students; middle-level binge

Table 2 Risk of Alcohol-Related Problems Comparing Students Who Were Infrequent Binge Drinkers or Frequent Binge Drinkers With Students Who Were NonBinge Drinkers Among College Students Who Had a Drink In The Past Year*

Reporting Problem	Nonbinge Drinkers, % (n = 6894)	Infrequent Binge Drinkers		Frequent Binge Drinkers	
		% (n = 4090)	Adjusted OR (95%)	% (n = 3291)	Adjusted OR (95% CI)
Have a hangover	30	75	6.28 (5.73–6.87)	90	17.62 (15.50–20.04)
Do something you regret	14	37	3.31 (3.00–3.64)	63	8.96 (8.11–9.95)
Miss a class	8	30	4.66 (4.15–5.24)	61	16.58 (14.73–18.65)
Forget where you were or what you did	8	26	3.62 (3.22–4.06)	54	11.23 (10.05–12.65)
Got behind in school work	6	21	3.70 (3.26–4.20)	46	11.43 (10.09–12.94)
Argue with friends	8	22	3.06 (2.72–3.46)	42	7.77 (6.90–8.74)
Engaged in unplanned sexual activity	8	20	2.78 (2.46–3.13)	41	7.17 (6.37–8.06)
Get hurt or injured	2	9	3.65 (3.01–4.43)	23	10.43 (8.70–12.52)
Damage property	2	8	3.09 (2.53–3.77)	22	9.48 (7.86–11.43)
Not use protection when having sex	4	10	2.90 (2.45–3.42)	22	7.11 (6.07–8.34)
Get into trouble with campus or local police	1	4	2.50 (1.92–3.26)	11	6.92 (5.44–8.81)
Require medical treatment of alcohol overdose	<1	<1	NS	1	2.81 (1.39–5.68)
Have five or more alcohol-related problems since the beginning of the school year§	3	14	4.95 (4.17–5.89)	47	25.10 (21.30–29.58)

*Problem occurred not at all or one or more times. Chi-square comparisons of nonbinge drinkers, infrequent binge drinkers, and frequent binge drinkers and each of the problems are significant at P<.001, except for alcohol overdose (P=.002). Sample sizes vary slightly for each problem because of missing values. OR indicates odds ratio: CI, confidence interval. See Table 1 for explanation of drinking classification.

†Adjusted ORs of infrequent binge drinkers vs nonbinge drinkers are significant at P<.001.

‡Adjusted ORs of frequent binge drinkers vs nonbinge drinkers are significant at P<.001, except for alcohol overdose, P<.01.

§Excludes hangover and includes driving after drinking as one of the problems.

Table 3 Alcohol-Related Driving Behavior for a 30-Day Period Comparing Students Who Were Infrequent Binge Drinkers or Frequent Binge Drinkers With Students Who Were Nonbinge Drinkers*

Driving Behavior	Nonbinge Drinkers		Infrequent Binge Drinkers			Frequent Binge Drinkers		
	Men, % (n = 2531)	Women, % (n = 4393)	Men, % (n = 1975)	Women, % (n = 2132)	Adjusted OR (95% CI)[†]	Men, % (n = 1630)	Women, % (n = 1684)	Adjusted OR (95% CI)[∞]
Drove after drinking alcohol	20	13	47	33	5.13 (4.67–5.64)	62	49	10.33 (9.34–11.42)
Drove after having five or more drinks	2	1	18	7	22.23 (16.89–29.26)	40	21	74.30 (56.56–97.58)
Rode with a driver who was high or drunk	7	7	23	22	4.73 (4.20–5.32)	53	48	15.97 (14.22–17.95)

*Chi-square comparisons of nonbinge drinkers, infrequent binge drinkers, and frequent binge drinkers and each of the three driving behaviors were all significant for men and women separately at P<.001. Sample sizes vary slightly for each question because of missing values. OR indicates odds ratio; CI confidence interval. See Table 1 for explanation of drinking classification.

[†]Adjusted OR of infrequent binge drinkers vs. nonbinge drinkers (sex combined) are significant at P<.001.

[∞]Adjusted OR of frequent binge drinkers vs. nonbinge drinkers (sex compared) are significant at P<.001.

410

schools (36% to 50% of students were binge drinkers) included 53 schools with 6455 students; and low-level binge schools (35% or less of students were binge drinkers) included 43 schools with 5043 students (for 10 students, information regarding school of attendance was missing). For two of the problems that occurred primarily or almost exclusively to women (sexual assault and experiencing an unwanted sexual advance), only women were included in the analyses.

Results

Characteristics of the Student Sample

This analysis is based on data from 17,592 undergraduate students at 140 US 4-year colleges. The student sample includes more women (58%) than men (42%), due in part to the inclusion of six all-women's institutions. This compares with national 1991 data that report 51% of undergraduates at 4-year institutions are women.[20] The sample is predominantly white (81%). This coincides exactly with national 1991 data that report 81% of undergraduates at 4-year institutions are white.[20] Minority groups included Asian/Pacific Islander (7%), Spanish/Hispanic (7%), black/African American (6%), and Native American (1%). The age of the students were distributed as follows: 45% younger than 21 years, 38% aged 21 to 23 years, and 17% aged 24 years or more. There were slightly more juniors (25%) and seniors (26%) in the sample than freshmen (20%) and sophomores (19%), probably because 30% of the students were transfers from other institutions. Ten percent of the students were in their fifth undergraduate year of school or beyond. Religious affiliation was discerned by asking students in which of the following religions they were raised: Protestant (44%), Catholic (36%), Jewish (3%), Muslim (1%), other (4%), and none (12%). Religion was cited as an important to very important activity among 36% of the students. Approximately three of five students (59%) worked for pay. Approximately half (49%) of the students had a grade-point average of A, A-, or B+.

Extent of Binge Drinking

Because of missing responses, there were 496 students excluded from bingeing analyses (ie, 17,096 were included). Most students drank alcohol during the past year. Only about one of six (16%) were nondrinkers (15% of the men and 16% of the women). About two of five students (41%) drank but were nonbinge drinkers (35% of the men and 45% of the women). Slightly fewer than half (44%) of the students were binge drinkers (50% of the men and 39% of the women). About half of this group of binge drinkers, or about one in five students (19%) overall, were frequent binge drinkers (overall 23% of the men and 17% of the women).

Binge Drinking Rates at Colleges

The figure shows that binge drinking rates vary extensively among the 140 colleges in the study. While 1% of the students were binge drinkers at the school with the lowest rate of binge drinkers, 70% of students were binge drinkers at the school with the highest rate. At 44 schools, more than half of the responding students were binge drinkers.

When the 140 colleges were divided into levels of bingeing rate, χ^2 analyses showed that several college characteristics were individually associated (at $P<.05$) with bingeing rate. Colleges located in the Northeast or North Central regions of the United States (compared with those in the West or South) or those that were residential (compared with commuter schools, where 90% or more of the students lived off campus)[21] tended to have higher rates of bingeing. In addition, traditionally black institutions and women's colleges had lower binge rates than schools that were not traditionally black or were coeducational colleges. Other characteristics, such as whether the college was public or private and its enrollment size, were not related to binge drinker rates.

Examination of whether college alcohol programs and policies have any association with binge drinking will be presented in a separate publication. There is little evidence to conclude that current policies have had strong impacts on overall drinking levels. Preliminary analyses suggest that individual binge drinking is less likely if the institution does not have any alcohol outlets within 1 mile of campus, or if it prohibits alcohol use for all persons (even those older than 21 years) on campus.

Drinking Patterns of Binge Drinkers

Table 1 indicates that our designations of binge drinker and frequent binge drinker are strongly indicative of a drinking style that involves more frequent and heavier drinking. Furthermore, intoxication (often intentional) is associated with binge drinking in men and women.

Binge drinking is related to age. Students who are in the predominant college age group (between 17 and 23 years) have much higher bingeing rates than older students. However, within the predominant college age group, students who are younger than the legal drinking age of 21 years do not differ in bingeing rates from students aged 21 to 23 years. In contrast to the modest effects of age, there is no relationship between year in school and bingeing, with rates of binge drinking virtually identical among students across the years of college attendance.

Alcohol-Related Health and Other Problems

There is a strong, positive relationship between the frequency of binge drinking and alcohol-related health and other problems reported by the students (Table 2). Among the more serious alcohol-related problems, the frequent binge drinkers were seven to 10 times more likely than the nonbinge drinkers to not use protection when having sex, to engage in unplanned sexual activity, to get

Table 4 Students Experiencing Secondary Binge Effects (Based on Students Who Were Not Binge Drinkers and Living in Dormitories, Fraternities, or Sororities*

Secondary Binge Effect	Low % (n = 801)	Middle % (n = 1115)	Adjusted OR (95% CI)[+]	High % (n = 1064)	Adjusted OR (95% CI)[∞]
			School's Bingeing Level		
Been insulted or humiliated	21	30	1.6 (1.3–2.1)	34	1.9 (1.5–2.3)
Had a serious argument or quarrel	13	18	1.3 (1.0–1.7)	20	1.5 (1.1–2.0)
Been pushed, hit or assaulted	7	10	1.4 (1.0–2.1)	13	2.0 (1.4–2.8)
Had your property damaged	6	13	2.0 (1.4–2.8)	15	2.3 (1.6–3.2)
Had to take care of drunken student	31	47	1.9 (1.6–2.3)	54	2.5 (2.0–3.0)
Had your studying/sleep interrupted	42	64	2.3 (1.9–2.8)	68	2.6 (2.2–3.2)
Experienced an unwanted sexual advance§	15	21	1.7 (1.2–2.3)	2.6	2.1 (1.5–2.8)
Been a victim of sexual assault or date rape	2	1	NS	2	NS
Experienced at least one of the above problems	62	82	2.8 (2.3–3.5)	87	4.1 (3.2–5.2)

*OR indicates odds ratio. CI, confidence interval.
[+]Adjusted ORs of students at schools with middle levels of bingeing vs students at schools with low levels are significant at $P < .05$.
[∞]Adjusted ORs of students at schools with high levels of bingeing vs students at schools with low levels are significant at $P < .05$.
§Based on women only.

into trouble with campus police, to damage property, or to get hurt or injured. A similar comparison between the infrequent binge drinkers and nonbinge drinkers also shows a strong relationship.

Men and women reported similar frequencies for most of the problems, except for damaging property or getting into trouble with the campus police. Among the frequent binge drinkers, 35% of the men and 9% of the women reported damaging property, and 16% of the men and 6% of the women reported getting into trouble with the campus police.

Drinking and Driving

There is also a positive relationship between binge drinking and driving under the influence of alcohol (Table 3). A large proportion of the student population reported driving after drinking alcohol. Binge drinkers, particularly frequent

binge drinkers, reported significantly ($P<.001$) higher frequencies of dangerous driving behaviors than nonbinge drinkers.

Number of Problems

Nearly half (47%) of the frequent binge drinkers reported having experienced
five or more of the 12 problems listed in Table 2 (omitting hangover and
including driving after drinking) since the beginning of the school year,
compared with 14% of infrequent binge drinkers and 3% of nonbinge
drinkers. The adjusted odds ratios indicate that frequent binge drinkers were
25 times more likely than nonbinge drinkers to experience five or more of
these problems, while the infrequent binge drinkers were five times more likely
than nonbinge drinkers to experience five or more problems.

Self-Assessment of Drinking Problems

Few students describe themselves as having a drinking problem. When asked
to classify themselves in terms of their current alcohol use, less than 1% of the
total sample (0.2%), including only 0.6% of the frequent binge drinkers, designated themselves as problem drinkers. In addition, few students have ever
sought treatment for a problem with alcohol.

A somewhat large proportion of students indicated that they had ever had
a drinking problem. Slightly more than one fifth (22%) of the frequent binge
drinkers thought that they ever had a drinking problem, compared with 12%
of the infrequent binge drinkers and 7% of the nonbinge drinkers.

Secondary Binge Effects

Table 4 reports on the percentage of nonbingeing students who experienced
"secondary binge effects," each of eight types of problems due to other
students' drinking at each of the three different school types (ie, schools with
high, middle, and low binge levels). For seven of the eight problems studied,
students at schools with high and middle binge levels were more likely than
students at schools with low binge levels to experience problems as a result of
the drinking behaviors of others. Odds ratios (adjusted for age, sex, race, marital status, and parents' college education) indicated that nonbingeing students
at schools with the high binge levels were more likely than nonbingeing
students at schools with low binge levels to experience secondary binge effects.

The odds of experiencing at least one of the eight problems was roughly
4:1 when students at schools with high binge levels were compared with
students at schools with low binge levels.

Binge Drinking in High School

Most students reported the same drinking behavior in high school as in college.
Almost half (47%) had not been binge drinkers in high school and did not
binge in college, while one fifth (22%) binged in high school and in college.
One fifth (22%) of the students were binge drinkers in college but not in high

school, while 10% were not binge drinkers at the time of the survey in college, but reported having been binge drinkers in high school.

Comment

To our knowledge, this is the first study that has used a representative national sample, and the first large-scale study to measure binge drinking under a sex-specific definition. Forty-four percent of the college students in this study were classified as binge drinkers. This finding is consistent with the findings of other national studies such as the University of Michigan's Monitoring the Future Project, which found that 41% of college students were binge drinkers,[13] and the Core Alcohol and Drug Survey, which found that 42% of college students were binge drinkers.[5] All three studies used a definition of bingeing over a 2-week period, but the other studies used the same five-drink measure for both sexes. Binge drinking was defined in terms of the number of drinks consumed in a single episode. No attempt was made to specify the duration of time for each episode. Future research might examine whether subgroup differences exist in duration and whether such differences are linked to outcomes.

A possible limitation of surveys using self-reports of drinking behavior pertains to the validity of responses; however, a number of studies have confirmed the validity of self-reports of alcohol and substance use.[22-34] Findings indicate that if a self-report bias exists, it is largely limited to the heaviest use groups[25] and should not affect such a conservative estimate of heavy volume as five drinks.

The results confirm that binge drinking is widespread on college campuses. Overall, almost half of all students were binge drinkers. One fifth of all students were frequent binge drinkers (had three or more binge drinking occasions in the past 2 weeks) and were deeply involved in a lifestyle characterized by frequent and deliberate intoxication. Frequent binge drinkers are much more likely to experience serious health and other consequences of their drinking behavior than other students. Almost half of them have experienced five or more alcohol-related problems since the beginning of the school year, one of three report they were hurt or injured, and two in five engaged in unplanned sexual activity. Frequent binge drinkers also report drinking and driving. Three of five male frequent binge drinkers drove after drinking some alcohol in the 30 days prior to the survey, and two of five drove after having five or more drinks. A recent national report that reviewed published studies concluded that alcohol was involved in two thirds of college student suicides, in 90% of campus rapes, and in 95% of violent crime on campus.[26]

Almost a third of the colleges in the study have a majority of students who binge. Not only do these binge drinkers put themselves at risk, they also create problems for their fellow students who are not binge drinking. Students who did not binge and who reside at schools with high levels of binge drinkers were up to three times as likely to report being bothered by the drinking-related behaviors of other students than students who did not binge and who reside at schools with lower levels of binge drinkers. These problems included being pushed, hit, or assaulted and experiencing an unwanted sexual advance.

Effective interventions face a number of challenges. Drinking is not typically a behavior learned in college and often continues patterns established earlier. In fact, one of three students in the present study was already a binge drinker in the year before college.

The prominence of drinking on college campuses reflects its importance in the wider society, but drinking has traditionally occupied a unique place in campus life. Despite the overall decline in drinking in US society, recent time-trend studies have failed to show a corresponding decrease in binge drinking on college campuses.[3,13] The variation in binge drinking rates among the colleges in this study suggest that colleges may unwittingly perpetuate their own drinking cultures through selection, tradition, policy, and other strategies. On many campuses, drinking behavior that would elsewhere be classified as alcohol abuse may be socially acceptable, or even socially attractive, despite its documented implication in automobile crashes, other injury, violence, suicide, and high-risk sexual behavior.

The scope of the problem makes immediate results of any interventions highly unlikely. Colleges need to be committed to large-scale and long-term behavior change strategies, including referral of alcohol abusers to appropriate treatment. Frequent binge drinkers on college campuses are similar to other alcohol abusers elsewhere in their tendency to deny that they have a problem. Indeed, their youth, the visibility of others who drink the same way, and the shelter of the college community may make them less likely to recognize the problem. In addition to addressing the health problems of alcohol abusers, a major effort should address the large group of students who are not binge drinkers on campus who are adversely affected by the alcohol-related behavior of binge drinkers.

This study was supported by the Robert Wood Johnson Foundation. We wish to thank the following persons who assisted with the project: Lloyd Johnston, PhD, Thomas J. Mangione, PhD, Anthony M. Roman, MD, Nan Laird, PhD, Jeffrey Hansen, Avtar Khalsa, MSW and Marianne Lee, MPA.

References

1. US Dept of Health and Human Services. *Alcohol and Health*. Rockville, Md: National Institute on Alcohol Abuse and Alcoholism: 1990.

2. Robert Wood Johnson Foundation. *Substance Abuse: The Nation's Number One Health Problem, Key Indicators for Policy*. Princeton, NJ: Robert Wood Johnson Foundation: October 1993.

3. Wechsler H., Issac N. Binge drinkers at Massachusetts colleges: prevalence, drinking styles, time trends, and associated problems. *JAMA* 1992; 267: 2929–2931.

4. Hanson DJ, Engs RC. College Students' drinking problems: a national study, 1982–1991. *Psychol Rep*. 1992; 71:39-42.

5. Presley CA, Meilman PW, Lyeria R. *Alcohol and Drugs on American College Campuses: Use, Consequence, and Perceptions of the Campus Environment. Volume 1: 1989–1991*. Carbondale, Ill: The Core Institute: 1993.

6. The Carnegie Foundation for the Advancement of Teaching. *Campus Life: In Search of Community.* Princeton, NJ: Princeton University Press; 1990.

7. Straus R., Bacon SD. *Drinking in College.* New Haven, Conn: Yale University Press: 1953.

8. Berkowitz AD, Perkins HW. Problem drinking among college students: a review of recent research. *J Am Coll Health.* 1986:35:21–28.

9. Saltz R, Elandt D. College student drinking studies: 1976-1985. *Contemp Drug Probl.* 1986:13:117–157.

10. Haworth-Hoeppner S., Globetti G., Stem J., Morasco F. The quantity and frequency of drinking among undergraduates at a southern university. *Int J Addict.* 1989:24: 829–857.

11. Liljestrand P. Quality in college student drinking research: conceptual and method-ological issues. *J Alcohol Drug Educ.* 1993:38:1–36.

12. Hughes S., Dodder R. Alcohol consumption patterns among college populations. *J Coll Student Personnel.* 1983:20:257–264.

13. Johnston LD., O'Malley PM., Bachman JG. *Drug Use Among American High School Seniors, College Students, and Young Adults. 1973-1990. Volume 2.* Washington, DC: Government Printing Office: 1991. US Dept of Health and Human Services publication ADM 91–1835.

14. Wechsler H., McFadden M. Drinking among college students in New England. *J Stud Alcohol.* 1979:40:969–996.

15. O'Hare TM. Drinking in college: consumption patters, problems, sex differences, and legal drinking age. *J Stud Alcohol.* 1990:51:536–541.

16. Engs RC, Hanson DJ. The drinking patterns and problems of college students: 1983. *J Alcohol Drug Educ.* 1985:31:65–83.

17. Brennan AF, Walfish S., AuBuchon P. Alcohol use and abuse in college students. I: a review of individual and personality correlates. *Int J Addict.* 1986:21:449–474.

18. Room R. Measuring alcohol consumption in the US: methods and rationales. In: Clark WB., Hilton ME., eds. *Alcohol in America, Drinking Practices and Problems.* Albany: State University of New York Press: 1991:26–50.

19. SAS Institute Inc. *SAS:STAT User's Guide Release 6.03 ed.* Cary, NC:SAS Institute Inc.: 1988.

20. US Dept of Education. *Digest of Educational Statistics.* Washington, DC: National Center of Educational Statistics: 1993:180–205.

21. *Barron's Profiles of American Colleges*: Hauppauge, NY: Barron's Educational Series Inc.: 1992.

22. Midanik L. Validity of self-reported alcohol use: a literature review and assessment. *Br J Addict.* 1988:83:1019–1030.

23. Cooper AM, Sobell MB, Sobell LC, Mausto SA. Validity of alcoholics' self-reports: duration data. *Int J Addict.* 1981:16:401–406

24. Reinisch OJ, Bell RM, Ellickson PL,. *How Accurate Are Adolescent Reports of Drug Use?* Santa Monica, Calif: RAND: 1991. RAND publication N-3189-CHF.

25. Room P. Survey vs sales data for the US Drink Drug Pract Surv. 1971:3:15–16.

26. CASA Commission on Substance Abuse at Colleges and Universities. *Rethinking Rites of Passage: Substance Abuse on America's Campuses.* New York, NY: Columbia University, June 1994.

Robert Wood Johnson Foundation. Substance Abuse: The Nation's Number One Health Problem, Key Indicators for Policy. Princeton, NJ: Robert Wood Johnson Foundation: October 1993.

Purging Bingeing

◆

ED CARSON

Erin and Jason don't think they drink excessively. "When I think of bingeing, I think of people drinking until they puke," says Erin, a 20-year old sophomore at the University of Oregon, adding that she usually stops at six drinks when she goes out on the weekend.

"I think drinking to get really drunk is stupid," says Jason, a 20-year-old junior. So what is a reasonable amount? "I usually have seven or eight beers," he says as he takes a gulp from his sixth glass.

But the public health establishment says both Erin and Jason are binge drinkers, defined as anyone who has had at least five drinks (sometimes four drinks for women) in one sitting during the previous two weeks. College drinking has attracted a lot of attention recently with the release of several studies reporting that some two-fifths of college students are binge drinkers. The studies say virtually all binge drinkers admit suffering some negative consequences, ranging from hangovers to sexual assaults. And they don't hurt just themselves. In a 1994 study by the Harvard School of Public Health, 82 percent of non-binge drinkers living in dorms, fraternities, or sororities said they had experienced "secondhand binge effect." As Selena, an 18-year old Oregon freshman puts it, "You always know when they come back from the bars at 4 a.m. screaming their heads off."

So last year, when the Center on Addiction and Substance Abuse at Columbia University (CASA) claimed the percentage of college women drinking to get drunk had more than tripled during the previous 15 years, the news media were quick to hype the finding that drinking on campus had reached "epidemic proportions." But as Kathy McNamara-Meis revealed in the Winter 1995 *Forbes MediaCritic*, CASA's conclusions were based on a misleading comparison of results from a 1977 survey of all college women and a 1992 survey of freshman women. Since freshmen drink more than any other class, such a comparison would suggest an increase in drunkenness even if nothing had changed. In fact, says David Hanson, a professor of sociology at the State University of New York at Potsdam who has studied alcohol use on campus for more than 20 years, "the evidence shows that the actual trend is as flat as your little sister's chest."

As this episode suggests, the problems associated with college drinking are overstated and misunderstood. Since college students have limited responsibilities, they can usually drink heavily without serious repercussions. Drunken college students do sometimes get into trouble, of course. But this is not a drinking problem; it is a drinking *behavior* problem.

ED CARSON IS *a staff reporter for* Reason. *From* Reason, *December 1995.*

For neoprohibitionists, alcohol itself is the problem. In their eyes, college students are children—children who can vote and serve in the military, but still children—who must be shielded from the pernicious effects of drinking. According to the federal Office for Substance Abuse Prevention, "for kids under 21, there is no difference between alcohol or other drug use and abuse." Yet most college students under 21 don't think they are doing anything wrong by drinking. "I'm not hurting anyone," says Derek, a 20-year old sophomore. "I'm just having a good time." Many college administrators say the 21-year purchase age just makes drinking more attractive.

"The 21 law makes alcohol a forbidden fruit and encourages underage students to drink," says Carl Wartenburg, dean of admissions at Swarthmore College. A 1994 survey by the CORE Institute at Southern Illinois University found that students under 21 drank more, and more often, than older students.

Underage students at the University of Oregon have little trouble obtaining alcohol. Most dorms have a no-use policy, but resident assistants just try to crack down on partying and encourage students to drink off campus. Fake IDs are everywhere. If they don't have IDs, students usually can find a party off campus or get someone older to buy for them.

Students may drink to let off steam, or drink to get drunk, or boast about how much they can drink without puking. But college drinking, by and large, remains social drinking. UO students could buy a half-rack of Henry Weinhard's Ale and drink at home. But instead they pay a lot more to drink at Rennie's or Max's because they want to be around other people.

Drinking isn't only something to do—it's something everyone can do together. It's how many freshmen begin meeting people. "You don't know anybody, and then somebody hands you a beer and pretty soon you're hanging out with a bunch of guys," says Eric, a 19-year old sophomore, remembering his first days in college. Freshmen drink hard early on: A 1995 Harvard study of college freshmen found that 70 percent binge drink in their social circle (and worship once or twice at the Temple of the Porcelain God), many decide to drink infrequently or not at all.

But others choose to drink throughout college. "When people ask me why college students drink," says Hanson, the sociologist, "I say, 'Why not?'" People in the "real world" have too little time and too many responsibilities to drink heavily night after night. They have to get up early five days a week, work all day, then go home to their families. Co-workers and family members count on them to live up to their obligations. College students are usually responsible only for themselves. All they have to do is go to a few classes and study when it's convenient. Michael Haines, coordinator of Health Enhancement Services at Northern Illinois University, notes that campus life is set up for binge behavior of all kinds. Students stay up one night cramming for a test, sleep in until noon the next day, then drink all night.

Research finds that college students who drink heavily have lower grades than those who drink moderately or not at all. But these students generally aren't chemistry majors whose grades and classes will be critical for graduate school and future careers. They tend to be business or social science majors who will probably end up in jobs that have little to do with their academic studies. "The truth is that most students can go out drinking several nights a week and get by," says Wartenburg, the Swarthmore dean.

College students get into trouble not because they drink to get drunk but because they get drunk to be irresponsible. "I was drunk" is a get-out-of-jail-free card for college students who act like idiots, get into fights, climb into construction equipment, or behave in other unacceptable or embarrassing ways. It works because friends know that drinking makes people lose control and they may want to use alcohol as an excuse for their own behavior, especially sexual behavior. According to the Harvard study, 41 percent of frequent binge drinkers engage in unplanned sexual activity, as opposed to only 4 percent for non-binge drinkers.

But unplanned does not mean unwanted. Students drink because they want to feel uninhibited. Men are less hesitant to approach women because they know that if their advances are rejected, they can laugh it off later, saying they were drunk. Women, who still face a double standard when it comes to sleeping around, can blame one-night stands on alcohol.

So men and women have a strong incentive to attribute sexual behavior to drinking, which can be dangerous. Men may be inappropriately aggressive, and willing women may later claim they did not consent. The popularity of the alcohol excuse also helps explain the higher rates of unplanned and unprotected sex while drinking, because halting "uncontrollable" sex to be responsible would destroy the illusion of chemical compulsion.

Although alcohol has consistent effects on motor skills among people of different cultures, its effects on behavior may have more to do with expectations than with pharmacology. Researchers at Washington University in Seattle have found that students who think they are drinking alcoholic beverages become more animated and aggressive, even if they've had only tonic water. Anthropologists have discovered that alcohol's behavioral effects are shaped by culture. In Europe, people grow up drinking beer or wine as a normal part of family life, so drinking is no big deal and generally doesn't cause problems. Americans, by contrast, have always been ambivalent about drinking. As Hanson notes, we "think dry and act wet": We associate drinking with negative behavior but do it anyway. In addition to a person's "set" (beliefs and expectations), the "setting" where drinking takes place has an important impact on drinking behavior. A young man having wine at a family dinner will not behave the same as he would at a bachelor party.

College drinking behavior usually resembles a bachelor party more than a family dinner, but it also varies more with the situation. When students go to a $3.00 all-you-can-drink kegger, they descend into a dimly lit, damp, smoky, and crowded basement. The beer is terrible, there's no place to sit, and everyone is pushing and shoving to get their money's worth before the keg runs out.

The only thing to do is drink fast and hard. Students at keggers are mostly underage because they have nowhere else to drink, thanks to the 21 law.

Things are usually more festive at college bars and fraternity functions. The beer is flowing, so students can relax and have a good, rowdy time. Drinking takes on a party atmosphere, which means strong sexual overtones. Bars and frat parties keep the music at a throbbing volume, making it difficult to talk.

But at the East 19th Street Café, one of five microbreweries near the UO campus, the music is turned down low so people can talk without shouting and savor the premium ales, porters, and stouts. The brew pubs are probably the closest college equivalent to an adult drinking environment. Some graduate students and twenty-somethings come to 19th Street, but most patrons are undergraduates who also spend a lot of time in the campus bars. No matter how much people had to drink, I never witnessed drunken or boorish behavior by anyone at a brewery.

With an understanding of how set and setting affect drinking behavior, social norms can be used to control problems. People used to wink and laugh at drunk driving. Now it's considered reckless and stupid, and drunk-driving fatalities have fallen dramatically. Many college administrators would like to design programs to encourage responsible drinking, but they are blocked by federal law. Thanks to the Drug-Free Schools and Community Act Amendments of 1989, universities must have an official no-use alcohol policy for students under 21 or risk losing federal funds, including student financial aid. "It's hard to teach people how to do something responsibly if it's illegal to do it at all," says Swarthmore's Wartenburg.

Nevertheless, some colleges are succeeding. In the late 1980s, officials at Northern Illinois University realized that the traditional approach of controlling consumption and keeping alcohol away from underage students wasn't working. A 1988 survey found that 43 percent of NIU students were binge drinkers, but students believed 70 percent were. NIU administrators thought that misperception of the campus norm was encouraging drinking. "What people feel is the norm has a rather potent influence on behavior," Haines, the NIU administrator, observes.

So with a slim budget of $6,000 the university began taking out ads in the campus paper during the 1989-90 school year reporting actual binge-drinking rates on campus. It also hired students to dress up like the Blues Brothers and hand out dollar bills to anyone who could report this information correctly. By 1995, perceived binge drinking had fallen to 43 percent. More important, actual binge drinking fell to 28 percent, and alcohol-related problems fell proportionally.

Officials at the University of Oregon are hoping to transplant Northern Illinois's success to their campus. Oregon is also one of many colleges that has set up substance-free dorms for students who want to avoid the mayhem in the regular dorms. "It's a great way for people who don't want to drink to avoid people who do," says Hanson. But there is probably a limit to what colleges and universities can do. The days when colleges served *in loco parentis* are long gone.

The best place for students to learn responsible drinking behavior is at home. "Children follow in their parents' footsteps," says Hanson. "What they learn in the home has more impact than what they pick up from friends or at school." Instead of allowing other students to teach their children "normal" drinking behavior, parents can teach their children to drink in moderation, with food, and in the company of adults.

Unfortunately, Hanson says, many parents are reluctant to teach their children responsible drinking when underage drinking is illegal outside the home and public health campaigns warn against sending "mixed messages." But accountability is not a mixed message. The principle that people are responsible for their behavior even when drinking should be drilled into young people's heads by parents as they are growing up and reinforced in college.

Not that college students would abandon keggers, campus bars, and frat parties altogether. College is not the real world, and responsible drinking has a different meaning there. "You gotta do it [drinking] in moderation," says Craig, a 23-year-old University of Oregon senior. "I think that you should go out once a week and get wasted—that's moderation."

"Drinking Age Has Simply Got to Go," Say Campus Riots

◆

PAMELA WHITE

(U WIRE) BOULDER, Colo.—The young are always the first to recognize hypocrisy. Unlike their elders, who've been shoveled so much manure over the years that they've grown numb to the smell, young people can tell almost immediately when society is feeding them a line. So it's no wonder that Boulder's young adults are incensed over the state's drinking laws.

Last weekend marked the first anniversary of the University Hill "beer" riots. And while the days here passed more or less without incident, riots rocked both Pullman, Wash., and East Lansing, Mich. In both cases, drinking laws were cited as one of the causes contributing to the unrest.

Old people, like me, have responded both to last year's violence and to recent events with scorn.

"They're rioting over beer?" we sniff disdainfully while shaking our graying heads, "How absurd."

Our disgust with the violence and its emotional and financial costs is well justified. Violence can only be justified in cases of self-defense, and even then, it is a tragedy. Rioting should never by condoned.

But when we casually dismiss the root of these young people's anger, we are missing the point. Their frustration has less to do with a desire to drink booze and more to do social justice.

At age 18, Coloradans can live on their own, but they can't drink a beer.

At age 18, they can gamble, but they can't drink a beer.

At age 18, they can commit themselves to another person for the rest of their lives in marriage, but they can't drink a beer.

At age 18, they can be parents, but they can't drink a beer.

They can vote, but they can't drink a beer.

But, worse of all, males 18 and over are required to submit to the draft, through which they might be forced on pain of imprisonment to risk their lives in military combat. But they can't drink a beer. Give them a tank, but not a tankard.

This is not an inconsistency. It's a travesty. To ask someone to lay down his life defending freedoms he has yet to enjoy is both unfair and just plain stupid.

I suppose the nation could choose to remedy this by raising the age at which men are required to register with the Selective Service, or better yet, by eliminating the accursed draft altogether.

From Colorado Daily, May 8, 1998.

It might also be a good idea to raise the age at which people can consent to marry to 21. Or better yet, 30. Imagine how few divorces there would be if we all waited to tie the knot until we know what the heck we're doing with our lives.

Still, the best solution might be the most difficult for Coloradans to embrace, afflicted with the curse of Puritanism as most Americans are. Rather than glamorizing alcohol by setting it up as a rite of passage into full adulthood, we should abolish the drinking age completely.

I came of age in Denmark, where there is no drinking age. And, yes, I got smashed more than a few times. But I did so under the watchful eyes of my Danish parents. By the time I was 18 and living on my own in Copenhagen, the idea of drinking to become intoxicated had become passé, replaced by the notion of having a good wine with dinner.

My Danish friends, who had lived all their lives knowing that alcohol was available to them, drank less than I did, most of them needing only one hang over to convince them that bingeing on booze was a bad idea.

On the other hand, their Swedish counterparts, who back then had a legal drinking age of 18, often spent weekends in Helsingor, retching and reeking of brandy bought at the duty free shop on the Helsingor ferry. (Their behavior has given rise to the Danish stereotype of Swedes as "drunken Swedes.")

Of course, it's not really fair to compare any place in the United States with any place in Scandinavia. They've managed to achieve a level of social justice and liberty there that we can only dream about.

Yet I'm not the first person in Boulder to call for the abolition of the drinking age. The call has been sounded time and time again by sincere people across the political spectrum. But it has always fallen on reactionary ears. Instead of taking the logical step and backing off, we now have tougher drinking laws and more rigid enforcement, forgetting, I suppose, that Prohibition has never worked and never will.

Last weekend, I watched as a dozen or more police converged on a party of 40, including about 23 underage drinkers. The cops were only doing their job, enforcing a law they've been asked to enforce. But the kids, other than drinking beer, weren't behaving badly—until the police arrived. Then the whole thing degenerated, with the hosts, who'd already been ticketed for providing alcohol to underage drinkers, refusing to cooperate with the cops, even trying to barricade the doors. This was, of course, a dumb thing to do.

Not surprisingly, police were frustrated and impatient. They'd tried the kid glove approach and had found a gauntlet dropped in their laps. The students were foul mouthed and furious.

"What do they expect us to do?" asked one young woman, who was over 21 and clearly not intoxicated. "Especially on the week before finals."

I felt sorry for all of them, police and partygoers alike. The cops were only doing their job. The kids were only doing what generation upon generation of American youth have done before them. The conflict between students and police is ultimately the result of actions taken by the federal government, which forced Colorado to raise its drinking age. When I was 18, some time shortly after the Pleistocene, 18 year olds were allowed to drink 3.2 beers.

Which brings us to the only real solution to this problem—political action. Young people might consider putting aside thoughts of keggers for the moment and think about writing to their state and federal representatives instead. Because folks in the State Legislature and Congress are, generally speaking, even older than I am, it might take a while to convince them to change our drinking laws, but it is the only way to permanently effect change.

Wisdom in a Bottle

◆

CAMILLE PAGLIA

O Auntie Mame:

I once again find myself in the spin cycle over the latest phase of screaming campus hysterics: "Binge Drinking." Though I'm the first person to call the recent death of the Louisiana State University student at the center of this episode a real tragedy, the doting uber-mothers and fathers of Clean Campus Living are now on a new warpath—probably since date rape and heterosexual AIDS have lost their novelty as crusades. Thankfully, I'm beyond their clutches, as I graduated from my university-cum-nursery school a couple of years back. My question to you, Madam Oracle, is: Do we need any more campus babysitting for "boys" and "girls" who 20 years ago, at their age, were considered very much ADULTS? Where's the common sense in these fools? Sounds like Carry Nation wields a sledge hammer, not an ax, these days! Quick— Pass me the poppers!

Shaken, Not Stirred

Dear Shaken:

The cultural savvy of Salon readers is well-demonstrated by your raffish sobriquet alluding to one of my favorite scenes in "Auntie Mame," where Mame's schoolboy nephew perkily mixes a very professional martini for the flabbergasted banker, Mr. Babcock: "Stir never shake—it bruises the gin!"

The authoritarian Big Mommy and Daddy who run the summer camps we call colleges can't decide what a student is these days: A thinking, breathing, exploring, risk-taking adult? Or a cash cow haltered and hidebound by the thick parental checkbook? I say let the herd out of the barn, and let the hooves fall where they may! Growing up means being allowed to take a tumble in your own dung.

The absurdity of the Louisiana State University case is that alcohol was banned on campus, as if the latter were in Puritan Salem rather than Xanadu Baton Rouge, La. Thus LSU students are forced to chug-to-the-max off campus to sustain their high and then endanger their lives and others' by driving home in a sodden state.

"Binge drinking" is a Dionysian response to Apollonian overcontrol of another area of life. I have always strongly opposed the draconian raising of the

---

ASK CAMILLE, *Camille Paglia's online advice for the culturally disgruntled.*

legal drinking age to 21 in this country, a highly politicized and infantilizing measure that deprived the majority of young people of their freedoms in order to constrain a tiny, careless minority responsible for traffic accidents.

Alcohol, with its ancient history and its standardized, quality-controlled modern commercial production, is far preferable to drugs or pills as a tool of youthful experimentation. Manipulation of mood and alteration of consciousness are important first stages in higher education—as long as one is not destroyed by them. Identity is developed by a temporary dissolution of the mental structure imposed by parents, teachers and other adults. Creativity in the arts especially profits from that dangerous, exciting fluidity. Teetotalers may be the spine of the nation, but drinkers are its heart and balls.

European universities would never dream of meddling in their students' private lives. But American universities have reverted to "in loco parentis" (in place of the parent)—the parietal rules and repressive oversight that my 1960s generation rebelled against and smashed. Administrators are locked in Machiavellian marriage with nosy, tuition-paying parents. Even the retiring president of Bryn Mawr College (a hotbed of p.c. feminism) recently complained to the *Philadelphia Inquirer* that today's parents won't let their children grow up and that they're overinvolved with micromanaging their Bryn Mawr daughters' lives by constant e-mail and phone calls.

It's not binge drinking that's the problem—it's the banality and mediocrity of American higher education that produces students' desperate lust for gusto. I have certainly seen many talented people destroyed by alcohol and drugs. But as William Blake said, "The road of excess leads to the palace of wisdom."

My sympathies are with the orgiasts—like Oscar Wilde, who quipped, "Work is the curse of the drinking class." And like Patsy Stone of "Absolutely Fabulous," whose Ivana-blond image, with a vodka bottle plastered to her lips, is printed on one of my favorite T-shirts. In vino veritas!

Binge Drinking as a Substitute for a "Community of Learning"

◆

KENNETH A. BRUFFEE

The Harvard School of Public Health found in 1993 that binge drinking is widespread on American college campuses, particularly among members of fraternities and sororities. The school's most recent report documents the disturbing fact that binge drinking has not declined in the five years since that first study. Even though the proportion of students who declare themselves teetotalers is slightly larger, the effects of binge drinking continue to be widespread and severe. They range from poor grades to destruction of property, assault, drunk driving, and death (*The Chronicle,* September 18, 1998).

To stem the tide of binge drinking, colleges have tried closing fraternities and sororities, punishing heavy drinkers, enlisting the help of liquor-store owners, and banning alcohol on their campuses. So far, those efforts have largely failed. One reason may be that missing from most of them, and from most research on the subject, is an understanding of why first-year students join fraternities and sororities in the first place.

I know why I joined one, many more years ago that I care to mention. I arrived on that gracious, learned, sophisticated campus to find myself among people—professors, administrators, upperclassmen (yes, all were men in those days)—who were committed (it seemed to me) to making me feel just how green, scared, lonely, and small-town I was. They all seemed vexed that I wasn't already what they hoped I would become. Administrators told me how much I had to learn and how hard I had to work to learn it. Professors told me how little they valued what I already knew, and how trivial and misleading would be anything that I learned from anyone but themselves. I was an intrusive rube. I didn't belong.

Most of my fellow freshmen seemed committed to making me feel like a rube, too. Today I think I know why, though I certainly did not know it then. They were trying as hard as I was to conceal from everyone, including themselves, that they, too, were green, scared, lonely, and small-town.

I joined a fraternity because I wanted, desperately, to belong.

Fraternity members were the only people on the campus who seemed to know what it meant to feel like a rube, who knew the depth and overwhelming intensity of an 18-year-old's need to belong. They knew how to marshal and exploit that need because they'd been there themselves not long before.

KENNETH A BRUFFEE *is a professor of English and director of the Honors Academy at Brooklyn College of the City University of New York. From* The Chronicle of Higher Education, *February 5, 1999.*

Fraternities seemed to be the only place on campus with a ready supply of friends for freshmen.

There were certainly no friends to be had where I thought I would achieve my most consequential goals as a college student—in my classes. I made no friends there until my last year in college, and then only by chance. Even today, most college students make few friends through their classes until late in their college careers, if at all.

That's one reason college students become binge drinkers.

Such a claim may sound like some kind of bad joke, so I hasten to explain.

Most of the talk about binge drinking, the research into it, and the administrative attempts to curb it assume a sharp distinction between the "academic" and the "social" connections of college students with their peers. Students also make that distinction. If you ask a cross section of college students about their friends, some may say they occasionally talk with a few of them about their course work and (if they admit at all to such eccentricities) their intellectual and aesthetic interests. With the rest of their friends, they'll say, such topics seldom come up.

It's peculiar, when you think about it, that most American colleges do not help entering students make friends through their course work. Presumably, one goal of liberal education is to enrich life with the kind of conversation that comes with substantive friendship. And when colleges actively provide students with the opportunity to make friends through their classes, they eagerly grasp the chance.

A study of 183 students who entered Brooklyn College in the fall of 1987 and took courses that were organized into "learning communities"—in which the same group of students was registered for three courses together—showed that 73 percent agreed with the statement that the experience "helps students make new friends more easily." The retention rate of the students studied was 73 per cent, compared with the college's normal average of 59 percent.

Many students who do make it to their junior and senior years are likely to concede (if only in private) that most of their friendships then tend to merge social interests with academic and aesthetic interests—from pursing genetic research to listening to Mozart concertos. By then their sense of belonging is rooted in the academic major they have chosen and in the new interests they have developed in elective courses.

Of course, some freshmen arrive on the campus in the company of old high-school friends. But those students, too—most of them similarly green, scared, lonely 18-year-olds—feel the pressing need to belong to the new world they have entered. And they, too, are willing to belong on any terms, even terms that require them to continue to keep their curiosity and thought deeply buried.

Those are the terms of membership that fraternities and sororities offer. In return, these social clubs provide companionship that is predictable, reliable, aesthetically unimaginative, and intellectually unchallenging. So-called "wild parties" and the binge drinking that fuels them are misguided attempts to breathe life into stultifying conventionality.

In contrast, many traditional college classrooms—organized around lectures and class discussions—offer surprise, change, and intellectual stimulation. But their structure emphasizes individual mastery, self-sufficiency, and exclusion of outside distractions. While encouraging individual achievement, such courses often foster little substantive social interaction among students.

Colleges can do a great deal more than they generally do to make classrooms a source of social engagement around substantive issues. One approach is collaborative learning and related ways of organizing course work, team projects, and peer tutoring.

Research can guide colleges in such efforts. We need to know whether collaborative learning actually does help students bring to the surface suppressed curiosity and thought, and, if so, how. Most of all, we need to know whether collaborative learning—especially, but not exclusively, during the first year of college—can give students opportunities to make friends in settings that are not merely social, vapid encounters, and, as a result, reduce the social desperation that drives students to binge drinking.

Granted, research is unlikely to show that collaborative learning is a universal solution to social problems in colleges. Research certainly will not demonstrate that collaborative learning alone can empty out fraternity and sorority houses.

But I am confident that research will show that collaborative learning can give entering college students a chance to experience a refreshingly new kind of social intimacy with their peers. It could help American colleges chip away at the problem of binge drinking, by helping to generate social cohesion, civil discourse, and, yes, even friendship among young people who arrive on campuses green, scared, lonely and small-town.

Smoking and the Tyranny of Public Health

◆

JACOB SULLUM

From a public health perspective, smoking is not an activity or even a habit. It is "Public Health Enemy Number One," "the greatest community health hazard," "the single most important preventable cause of death," "a pediatric disease," "the manmade plague," "the global tobacco epidemic." It is something to be stamped out, like smallpox or yellow fever. This view of smoking is part of a public health vision that encompasses all sorts of risky behavior, including not just smoking and drinking, using illegal drugs, overeating, failing to exercise, owning a gun, speeding, riding a motorcycle without a helmet—in short, anything that can be said to increase the incidence of disease or injury.

Although this sweeping approach is a relatively recent development, we can find intimations of it in the public health rhetoric of the 19th century. In the introduction to the first major American book on public health, U.S. Army surgeon John S. Billings explained the field's concerns: "Whatever can cause, or help to cause, discomfort, pain, sickness, death, vice, or crime—and whatever has a tendency to avert, destroy, or diminish such causes—are matters of interest to the sanitarian." Despite this ambitious mandate, and despite the book's impressive length (nearly 1,500 pages in two volumes), *A Treatise on Hygiene and Public Health* had little to say about the issues that occupy today's public health professionals. There were no sections on smoking, alcoholism, drug abuse, obesity, vehicular accidents, mental illness, suicide, homicide, domestic violence, or unwanted pregnancy. Published in 1879, the book was instead concerned with things like compiling vital statistics; preventing the spread of disease; abating public nuisances; and assuring wholesome food, clean drinking water, and sanitary living conditions.

A century later, public health textbooks discuss the control of communicable diseases mainly as history. The field's present and future lies elsewhere. "The entire spectrum of 'social ailments,' such as drug abuse, venereal disease, mental illness, suicide, and accidents, includes problems appropriate to public health activity," explains *Principles of Community Health*. "The greatest potential for improving the health of the American people is to be found in what they do and don't do and for themselves. Individual decisions about diet, exercise, stress, and smoking are of critical importance." Similarly, *Introduction to Public Health* notes that the field, which once "had much narrower interests," now "includes the social and behavioral aspects of life—endangered by contemporary stresses, addictive diseases, and emotional instability."

MR. SULLUM *is a syndicated columnist and senior editor at* Reason *magazine. This article is adapted from* For Your Own Good: The Anti-Smoking Crusade and the Tyranny of Public Health, *published this year by the Free Press. From* Consumers Research Magazine, *July 1998.*

The extent of the shift can be sensed by perusing a few issues of the American Public Health Association's journal. In 1911, when the journal was first published, typical articles included "Modern Methods of Controlling the Spread of Asiatic Cholera," "Sanitation of Bakeries and Restaurant Kitchens," "Water Purification Plant Notes," and "The Need of Exact Accounting for Still-Births." Issues published in 1995 offered articles like "Menthol vs. Nonmenthol Cigarettes: Effects on Smoking Behavior," "Compliance with the 1992 California Motorcycle Helmet Use Law," "Correlates of College Student Binge Drinking," and "The Association Between Leisure-Time Physical Activity and Dietary Fat in American Adults."

In a sense, the change in focus is understandable. After all, Americans are not dying the way they once did. The chapter on infant mortality in *A Treatise on Hygiene and Public Health* reports that during the late 1860s and early 1870s two-fifths to one-half of children in major American cities died before reaching the age of five. The major killers included measles, scarlet fever, smallpox, diphtheria, whooping cough, bronchitis, pneumonia, tuberculosis, and "diarrheal diseases." Beginning in the 1870s, the discovery that infectious diseases were caused by specific microorganisms made it possible to control them through vaccination, antibiotics, better sanitation, water purification, and elimination of carriers such as rats and mosquitoes. At the same time, improvements in nutrition and living conditions increased resistance to infection.

Americans no longer live in terror of smallpox or cholera. Despite occasional outbreaks of infectious diseases such as rabies and tuberculosis, the fear of epidemics that was once an accepted part of life is virtually unknown. The one exception is AIDS, which is not readily transmitted and remains largely confined to a few high-risk groups. For the most part, Americans are dying of things you can't catch: cancer, heart disease, trauma. Accordingly, the public health establishment is focusing on those causes and the factors underlying them. Having vanquished most true epidemics, it has turned its attention to metaphorical epidemics of unhealthy behavior.

In 1979 Surgeon General Julius Richmond released *Healthy People: The Surgeon General's Report on Health Promotion and Disease Prevention,* which broke new ground by setting specific goals for reductions in mortality. "We are killing ourselves by our own careless habits," Secretary of Health, Education, and Welfare Joseph Califano wrote in the introduction, calling for "a second public health revolution" (the first being the triumph over infectious diseases). *Healthy People,* which estimated that "perhaps as much as half of U.S. mortality in 1976 was due to unhealthy behavior or lifestyle," advised Americans to quit smoking, drink less, exercise more, fasten their seat belts, stop driving so fast, and cut down on fat, salt, and sugar. It also recommended motorcycle helmet laws and gun control to improve public health.

Public health used to mean keeping statistics, imposing quarantines, requiring vaccination of children, providing purified water, building sewer systems, inspecting restaurants, regulating emissions from factories, and reviewing drugs of safety. Nowadays it means, among other things, banning cigarette ads, raising alcohol taxes, restricting gun ownership, forcing people to buckle their seat belts, and making illegal drug users choose between prison and "treatment." In the past, public health officials could argue that they were protecting people from external threats: carriers of contagious diseases, fumes and the local glue factory, contaminated water, food poisoning, dangerous quack remedies. By contrast, the new enemies of public health come from within; the aim is to protect people from themselves rather than each other.

Treating risky behavior like a contagious disease invites endless meddling. The same arguments that are commonly used to justify the government's efforts to discourage smoking can easily be applied to overeating, for example. If smoking is a compulsive disease, so is obesity. It carries substantial health risks, and people who are fat generally don't want to be. They find it difficult to lose weight, and when they do succeed they often relapse. When deprived of food, they suffer cravings, depression, anxiety, and other withdrawal symptoms.

Sure enough, the headline of a March 1985 article in *Science* announced, "Obesity Declared a Disease." The article summarized a report by a National Institutes of Health panel finding that "the obese are prone to a wide variety of diseases, including hypertension, adult onset diabetes, hypercholesterolemia, hypertriglyceridemia, heart disease, cancer, gall stones, arthritis, and gout." It quoted the panel's chairman, Jules Hirsch: "We found that there are multiple health hazards at what to me are surprisingly low levels of obesity. Obesity, therefore, is a disease."

More recently, the "epidemic of obesity" has been trumpeted repeatedly on the front page of the *New York Times*. The first story, which appeared in July 1994, was prompted by a study from the National Center for Health Statistics that found the share of American adults who are obese increased from a quarter to a third between 1980 and 1991. "The government is not doing enough," complained Philip R. Lee, an assistant secretary in the Department of Health and Human Services. "We don't have a coherent, across-the-board policy." The second story, published in September 1995, reported on a *New England Journal of Medicine* study that found gaining as little as 11 to 18 pounds was associated with a higher risk of heart disease—or, as the headline on the jump page put it, "Even Moderate Weight Gains Can Be Deadly." The study attributed 300,000 deaths a year to obesity, including one-third of cancer deaths and most deaths from cardiovascular disease. The lead researcher, JoAnn E. Manson, said, "It won't be long before obesity surpasses cigarette smoking as a cause of death in this country."

In his book *The Fat of the Land,* journalist Michael Fumento argues that obesity, defined as being 20% or more above one's appropriate weight, is only part of the problem. (See also "Busting the Low-Fat Dieting Myth," *Consumer Reports*, October 1997.) According to a 1996 survey, 74% of Americans exceed the weight range recommended for optimal health. "So instead of talking about a third of Americans being at risk because of being overweight," he writes, "we really should be talking about somewhere around three fourths."

If, as Philip R. Lee recommended, the government decides to do more about obesity—the second most important preventable cause of death in this country, soon to be the first—what would "a coherent, across-the-board policy" look like? As early as June 1975, in its *Forward Plan for Health,* the U.S. Public Health Service was suggesting "strong regulations to control the advertisement of food products, especially those of high sugar content or little nutritional value." But surely we can do better than that. A tax on fatty foods would help cover the cost of obesity-related illness and disability, while deterring overconsumption of ice cream and steak.

Lest you think this proposal merely facetious, it has been offered, apparently in all seriousness, by at least one economist, who wrote, in the *Orlando Sentinel:* "It is somewhat ironic that the government discourages smoking and drinking through taxation, yet when it comes to the major cause of death—heart disease—and its spiraling health-care costs, politicians let us eat with impunity . . . . It is time to rethink the extent to which we allow people to impose their negative behavior on those of us who watch our weight, exercise and try to be as healthy as possible."

Kelly Brownell, a professor of psychology at Yale University who directs the school's center for Eating and Weight Disorders, has also suggested a "junk food" tax, along with subsidies for healthy foods. "A militant attitude is warranted here," he told the *New Haven Register* last year. "We're infuriated at tobacco companies for enticing kids to smoke, so we don't want Joe Camel on billboards. Is it any different to have Ronald McDonald asking kids to eat foods that are bad for them?"

Of course, a tax on certain foods would be paid by the lean as well as the chunky. It might be more fair and efficient to tax people for every pound over their ideal weight. Such a market-based system would make the obese realize the costs they impose on society and give them an incentive to slim down.

If this idea strikes most people as ridiculous, it's not because the plan is impractical. In several states, people have to bring their cars to an approved garage for periodic emissions testing; there's no logistical reason why they could not also be required to weigh in at an approved doctor's office, say, once a year, reporting the results to the Internal Revenue Service for tax assessment. Though feasible, the fat tax is ridiculous because it's an odious intrusion by the state into matters that should remain private. Even if obesity is apt to shorten your life, most Americans would (I hope) agree, that's your business, not the government's. Yet many of the same Americans believe not only that the state should take an interest in whether people smoke but that it should apply pressure to make them stop, including fines (a.k.a. tobacco taxes), tax-supported nagging, and bans on smoking in the workplace.

In a 1977 talk show appearance, New York City lung surgeon William Cahan, a prominent critic of the tobacco industry, explained the rationale for such policies: "People who are making decisions for themselves don't always come up with the right answer." Since they believe that smoking is inherently irrational, tobacco's opponents tend to assume that smokers are stupid, ignorant, crazy, or helpless—though they rarely say so in such blunt terms. They understandably prefer to focus on the evil tobacco companies, portraying smokers as their victims.

Yet there is a palpable undercurrent of hostility toward smokers who refuse to get with the program. On two occasions in recent years, I was sitting at a (smoke-free) table with a group that included both a smoker and a busybody who took it upon himself to berate the smoker for his unhealthy habit. In both cases, the smoker, constrained by politeness, offered only the mildest of objections, and no one intervened on his behalf. Imagine what the reaction would have been if, instead of a smoker, the meddler had zeroed in on a chubby diner, warning him about the perils of overeating and lack of exercise. I suspect that the other diners would have been appalled, and the target, in turn would have been more likely to offer the appropriate response: Mind your own damned business. It seems we have special license to pick on smokers as a way of demonstrating our moral superiority.

The same sort of arrogance can be observed among public health specialists, but they are more consistent. Because the public health field developed in response to deadly threats that spread from person to person and place to place, its practitioners are used to dictating from on high. Writing in 1879, John S. Billings put it this way: "All admit that the state should extend special protection to those who are incapable of judging of their own best interests, or of taking care of themselves, such as the insane, persons of feeble intellect, or children; and we have seen that in sanitary matters the public at large are thus incompetent."

Billings was defending traditional public health measures aimed at preventing the spread of infectious diseases and controlling hazards such as toxic fumes. It's reasonable to expect that such measures will be welcomed by the intended beneficiaries, once they understand the aim. The same cannot be said of public health's new targets. Even after the public is informed about the relevant hazards (and assuming the information is accurate) many people will continue to smoke, drink, take illegal drugs, eat fatty foods, buy guns, speed, eschew seat belts and motorcycle helmets, and otherwise behave in ways frowned upon by the public health establishment. This is not because they misunderstood; it's because, for the sake of pleasure, utility, or convenience, they are prepared to accept the risks. When public health experts assume these decisions are wrong, they are indeed treating adults like incompetent children.

One such expert, writing in the *New England Journal of Medicine* two decades ago, declared "The real malpractice problem in this country today is not the one described on the front pages of daily newspapers but rather the malpractice that people are performing on themselves and each other . . .. It is a crime to commit suicide quickly. However, to kill oneself slowly by means of an unhealthy lifestyle is readily condoned and even encouraged."

The article prompted a response from Robert F. Meenan, a professor at the University of California School of Medicine in San Francisco, who observed: "Health professionals are trained to supply the individual with medical facts and opinions. However, they have no personal attributes, knowledge, or training that qualifies them to dictate the preferences of others. Nevertheless, doctors generally assume that the high priority that they place on health should be shared by others. They find it hard to accept that some people may opt for a brief, intense existence full of unhealthy practices. Such individuals are pejoratively labeled 'noncompliant' and pressures are applied on them to re-order their priorities.

The dangers of basing government policy on this attitude are clear, especially given the broad concerns of the public health movement. According to John J. Hanlon's *Public Health Administration and Practice*: "Pubic health is dedicated to the common attainment of the highest levels of physical, mental, and social well-being and longevity consistent with available knowledge and resources at a given time and place." The textbook *Principles of Community Health* tells us: "The most widely accepted definition of individual health is that of the World Health Organization: 'Health is a state of complete physical, mental, and social well being and not merely the absence of disease or infirmity.'" A government empowered to maximize health is a totalitarian government.

In response to such fears, the public health establishment argues that government intervention is justified-because individual decisions about risk affect other people. "Motorcyclists often contend that helmet laws infringe on personal liberties," noted Surgeon General Julius Richmond's 1979 report *Healthy People*, "and opponents of mandatory [helmet] laws argue that since other people usually are not endangered, the individual motorcyclist should be allowed personal responsibility for risk. But the high cost of disabling or fatal injuries, the burden on families, and the demands on medical care resources are borne by society as a whole." This line of reasoning, which is also used to justify taxes on tobacco and alcohol, implies that all resources—including not just taxpayer-funded welfare and health care but private savings, insurance coverage, and charity—are part of a common pool owned by "society as a whole" and guarded by the government.

As Meenan noted in the *New England Journal of Medicine:* "Virtually all aspects of life-style could be said to have an effect on the health or well-being of society, and the decision (could then be) reached that personal health choices should be closely regulated." Writing 18 years later in the same journal, Faith T. Fitzgerald, a professor at the University of California, Davis, Medical Center, observed: "Both health-care providers and the commonwealth now have a vested interest in certain forms of behavior, previously considered a person's private business, if the behavior impairs a person's 'health.' Certain failures of self-care have become, in a sense, crimes against society, because society has to pay for their consequences . . ... In effect, we have said that people owe it to society to stop misbehaving, and we use illness as evidence of misbehavior."

Most public health practitioners would presumably recoil at the full implications of the argument that government should override individual decisions affecting health because such decisions have an impact on "society as a whole." Former Surgeon General C. Everett Koop, for his part, seems completely untroubled. "I think that the government has a perfect right to influence personal behavior to the best of its ability if it is for the welfare of the individual and the community as a whole," he writes. This is paternalistic tyranny in its purest form, arrogating to government the authority to judge "the welfare of the individual" and elevating "the community as a whole" above mere people. Ignoring the distinction between self-regarding behavior and behavior that threatens others, Koop compares efforts to discourage smoking and other risky behavior to mandatory vaccination of school children and laws against assault.

While Koop may simply be confused, some defenders of the public health movement explicitly recognize that its aims are fundamentally collectivist and cannot be reconciled with the American tradition of limited government. In 1975 Dan E. Beauchamp, then an assistant professor of public health at the University of North Carolina, presented a paper at the annual meeting of the American Public Health Association in which he argued that "the radical individualism inherent in the market model" is the biggest obstacle to improving public health. "The historic dream of public health that preventable death and disability ought to be minimized is a dream of social justice," Beauchamp said. "We are far from recognizing the principle that death and disability are collective problems and that all persons are entitled to health protection." He rejected "the ultimately arbitrary distinction between voluntary and involuntary hazards" and complained that "the primary duty to avert disease and injury still rests with the individual." Beauchamp called upon public health practitioners to challenge "the powerful sway market-justice holds over our imagination, granting fundamental freedom to all individuals to be left alone."

Of all the risk factors for disease and injury, it seems, freedom is the most pernicious. And you thought it was smoking.

Turkey Police, Beware

◆

Richard Berman

Food police cut more than calories by whacking feast foods. Somewhere in America, a family will eat a Thanksgiving dinner the food police would be proud of. Warm aromas of mashed tofu with fresh, creamy canola oil, baked yams with a pinch of salt-free substitute on them, boiled onions and soy-bread stuffing with low-sodium vegetable broth gravy fill the house with an air of excitement. Everyone waits for the pièce de résistance and out of it comes: A steaming, gleaming tofurky (tofu molded into a turkey), complete with fermented soy drumsticks.

In an effort to change American eating habits to conform to their puritanical vision, groups such as the Center for Science in the Public Interest, the Vegetarian Society and People for the Ethical Treatment of Animals are perverting the way Americans look at food. Nowhere is this more prevalent than in their attacks on our feast foods, those meals we eat only on special occasions. Every year the talking heads appear on the air to demonize holiday fare as unholy bastions of what CSPI calls food porn. The weeks before Thanksgiving host the now-traditional parade of health scares, tips, pranks and even outright terrorism as nanny state activists jostle for the media attention.

Mothers against Drunk Drivers uses Thanksgiving to move almost seamlessly from its "Deadly Days of Summer" (Memorial Day to Labor Day) to its "Tie One On" (Thanksgiving to New Year's Eve) campaign. Both are intended to scare us away from even responsible drinking. As MADD's President, Karolyn Nunnallee says, "we will not tolerate drinking and driving, period." So much for any holiday cheer for those not sleeping over.

On the food front, a widely reported study—purposely released days before last Thanksgiving—claimed that just one fatty meal could induce a heart attack. (That'd sure put a damper on the giblet gravy.) Less reported was that the study surveyed only 18 men, hardly a significant medical development. That same week, other scientists released overblown warnings about malonaldehyde in turkey, arsenic in mashed potatoes, and aflatoxins in walnuts. Such arguments stretch believability. According to the American Council on Science and Health, one must each 3.8 tons of turkey to develop cancer from malonaldehyde. A legion of chipmunks couldn't eat enough nuts to give one of them cancer.

Richard Berman *is founder of the Guest Choice Network, a nationwide coalition of restaurant and tavern operators. "Turkey Police, Beware," by Richard Berman, from* The Washington Times, *Nov. 26, 1998, p. A19. Copyright © 1998 News World Communications, Inc. Reprinted with permission of* The Washington Times. *Visit our web site at http://www.washtimes.com.*

The science and the public interest group CSPI does its part for the holidays and its annual press conference warning us that "consumers need to treat every turkey as though it harbors a feast of bacteria." The group goes so far as to campaign against stuffing turkeys, for fear of salmonella or food poisoning. Isn't that why we cook our turkeys? Radical vegetarians and PETA go further, protesting everything from barbecue to the Easter ham to (again) that icon of American food, the Thanksgiving turkey. Calling the holiday "murder on turkeys," PETA suggests we eat tofurky instead.

More sinister are the antics of the Animal Avengers, which in 1996 created a scare in Vancouver, Canada, by saying the group had laced turkeys with rat poison. Another group, the Animal Rights Militia, pulled the same trick in 1994. Such relentless attacks have done more than just cut calories from our dinner plate. Thanksgiving and the winter holidays are a time for family, reunions, friends and for literally giving thanks for what we have. Food, drink, and yes, even smoking, is often part of this experience. On an even deeper level, feast foods help define who we are as an individual, as a family and as a regional or ethnic group. "There are all kinds of signposts on people's Thanksgiving table that give away who they are," *New York Times* food editor Ruth Reichl said.

Author Irene Chalmers, whose book *Food* discusses the social, psychological and emotional aspects of special meals, goes further: "The construction of the meal at holidays is a way of holding hands with past and future generations." Disrupt that, she says, and the link is broken.

The incessant (and usually bogus) health scares that emasculate our beloved family recipes do just that. They scour away the joy of cooking grandmother's stuffing or Aunt Mae's yams with brown sugar and molasses. "We are a society obsessed with the harmful effects of eating," said University of Pennsylvania Professor Paul Rozin.

Such an unhealthy obsession makes that tofurky look almost palatable. At least it's safe, so the logic goes. Few of us still go over the river and through the woods for a Thanksgiving at grandma's house. But all of us have warm memories of feasts gone by. And after the meal, the hours of conversation punctuated by coffee or brandy bind the day up into a sensation that hangs with us, sometimes forever. But those memories are being replaced by anguish over naked statistics, animal rights and cancer scares. And that's not a lot to be thankful for.

READINGS 3

Lying

Lying
Moral Choice in Public and Private Life

◆

SISSELA BOK

Introduction

When regard for truth has been broken down or even slightly weakened, all things will remain doubtful. — St. Augustine, "On Lying"

Doth any man doubt, that if there were taken out of men's minds vain opinions, flattering hopes, false valuations, imaginations as one would, and the like, but it would leave the minds of a number of men poor shrunken things, full of melancholy and indisposition, and unpleasing to themselves? —Bacon, "Of Truth"

After prolonged research on myself, I brought out the fundamental duplicity of the human being. Then I realized that modesty helped me to shine, humility to conquer, and virtue to oppress. —Camus, *The Fall*

Should physicians lie to dying patients so as to delay the fear and anxiety which the truth might bring them? Should professors exaggerate the excellence of their students on recommendations in order to give them a better change in a tight job market? Should parents conceal from children the fact that they were adopted? Should social scientists send investigators masquerading as patients to physicians in order to learn about racial and sexual biases in diagnosis and treatment? Should government lawyers lie to Congressmen who might otherwise oppose a much needed welfare bill? And should journalists lie to those from whom they seek information in order to expose corruption?

We sense differences among such choices; but whether to lie, equivocate, be silent, or tell the truth in any given situation is often a hard decision. Hard because duplicity can take so many forms, be present to such different degrees, and have such different purposes and results. Hard also because we know how questions of truth and lying inevitably pervade all that is said or left unspoken within our families, our communities, our working relationships. Lines seem most difficult to draw, and a consistent policy out of reach.

I have grappled with these problems in my personal life as everyone must. But I have also seen them at close hand in my professional experience in teaching applied ethics. I have had the chance to explore particular moral quandaries encountered at work, with nurses, doctors, lawyers, civil servants, and many others. I first came to look closely at problems of professional truthtelling and deception in preparing to write about the giving of placebos. And I

FROM SISSELA BOK, Lying: Moral Choice in Public and Private Life *(1978), Pantheon Books.*

grew more and more puzzled by a discrepancy in perspectives: many physicians talk about such deception in a cavalier, often condescending and joking way, whereas patients often have an acute sense of injury and of loss of trust at learning that they have been duped.

I learned that this discrepancy is reflected in an odd state of affairs in medicine more generally. Honesty from health professionals matters more to patients than almost everything else that they experience when ill. Yet the requirement to be honest with patients has been left out altogether from medical oaths and codes of ethics, and is often ignored, if not actually disparaged, in the teaching of medicine.

As I widened my search, I came to realize that the same discrepancy was present in many other professional contexts as well. In law and in journalism, in government and in the social sciences, deception is taken for granted when it is felt to be excusable by those who tell the lies and who tend also to make the rules. Government officials and those who run for elections often deceive when they can get away with it and when they assume that the true state of affairs is beyond the comprehension of citizens. Social scientists condone deceptive experimentation on the ground that the knowledge gained will be worth having. Lawyers manipulate the truth in court on behalf of their clients. Those in selling, advertising, or any form of advocacy may mislead the public and their competitors in order to achieve their goals. Psychiatrists may distort information about their former patients to preserve confidentiality or to keep them out of military service. And journalists, police investigators, and so-called intelligence operators often have little compunction in using falsehoods to gain the knowledge they seek.

Yet the casual approach of professionals is wholly out of joint with the view taken by those who have to cope with the consequences of deception. For them, to be given false information about important choices in their lives is to be rendered powerless. For them, their very autonomy may be at stake.

There is little help to be found in the codes and writings on professional ethics. A number of professions and fields, such as economics, have no code of ethics in the first place. And the existing codes say little about when deception is and is not justified.*

The fact is that reasons to lie occur to most people quite often. Not many stop to examine the choices confronting them; existing deceptive practices and competitive stresses can make it difficult not to conform. Guidance is hard to come by, and few are encouraged to consider such choices in schools and colleges or in their working life.

As I thought about the many opportunities for deception about the absence of a real debate on the subject, I came to associate these with the strik-

---

* Scholars in many fields have had no reason in the past to adopt a code of ethics. But some are now exerting so much influence on social choice and human welfare that they should be required to work out codes similar to those that have long existed in professions like medicine or law.

ing recent decline in public confidence not only in the American government, but in lawyers, bankers, businessmen, and doctors. In 1960, many Americans were genuinely astonished to learn that President Eisenhower had lied when asked about the U-2 incident, in which an American spy plane and pilot had been forced down by the Soviet Union. But only fifteen years later, battered by revelations about Vietnam and Watergate, 69 percent of the respondents to a national poll agreed that "over the last ten years, this country's leaders have consistently lied to the people."

The loss of confidence reaches far beyond government leadership. From 1966 to 1976, the proportion of the public answering yes to whether they had a great deal of confidence in people in charge of running major institutions dropped from 73 percent to 42 percent for medicine; for major companies from 55 percent to 16 percent; for law firms from 24 percent (1973) to 12 percent; and for advertising agencies from 21 percent to 7 percent.

Suspicions of widespread professional duplicity cannot alone account for the loss of trust. But surely they aggravate it. We have a great deal at stake, I believe, in becoming more clear about matters of truth-telling, both for our personal choices and for the social decisions which foster or discourage deceptive practices. And when we think about these matters, it is the reasons given for deceiving which must be examined. Sometimes there may be sufficient reason to lie—but when? Most often there is not—and why? Describing how things are not enough. Choice requires the formulation of criteria. To lie to the dying, for example, or to tell them the truth—which is the best policy? Under what circumstances? And for what reasons? What kinds of arguments support these reasons or defeat them? [. . .] If we have all been poorly served by the dominant practices, then the most important remaining questions are: What are the alternatives, for society and for each of us individually, to merely going along with such practices? And how can we act so as to change them? What institutional and personal incentives may be needed? And what real risks might dissuade would-be liars? [. . .]

Is the "Whole Truth" Attainable?

> "I was born for this, I came into the world for this: to bear witness to the truth; and all who are on the side of truth listen to my voice."
> "Truth?" said Pilate, "what is that?" — John 18:37

> If, like the truth, the lie had but one face, we would be on better terms. For we would accept as certain the opposite of what the liar would say. But the reverse of truth has a hundred thousand faces and an infinite field. — Montaigne, *Essays*

> Like freedom, truth is a bare minimum or an illusory ideal (the truth, the whole truth, and nothing but the truth about, say, the battle of Waterloo or the *Primavera*.) — J.L. Austin, "Truth," *Philosophical Papers*

The "Whole Truth"

Is it not naïve to set forth on a general exploration of lying and truth-telling? Some will argue that the task is impossible. Life is too complex, they will say, and societies too diverse. How can one compare the bargaining in an Eastern bazaar, the white lies of everyday life, the lie for national defense, and that to spare a dying child? Is it not arrogant and myopic to conceive of doing so?

And even if these variations could somehow be encompassed, the argument continues, how can we ever attain the truth about any complex matter—the battle of Waterloo, in Austin's example—or even a single circumstance? How can one, in fact, do full justice to the words used in court: "The truth, the whole truth, and nothing but the truth"?

These words mock our clumsy efforts to remember and convey our experiences. The "whole truth" has seemed so obviously unattainable to some as to cause them to despair of human communication in general. They see so many barriers to prevent us from obtaining truthful knowledge, let alone communicating it; so many pitfalls in conveying what we mean.

How can a physician, for example, tell the "whole truth" to a patient about a set of symptoms and their causes and likely effects? He certainly does not know all there is to know himself. Even all he does know that might have a bearing—incomplete, erroneous, and tentative though it be—could not be conveyed in less than weeks or even months. Add to these difficulties the awareness that everything in life and experience connects, that all is a "seamless web" so that nothing can be said without qualifications and elaborations in infinite regress, and a sense of lassitude begins to steal over even the most intrepid.

This book is intended as a reply to such arguments. The whole truth is out of reach. But this fact has very little to do with our choices about whether to lie or to speak honestly, about what to say and what to hold back. These choices can be set forth, compared, evaluated. And when they are, even rudimentary distinctions can give guidance.

If arrogance there be, it lies rather in the immobilizing impatience with all that falls short of the "whole truth." This impatience helps explain why the contemporary debate about deception is so barren. Paradoxically, the reluctance to come to grips with deception can stem from an exalted and all-absorbing preoccupation with *truth*.

"Truth"—no concept intimidates and yet draws thinkers so powerfully. From the beginnings of human speculation about the world, the question of what truth is and whether we can attain it have loomed large. Every philosopher has had to grapple with them.* Every religion seeks to answer them.

One pre-Socratic Greek tradition saw truth—*aletheia*—as encompassing all that we remember: singled out through memory from everything that is

---

* A glance at the Index of the recently published *Encyclopedia of Philosophy* reveals the contrast. As mentioned in the Introduction, it has no reference to "lying" or "deception." "Truth," on the other hand, receives over 100 references.

destined for Lethe, "the river of forgetfulness." The oral tradition required that information be memorized and repeated, often in song, so as not to be forgotten. Everything thus memorized—stories about the creation of the world, genealogies of gods and heroes, advice about health—all partook of truth, even if in another sense completely fabricated or erroneous. In this early tradition, repeating the songs meant keeping the material alive and thus "true," just as creating works of art could be thought of as making an object true, bringing it to life.

Only gradually did the opposition between truth and error come to be thought central to philosophy, and the nature of verification itself spotlighted. The immense preoccupation with epistemology took hold with Plato and has never diminished since. In logic, in epistemology, in theology, and in metaphysics, the topic of "truth" has continued to absorb almost limitless energies. And since the strands from these diverse disciplines are not always disentangled, a great many references to "truth" remain of unsurpassed vagueness.

Truth and Truthfulness

In all such speculation, there is great risk of a conceptual muddle, of not seeing the crucial differences between two domains: the *moral* domain of intended truthfulness and deception, and the much vaster domain of truth and falsity in general. The moral question of whether you are lying or not is not *settled* by establishing the truth or falsity of what you say. In order to settle this question, we must know whether you *intend your statement to mislead.*

The two domains often overlap, and up to a point each is indispensable to the other. But truth and truthfulness are not identical, any more than falsity and falsehood. Until the differences are seen, and the areas of overlap and confusion spotlighted, little progress can be made in coping with the moral quandaries of lying.

The two domains are sometimes taken to be identical. This can happen whenever some believe that they have access to a truth so complete that all else must pale by comparison. Many religious documents or revelations claim to convey what is true. Those who do not accept such a belief are thought to live in error, in ignorance, even in blindness. At times, the refusal of nonbelievers to accept the dogma or truth revealed to the faithful is called, not merely an error, but a lie. The battle is seen as one between upholders of the faith and the forces of deception and guile.* Thus Bonhoeffer writes that:

> Jesus calls Satan "the father of the lie." (John 8:44) The lie is primarily the denial of God as He has evidenced Himself to the world. "Who is a liar but he that denieth that Jesus is the Christ?" (1 John 2:22)

---

* The confusion between "error" and "lie" underlying such a belief occasionally gives rise to the conclusion that those who are in possession of the truth—and thus not liars—are both infallible and incapable of lying. In order to sort out just what is meant by any one such claim, it is necessary to ask: Is the person believed infallible incapable of lying? of other forms of deceit? of being wrong? of being deceived? and with respect to what forms of knowledge? *Cf* a Sufi saying: "The pious would not deceive and the intelligent man cannot be deceived." *A Sufi Rule for Novices*, ed. Menahem Wilson (Cambridge, Mass: Harvard University Press, 1975), p. 41.

Convinced that they know the truth—whether in religion or politics—enthusiasts often regard lies for the sake of this truth as justifiable. They may perpetrate so-called pious frauds to convert the unbelieving or strengthen the conviction of the faithful. They see nothing wrong in telling untruths for what they regard as a much "higher" truth.

In the history of human thought, we find again and again such a confusion of the two domains. It is not unrelated to the traditions which claim the truth exists, that it can be revealed, that one can hope to come face to face with it. Even Nietzsche, at war with such traditions, perpetuates the confusion:

> There is only *one* world, and that world is false, cruel, contradictory, misleading, senseless. [. . .] We need lies to vanquish this reality, this "truth," we need lies in order to live. [. . .] That lying is a necessity of life is itself a part of the terrifying and problematic character of existence.

The several meaning of the word "false" only add to the ease of confusing the two domains. For whereas "false" normally has the larger sense which includes all that is wrong or incorrect, it takes on the narrower, moral sense when applied to persons. A false person is not one merely wrong or mistaken or incorrect; it is one who is intentionally deceitful or treacherous or disloyal. Compare, to see the difference, a "false note" and a "false friend"; a "false economy" and a "false witness."*

Any number of appearances and words can mislead us; but only a fraction of them are *intended* to do so. A mirage may deceive us, through no one's fault. Our eyes deceive us all the time. We are beset by self-delusion and bias of every kind. Yet we often know when we mean to be honest or dishonest. Whatever the essence of truth and falsity, and whatever the sources of error in our lives, *one* such source is surely the human agent, receiving and giving out information, intentionally deflecting, withholding, even distorting it at times.† Human beings, after all, provide for each other the most ingenious obstacles to what partial knowledge and minimal rationality they can hope to command.

We must single out, therefore, from the countless ways in which we blunder misinformed through life, that which is done with the *intention to mislead;* and from the countless partial stabs at truth, those which are intended to be truthful. Only if this distinction is clear will it be possible to ask the moral question with rigor. And it is to this question alone—the intentional manipula-

---

* To further complicate matters, there are, of course, many uses of "false" to mean "deceitful" or "treacherous" which do not apply directly to persons, but rather to what persons have intended to be misleading. A "false trail," a "false ceiling," or a "false clue" carry different overtones of deceptiveness.

† Messages between human beings can suffer from a number of unintended distortions or interferences, originating either at the source, en route, or at the reception. The speaker, for example, may be mistaken, inarticulate, or using a language unknown to the listener. En route, the message may be deflected by outside noise, by atmospheric conditions, by interruption. At the receiving end, deafness, fatigue, language problems, or mental retardation may affect the reception of the message.

tion of information—that the court addresses itself in its request for "the truth, the whole truth, and nothing but the truth."

But one obstacle remains. Even after the two domains of the ethical and the epistemological are set apart, some argue that the latter should have priority. It is useless to be overly concerned with truthfulness, they claim, so long as one cannot know whether human beings are capable of knowing and conveying the truth in the first place. Such a claim, if taken seriously, would obviously make the study of truth-telling and deception seem pointless and flat. Once again, the exalted and all-absorbing preoccupation with "truth" then comes to nourish the reluctance to confront falsehood.

Skeptics have questioned the certitudes of their fellows from the earliest times. The most extreme among them have held that nothing can be known at all; sometimes they have gone very far in living out such a belief. Cratylus, a contemporary of Socrates, is said to have refused discussion of any kind. He held that the speakers and the words in any conversation would be changing and uncertain. He therefore merely wiggled his finger in response to any words to show the he had heard them but that a reply would be pointless. And Pyrrho, in the third century B.C., denied that anything could be known and concluded that nothing could therefore be said to be honorable or dishonorable, just or unjust.

For these radical skeptics, just as for those who believe that complete and absolute truth can be theirs, ethical matters of truth-telling and deception melt into insignificance by comparison with the illumination of truth and the dark void of its absence. As a result, both groups largely ignore the distinctions between truthfulness and falsehood in their intense quest for certainty regarding truth.

But the example of Cratylus shows how difficult it is to live up to thoroughgoing skepticism. Most thinkers who confuse intentional deception and falsity nevertheless manage to distinguish between the two in their ordinary lives. And those who consider the study of "truth" to be prior to any use of information put such concerns aside in their daily routines. They make informed choices of books and libraries; of subway connections and tools and food; they take some messages to be more truthful than others, and some persons as more worthy of their trust than others. [. . .]

For all these reasons, deception commands little notice. This absence of real analysis is reflected also in teaching and in codes of professional ethics. As a result, those who confront difficult moral choices between truthfulness and deception often make up their own rules. They think up their own excuses and evaluate their own arguments . . .[O]ne deserves mention here, for it results from a misuse of skepticism by those who wish to justify their lies, giving rise to a clearly fallacious argument. It holds that since we can never know the truth or falsity of anything anyway, it does not matter whether or not we lie when we have a good reason for doing so. Some have used this argument to explain why they and their entire profession must regretfully forgo the virtue of veracity in dealing with clients. Such a view is stated, for example, by an eminent physician in an article frequently referred to in medical literature.

> Above all, remember that it is meaningless to speak of telling the truth, the whole truth, and nothing but the truth to a patient. It is meaningless because it is impossible—a sheer impossibility. [. . .] Since telling the truth is impossible, there can be no sharp distinction between what is true and what is false.
>
> [. . .] Far older than the precept, "the truth, the whole truth, and nothing but the truth," is another that originates within our profession, that has always been the guide of the best physicians, and, if I may venture a prophecy, will always remain so: So far as possible, do no harm. You can do harm by the process that is quaintly called telling the truth. You can do harm by lying. [. . .] But try to do as little harm as possible.

The same argument is often used by biomedical investigators who claim that asking subjects for their informed consent to be used in research is meaningless because it is impossible to obtain a *genuinely* informed consent. It is used by government officials who decide not to inform citizens of a planned war or emergency measure. And very often, it is then supplemented by a second argument: Since there is an infinite gradation between what is truthful and what is deceitful, no lines can be drawn and one must do what one considers best on other grounds.

Such arguments draw on our concerns with the adequacy of information to reach a completely unwarranted conclusion: one that gives *carte blanche* to what those who lie take to be well-meant lies. The difference in perspectives is striking. These arguments are made by the liar but never by those lied to. One has only to imagine how the professionals who argue in this way would respond if their dentists, their lawyers, or their insurance agents used similar arguments for deceiving *them*. As dupes we know what as liars we tend to blur—that information can be more or less adequate; that even where no clear lines are drawn, rules and distinctions may, in fact, be made; and that truthfulness can be required even where full "truth" is out of reach.

The fact that the "whole truth" can never be reached in its entirety should not, therefore, be a stumbling block in the much more limited inquiry into questions of truth-telling and falsehood. It is possible to go beyond the notion that epistemology is somehow prior to ethics. The two nourish one another, but neither can claim priority. It is equally possible to avoid the fallacies which arise from the confusion of "truth" and "truthfulness," and to draw distinctions with respect to the adequacy and relevance of the information reaching us. It is therefore legitimate to go on to define deception and to analyze the moral dilemmas it raises.

Defining Intentional Deception and Lying

When we undertake to deceive others intentionally, we communicate messages meant to mislead them, meant to make them believe what we ourselves do not believe. We can do so through gesture, through disguise, by means of action or inaction, even through silence. Which of these innumerable deceptive messages are also lies? I shall define as a lie any intentionally deceptive message which is *stated*. Such statements are most often made verbally or in writing, but can of course also be conveyed via smoke signals, Morse code, sign language, and the like. Deception, then, is the larger category, and lying forms part of it.*

This definition resembles some of those given by philosophers and theologians, but not all. For it turns out that the very choice of definition has often presented a moral dilemma all its own. Certain religious and moral traditions were vigorously opposed to all lying. Yet many adherents wanted to recognize at least a few circumstances when intentionally misleading statements could be allowed. The only way out of them was, then, to define lies in such a way that some falsehoods did not count as lies. Thus Grotius, followed by a long line of primarily Protestant thinkers, argued that speaking falsely to those—like thieves—to whom truthfulness is not owed cannot be called lying. Sometimes the rigorous tradition was felt to be so confining that a large opening to allowable misstatements was needed. In this way, casuist thinkers developed the notion of the "mental reservation," which, in some extreme formulations, can allow you to make a completely misleading statement, so long as you add something in your own mind to make it true. Thus, if you are asked whether you broke somebody's vase, you could answer "No," adding in your own mind the mental reservation "not last year" to make the statement a true one.

Such definitions serve the special purpose of allowing persons to subscribe to a strict tradition yet have the leeway in actual practice which they desire. When the strict traditions were at their strongest, as with certain forms of Catholicism and Calvinism, such "definitional" ways out often flourished. Whenever a law or rule is so strict that most people cannot live by it, efforts to find loopholes will usually ensue; the rules about lying are no exception.

I see nothing wrong with either a narrow or a wider definition of lying, so long as one retains the prerogative of morally evaluating the intentionally misleading statements, no matter whether they fall within the category of lying or outside it.* But a narrower definition often smuggles in a moral term which in itself needs evaluation. To say, for instance, that it is *not* lying to speak falsely to those with no right to your information glides over the vast question of what it means to have such a right to information. In order to avoid this difficulty, I shall use instead a more neutral, and therefore wider, definition of a lie: an intentionally deceptive message in the form of a *statement*. [. . .]

---

* It is perfectly possible to define "lie" so that it is identical with "deception." This is how expressions like "living a lie" can be interpreted. For the purposes of this book, however, it is best to stay with the primary distinction between deceptive *statements*—lies—and all the other forms of deception.

Augustine on Lying*

The first type of lie is a deadly one which should be avoided and shunned from afar, namely, that which is uttered in the teaching of religion, and to the telling of which no one should be led under any condition. The second is that which injures somebody unjustly: such a lie as helps no one and harms someone. The third is that which is beneficial to one person while it harms another, although the harm does not produce physical defilement. The fourth is the lie which is told solely for the pleasure of lying and deceiving, that is, the real lie. The fifth type is that which is told from a desire to please others in smooth discourse. When these have been avoided and rejected, a sixth kind of lie follows which harms no one and benefits some person, as, for instance, when a person, knowing that another's money is to be taken away unjustly, answers the questioner untruthfully and says that he does not know where the money is. The seventh type is that which is harmful to no one and beneficial to some person, with the exception of the case where a judge is questioning, as happens when a person lies because he is unwilling to betray a man sought for capital punishment, that is, not only a just and innocent person but even a criminal, because it belongs to Christian discipline never to despair of the conversion of anybody and never to block the opportunity for repentance. Now, I have spoken at length concerning these last two types, which are wont to evoke considerable discussion, and I have presented my opinion, namely, that by the acceptance of sufferings which are borne honorably and courageously, these lies, too, may be avoided by strong, faithful, and truthful men and women. The eighth is that type of lie which is harmful to no one and beneficial to the extent that it protects someone from physical defilement, at least, from that defilement which we have mentioned above. Now, the Jews considered it defilement to eat with unwashed hands. If anyone considers that as defilement, then a lie must not be told in order to avoid it. However, we are confronted with a new problem if a lie is such that it brings injury to any person, even though it protects another person from that defilement which all men detest and abhor. Should such a lie be told if the injury resulting from it is not in the nature of the defilement of which we have been treating? The question here does not concern lying; rather, it is whether harm should be done to any person, not necessarily through a lie, so that such defilement may be warded off from another person. I am definitely inclined to oppose such a license. Even though the most trivial injuries are proposed, such as that one which I mentioned above in regard to the one lost measure of grain, they disturb me greatly in this problem as to whether we ought to do injury to one person if, by that wrong, another person may be defended, or protected against defilement. But, as I have said, that is another question.

---

* From Augustine, "Lying," In *Treatises on Various Subjects*, ed. R.J. Deferrari, Fathers of the Church (New York: Catholic University of America Press, 1952), vol. 14, chap. 14. From Appendix to Sissela Bok, *Lying: Moral Choice in Public and Private Life*.

*Augustine Against Lying**

You have sent me much to read, dear brother Consentius, you have sent me much to read. [. . .] I am quite delighted with your eloquence, with your memory of sacred Scripture, with your adroitness of mind, with your distress in stinging indifferent Catholics, with your zeal in raging against even latent heretics. But I am not persuaded that they should be drawn out of hiding by our lies. For, why do we try with so much care to track them and hunt them down? Is it not so that, when they have been caught and brought into the open, we may either teach them the truth themselves or else, by convicting them of error, keep them from harming others? Is it not, in short, so that their falsehood may be blotted out or guarded against and God's truth be increased? Therefore, how can I suitably proceed against lies by lying? Or should robbery be proceeded against by means of robbery, sacrilege by sacrilege, and adultery by adultery? "But if through my lie the truth of God has abounded," are we, too, going to say, "why should we not do evil that good may come from it?" You see how much the Apostle detests this. But what is it to say: "Let us lie in order to bring lying heretics to the truth," if not the same as saying, "Why should we not do evil that good may come from it?" Or is lying sometimes a good or sometimes not an evil? Why, then, has it been written "Thou hatest all the workers of iniquity: thou wilt destroy all that speak a lie?" He has not made exception of some or said indefinitely: "Thou wilt destroy tellers of lies," so as to allow that certain ones be understood, but not every one. But he has brought forth a universal proposition, saying: "Thou wilt destroy all that speak a lie." Or, because it has not been said: "Thou wilt destroy all that speak any lie or that speak any lie whatsoever," are we to think, therefore, that room has been made for a certain kind of lie and that God wilt not destroy those who tell a certain kind of lie, but only those who tell unjust lies, not any lie whatsoever, because there are found just lies, too, which ought actually to be matter for praise rather than reproach? . . .

Often, in human affairs, human sympathy overcomes me and I am unable to resist when someone says to me: "Look, here is a patient whose life is endangered by a serious illness and whose strength will not hold out any longer if he is told of the death of his dearly beloved only son. He asks you whether the boy is still alive whose life you know is ended. What will you answer when, if you say thing except He is dead or He is alive or I don't know, the patient will believe that he is dead, because he realizes that you are afraid to say and do not want to lie? It will be the same no matter how hard you try to say nothing. Of the three convincing answers, two are false. He is alive and I don't know, and you cannot utter them without lying. But, if you make the one true answer, namely, that he is dead, and if the death of the anguished father follows hard

From Augustine, "Against Lying," in *Treatises on Various Subjects,* ed. R.J. Defarrari, Fathers of the Church (New York: Catholic University of America Press, 1952), vol. 16, chaps. 1, 2, 18. From Appendix to Sissela Bok, *Lying: Moral Choice in Public and Private Life.*

upon it, people will cry that he was slain by you. And who can bear to hear them exaggerate the evil of avoiding a beneficial lie and of loving homicide as truth?" I am moved by these arguments—more powerfully than wisely! . . .

Immanuel Kant
On a Supposed Right to Lie from Altruistic Motives*

In the journal *France,* for 1797, Part VI, No. 1, page 123, in an article entitled "On Political Reactions" by Benjamin Constant, there appears the following passage:

> The moral principle, "It is a duty to tell the truth," would make any society impossible if it were taken singly and unconditionally. We have proof of this in the very direct consequences which a German philosopher has drawn from this principle. This philosopher goes so far as to assert that it would be a crime to lie to a murderer who has asked whether our friend who is pursued by him had taken refuge in our house.

The French philosopher on page 124 refutes this principle in the following manner:

> It is a duty to tell the truth. The concept of duty is inseparable from the concept of right. A duty is that which is one being corresponds to the rights of another. Where there are no rights, there are no duties. To tell the truth is thus a duty: but it is a duty only in respect to one who has a right to the truth. But no one has a right to a truth which injures others.

Now the first question is: Does a man, in cases where he cannot avoid answering "Yes" or "No," have a right to be untruthful? The second question is: Is he not in fact bound to tell an untruth, when he is unjustly compelled to make a statement, in order to protect himself or another from a threatened misdeed?

Truthfulness in statements which cannot be avoided is the formal duty of an individual to everyone, however great may be the disadvantage accruing to himself or to another. If, by telling an untruth, I do not wrong him who unjustly compels me to make a statement, nevertheless by this falsification, which must be called a lie (though not in a legal sense), I commit a wrong against duty generally in a most essential point. That is, so far as in me lies I cause that declarations should in general find no credence, and hence that all rights based on contract should be void and lose their force, and this is a wrong done to mankind generally.

Thus the definition of a lie as merely an intentional untruthful declaration to another person does not require the additional condition that it must harm another, as jurists think proper in their definition (*mendacium est falsiloquium in*

---

* From Immanuel Kant, *Critique of Practical Reason and Other Writings in Moral Philosophy,* ed. and trans. Lewis White Beck (Chicago: University of Chicago Press, 1949), pp. 346-50. From Appendix Sissela Bok, *Lying: Moral Choice in Public and Private Life.*

praeidicium alterius). For a lie always harms another; if not some other particular man, still it harms mankind generally, for it vitiates the source of law itself.

This benevolent lie, however, can become punishable under civil law through an accident (*casus*), and that which escapes liability to punishment only accident can also be condemned as wrong even by external laws. For instance, if by telling a lie you have prevented murder, you have made yourself legally responsible for all the consequences; but if you have held rigorously to the truth, public justice can lay no hand on you, whatever the unforeseen consequences may be. After you have honestly answered the murderer's question as to whether this intended victim is at home, it may be that he has slipped out so that he does not come in the way of the murderer, and thus that the murder may not be committed. But if you had lied and said he was not at home when he had really gone out without your knowing it, and if the murderer had then met him as he went away and murdered him, you might justly be accused as the cause of his death. For if you had told the truth as far as you knew it, perhaps the murderer might have been apprehended by the neighbors while he searched the house and thus the deed might have been prevented. Therefore, whoever tells a lie, however well intentioned he might be, must answer for the consequences, however unforeseeable they were, and pay the penalty for them even in a civil tribunal. This is because truthfulness is a duty which must be regarded as the ground of all duties based on contract, and the laws of these duties would be rendered uncertain and useless if even the least exception to them were admitted.

To be truthful (honest) in all declarations, therefore, is a sacred and absolutely commanding decree of reason, limited by no expediency . . .

Lies, Damn Lies, and Statistics

◆

JONATHAN RAUCH

I'm going to say this again. I did not have sexual relations with that woman, Miss Lewinsky. —President Clinton, January 26

The murder rate in Holland is double that in the United States. . . . That's drugs.—drug czar Barry McCaffrey, July 13

Which of the two quotations above is the more appalling? I suppose most people would choose President Clinton's, and I suppose, on balance, I would, too. Still, the choice isn't altogether obvious—or, at least, it shouldn't be.

The word "lie"—like the word "is" and the word "sex"—is a term that tends to be used rather loosely. Recently St. Martin's Press sent me a new book called *The 15 Biggest Lies in Politics,* by the journalist Major Garrett and the former congressman Timothy J. Penny. The 15 "lies" turn out to include "The abortion debate matters," "Medicare works," and "Democrats are compassionate."

This book, luckily, is more sophisticated than its title (this is still true of books, sometimes), and it begins usefully with what the authors call a "hierarchy in the art of political lying." At the bottom are lies of decorum, which are harmless and even useful. "Demagogic lies" and "lies meant to conceal political cowardice" are worse, but also have their uses. Most people, however, would probably agree with Garrett and Penny that the exculpatory personal lie deserves only opprobrium: "The most-damaging lies are those politicians tell about their ethical conduct, hoping the ugly truth never emerges." Now who has done that sort of lying lately?

By contrast, Barry McCaffrey's statement of July 13 seems pretty innocent. As he was about to leave for Europe, the drug czar called the Netherlands' liberal drug policies an "unmitigated disaster." When the Dutch—no doubt, looking at the non-unmitigated success of American drug policies—expressed dismay, McCaffrey fired back that in 1995 the Dutch murder rate was double America's, and that other crime was worse, too.

The claim that the Netherlands is a more murderous place than America seems roughly as plausible as the claim that oral sex is not sex; and, in fact, in 1995 the Dutch murder rate was less than a quarter of the American rate. The Netherlands, population 15.5 million, had fewer murders that year than did Houston, population 1.7 million.

What may have begun as a simple mistake, however, became more ethically complicated when, the next day, the misstatement was pointed out to

---

McCaffrey, not least by the flabbergasted Dutch. A mistake uncorrected is no longer just a mistake, and McCaffrey did not issue a correction. In an August interview with the *Dallas Morning News,* he seemed pleased with himself. "The other thing we did during the visit was, I started laying down other people's comparative data," he said. "God, did it annoy them."

Asked recently if the murder comment still stands, a spokesman for McCaffrey responded with a Clintonesque step to the side. "We have said if we are wrong, speak to Interpol—it's not our statistics, it's (their) reporting." But Franklin Zimring, a University of California (Berkeley) law professor who is an authority on crime, says that the Interpol numbers are raw and unaudited; and, as the Dutch pointed out right away, the numbers cited by McCaffrey for the Netherlands (though not for the US) included not only murders but attempted murders. "If you want to walk the streets safely, Amsterdam is still a good place for a vacation," Zimring says. "And, more importantly, McCaffrey knows this. Folks have been going after him on this. And the notion of hiding behind the unaudited Interpol data—they can do that if they want, but they know what they're doing."

We find ourselves, here, deep in the misty jungle between outright lying ("I did not have sexual relations," etc.) and ordinary political spin. This twilight and primeval region is the preserve of a strange but common animal, the policy lie. Actually, "Lie" is not exactly the right word, since the hallmark of the policy lie is that it intends not to deceive so much as to silence or browbeat an opponent, and it aims not so much at personal gain as at keeping some policy or other alive until next week.

According to the National Association of Attorneys General, 40 states have sued the tobacco industry, demanding to be reimbursed for Medicaid and other health-program costs resulting from smoking. The only problem is that there are no such costs. In fact, the states, like the federal government, make a nice profit on smokers, even after health costs are factored in: Smokers pay high state cigarette taxes while they're alive, and then they die younger than nonsmokers, thus not living to accumulate as much in medical and nursing benefits. W. Kip Viscusi, an economist at Harvard Law School, figures that Florida, which settled with Big Tobacco for $13 billion in alleged damages, also profited by a net of 42 cents on every pack of cigarettes sold. A policy lie allows the attorneys general to strike righteous poses, when in fact they are merely greedy.

In 1996, the opponents of California's Proposition 209, which banned affirmative action in state programs, knew they had an uphill battle against public opinion. So they set out to convince the public that a vote for 209 was in fact a vote to legalize discrimination against women (there are lots of female voters). "Women could get fired if they had children or if they got pregnant," said Patricia Ireland, the head of the National Organization for Women. The chairman of the state Democratic Party said that 209 would repeal girls' athletic programs. And so on. The charge was not only false but bizarre. (The voters weren't fooled.) Or again: Instead of defending their policies of setting much lower admissions standards for blacks than for whites, elite universities and law schools have simply denied that the policies exist. Again, the lying fooled no one, though it did help discredit affirmative action.

Henry James once wrote, "The simplest division it is possible to make of the human race is into the people who take things hard and the people who take them easy." Where political lying is concerned, I'm in the easygoing camp. Stuart Taylor Jr., the proprietor of the column next door, has proposed a group called CRALP: Citizens Repelled by All Lying Politicians. I would join CRALP, but my own chapter would be called Citizens Responding with Amusement to Lying Politicians. The important thing, in my version of CRALP, is to distinguish the really loathsome or hurtful lies from the banal stretchers of everyday political and personal life.

Still, I concede that this is an issue of temperament rather than morals, and that outrage is a reasonable response to lies in public life. So, to the outraged, I propose a deal. Stay outraged, but look a little less at intentions and legality, and more at real-world charm.

Bill Clinton's lie about sex was legally wrong and morally shabby. But the lie—as distinct from the consequences of its exposure—didn't do very much real-world damage. In fact, the country would have been much better off if Clinton had gotten away with it. Personal lies and policy prevarication co-exist in a curiously transverse relationship: Shabby lies of self-preservation usually cause only retail damage, whereas even well-intentioned policy dissembling can do mischief wholesale.

On August 4, 1964, Washington got word that the North Vietnamese had launched a nighttime attack on two U.S. destroyers in the Gulf of Tonkin. The North Vietnamese had already skirmished with an American destroyer in the area two days earlier, and the Johnson administration took the second attack to Congress as justification for a broad grant of war-making powers. What the administration did not say was that reports from the scene were conflicting and confused. Owing to the dark night and the rough weather, not even the men in the gulf were sure whether they had been shooting at real enemies or phantoms. Congress gave Johnson his authority to "take all necessary measures" in Vietnam—but the attack that justified this mandate had not occurred.

The country is still living with the consequences of the Johnson administration's Gulf of Tonkin not-quite-lie. Dishonest non-defenses of affirmative action have inflamed racial resentment; the states' tobacco suits will cost smokers billions of dollars that they do not properly owe; nonsense about the Dutch murder rate fuels obsessive drug-war overkill.

So here is a suggestion: Barry McCaffrey should manfully step forward and declare, for the record, that America is a more criminally lethal country than the Netherlands. He should come clean and admit the obvious, instead of hiding behind legalisms and technical dodges. Then we can forgive him, and put this whole sorry episode behind us.

Is It Ever Right to Lie? The Philosophy of Deception
◆

Robert C. Solomon

No matter what you think of his politics or his personality, it is hard not to sympathize with President Clinton. The economy is booming, war is on the horizon, yet the press is rabid about sex in the White House. Of course, even in this "puritan" culture, there are few who would insist that the President should be impeached because of his by now well-known sexual proclivities. Rather, the question is: Did he lie (or tell someone else to)?

The importance of this question was summarized by one Congressman who pointed out that if the president would lie about one thing, he would lie about another.

For a philosopher, that argument raises all sorts of interesting questions. Is it ever right to lie? Is a lie told to embellish an otherwise tedious narrative just as wrong as a lie told to cover up a misdeed and avoid punishment? Is a lie told in desperation any less wrong than a calculated, merely convenient lie? Is a lie told out of self-deception more or less wrong than a clearheaded, tactical lie? (Is the former even a lie?) Are all lies wrong? Or does deception serve such important functions as protecting us from harm, especially emotional harm?

Let's start with the basics: Is it ever right to lie? Common sense surely says "Yes, sometimes." But legions of philosophers and other moralists have answered "No," and then tried to make sense of this indefensible position. Insisting that lying is always wrong—as Thomas Aquinas and Immanuel Kant did, for example—appeals to our desire for absolutes. But then, of course, what about the example from freshman philosophy: The Nazis come to your door asking if you are hiding a Jewish family. You are. Should you say "No"? Or, on a mundane level, your spouse or lover walks in with an utterly silly new hairdo and asks, "Do you like it?" Does morality dictate that you ruin the evening? Or can you, in both cases, finesse the answer, not lying but not telling the truth, either, perhaps by avoiding an answer to the question?

If a person would lie about one thing, does it follow that he or she would lie about another? That depends. The demand for honesty is contextual. It depends on what the truth concerns. The Bible tells us not to bear false witness against our neighbor. Perjury, we can agree, is wrong: The consequences can be awful. In a trial, a jury's assumption that a person who lies about one thing will lie about another is perfectly justified.

But it seems to be absolutely crucial to distinguish here between public and private life. Perjury, by its very nature, is public, as is politics. Sex, with a

---

Robert C. Solomon *is a professor of philosophy at the University of Texas at Austin, and the author, with Kathleen M. Higgins, of* A Short History of Philosophy *(Oxford University Press, 1996). From* The Chronicle of Higher Education, *February 27, 1996.*

few obvious exceptions, is part of our private life. And just about everyone is less than forthright about sex. Lying about sex, while it may have grave significance for people in an intimate relationship, has nothing to do with one's public credibility. Indeed, when publicly asked a rudely inappropriate question about one's private (adult, consensual) sex life, it seems to me not only natural but even obligatory to lie, finesse, or refuse to answer.

Nietzsche once asked. "Why must we have truth at any cost, anyway?" It was an odd question, coming from the philosopher who prided himself, above all, on his brutal honesty, and it is an obscene question, in any case, for a profession that sees itself as seeking solely the truth. Even philosophers who challenge the very idea of truth—not just Nietzsche and Buddhist Nagarajuna, but also Jacques Derrida and Richard Rorty—are unforgiving when it comes to deception, misrepresentation, and "creative misreadings," at least of their own work. Philosophers in general insist on the truth even if they do not believe in "the Truth." They despise deception and ridicule self-deception.

The Australian philosopher Tony Coady probably speaks for most philosophers when he writes, "Dishonesty has always been perceived in our culture, and in all cultures but the most bizarre, as a central human vice." But, he adds, "we should note that this perception is consistent with a certain hesitancy about what constitutes a lie and with the more than sneaking suspicion that there might be a number of contexts in which lying is actually justified." Plato defended "the noble lie," and the English ethicist Henry Sidgwick suggested that a "high-minded lie" in the direction of humility might do us all a great deal of good.

Not all untruths are malicious. Telling the truth can complicate or destroy social relationships. It can undermine precious collective myths. Honesty can be cruel. Sometimes, deception is not a vice but a social virtue, and systematic deception is an essential part of the order of the (social) world. In many countries—Japan and Western Samoa, for example—social harmony is valued far more than truthfulness as such. To tell another person what he or she wants to hear, rather than what one might actually feel or believe, is not only permitted but expected.

Could we not begin to see our own enlightened emphasis on "seeking the truth at all costs" (as Ernst Jones wrote admiringly of Sigmund Freud) as one more ethnocentric peculiarity, another curious product of our strong sense of individualism, and a dangerously unsociable conception?

Behind the blanket prohibition on lying, we can discern the outlines of a familiar but glorious philosophical metaphor: The truth is bright, simple, the Holy Grail of Rationality, while dishonesty is dark and devious, the path to irrationality and confusion. But philosophy, one begins to suspect, has overrated those metaphors of clarity and transparency. The obvious truth is that our simplest social relationships could not exist without the opaque medium of the lie. The best answer to the question "What are you thinking?" is often "Oh, nothing." Perhaps deception, not truth, is the cement of civilization—a cement that does not so much hold us together as safely separate us and our thoughts. Some things are better left in the dark.

In contrast to Kant, for whom the rule against lying was a moral law, a "categorical imperative" never to be overridden, utilitarian philosophers insist that lying is wrong only because a lie does, in fact, cause more harm than good. There is no absolute prohibition here, rather perhaps a "rule of thumb," and there may well be many cases, such as the "white lies" described above, in which lying causes no harm and may even be commendable. The problem, as Nietzsche so wisely complains (in characteristic opposition to Kant) is "not that you lied to me, but that I no longer believe you." It is not the breach of the principle against lying that is so troublesome, nor is it the consequences of the lie or the character of the liar: It is that lying compromises and corrupts our relationships.

In other words, the wrongness of lying does not have to do primarily with breaches of principle or miscalculations of harm and good, even if these weigh heavily in particular cases—in a court of law or a Congressional hearing, for example. Lying is wrong because it constitutes a breach of trust, which is not a principle but a very particular and personal relationship between people. And in sexual relations, while personal trust is of the utmost importance, it has nothing to do with, and no necessary correlation with, public trust.

What is wrong with lying, in other words, is not exactly what philosophers have often supposed. Lying undermines relationships by undermining trust. But trust may just as often be supported by mutual myths, by religious faith, by a clear understanding of what is private and personal and what is "the public's right to know." Trust is usually violated by lies, but trust can be more deeply damaged by a violation of personal boundaries, which in turn may invite lies and deception to protect what has been violated.

What further complicates questions about lying and deception is the familiar phenomenon of self-deception. It is always easiest, the old adage tells us, to tell the truth. But next-easiest is to believe your own lie, to become so submerged in its network of details and implications that the continuation of the lie—as Aristotle argues—becomes second nature.

Discussions of lying too often focus on the straightforwardly cynical, self-interested lie and ignore the more common species of lying that includes self-deception as well. But transparency to ourselves can be just as intolerable as transparency to others, and for just the same reason. The recognition of one's own motives and the significance of one's own thoughts can be devastating to one's self-image and sense of well-being. And so we disguise, hide, distract ourselves from those facets and the self that are less than flattering. As Nietzsche puts it, "'I have done that,' says my memory. 'I cannot have done that,' says my pride, and remains inexorable. Eventually, memory yields."

Deception and self-deception are part and parcel of our engagements in the world, including, not least, the development and maintenance of our sense of ourselves. Lying can sometimes be a way of protecting our private lives, especially in the midst of a press-plagued public life. Within one's personal life, within the so-far unbreached walls of the Clintons' bedroom, for example, there is, no doubt, a continuing drama of Shakespearean proportions. But that is where this business about sex and lying about it should remain.

As for all of those inappropriate questions from otherwise distinguished journalists, special persecutors, and the curious public, they deserve no answer, or an evasion or even a lie for an answer. Clinton's sex life and what he says about it do not have anything to do with Clinton's credibility or ability to govern (which are other questions altogether). A lie or an invitation to lie that is provoked by a breach of sacred personal boundaries is in moral limbo, and no violation of a public trust.

Yes, Sometimes Lying Is Right Action to Take

◆

Lorraine Dusky

Some years ago, I told a lie to protect one person's feelings and another's reputation. Yes, I had chopped down the cherry tree just as I had been accused, and I had not done it alone. To say that I'd done the deed would have drawn in another person who had much to lose if the truth were out, and it was clear no good could come of that. Several people would be hurt. Yes, this involved infidelity and, no, I'm not going to go further.

There are times when the cost of telling the truth is greater than the worth of honesty. It is not only that one has to stand up and take the consequences for one's misdeed, but it is also that other individuals will be irreparably harmed by the truth-telling. Then lying is the only noble course there is.

History gives us significant examples of this as recently as the '50s. Then an out-of-control, self-anointed special investigator, Joe McCarthy, wanted to get at the "truth" of the Red Menace in this country. All sorts of people were hauled before his Senate committee and the House Un-American Activities Committee and asked to be truthful about those they believed had communist leanings. Whom do we admire today? The finks who told the "truth," named names and got off with their jobs intact, or those who were blacklisted because they didn't? Early Christian history is rife with stories of martyrs who sacrificed their own lives rather than name other Christians. The same is true of the Resistance during the last World War. Certainly the Underground Railroad, which secretly transported slaves to their freedom, involved "lying" to keep it thriving.

Lying Spares Pain

Today many children in adoptive families "lie" when asked if they were searching for, or have made contact with, their first families. They want to spare their adoptive parents any pain. Doctors and parents sometimes "lie" to terminally ill children, and adult children sometimes "lie" to their terminally ill parents. In the name of truth-telling, a great many relationships have been gratuitously damaged and countless feelings hurt.

Which brings us to Bill Clinton. Let's say that when Monica Lewinsky's name surfaced in the Paula Jones suit, he did not tell the truth about his relationship with the former White House intern. Not answering would have been the same as an admission of guilt. So Clinton, responding in the only way that would protect the honor of his wife, his daughter, the young woman in question, her family and, yes, himself, perhaps was not truthful. Think, for a moment, what the truth would do.

Lorraine Dusky *is a freelance writer living in New York and is the author of* Still Unequal: The Shameful Truth about Women and Justice in America. *From* USA Today, *March 5, 1998.*

Hillary Clinton, who has had to endure some embarrassment before over Clinton's peccadilloes, would be humiliated much further. Their teenage daughter, Chelsea, would be publicly embarrassed. And Lewinsky? We've heard that she has asked: Who will ever hire me? Who will ever date me? Who, indeed? Now Lewinsky faces the threat of indictment.

Sure, Clinton Stood to Gain, But . . .

It goes nearly without saying what Clinton stood to gain by insisting that no improper relationship existed: his marriage, his dignity, perhaps even his presidency. And if it were later revealed that he was lying about it under oath, he would be in much more serious trouble than if he simply told the truth.

Considering all that has transpired since that day some six weeks ago, just possibly it would have been more self-serving to tell the "truth," if that's what it is, and confess to the nation. Judging by Clinton's popularity, he would have been pardoned by the public. His family probably would have forgiven him also. And Ken Starr, the McCarthy of our times, would have nothing to investigate. No matter what comes out about Lewinsky, legally it is of no use to the Jones team, since it's been ruled inadmissible in her trial. But Lewinsky? Ah, well she would have been trashed in the process. Would truth then have been the more honorable course? Resoundingly, no.

So, no matter what the reality of the situation, no matter what we think of our president's fatal flaws, Clinton took the high road: He said that no improper relationship existed. He responded with the sense of decency we all hope someone would draw upon if our daughter, sister or mother were named as a corespondent in such an affair. And he may have told a lie in the process.

While we might not readily compare Clinton to Antigone, the lines Sophocles gave her are relevant here: "What divine justice have I disobeyed?" she says as she is led to her death for disobeying the king. "The wise will know my choice was right."

Apparently the American public knows, too. Regardless of the consequences yet to come, Clinton made the right choice.

Response: If Lying Is OK, How Do We Determine Truth?

Free-lance writer Lorraine Dusky's assertion that sometimes lying is "the only noble course" produced a flood of letters to the editor disagreeing with her. Here are the comments of a few:

> After reading Lorraine Dusky's article, "Yes, sometimes lying is right action to take, " I had to step back and ponder. Let's follow this argument to its logical conclusion. If it's all right to lie sometimes, why have a court system where we swear under oath to speak the truth? Why look for truth and try to determine justice in this society if lying "is some-

times all right"? The obvious conclusion is that there is no right or wrong, and everything is relative as long as one can justify that the reason he or she is lying is for a good purpose.

This sounds like those who believe that government should take care of society and we don't have to take personal responsibility or be accountable. What a fantastic model this would be for our children.

Dusky's logic that sometimes lying is a noble course to take fails me. Following her argument, we could hold that objective journalism would be out the window because if it's all right to lie sometimes, who knows if what is being reported is the truth or a justifiable lie? We could just live in a world of make-believe and decide "who we need to protect from the truth" by lying at will.

And when people don't have a logical argument to back up their position, it seems the tactic to take is to denigrate the other side. This sounds like name-calling from my kindergarten days or, better yet, character assassination as I have come to know it as an adult. We have an independent counsel, Kenneth Starr, who was appointed by President Clinton's attorney general, Janet Reno, and a three-judge panel to do the job he is doing. But all the pundits can do is try to undermine his character.

The truth is, if we come to the point where we justify lying and cover-up for any reason, read the history books and you will find that the moral corruption of a nation is always the pathway to destruction. It seems character may count after all.

Elaine E. Mason
Burke, Va.
From USA Today, *March 9, 1998.*

A Sign of Moral Decline

Lorraine Dusky's advocacy of lying is a shocking indication of the degree of moral degradation to which we have fallen as a nation. How dare she!

There's a sharp difference between not telling all you know and telling something you know not to be true. The former is honorable, motivated by decency, and is protective of others regardless of personal cost. The latter is dishonorable, motivated by deceit and the desire to protect oneself, at any cost, from receiving the just deserts of personal wrongdoing. Especially in sworn testimony.

It has not been proved the president lied under oath, or urged others to. If he did, only the morally bankrupt would seek to whitewash this action.

Rick Huff
Tucson, Ariz.
From USA Today, *March 9, 1998.*

The Truth

Seldom has an article almost made me physically sick the way the column by Lorraine Dusky does.

Her examples of acceptable lying involve life and death and persecution. To lump President Clinton's alleged lie with horrors like the Christian martyrs, the Underground Railroad days, war Resistance fighters and the McCarthy era is silly.

To imply that the truth can hurt Hillary Rodham Clinton suggests that she does not know her husband better than any person or that she is naïve or not too bright; these do not fit this very intelligent lady. And their daughter, Chelsea, has been hearing negatives about her father for years. She is adult enough to deal with difficult situations.

The only person who can be hurt by the truth now is the president, and his place in history. Ironically, had he admitted he had a problem and reviewed it with the American people, it probably would be over, just a footnote in history. Americans have a great capacity for forgiveness.

Is it any wonder that more people are willing to try to lie their way out of difficult situations? If it is OK for our leaders, why isn't it OK for everyone?

If children learn from what they see, their not being truthful will be a big price for the country to pay.

Barbara A. Volz
Sugarcreek, Ohio
From USA Today, *March 9, 1998.*

Credits

Index